The Controversial Sholem Asch

The Controversial Sholem Asch:

An Introduction to his Fiction

Ben Siegel

Bowling Green University Popular Press
Bowling Green, Ohio 43404

Library of Congress Catalog Card No.: 76-43446

Copyright © 1976, Bowling Green University Popular Press

ISBN: 0-87972-076-X

Cover design by Gregg Swope

For RUTH

Contents

Preface

This study is the first critical biography in English of Sholem Asch, who did little in his lifetime to make such a task an easy one. Asch was not a "tidy" writer. He lived in many cities and countries, wrote tirelessly, and kept little record of his numerous novels, stories, and essays—much less of the countless Yiddish, Hebrew, and European periodicals and newspapers (most of them now long defunct), or editions and translations, in which his writings appeared. Some items were translated several times in the same language; others remained in the Yiddish or were translated from one foreign version to another, rather than from the original Yiddish. (Willa and Edwin Muir, for example, based their English version of *Three Cities* on the German translation, as they did not know Yiddish.) Several major novels appeared in many languages before finding Yiddish publication. Matilda Asch kept after her husband to compile a master list of his published writings, but he repeatedly put off the task. An avid collector of paintings and sculptures, books and religious artifacts, he included always among his treasures a bookcase of his own publications, but his gathering was never complete.

Much work remains to be done on Asch's life and writings. (The late Samuel Charney ["S. Niger"] made a valiant start in his *Sholem Asch, His Life and His Work*, a volume that cries for translation from the Yiddish.) My own shelves groan under materials for which there is no room in this introductory study. Indeed, limitations of length and format have forced several hard decisions. As this book aims primarily at readers of English, I have emphasized those Asch works available (often with difficulty) in English. Most are out-of-print and to be found only in the large university and municipal libraries. (At this writing, only *Moses, Salvation, Three Cities,* and *God of Vengeance* may validly be described as "in print.") Of course, I have found it necessary to discuss some fiction and non-fiction that have remained in Yiddish; these I deal with more briefly. Conversely, I have summarized the plots of many novels and stories more fully than would be necessary were these writings still in print and on class reading-lists. And only those readers familiar with Yiddish can appreciate the difficulties in transliterating—with total consistency in spelling—Yiddish words or titles into English. (For a concise discussion of the problems involved, see Ronald Sanders, *The Downtown Jews* [New York: Harper & Row, 1969], pp. 455-60.) After much thought and travail,

I opted for "a humane inconsistency" (Sanders, p. 456) in an attempt to approximate the Yiddish spellings prevailing at the time Asch was writing. Not all readers of Yiddish will be pleased, but few should be confused or misled. And clarity has here been my most immediate goal.

For I have tried to establish a basis for future discussion of Asch's literary contribution, discussion that hopefully will be free of past rancors or partisanship. In striving to reduce his long life and voluminous output to a semblance of order, I felt that a straight chronological approach promised the best results. Not surprisingly, however, certain writings—especially among the plays, short tales, and essays—tended to "cluster" and to disrupt my neat time scheme. Even more significantly, perhaps, I decided I could better tell my story by stringing Asch's writings on a biographical thread, rather than by confining his "life" to an opening chapter.

Many persons have contributed to this study—publishers, editors, and librarians, as well as correspondents, colleagues, and friends. First acknowledgements must go to Samuel Brier and William Davenport, of Claremont. Mr. Brier, a Yiddishist and raconteur, a lover of good books, good paintings, and good talk (especially in Yiddish), did much to lighten my labors with his recollections of Sholem Asch and his rich knowledge of the Yiddish language and the special world of Yiddish letters and journalism. Professor Davenport, longtime friend, mentor, and collaborator, with sharp eye, keen wit, and unfailing good humor, caught many a slip in manuscript style, logic, and tone. And special thanks must go to Mr. Joseph Singer, of Teaneck, New Jersey, whose translating skills and sensitivity to Yiddish-English nuances are widely recognized, and who offered here invaluable suggestions, corrections, and encouragement.

Others also helped beyond the point of mere courtesy. Solomon Rosenberg placed at my disposal materials and memories of a decade spent as Sholem Asch's secretary. Earle H. Balch did not allow illness to prevent his writing me detailed accounts of his close collaboration with Asch in preparing (as Senior Editor at Putnam's) several of the later novels for English publication. The late Maurice Samuel, who needs no introduction to readers of serious literature, augmented, with candid private impressions, his published observations on his role as Asch's major English translator. Others adding significant literary materials and personal anecdotes were Louis Zara of New York, Joseph Leftwich of London, Helen Grace

Carlisle of Stamford, Connecticut, and Gertrude Asch Gelber of Los Angeles.

In addition, I am indebted to Kate Mollinoff and Gershom Pomerantz for useful clippings and information, as well as to Milton Tunick, Charles Hinton, and Gerda Bikales for letters relating personal experiences with Asch or his family. I am grateful to Peter Israels and Walter Minton of Putnam's, who permitted me free use of Asch's published English writings; to William Charney, who arranged for me to borrow from the archives of the YIVO Institute for Jewish Research the Asch manuscripts and materials compiled by his noted father, Samuel Charney; and to Ezekiel Lifschutz, archivist at YIVO, who gathered and made available the Charney items and others. Indeed, many librarians extended valuable assistance. Dorothy W. Bridgwater, Head Reference Librarian at the Yale University Library, and Marjorie G. Wynne, Research Librarian of the Beinecke Rare Book and Manuscript Library at Yale, carefully compiled and shared with me photocopies of their Asch holdings. On my own campus, a tireless and uncomplaining library staff helped me track and borrow a seemingly endless list of Aschiana from the Library of Congress and scattered university libraries. Colleagues and students also helped, and to them many thanks.

But how does one thank Sharon and Kenneth, who all too often found Dad locked away behind his study door with "a Sholem Asch"? Or, how does one say thanks to Ruth, a tireless typist and tough, tough critic of her husband's writing?

Ben Siegel
California State
Polytechnic University,
Pomona

Chapter 1
Sholem Who?

During the 1940's and early 1950's Sholem Asch was for most reading Americans and Europeans the best-known "Yiddish" writer. Only Isaac Bashevis Singer, in recent years, has challenged this distinction. Coffee tables around which a Yiddish word had never been spoken sported bookclub copies (translated of course) of *The Nazarene, The Apostle,* and *Mary.* Cocktail debaters evaluated animatedly Asch's fidelity to or distortion of scriptural narrative. But when Asch died, in England in 1957, his funeral, though well publicized, was sparsely attended.

Jewish apathy to his passing contrasted sharply with the expressed attitude toward the deaths of other prominent Yiddish writers. An approximate 100,000 Warsaw Jews had followed Isaac Leib Peretz's funeral procession in 1915, and another 100,000 had lined New York streets in 1916 to mourn Sholom Aleichem. Wrapped in his large woolen prayer shawl, Sholem Asch was buried quietly in the West London (Reform) Synagogue's cemetery in Hoop Lane, Golders Green. He had often requested a traditional burial. He had wished also to lie in Israel, in the Tel Aviv suburb of Bat Yam, where he lived his last two years. But his wife decided he should remain in England, where he and his writing generally had been well received.

Asch spent his last day, July 10, as he had most of his adult life—at his desk writing, swiftly, very swiftly, his one hand writing, the other pressed against his head.[1] He wrote always in Yiddish, moving from right to left, "in uneven lines, the writing becoming smaller at the end of a line and at the bottom of a page, as if he were anxious to get more in."[2] To die virtually pen in hand seems almost symbolically fitting for Asch. He would have appreciated the inherent drama; undoubtedly, had he been able, he would have worked the scene into a story. His sudden death ended the career of one of this century's most prolific and controversial writers. The first Yiddish author to rank among the West's leading contemporary novelists, he was also the most translated and widely

1

read of modern Yiddishists. Obituary articles in the world press
generally were favorable; his more acrid critics, sensibly, were
silent, having said their worst while he lived. They could add
nothing now to the bitterness of his last years. His final relevance
would be determined by future readers and critics. Today, mention
of Asch still evokes animated responses from older Jewish readers.
Not even death and time have made him a neutral figure.

I   Charges and Rejoinders

Their elders' impassioned reactions, however, baffle young
readers, Jewish and non-Jewish. Who, they ask, was Sholem Asch?
(How pained that proud and dedicated man would be by the
question. He could not understand why the Nobel Prize Committee
repeatedly ignored him.) Few writers have written more than
he—novels, plays, stories, and essays. That, perhaps, was the
problem: had he written less and more carefully, his name now
might not be lost upon the young. If today's readers do not know
Asch, his contemporaries never quite understood him. They called
him everything from God's "true advocate" and "seer of reality" to
charlatan and apostate. Contention marked his life and career. Yet
he secured his place among the Yiddish literary masters. Despite
harsh attacks by assorted intellectuals, journalists, and religious
spokesmen, the Yiddish-speaking masses for years literally
revered him.

His fictionalized lives of Jesus, Paul, and Mary, however, did
much to change Jewish public opinion toward him. In these novels
Asch reconstructed the ancient settings with meticulous detail and
deep moral awareness, but he stretched scriptural narrative to
emphasize the religious ties linking Jew and Christian; an
inveterate idealist, he hoped to help create a climate of mutual
understanding that might lead to a better world. Instead, his
"interfaith" efforts led to a broadside of acclaim and suspicion,
praise and abuse, bestsellers and near isolation. Most painful and
confusing were the apostasy charges. These he tried to answer: Did
not his stories and essays shout that Sholem Asch was a Jew? that
he wrote as a Jew and was interested chiefly in Jews as subjects
and readers? Had he not rejected an American publisher for
insisting he list himself merely as S. Asch because "Sholem"
sounded too Jewish? His replies were lost in the din raised by his
critics, most of whom were shouting from rancor and envy.

Like many a Hebrew and Yiddish writer, Asch came from a

Jewish small town or *shtetl*. Exposed to no formal learning other than the Bible and other Hebrew religious writings until he was eighteen, he was essentially self-educated. But he was never provincial. Poland's orthodox Jews viewed European culture as profane, even sinful. Young Sholem, however, determined to acquire a Western education. He succeeded, exhibiting amazing intellectual vigor and self-discipline. At twenty-one he published a cluster of sketches that won quick acceptance among East Europe's Jews, and he followed these with other tales and plays. He wanted to articulate much of Jewish life, past and present. His special concern was that a coherent Jewish identity assert itself despite all Diaspora obstacles. Writing with a fervor and pride often "untempered by reason," [3] Asch employed every literary form but verse; if he placed the Jew at the center of every work, he revealed in each a strong awareness of the outside world and the Jew's place, or lack of place, in it. He was proud of the Jew as Jew—the one who retained his identity despite being devoured or engulfed by others. "It is the spirit of the Jewish faith kept alive through the ages," Asch declared, "that I must describe." [4]

He soon proved a writer of scope and variety who sought always new areas for descriptive narrative. When contemporary Jewish life seemed flat, he turned easily to the past for plots and characters. Time and space were sources of inspiration rather than barriers; he could depict knowingly each period and locale's fine points and special tensions—from Moses to Miami, from Polish *shtetl* and Israeli kibbutz to Renaissance Rome, Weimar Berlin, and New York's East River. Prophets and priests, peasants and scholars, merchants and laborers move convincingly through his pages. St. Petersburg's officials and aristocrats emerge as vividly as Warsaw's thieves and pimps. No other writer presents so rich a Diaspora life. Asch grasped clearly such modern phenomena as the rise of the Enlightenment (*Haskala*) and radicalism among East Europe's Jews, and the effects on these Jews of the First World War, Russian Revolution, emigration to America, and Palestine settlement. He had a sure hand for the sweeping brushstroke and a sharp eye for dramatic externals—for panoramic vistas, moving masses, and strong contrasts. With the fine detail he was less certain. When his emotions and imagination had been fired, however, he could bring a colorful individual to life. Yet many of his figures run to representative types, if not stereotypes.

Several themes recur in Asch's fiction, but most frequent are those of man's faith, goodness, and generosity. Christian violence repels and intrigues him, while Jewish survival and martyrdom inspire him; martyrdom represents for him, as Joseph Landis puts it, a fusion of "violent endurance and the endurance of violence."[5] With Asch, to admire often means to idealize, and he admires most those who exemplify faith or goodness. These include not only scholars, rabbis, patriarchs, and martyrs, but lovers (young and old), virtuous matrons and chaste maidens, and often entire Jewish hamlets. Indeed, his "good" people frequently are also tough thieves, prostitutes, pimps, and brothel owners. Two character types dominate his tales: the pious Jew who disdains violence and embraces morality and study and the burly worker whose labors endow him with the muscle and spirit to take and give blows. Asch reveres them both, and even his roughest toughs, though uncouth and unlettered, remain loyal to Judaic traditions and concerns. In a sense, Asch had both types in his own family. His brothers were tall, brawny fellows who, in helping their father in his tavern and cattle-buying, dealt with peasants and butchers. His much older half-brothers (from his father's first wife) were more pious Hasidim.

II   Literary Comparisons, Habits, and Themes

Asch wrote almost daily for over a half-century. He wrote wherever he went, and he resided or traveled widely in Poland, Germany, Switzerland, Austria, England, France, the United States, and Israel. His writings reflect his cosmopolitan interests and deep concern for the people and conditions he encountered. At least a half-dozen novels and a score of short stories merit attention today. These prove a small segment of his vast output, but few authors can claim much more. His fiction divides loosely into three broad categories. First are the tales, novels, and plays of East European (primarily Polish) Jewish life. Second are the tales and novels of Jewish life in America. Third are the five Biblical novels: two center on Old Testament figures, while the others form a New Testament trilogy that argues a common spiritual and cultural matrix for Judaism and Christianity. Smaller groupings center on the Holocaust (the Nazi slaughter of Jews) and on modern Israel.

Friendly critics dubbed Asch a "Yiddish Maupassant," "Yiddish Charles Dickens," and "Yiddish Gorky." (A "Yiddish Mark Twain" had been assigned to Sholom Aleichem.) Never accurate, such analogies are here especially misleading. Asch's work is not easily classifiable. Scenes, incidents, and characters are reminiscent occasionally of Dickens's droll caricatures. His sexual frankness at a time when this was rare in "serious" literature fleetingly resembles Maupassant's treatment of sexual relationships. And he did share Gorky's deep sympathy for the poor, weak, and toiling. Yet Sholem Asch, as man and artist, remained always different, distinct, and himself. An impulsive, frequently generous man, he could be childish and bad-tempered. His public tears and private outbursts—of joy as well as anger—repeatedly evoked concern or amusement. "A more sensitive and emotional man," recalled the Russian actor-dramatist Nikolai Chadotov, "I have never seen in my life." [6] Often he presented valuable objects in his home to friends who had admired them. But he was capable of asking—as he did several times—that these gifts be returned.

Spontaneous and imaginative, Asch was both realist and romanticist, naturalist and idealist, novelist and essayist, playwright and journalist. Avoiding literary schools and theories, he relied mostly on his own taste and judgment; these did not always prove reliable, and his methods and "styles" frequently were excessively varied or uneven. Indeed many novels and stories are ignored today because their language and construction appear inconsistent, melodramatic, faulty. But his best efforts are distinguished by charming simplicity and original treatment and have proved durable "standards" of Jewish, Yiddish, and world literature. His reputation has suffered considerably since his death—in part perhaps deservedly and in part from critics who assume that prolific writers who appeal to general readers in novel, short story, and drama are not to be taken seriously. Asch's versatility and productivity made it difficult for many lay and professional critics to appreciate his creativity, energetic imagination, or dedication to his craft. Furthermore, Asch was primarily a storyteller in an age dominated by the fictionalized case study or by the tale of introspection or absurdity. He was attracted instead to the wide-spectrum chronicle and the mood-piece or tonal impression. He accepted freely the prime obligation of the teller of tales—to engage his listener, to entertain and give him satisfaction. Like Dickens, Theodore Dreiser, or Thomas Wolfe, Sholem Asch attempted to articulate all he observed, heard, or experienced. [7]

He endowed literature with rich, vivid portraits of the Jewish experience through its rich history. His range was wide, his imagination deep, his vigor unflagging, his dedication unwavering.

To East Europe's Jews, he was for several decades a living legend. Such early plays as *God of Vengeance* and *The Days of the Messiah* and novels like *The Little Town, Sanctification of the Name, Mottke the Thief, The Witch of Castile, Three Cities*, and *Salvation* quickly became hallmarks of Yiddish literature. Tall and straight (if early given to fleshiness), with a thick head of hair he would carry to the grave, his strong features emphasized by a heavy mustache, and always immaculately attired, Asch epitomized the successful man-of-letters. He spent much of his last forty-seven years in the English-speaking world, but he wrote exclusively in Yiddish. In turn, he was never accepted as an "American" author. This "neglect" moved Oscar Cargill to lament that whereas "Sholem Asch had adopted America . . . America had not adopted Asch."[8]

Success had come to Asch early, perhaps too early for him to develop sound writing habits. As a teenager he had set down brief impressions in Hebrew. At twenty, at "Yal" Peretz's suggestion, he switched to Yiddish, his mother tongue, and soon published a novella of patriarchal life entitled *The Little Town*. A cluster of nostalgic, sentimental sketches of a *shtetl* gasping its last, this modest narrative was reinforced by recollections of his native Kutno and proved his first success. The next year his play *God of Vengeance* was produced, and the "controversial" Sholem Asch was born; the play's harsh depiction of Jewish city life's seamier aspects stirred loud resentment in Jewish circles. But its Berlin production by the famed Max Reinhardt spread the Asch name through Europe. At twenty-five this unlettered young novelist-playwright from the Polish provinces had seen his play produced in St. Petersburg, Warsaw, and New York. Asch wrote nothing for the stage after the 1920's, but by that time he had authored around twenty plays and had won wide popularity in the Yiddish theater. Numerous dramatizations of his novels, however, were produced after that, including his own adaptation of *Mottke the Thief*.

From the start Asch's writing found non-Yiddish readers. His earliest works were translated into Polish, Russian, German, and over twenty other languages. Twenty-seven works have appeared in English alone, of which most are novels. This rapid success beyond the Jewish Pale stirred the envy of some Yiddish literati, an envy that followed him to the grave and after. Proud, stubborn, outspoken, Asch repeatedly provided his critics with issues. (His comments about the rite of circumcision, for instance, as well as his acceptance of a Polish government medal, caused bitter debate for years in Jewish circles.) His writings, too, were a recurrent irritation to some. Those angered by *God of Vengeance* were ruffled again by *Mottke the Thief;* the blunt account of a picaresque vagabond forced by events to become a thief, murderer, and pimp, *Mottke* won (despite a painfully sentimental conclusion) quick acceptance as a Yiddish literary and theatrical classic. But to many it proved once more Asch's prurient opportunism, a charge they renewed during the later tumult over his "Christological" novels. Most Jewish critics and readers, however, hailed Asch as a master chronicler of their history and foibles. If he scored their frailties, he emphasized also their courage, forbearance, and generosity. On balance, Sholem Asch spoke knowingly and eloquently, they agreed, for his fellow Jews. Certainly no Jewish cause, several commentators pointed out, lacked his impassioned voice and tireless pen.

Jewish critics use the 1930's to divide his writings into two parts. For them the first period is unquestionably the greater: Asch devoted his efforts then almost exclusively to Jewish life and history. The 1930's found him at the peak of his fame and creative powers. By that time he had spent some years in the United States and long been an American citizen; also, he had published in English four short novels (*America, Uncle Moses, Chaim Lederer's Return, Judge Not—*) on Jewish life transplanted to the New World. Early in the decade Asch gained his first large American readership with an expansive Russian Revolution trilogy, *Three Cities*, and followed it quickly with *Salvation*, the novel he considered the "cornerstone of his literary structure."[9] With *Salvation* he won back many Jewish readers whom his previous works had antagonized; it also did much to restore his early luster with even the most parochial critics: they could find little to quarrel with in this extended eulogy to a lost Hasidic world. His *Salvation* was an achievement hard to equal, and Asch's next efforts, *The War Goes On*, a novel of inflation-ridden Weimar Germany, and *Song of the Valley*, fell far short. His mind during those troubled years had been increasingly on the grim events in Germany and on Palestine, with its slowly spreading Jewish settlements. Thus *Song of the Valley* was a thinly fictionalized account of one kibbutz group's tenacious fight to survive. A lesser work than its immediate predecessors, it served primarily to reaffirm Asch's pride in Jewish courage and accomplishment in the face of crushing opposition and hardships.

III The Bitter Years

Asch's popularity with Jewish readers then was unrivaled, and his trips and lectures on behalf of beleaguered European Jews made him a world figure. Ludwig Lewisohn included him, in 1936, on a list of the "Ten Outstanding Jews" then living, a distinction that grouped him with Einstein, Freud, Henri Bergson, and Martin Buber. His concern for modern Palestine provided a threshold into the Biblical past, and with *Song of the Valley* finished he settled down to his long-planned novel of Jesus. Publication of *The Nazarene* (1939) brought immediate returns: new fame, large royalties, and a torrent of Jewish hostility that changed his life. After four decades of writing in the revered tradition of Mendele, Peretz, and Sholom Aleichem, and as a near-idol of the Yiddish-reading masses, Asch became overnight the target for a wave of journalistic abuse surpassing easily the bitter Jewish reactions to Freud's speculative *Moses and Monotheism*. A sad but familiar cycle ensued: the attacks increased curiosity about the infamous book and spurred sales; as *The Nazarene* climbed the best-seller charts, Asch's critics grew more vitriolic.

Some critics and readers may have expected a shamefaced admission of wrongdoing; instead, they got two more "Christo-logical" novels, *The Apostle* (1943) and *Mary* (1949). These three books lodged him for a decade on American bookclub and best-seller lists and in the leading book-review sections. They also made him the most debated Jewish writer of his time, filled his last years with acrimony, and gained him the surprised anger and rejection of much of the Jewish journalistic world. Numerous spokesmen accused him of apostasy and venality, of courting Christian favor, and of harboring arrogant hopes of a Nobel Prize. He had distorted Jewish history and thought, they charged, and his glorification of Mary and Paul surpassed in bias depictions by Christian writers. But why, they puzzled, had he reversed so suddenly? Why was he no longer content to pursue readers and recognition with his familiar subjects, themes, and attitudes? Asch replied by vehemently denying defection from Jewish tradition. His interest in Jesus, Paul, and Mary, he insisted, stemmed from their being Jews and essential figures in Jewish history, and he wanted to help bridge the two-millennia gap between Judaism and Christianity. Nor was this interest sudden or new; he had planned a life of Jesus, Asch declared, even before his first Palestine trip in 1906.

His explanations only intensified the confusion and division among Jewish literati and readers. Many found it hard to scorn the revered author of so many Yiddish classics. Others defended a novelist's right to be free with history. The most savage attacks came from the *Jewish Daily Forward* and its famed editor, Abraham Cahan (who had serialized most of Asch's previous fiction), and from a defamatory book, *The Christianity of Sholem Asch*, by *Forward* columnist Herman (Chaim) Lieberman. A telling blow was landed also by the respected Maurice Samuel, who had translated *The Nazarene* and *The Apostle* but now refused to translate *Mary*. Asch was denounced in editorials, letters, and pulpits, and even threatened with physical assault. Jewish reaction abroad—in Britain especially—was softer than in America, and in Israel, despite a vocal but limited opposition, he was received warmly during his last years. East Europe's survivors there welcomed the famed *shtetl* chronicler of their youth. When Asch died during a London visit, the Israeli ambassador to England, Eliahu Elat, expressed to the family his government's condolences and made the stance official by attending the funeral. Even the religiously conservative *London Jewish Chronicle* finally saw fit to pay Asch tribute and to defend him from the charges of apostasy. [10]

Few writers devoted more time and effort to self-improvement. Few traveled so widely or sought out so many people of diverse occupations and social levels. Few took more seriously than he the vocation of writing. Never waiting for his muse, Asch strove daily to activate his imagination, partly by dogged determination, partly by changing his environment when he felt that would help. But mostly he simply isolated himself at his desk for weeks at a stretch. He was no timeserver. He spoke out at great cost for his convictions. Not a profound thinker, he re-created or recaptured a world rich in characters, but they were often recognizable figures moving on a familiar surface. He saw history, society, morality in large dimensions, for their more subtle complexities repeatedly eluded him. He could give life and color to old impressions, but too frequently he could not provide a new insight without a vitiating sentiment or moralism. Never did he define precisely the "faith" he championed in fiction and non-fiction. His doctrine seemed to waver uncertainly about God and man, miracle and tradition, divine law and simple decency. A creed's historic or psychological results interested him more than did its spiritual substance. He focused less on a religious victim's inner anguish than on his physical courage and pain.[11]

If the great novelist is one who transmutes human confusion into coherent patterns of harmonious impression and deep insight, Asch only rarely achieved greatness. His lesser achievement was to give to numerous basic human experiences a memorable, lasting intensity. Perhaps English critic Roger Pippett best summed-up Asch's accomplishment: "If ever I have to discuss the essentials of Jewish literature I shall shelter behind the tall figure of Sholem Asch. For in his stories you will find that lyric quality, as though death and terror were simply the notes in an age-old song."[12] Many writers would settle gladly for a similar epitaph.

IV   In the *Shtetl*

Sholem Asch was born in Russian Poland, in Kutno near Warsaw, on November 1, 1880.[13] He was the eleventh of Moshe Asch's fifteen children. Stemming from a family of ritual slaughterers, Moshe Gombiner Asch was modestly versed in Talmud, a generous donor to charity, and by vocation a cattle-and-sheep merchant and an innkeeper. Years after his death he would be eulogized by his author-son as having had an "unswerving belief in the universalness [*sic*] of God and a deep, understanding love of man."[14] He also served as prototype for several of his son's idealized patriarchs, most specifically Reb Shlomo Nagid and Reb Israel Zyclinski ("Kola Street"). Malka Asch, Sholem's mother, was a Widowsky, a family noted in Lenchitz for its piety. She was her husband's second wife and much younger (and taller) than he. His father's house was for Sholem a warm but somewhat divided place. On one side were his five older half-brothers who were adhering Hasidim and wore black gabardine. One the other, and filling the house, were his four sisters and five brothers; the latter were large, robust men who consorted with tradesmen, laborers, and peasants and who liked the good life. These brothers and their sisters later came to America and, in general, prospered.

Despite his heavy burden, Moshe Asch kept his family in comfortable circumstances, seeing to it that all his sons got some religious instruction. Sholem was the designated "scholar" among them. Bright, inquisitive, articulate, he fanned his pious parents' hopes for a rabbinical son; they enrolled him in Kutno's best religious school or *cheder*, where the more affluent townsmen sent

their children. But Moshe Asch did not rely entirely on others to
instruct his son in God's ways. "The Bible was the first book,"
Sholem Asch noted later, "that I had ever held in my hand. From it
my father taught me the alphabet. It was my textbook and my book
of boyish joy, my grammar and my storybook, my geography and
my history book. One might say that in my childhood I studied no
other branch of knowledge but that which shines out of the
Bible. . . . Through it I obtained a conception of the manifold joyful
things of nature."[15] This early exposure proved lasting. The Bible
remained a lifelong prism for Asch's vision; he not only derived
from it constant literary inspiration but became a zealous collector
of rare Biblical editions and incunabula.

His Hebrew school, however, emphasized Talmud rather than
Bible. From early morning until late evening, he would recall, he
studied the Talmud's intricate canonical law. "I was not allowed
much time to read the Bible. Nor was I permitted to occupy myself
very often with the Haggadah, that part of Jewish writings which
expounds the law through parables and tales. . . . That was
regarded as pastime."[16] Young Sholem appears to have been (like
the youthful Yechiel in *Salvation*) a thoughtful and solemn little boy
who felt caught up in two very different worlds. One seemed small
and temporary; the other appeared true, vast, eternal, and
embodied in the Bible's small Hebrew letters. A Jewish child in
Eastern Europe did not spend his days in this world's fields and
streams but in those where Abraham, Isaac, and Jacob grazed and
watered their flocks. For gentile lads summer may have been the
happiest time, but for the Jewish boy it was the saddest; he then
had to spend his weekdays in the dark schoolroom, plus three
weeks mourning the Temple's destruction.

The school Asch attended was segregated from that of his
Polish neighbors; the teacher tended to be severe, and both
Hebrew and Yiddish had to be learned flawlessly. Winters brought
their special hardships. Years later, reminiscing in his comfortable
home in Miami Beach, Asch sighed that he had arisen every
morning at four, "and four in the morning is much colder in Poland
than it is in Miami! We had to haul our own water to wash in and
more frequently it was not water at all, but ice!"[17] The week's
happiest moments for devout young Sholem were provided by the
Sabbath. Its benediction of lighted candles and bright silver
seemed "not as a day of temporal life, but as one of the days which
awaited us in the next world. . . . When I saw the gentile 'Strusch'

(porter) [*sic*] sweep the yard while we sat at the dazzling white-covered table, I broke into copious tears because God had created such luckless people as the *goyim*." [18]

Yet despite his rigorous studies, Sholem did find some time to play and to ask questions. A doting Malka Asch, when past eighty, remembered how her small son's active presence would brighten a room,[19] how he had loved riding horseback on the window sill, and how he had pestered her repeatedly to explain why God had divided mankind into Jew and gentile.[20] With her large, boisterous brood, Malka Asch undoubtedly had little time or patience for metaphysics, but the question would echo through her son's writings. A tall, strong-willed woman, she left an indelible, if curious, mark on her adoring son and his work: nearly every Asch hero has a mother-fixation.

Asch's boyhood may be glimpsed from personal comments in essays and interviews, and from such *shtetl* narratives as *The Little Town*, *Reb Shlomo Nagid*, "Kola Street," and *Salvation*, among others, for in these he draws heavily upon Kutno memories. In "Kola Street," for instance, he describes his native area with its peasants and Jews. The region, he states, is a triangular area "along the bend of the Vistula . . . a region poor in water and sparse in forests. . . . Flat and monotonous are its fields, and the peasant who cultivates them is as plain as the potatoes they yield." Valuing his horse above family and other possessions, the peasant "is like a clod of earth into which God has breathed a soul. . . . He is a man without guile—'I am as God made me.' When he is friendly he will give you his very shirt; but when he gets mad he will take his revenge, let it be at the cost of his life." [21]

But young Sholem naturally assumed the earth, like Kutno, was inhabited primarily by Jews. Gentiles existed simply to put out lights on the Sabbath and do the other menial work not permitted Jews on the day of rest. Their other activities hardly seemed fruitful. Every Tuesday and Friday, Asch notes in *Salvation*, peasants filled the market place and air with cursing, guffawing, screaming, haggling, and whip-cracking—seemingly oblivious of the approaching Sabbath. Only Sunday brought a change; they then moved quietly behind carefully groomed horses and, dressed in their best, camped about the church.[22]

Asch's pride is clear when he describes the region's hardy outdoor Jews, those lacking the painfully familiar indoor frailty and pallor.

The Jew native to this region partakes more of the flavor of wheat and of apples than of the synagogue and the ritual bath. . . . Among the Jews there are the renowned fishermen of the Lonsk ponds . . . [as well as] the sturdy teamsters who take Litvaks to the frontier where the railway has not yet penetrated; and the big horse-dealers who sell the horses bred and nurtured by the peasants to Germans coming from Torun and Berlin. . . . Throughout the week the Jew stays in the village sharing the peasant's life. For the Sabbath he comes to town to attend services at the Three-Trade Synagogue, where fishermen, cattlemen, and teamsters divide the honors among them, and where they discuss the events of the week. ("Kola Street," p. 261.)

The Asch house nestled amid a cluster of Jewish dwellings encircling the old synagogue; some gentiles also lived within this enclave. Linked by a common exposure to poverty and the harsh winters, Jews and Christians dwelled peaceably enough most of the year. But religious holidays proved troublesome. Christmas was not bad, Asch recalled, for Christians then were kindly disposed towards their neighbors. Easter, however, brought problems. On Holy Thursday the Christians would celebrate the Feast of Corpus Christi by leading a procession of holy images through the poor Jewish street, and no Jew dared appear outside his house.

One Holy Thursday proved memorable. Young Sholem had been peeping through a crack in the shades when he saw "what appeared to be a figure of a Jewish rabbi with a beard and wearing a Hebrew inscription on his head. From an open wound in his naked body, streams of blood seemed to be pouring down. I started to cry and called out, 'Mother, the gentiles have killed another Jew!' Actually it was a life-size figure of Christ on the crucifix. This impression has always remained with me."[23] (Using this experience in *Salvation*, Asch has his child-hero stumble into the crowd and barely escape with his life and the loss of a side curl.)

Yet Jews and gentiles mostly got along in the town, where they shared civil authority. Beyond the town limits, however, the gentiles were sole rulers and repeatedly reminded the Jews that the fields and streams did not belong to them. On Friday afternoons Jews bathing in the Vistula in preparation for the Sabbath might be beset by whip-wielding young gentiles. The latter also controlled the local lake in which young Sholem loved to swim. To get to the lake he had to pass through the gentile cobblers' lane. One June afternoon, during a Pentecost when he was about seven, he was sneaking toward the lake when three or four boys his own age caught him. They were armed with sticks and accompanied by two dogs. Pushing him into the dust, they threatened to rip his new Passover coat unless he answered a "simple" question: "Did you kill Christ? Did you?" He knew the Christian God was called Jesus, but "Christ" was unknown to him. Afraid to return home with a torn coat, he confessed to the murder. "I was not the first to plead guilty to an uncommitted crime under the torture of an inquisition." He then learned such confessions avail little, as the boys immediately beat him and tore his coat.[24]

Thus his first encounter with "Christ" came to him, Asch would remember sadly, "not through good works, nor through faith and compassion, in accordance with the teaching of Jesus the Nazarene; it came to me through fear and terror, through blood and fire. Every Christian holiday in my childhood years was turned into days of fright and suffering."[25] He never overcame these early fears. Years later he declared that "Churches for me are forbidden fruit. . . . In my early childhood, the two crosses on the towers of the Gothic church in my town, I am sorry to say, had always frightened me and awakened all the terror in my blood inherited from ancestors of long martyrdom."[26] Indeed Jesus' mere name evoked for him "all the torments which the Christian world has made us endure throughout the years of our history." Hence "that name arouses no pride in Israel, no hope and solace, as might be expected, but only fear, pain, and terror. And these lines are intended as nothing more than a way of justifying myself against those boys of the cobblers' lane who are still holding me even today by my side curls and tail of my coat in terror of their savage dogs."[27] Asch never lost his fear of dogs, but in time Christ took on for him very different connotations, often to his coreligionists' consternation. "I have never separated Christ from the Jewish people," he told an interviewer. "On the contrary, I have always considered, from my earliest youth, that Christ is the everlasting sufferer for the sins which are committed by all of us."[28] Asch saw no contradiction in his responses to the image and concept of Jesus of Nazareth. Most Jews, however, have been more prone to accept Jesus Christ as a tangible symbol of their suffering at Christian hands than as emblematic of their own collective sinfulness.

V   From Talmud to Enlightenment

Upon finishing *cheder*, Sholem moved on to the House of Study to learn on his own. Even as he poured over Talmud folios, he became aware of major social changes. New ideas abroad in the

Jewish world had penetrated the city ghettos; now the Enlightenment was asserting itself among Kutno's young people. Sholem soon read enough "profane" literature to consider himself too worldly to become a rabbi or Talmudic scholar. He was also too interested in nature, too fond of wandering the woods and observing its wonders, and too interested in human foibles. No, the rabbinate, he decided, was not for him.

The local culture center for Asch and his friends was the home of classmate Abraham Glicksman. The only "enlightened" Jewish house in Kutno, it boasted a library of German classics. As the young people gleaned German from Moses Mendelssohn's German translation of the Psalms (printed in Hebrew alphabet), they read Schiller, Goethe, Heine—and Shakespeare. Heine's poetry moved Asch to memorize lengthy passages, and he developed a deep fondness for German literature.[29] In Kutno secrets were few, and Sholem Asch soon was counted among the community's growing circle of *maskilim*, or secular intellectuals. Then he began experiencing a strong compulsion to write. Publisher Reuben Brainin recalls in his memoirs having received, about 1896, ungrammatical effusions in Hebrew from Asch. The latter was sixteen and these were his first literary efforts. Brainin emphasizes the numerous grammatical errors and relates his impression that Asch had dipped a whittled stick in charcoal and water to put his immature reflections on paper.[30] Brainin's tone does him little credit. Asch was displaying his determination to overcome a limited education and become a writer.

Apparently his new secular outlook was embarrassing to his family in so orthodox a community as Kutno. At seventeen he was sent to relatives in a nearby village, where he became a Hebrew teacher for the Jewish children and an observer of the Polish peasants and simple, toiling Jews. "This was my first schooling in life," he later declared. "Until that time I was a completely orthodox believing Jew. Later I was convinced that the simple Jew, the *folkmensch*, the common man, stands on a much higher ethical level than the learned Hasid."[31] He would never lose this conviction.

After some months in the village, Asch spent the next two years in Wloclawek (Vlotslavsk in Russian), a Vistula River port and industrial center. He tried a variety of jobs there before he settled down to writing letters for people who could not write. He enjoyed most the love letters, he confessed, for these gave him glimpses into life's "hidden corners" and served as a part of his "higher schooling." [32] He was reading Tolstoy, Hauptmann, and especially Boleslaw Prus, a Polish novelist of peasant life. [33] He also was finding much to admire in Hebrew and Yiddish poetry and fiction, and soon fell under the "strong influence" of Isaac Leib Peretz. [34] He literally memorized Peretz's slender volume of Hebrew love poems entitled *The Flute* [*Ha-Ugav*] and read and re-read the latter's best-known Yiddish satires, "The Hasidic Hat!" and "Bontche the Silent." [35]

He himself was writing solely in Hebrew; he was trying hard to master the short story or sketch, which he considered the most effective medium for the myriad images and thoughts now crowding his imagination. Since childhood he had observed closely the people and customs about him. In 1899, when he left Kutno and the provinces for Warsaw, he carried a folder of Hebrew sketches of the small-town Jewish life he knew so well. A year after his arrival, these sketches (revised and most of them transposed into Yiddish) would launch his career.

Chapter 2
Warsaw and Early Success

Asch traveled by boat along the Vistula to Warsaw, at that time Europe's center of Jewish culture. He carried his *shtetl* sketches and a few poems. Upon arrival he went almost immediately to the famed Isaac Leib Peretz (1852-1915); the latter was then at the peak of his reputation and powers and considered (with Mendele and Sholom Aleichem) a "father" of modern Yiddish literature. A vibrant, engaging conversationalist, Peretz liked relating his stories to friends before putting them on paper. He shared Mendele's biting wit and a subdued form of Sholom Aleichem's humor. A close student of European thought and writing, he was steeped also in Hebrew scripture and lore, and he filled his fiction with allusions to Bible, Talmud, and the sages. His humanism and sophistication had failed, however, to make him a narrow secularist; on the contrary, a persistent pietism moved Peretz to delve into ghetto legend, especially the wondrous tales of the Hasidim. Indeed, his re-evaluation of the Hasidic movement and its stories not only popularized literary Hasidism but also prepared the way for such later exponents of the Hasidic tale as Asch, Martin Buber, and Isaac Bashevis Singer. Recognizing his contribution, his contemporaries credited Peretz with having given new scope and stature to modern Yiddish literature.

I Peretz and "Madja"

"Yal" Peretz's warmth and generosity attracted young Yiddish writers, who made his home, at Ceglana 1, a veritable Hasidic court. David Pinski, Hirsh David Nomberg, Zalman Schneour, Abraham Reisen, and Moshe Nadir were among the disciples Asch found gathered around the master. Older writers "feared and avoided Peretz," claims critic Alexander Mukdoni; "their ideas and styles were fixed, and they feared his power and influence."[1] But younger writers welcomed his assistance. He read and corrected their manuscripts and helped the newcomers (most of them ex-Talmud students from the provinces) publish their efforts. Asch later repeatedly acknowledged Peretz's friendship and financial aid in his time of "greatest need";[2] this aid also included, apparently, help in freeing him from military service. Obviously Asch had this debt in mind when in *Three Cities* he has a "Warsaw novelist" help a young provincial writer establish himself.

A severe but friendly judge, Peretz was quick to praise creativity or originality. "He had one great gift which helped to discover new talent," Asch would recall. "He seemed to sense the 'soul' of everything that was read to him. . . . And the moment he penetrated the intrinsic significance of a piece of writing, he was willing to overlook many external flaws."[3] Certainly the somber, sentimental Hebrew sketches and verses Asch now presented for evaluation exhibited many such "external flaws." Reading Asch's first story, Peretz remarked, "A bird is breaking through the shell—who knows whether it will be an eagle or a crow?"[4] But whatever his doubts, he recognized in this tall, fervent young man a budding talent. Peretz himself had written in Russian, Polish, and Hebrew before gaining his reputation, after forty, as a Yiddish writer. Seeing Asch's knowledge was limited to traditional Jewish lore and small-town life, he advised the youth to return home and rewrite his stories in Yiddish, to achieve greater naturalness and fluency. When Asch agreed, the master welcomed him to his inner circle.

A few months later Asch returned to Warsaw to read Peretz his first tales in Yiddish. Peretz recommended them to Dr. Joseph Luria, editor of *The Jew*, and Asch's first published story, "Little Moses," appeared there. Asch followed it two issues later with "The Grandfather" and "The Hanukah Lamp," and with six more sketches during the next year. Soon after "Little Moses" was published, one of his few remaining Hebrew tales, "On the Way," was included in David Frishman's weekly, *The Post*. His first efforts being well received, Asch produced stories for Warsaw's leading Yiddish newspapers, *The People's Times* and *Today*.[5] He established himself quickly as the master's most ambitious, prolific disciple. Peretz was pleased to see his judgment so soon vindicated, but Asch's young rivals, some of whom had built small reputations before his arrival in Warsaw, now found it difficult to accept with total good grace his near-meteoric success. In later years several repeatedly disparaged his work and character. They refused to admit that Asch's rapid progress reinforced their own efforts to establish Yiddish as a respected literary medium; nor did they acknowledge that his subsequent breakthrough to the larger European world of theater and letters added new luster to all Yiddish writing.

As 1900 drew to a close, Asch was a recognized young writer. His career and the new century were beginning together. Fervent, idealistic, hard-driving, he impressed everyone with his obvious talents. His appearance was an added asset. He had a strong face and a thick shock of dark hair, while at six feet one he towered over most acquaintances. Jewish intellectual circles took him up, and at twenty, only months from the *shtetl*, he found himself a near-celebrity. The world was bright and exciting. His stories were being published and praised, and he kept meeting clever, active people; among these was the beautiful Matilda Spiro, daughter of a respected Hebrew teacher and writer.[6] Ardent socialists, the Spiros were deeply involved in Warsaw's political and social ferment. To young Sholem Asch they must have seemed as exciting a family as the Hurvitzes in *Three Cities* do to young Zachary Mirkin upon his arrival in Warsaw.

Sholem and Matilda married in 1901, and for the next 56 years "Madja" devoted herself to her husband and his work, sharing his every interest, and defending him when necessary from enemies, critics, and friends. A year later their son Nathan was born. Nathan would grow up to experience fully the American Depression and to write political articles, stories, movie scenarios, and five novels (one causing a celebrated obscenity trial); his last published piece would be a soul-searching memoir of his relationship with his father. Two other sons, Moses and John, and a daughter, Ruth, would follow.[7]

II The Yiddish Literary Tradition

Asch learned much from earlier writers, Jewish and non-Jewish. Among Jewish authors, Mendele Mocher Sforim (Mendele the Bookseller)[8] had probably the most direct effect. Peretz was a generous and wise patron, but for Asch he did not prove a lasting influence. To discuss Asch, a critic must glance at least at the Yiddish literary tradition; he must also treat Jewish literature and Yiddish literature as near synonyms. Yiddish is, of course, a quite distinct language. Its alphabet and many of its words derive from the Hebrew of the Old Testament and Talmud. Yet it is basically a German dialect—one that originated in the four-teenth and fifteenth centuries, when German Jews migrating to

Poland carried along their Middle High German speech. Viewing the new homeland as less culturally advanced than the old, these Jews clung to their earlier idiom. The Yiddish that emerged provided Eastern Jewry with its *mamme-loshen* (mother tongue) for the next five centuries. Time, naturally, brought new ingredients. If an elaborate daily religious ritual perpetuated the rich Hebrew component, Jewish contact with Polish and Russian life introduced a strong Slavic element. Indeed Yiddish, being the patois of a transient people, had to prove flexible enough to absorb linguistic elements from various tongues.

In 1880, when Asch was born, Yiddish had little status as a language. "Modern" Jews used their respective European vernaculars; the orthodox condescended to Yiddish as their daily idiom, but they wrote only in Hebrew—stretching the scriptural vocabulary to cover contemporary needs. The next two decades, however, saw sharp changes: Zionism and the Russian pogroms wrought an ethnic awakening, and Europe's Jews felt they needed a living language. Some still turned to Hebrew, but most Jewish writers—led by Mendele, Sholom Aleichem,[9] and Yal Peretz— adopted Yiddish. Ironically, its very "flexibility" could have obliterated Yiddish as an effective medium had it not produced a vital modern literature that appeared abruptly and flowered quickly. In two generations, one commentator has observed, "a brawling . . . jargon, a gibberish shady in pedigree and flabby in syntax, ignored by the world and despised by its own users,"[10] somehow developed a literature of beauty, vigor, and truth. Yet the impetus to Yiddish was as much social as literary. At century's end, economic and political unrest, spreading from the Jewish Pale of Settlement to New York's Lower East Side, gave a new thrust to Yiddish. As the vernacular of the masses, it became the obvious propaganda vehicle for the emerging Jewish Socialist (or Bundist) movement; in fact, activists all along the Jewish political spectrum turned to Yiddish to disseminate their ideas.[11]

Mendele, Peretz, and Sholom Aleichem, preceding Asch by a generation, were primarily responsible for fashioning Yiddish prose into an effective literary vehicle. Adding Hebrew, Russian, and Polish words to the Yiddish lexicon, they and their contemporaries refined and enriched it stylistically and substantively. "They found a housemaid literature of tawdry romances and popular songs," wrote a critic, and then "they proceeded to dignify it by expressing a nation's suffering and to inspire it by voicing a nation's ideals."[12] Heirs to a difficult age, these authors rejected romanticism to depict Jewish life with candor, humor, and bite. They combined stinging satire of ghetto filth and fanaticism with a tender sympathy for the people. A powerful Yiddish press and a loyal reading public developed, and with them a vigorous poetry and prose. Yiddish drama lagged behind for a time as unimaginative, conservative producers, interested only in sure-fire but shoddy melodramas, restrained and repressed serious creativity.

Asch's literary generation included novelists David Pinski, Joseph Opatoshu, Zalman Shneour, and Israel Joshua Singer—all of whom grew to maturity under the influence of the three "fathers." They found themselves writing about a Jewish world verging on dust and ashes due to age, change, persecution, and war. Like their predecessors, they started their careers by portraying life in the outmoded *shtetl.* But new times and conflicting pressures soon reshaped their views of Jewish life. Asch and the others had been born during the last days of the Jewish Enlightenment, when its followers, moved by nostalgia and a sense of loss, were beginning to romanticize Hasidism and even to view the ghetto more sympathetically. Feeling themselves a part of both the older and newer worlds, these younger writers rejected the static and merely venerable to portray a life in transition, a life in which their roots were immediate and deep but one which they recognized as no longer viable. Anxious to catch and describe this disappearing world, they concentrated upon movement and change, pausing reluctantly over individual foibles or idiosyncrasies. Everything they saw and recorded was aimed primarily at emphasizing this dynamic, often traumatic, transition. Their novels and tales seem now but segments of a vast, portentous drama of movement, a drama in which countless vital individuals emerge briefly only to be swept aside by larger events.

Together, these young novelists fashioned a modern Yiddish fiction that proved predominantly naturalistic and vivid, as well as often erotic, coarse, and vital. Influenced also by Tolstoy, several later wrote massive chronicles of the shifts in Jewish family life. Even Asch's small set piece *The Little Town* conveyed this "movement." In addition, a sense of urgent social change was integral to Judaism's prophetic tradition—in which prophecy involved not only foretelling the future but ideas related to change. This Hebrew conception of eternal flux (in contrast to Hellenism's emphasis on the present or *carpe diem*) was absorbed into Yiddish literature. Hence Asch and his contemporaries thought in terms of transience and variety of technique rather than the permanence or "purity" of art, of collective trends rather than individual character; their men and women were less individuals than generic types or forces acting and acted upon. The protagonists of their longer novels tended to be the entire folk, whose members re-experienced the archetypal Jewish role of a wandering people put to repetitive tests of fortitude and endurance. Their novels, stories, and plays embodied as much history and social protest as "fiction," since their materials proved inseparable from the gentile contexts they contained and reflected.[13]

A young Yiddish novelist at the century's turn, therefore, had rich materials to feed his imagination. Asch, moving between Kutno and Warsaw, observed the Russian Empire on the eve of Bolshevism. So cataclysmic were each day's social changes that life appeared often a harshly realistic historical pageant. Yet the Hasidism he knew so well had inclined him towards the mystical or Messianic, as well as to a sort of sensual pietism. God, for the true Hasid, was revealed in all natural phenomena, and in Kutno young Sholem had felt close to nature's orchards, forests, and trees. Thus did sharply diverse forces—realistic and religiously romantic—combine to shape his vision and imagination.

Asch now published two small collections of Hebrew stories, and then early in 1903 he brought out a first book of twelve Yiddish sketches aptly titled *In An Evil Time*.[14] The critics, led by the prominent Dr. Isidor Eliashev ("Bal Makhshoves"), reviewed the volume warmly; they found in its somber vignettes of small-town Hasidic life an idyllic lyricism that set them apart from those of such older writers as Jacob Dinesohn, Isaac Joel Lienetsky, and even Yal Peretz. Like Peretz, Asch appreciated the human values beneath the town's dusty provincial surface and Hasidism's ritualistic crudities. Yet he was not blind to the town's soul-stifling poverty and rigidity, and his tales were marked by a hapless melancholy and sorrow. Their most distinct resemblance, however, was to Mendele's stories. Loving the simple provincial Jew, both Mendele and Asch emphasized his ties to his physical world. They acknowledged also the close, if paradoxical, bonds between nature and the most sophisticated cosmopolitan Jew.[15] Both relished detailing Jewish communal hopes, feelings, and manners, and both traced repeatedly the steady ossifying of once-vital group responses to life and faith into cold ritual and custom. In satirizing ghetto squalor, ignorance, and vulgarity, Mendele was often more the disinterested, ironic naturalist than an involved and sympathetic chronicler. Only in his later writings did he manage to be both ironic and tender, precise and compassionate—as well as sardonic.

Asch, however, exuded always a warm concern for his people and their fates. If he rejected early the fashionable literary moods of parochialism and isolation, he soon romanticized the Jewish community's underlying patriarchal structure, with its peculiar idealism, harmony, and unity. Seeing that life as a totality rather than a fragmented entity, he treated it with greater empathy and less objectivity than had his predecessors. Less satiric and detached than Mendele, he linked his stories more tightly to the world he described. Mendele aimed always to instruct. But Asch, wishing primarily to re-create the spirit animating Jewish life, was tempted to depict the distant or near past in fervently lyric and idyllic terms. As he came to favor setting and description over character and action, he allowed his prose to grow "softer," to become more sensuous; consequently, his rustic characters and pastoral settings lost the realism, bite, and pathos of Mendele and the older Yiddish writers. Instead, his tales began to reveal the easy sentiment, inflated rhetoric, and imprecise diction that marred so much of his later writing.

III The *Shtetl* and Its People

Yal Peretz advised every disciple who had proved himself a competent story writer to try a novel. When he suggested that Asch do so, the latter agreed. "That's right," he told his friend Abraham Reisen. "Another story, another sketch, another poem, but we must have a novel. With short stories and poems alone one doesn't achieve greatness."[16] Yet his first longer narrative was a relatively cautious and modest effort. Appearing serially in 1904, *The Little Town*[17] proved less novel than tone poem, with its scenes and episodes vaguely reminiscent of Eden Phillpotts' *Widecombe Fair*. Drawing upon Kutno memories and his relatives there, Asch apotheosizes the Polish *shtetl* and the serene patriarchal life it boasted before time and catastrophe demolished all. Oscar Cargill has characterized Asch's idyllic hamlet as "a Polish Cranford on the Vistula, though the characters are more robust and certainly more carnal than those in Mrs. Gaskell's story."[18] Here the early Asch is at his best. In disciplined prose that is both lyric and vigorous, he integrates the gestures and incidents of daily life into a harmonious genre portrait. His sensitive depictions of lush bordering woods and mighty Vistula, on whose banks the town nestles, enhance the pastoral effect. The townsmen reveal an earthiness and love of nature uncommon in Yiddish fiction. "The first Yiddish writer to paint the out-of-doors with pagan joy," Asch was, according to Charles Madison, "the first to luxuriate in the description of sensuous beauty for its own sake."[19]

This short narrative proved Asch's first major success and secured his place in Yiddish literature. Despite his later world fame, he remained for East Europe's Jews the venerated chronicler of *The Little Town* and the later *Reb Shlomo Nagid*. The critics hailed its "romantic realism" as a fresh approach to both the old Jewish life and modern Yiddish writing. While recognizing Asch's slight debt to Peretz's Hasidic tales, they welcomed his departure from the barbed satire of Mendele and older Yiddish authors. This earlier group had ridiculed such Jewish Pale towns as "symbols of Jewish petrifaction and superstitious resistance to enlightenment."[20] To be fair, these writers did not lack sympathy or affection for their fellow Jews, for they saw them as having borne a heavy cross for two thousand years.[21] But they were neither blind to Jewish faults nor reluctant to castigate them. Self-pity—communal or individual—was their special target.

Asch avoids the abhorrence of the "ghetto spirit" so evident in Peretz and Sholom Aleichem to revel in admiration for his little Jews. Revealing elements of that "soil romanticism" he later expanded into a distinctive manner, he fixes a romantic halo around his characters and their despised *shtetl;* he finds beauty in its filthy streets, charm and elevation in its gray daily existence. Czarist oppression and cruelty, pervasive in Sholom Aleichem and Yal Peretz's towns and villages, are lacking here. No crushing miseries are in evidence, only peace and contentment. Asch does not see the *shtetl* exclusively in Jewish terms but as a composite of Jewish townsmen and gentile peasants—all existing happily far from Europe's cultural mainstream. So loving is he toward his characters that they evoked charges of sentimentality and parochialism—with even one generally admiring critic, Isidor Eliashev, dismissing the Jewish ones as "children with beards and earlocks."[22] And these do reveal here the virtues and vices that result from a lack of distance or separation from their creator. They can not be mistaken for anything but Jews, yet they are not the living Russian-Polish Jews of three or four generations ago; they are, instead, highly transformed and idealized beings drawn from an impressionable childhood and shaped undoubtedly by the sharp contrasts offered to the Warsaw ghetto's careworn inhabitants among whom Asch now lived. They filtered through his memory and imagination as kind, wholesome rustics sharing the peasantry's carnal robustness but grounded in their fathers' revered faith and customs and as exuding a perpetual holiday or Sabbath exuberance.

The action of *The Little Town* covers nine months (early spring to late fall) in the community of Kasner. The setting is serene, nature bountiful, and life almost devoid of poverty and fear. Their trust in God enables the townspeople to cope firmly with life. "The Jews are one people with one God, and they all await the same Messiah," observes Asch, "but every little village has its own look, its own customs, one might say its own soul, with which it stamps its inhabitants."[23] In Kasner the people seem stamped with God's goodwill. The reader arrives with a lone pack-bearing "wayfarer" in the spring thaw. Black fertile soil emerges from the snow, and crows dot the bare white branches. Carnival entertainers appear, perform, and disappear. Soon the nights warm as summer replaces spring. Happy mothers and infants fill the doorways while prankish boys race about and young girls exchange secrets. Jews and peasants feel themselves in harmony with nature. In late afternoon the air fills with sacred and secular songs that blend with a synagogue student's sorrowful melody.

Somber notes are scarce here, but a few are heard. The local Hasidim displace the craftsmen's unlettered but saintly rabbi with their own "wonder" rabbi, the synagogue burns, and on market day it rains—and always the future poses uncertainties. But these weekday motions soon are replaced by Friday's late afternoon bustle: the community must usher in the Sabbath. School boys then hurry with their fathers from barber to bathhouse, peddlers return to town, Hasidim arrive to visit their rabbi, and even the peasants feel festive and get drunk. A "Friday feeling" pervades as the sun shines brightly on all. But soon a dark quietude settles in and Sabbath candles fill the windows.

Summer fades quickly into the awesome month of Elul with its High Holy days and ensuing Succoth festivities. These then give way to the fall's drab pattern, and life resumes a grayish hue. Winds scatter dead leaves through the streets and roads turn muddy. A traveling yarn dealer (winter's "first bird") heralds the cold season by hawking his wool. He is followed by a sad-eyed Jew making his annual collection of charity boxes for the Holy Land—and by an array of peddlers, beggars, orphans, lonely women, booksellers, and the sick coming to be cured by the new wonder rabbi. Over them all, intones Asch, rests

a kind of Jewish charm, a spirit of familiarity with the other world of mystery, a veil, like the coat of dust that lies upon ancient holy books. One might have imagined that such a Jewish world actually existed somewhere—a Jewish world consisting of one immense house of prayer, where the whole Jewish community lived as though in a case of discarded leaves out of the scriptures, enveloped in holy dust, and that upon all this there lay the spirit of Jewish family love and of longing. [24]

The successful lumber merchant Yechezkel Gombiner (a thinly disguised Moshe Gombiner Asch) and his family link the various vignettes of town life. Pious, humble, and generous, Reb Yechezkel opens his door to all. No inept *luftmensch* (like Sholom Aleichem's Menachem Mendel or Mendele's Benjamin the Third), he is a hard-headed entrepreneur with a quick eye for any sound venture. Convinced that God shares in every endeavor, he adheres to the holy law's moral principles. When a spring ice floe threatens his logs, Reb Yechezkel refuses to work his men in the dark. "God's mercy," he declares, "will guard the rafts overnight." His voice is heard, for at dawn the ice bypasses his rafts. His good fortune continues when he encounters a fellow merchant with a son fresh from the Yeshiva: the lad will make a fine husband for his daughter Leabeh. The match is arranged, and Reb Yechezkel sheds happy tears at the prospect of a learned son-in-law. For the Gombiners, life in Kasner promises much.

When the first snow arrives, the lone wayfarer leaves. The evening is peaceful and the moon floats clear and bright. Schoolboys returning home extinguish their lanterns to walk by moonlight between snow-laden poplars. Night stillness absorbs their laughter as the *shtetl* fades into darkness—and history.

These early sketches hold up well. Had Asch retained the lucid, understated language he exhibits here, he would rate as a fine stylist. His approach is almost elliptical and oblique, with much left to the reader's imagination. His young rivals must have learned much from his technique, but Asch himself was to grow increasingly discursive and didactic. Many later traits are already evident, especially his appreciation of nature as tangible evidence of God's hand and spirit. His desire for harmony between Christian and Jew, his admiration for the unlettered but devout Jewish laborer (and simple peasant), and his reservations—mingled with admiration—for the Hasidim are also to be seen. Visible too is his eagerness to describe Jewish holidays, feasts, and foods, and their bustling preparations. Asch loves the generous host, custom, or act; he dislikes the mean in mind, deed, or spirit. He catches a figure or personality in a few words or gestures, shaping each into a *shtetl* or ghetto type of vivid idiosyncrasy. His numerous characters are varied, but they were fated to become painfully familiar. Here, however, setting rather than character predominates. Town, river, and soil, even the lumber, grain, and livestock, overshadow the little people and their problems.

The *shtetl* fascinated Asch as a subject, and he returned to it repeatedly. Several early protagonists are town elders who take on communal responsibilities with the solemnity of an ancient patriarch. Their fellow Jews accept these shepherds as they do life, without question or hesitancy. These leaders do their appointed tasks, praise God at every opportunity, and enjoy peace and plenty. They see themselves as God's trustees, their wealth as His gifts, and their charity and benevolence merely as His means of distributing aid to the needy. The poor take their help as from a father. Yet in fashioning such portraits Asch was indulging in nostalgia, for the traditional Jewish town was disintegrating when he was born. As the old order dissolved, so did the patriarchal mold of communal life; long-humble social groups (butchers, bakers, teamsters, peddlers), now grown assertive, were insisting on new modes of expression and advancement. Aggressive and ambitious, they flaunted their physical prowess and defied tired conventions. Every town had a street harboring this recently aroused element. Most of its members remained within the Czar's law, but some moved beyond legal bounds. Soon even the smallest Jewish town boasted a miniature "underworld" that cried for portrayal, and Asch was among the few to undertake the task.

He wrote, almost simultaneously with *The Little Town,* a cluster of tales about these new shaded Jewish figures and life-styles; they reveal his (and his literary generation's) revolt against the "excessive refinement and thinness"[25] of Sholom Aleichem, Peretz, and the other older writers. These stories display also Asch's other descriptive tendency—his unblinking realism, a realism that, at first glance, seems to differ sharply from the romanticism of *The Little Town.* Yet tales like "Kola Street," "Daughter of the Upper Class," and "Abandoned" mix romanticism and realism to depict not only his familiar patriarchs but burly laborers and thieves of raw strength and emotions who yearn for a better life. Asch returns often to the tough workmen who have outgrown humble origins but have not won social acceptance. The more respectable citizens scorn them as roughnecks—till danger threatens the community or till a laborer scores a business success. For the upright elders often need money. In *God of Vengeance, Mottke the Thief,* and *Salvation,* Asch develops these ideas fully, but in "Kola Street," and "Daughter of the Upper Class" he presents briefer treatments. In the first he revels in the strength and courage of the Three-Trade Synagogue's butchers, teamsters, and fishermen who rout in pitched battle their hostile gentile neighbors. They see to it that in their town no Jewish scholar or merchant is beaten by carousing peasants or soldiers. Yet these same scholars and merchants dismiss the Kola Streeters as illiterate rabble, who are sometimes useful. For Asch, however, this rough element embodies a courage and generosity of spirit sadly lacking in their social superiors.

His "Daughter of the Upper Class" centers on an unlettered teamster named Mattes, who by ambition and ability rises to wealthy wagon owner and carrier. His companions have been wagon drivers, stable boys, and servant maids, but now he wants a more genteel life. A clever matchmaker helps Mattes marry the daughter of an upperclass merchant who needs his money. Much taken with his wife's refined manners and demeanor, Mattes tries hard to improve himself, to acquire a respectable veneer. He succeeds only enough to create a gulf between himself and his former companions, who are now his employees and consider him of another class. Trying to join their Sabbath amusements, he feels himself an outsider. He has risen from his former station without having reached his new one; a tough entrepreneur buoyed by success, Mattes is also a man torn by loss and uncertainty.

For that matter, Sholem Asch, the brilliantly successful young author and recent husband and father, caught up quickly by Warsaw's cultural and intellectual circles, may have been experiencing some discomfiting identity twinges of his own.

IV   The Early Plays

The Warsaw of 1904 was an exciting city for a promising Yiddish writer. Still in its "first efflorescence," Yiddish literature had won approval from influential continental intellectuals. Translations of *The Little Town* into Russian, Polish, and German thrust Asch into contact with European editors, publishers, and writers, some of whom made him as aware of social and political happenings as literary ones. European life was more turbulent than usual, and Asch, having left the provinces but four short years before, had to struggle to absorb the recent art trends and new political issues rocking Czarist Russia; he complained that he felt "ignorant and puerile" and uncertain of his literary direction.[27] For guides he chose the masters Tolstoy and Dostoevsky and two current radical "prophetic" writers, Maxim Gorky and Mikhail Artzybashev; these, plus his wife Matilda and her family, combined to make him a strong advocate of both the revolutionary movement and the Social Democrats.

In later years Asch paid homage to a varied list of authors, singling out Cervantes and Dickens as having exerted the strongest influences on him.[28] The claim has some validity, but at this time the Russian writers were shaping his thought and technique. He even translated a Tolstoy short novel into Yiddish to grasp the master's plot and character development. (One story long popular in Jewish circles held that Asch's early tales had won Tolstoy's admiration and that when members of the St. Petersburg Dramatic Club talked of blackballing Asch because he was a Jew, Tolstoy threatened to leave the club.[29] If apocryphal, and whatever the facts, this is one of those stories that *should* be true.) Convinced that translating was teaching him much about the novel, Asch turned several other Russian works into Yiddish. Few who later criticized his craftsmanship could boast a similar dedication. At different times Asch praised a number of novelists, especially two contemporaries, Thomas Mann and Ernest Hemingway (to whom he was introduced by his son Nathan), but he reserved always for Dostoevsky his strongest admiration. When in late years he described to a friend, novelist Louis Zara, his feelings upon re-reading *The Idiot,* Asch bowed his head, placed a hand over his eyes, and declared: "Dostoevsky's characters, we have done nothing like that in our time!"[30]

But young Asch, new to the larger European scene, needed

immediate guides if he were to deal convincingly with contemporary issues. He seemed to find just the right blend of liberal socialism and literary realism in Gorky's *The Lower Depths* (1902) and Artzybashev's *Sanine* (1907). These and similar works inspired him to portray in his own fiction Poland's seething city life and spreading revolutionary anger. A zealous convert to the cause of the underdog, he quickly wrote stories and plays that emphasized the essential, if somewhat distorted, humanity of social misfits and outcasts. In "Abandoned,"[31] for instance, Asch has an infant's cries awaken paternal emotions in a hardened criminal. Tough, thieving Burih Kulock finds his wife has deserted him and their infant son. Raging and vengeful, he tries also to abandon the "damned brat," but the child's wail forces him to rationalize that even a dog does not abandon its young, and soon Burih is reduced to begging food for the two of them.

Asch launched his career as a dramatist in 1904 with *The Return*, a highly rhetorical two-acter in the same social-religious vein as his fiction. But here, as in his other early dramas, he focused on his generation's search for viable alternatives to both religious and secular parochialism. Neither orthodoxy nor nihilism, he made clear, offered young people reliable solutions. Set in the 1870's, *The Return* has for hero a *yeshiva* student, David, who turns skeptic and deserts wife and child for the big city's promised freedom. There he samples various ideologies and movements, only to return home years later devoid of faith or ideal. He has little hope of regaining either. "One can believe only once in Him who is believed!" he declares. "I went out into the world, crumpled my soul and scattered the pieces; each piece bore a different name."[32] Asch followed this play with several others; like his tales and novels, his plays were spiced with a sharp mix of scholars and saints, scoffers and vagabonds. All prove wanderers in search of self and soul,[33] for despite his new socialist sympathies his prime concern in these first dramas remained essentially religious. He was bothered particularly by the inevitable tensions between tradition and flux, as well as by those resulting from the spiritual bankruptcy of quasi-emancipated middle-class Jews and their children's frenetic gropings for new beliefs and values.

To discuss coherently the many plays Asch was turning out at this time would be pointless, even were it possible. His *The Times of the Messiah* (1906), *Winter* (1906), *The Sinner* (1908), *Prestige* (1909), and the later *The Inheritors* (1913) and *Our Faith* (1914) are but a few of the early efforts not yet wholly lost; all deal, somewhat variously, with the three-way confrontation of orthodoxy, heterodoxy, and social change. This recurrent struggle has fascinated many Yiddish writers but none more so than Asch. In *Winter*, [34] for instance, an older sister who has allowed her marriage opportunities to pass now must stand aside, despite tradition, and permit her younger sister to marry. For even the most convention-bound and sentimental Jews (here exemplified by the girls' widowed mother) occasionally must compromise, Asch makes clear, with practical necessity. He returned to this idea in *Our Faith*, [35] an unabashed melodrama in which the religious and emotional consequences of a mixed marriage are diluted by his too-eager emphasis on love's triumph over prejudice.

Even in these first years Asch revealed his compulsive need to challenge traditional thinking on Jewish ritual and custom. His plays of this period also feature protagonists fleeing their Jewishness to enter the larger world. Sometimes their apostasy involves the flaunting of sexual mores, as in his one-act *The Sinner* [36] where a Jewish community struggles to bury a renegade who has flouted holy law. The deadman's black-veiled mistress sobs as the seedy little cemetery refuses his body; each grave turns up bones, spouts water, or produces an impeding stone. The community then makes a final effort to gain the sinner a resting place: amid the elders' prayers to heaven and appeals to the earth, each townsman surrenders to the corpse one of his own good deeds—and seven bricks are placed in the fire to test the deadman's Jewishness. As the woman in black kneels in silent prayer, six bricks split and fall out of the flames. Then the last cracks—but fails to split, proving that even a flawed soul is not easily cast aside. Despite everything, the rabbi declares, the sinner has remained a Jew and the cemetery must receive him. When he is finally buried, his mistress throws her black veil on the grave. Neither one has anything more to hide.

Melodramatic, sentimental, and occasionally ambiguous, these early plays reveal Asch's talents to be descriptive and lyric rather than dramatic. In each his strength derives from a realistic detailing of time and place and from a sound ear for idiom and tradition—all handled with compassionate understanding. In *Winter*, for instance, his extended portrayal of the Jewish stock character of the bypassed older sister, and her anguish, undoubtedly wrenched from his audiences tears of recognition and sympathy. Yet all must have approved his insistence that nothing must prevent the younger sister from avoiding a similar fate. If *The Sinner* seems a less decisive and more puzzling effort, it strikes the same note of pragmatic necessity. Here the communal disdain for the woman in black is presented uncritically, for despite her obvious devotion to the dead man she symbolizes his wickedness; thus her ostracism is part of the punitive process necessary to cleanse his soul of earthly taint.

At this point Asch is still the novice dramatist clumsily dependent on irrelevant stage directions and author's asides. Actions and emotions are externally motivated, and didactic passages clash with the lyric ones. Even his more effective plays, like *The Times of the Messiah* and *God of Vengeance,* include polemical segments from earlier short stories that are not fully integrated into the structure and plot. Yet despite such shortcomings, Asch displays a slowly stirring dramatic sense and more rapidly developing narrative skills. In these plays and those that followed, Asch identified strongly with his own skeptical generation's desperate search for a viable faith. For this sense of loss and deprivation, he held the preceding generation primarily responsible. Moral tensions in *The Times of the Messiah,*[37] for instance, produce a three-generation encounter—that of pious grandparents, agnostic middle-aged parents, and idealistic youths; the young people are embittered by their own and their parents' failure to find a convincing moral or religious code.

These issues are re-examined somewhat more realistically in *The Inheritors,* wherein a cultivated banker, proud of his enlightened rationalism, is appalled to discover that his children despise him for his single-minded devotion to business. His oldest son soon leaves home to work for social causes, while his daughter is kept from entering a convent only by her pious grandfather. These last two figures give clearest voice to the play's theme. "How can I be silent," asks the old man, angered that his granddaughter's planned acceptance of Christianity is meeting little parental resistance,

"when I see my light growing dim, my child making nothing of all that I and my parents have saved with their blood? Should I say nothing when I see the pit into which I and everyone coming after me are falling into, as in a black hell. Do you call this tolerance?"

The girl also blames her parents for her religious confusion. "They gave me everything," she declares, "except one thing—faith. A God they did not give me . . . that which every person needs for his daily existence—a faith, love of God, love toward people. . . . I am no philosopher, I am not interested in whether or not there is a God, I need faith . . . in a dark hour. I should have someone to pray to, someone to appeal to for help." [38]

Asch continues his attack on Jewish philistine life and values in *Prestige*, [39] a play resembling *The Cherry Orchard* but lacking Chekhov's light, ironic touch. Here, too, a proud but impoverished aristocratic house falls through listlessness and effete gentility to vigorous, vulgar, newly prosperous menials. Asch dissects sharply middle-class materialism, but where Chekhov's bitingly satiric analysis of social displacement achieved genuine pathos, Asch's blunt assault culminates in bathos. These last three plays underscore their author's strong and weak traits. At times their characters appear vital and convincingly motivated: they seem capable of shedding old lives, surviving possible violence and bloodletting, and assimilating into harsh new environments. But in straining for social significance, Asch often overextends themes and characters; his people then are not so much unique individuals as blurred ideological types voicing prepared dialogue. Their strongly emphasized moral issues gave these plays an immediate, if limited, thematic interest, but their melodramatic style rendered them unsuitable for later, more sophisticated audiences.

European and American readers would discover Asch through wide-scope novels like *Three Cities* and *The Nazarene*. But for over three decades the Jewish working masses (many of whom never read beyond their Yiddish newspapers) knew Asch primarily, and viscerally, through his minor plays. The best and worst elements of these early theatricals are all evident in his major stage effort, *God of Vengeance*, which some critics detested and other hailed as the greatest of modern Jewish dramas. [40]

V   Controversy and *God of Vengeance*

When the Revolution of 1905-6 flared, Asch sympathized strongly with the socialist workers and intellectuals. But he quickly became aware of the uprising's uncertainties and terrors. In fact, he soon found it difficult, and finally impossible, to remain in Poland. His marriage to Matilda Spiro implicated him by association in her family's activities. Several Spiros were active revolutionaries. Matilda's brother Isaac, a Social Democrat, was hanged by the Czar for seditious activity. Her sister Basha, a rebel organizer, gained fame during the Warsaw fighting by carrying weapons under her long cloak to various distributing points. Sentenced to death by a Czarist tribunal, Basha also was accused falsely by socialist rivals of being a double agent. She fled from both sides to the Polish countryside, but later the government exiled her to Siberia.[41] Matilda's political activism was limited to extending her relatives occasional assistance, but this was enough to make the government suspect her husband's loyalty. Asch hardly helped matters when he published his biased impressions of the revolt in a slender pamphlet entitled *Moments*.[42] Later he wove this material into his fiction.

Not only the Czarists but his Jewish compatriots found Asch nettling. Besides questioning Jewish customs in his fiction, he spoke out on them publicly. He soon embroiled himself in a debate involving the ancient Jewish rite of circumcision. An infant had died before his eighth day (or was stillborn) and his father refused to have him circumcised. A question arose: should he be buried in a Jewish cemetery? Jewish law, after all, prescribes circumcision before burial. The case attracted wide attention and divided Polish Jewry. Asch held with the "modernists" that any child of Jewish parents was entitled to all Jewish rites; circumcising the dead child, he declared, would be a "barbarous" act. Other prominent figures expressed the same sentiment, but some writers and journalists, envious of Asch's rapid success, made him their prime target.[43] So vitriolic were they that Yal Peretz warned him he was risking ostracism by deprecating so cherished a tradition as circumcision. Yet he defended Asch publicly. "If one wishes to stop the mouth of an artist with dirty rags," stated Peretz, "we must declare: 'Dirty people, hands off!' "[44] Indeed, the resultant bitterness did follow Asch for years. Undaunted, he soon stirred Jewish emotions again, this time with a sensationalistic drama in which the holiest of Jewish religious objects, a *Sefer Torah* or scroll of the law, is placed in a brothel. Wherever it played, *God of Vengeance* not only aroused the Jewish press but managed also to antagonize (for different reasons) non-Jewish sensibilities.

Asch would not officially leave Poland until 1912, but now he began taking his family out of the country for months at a time. Political and social pressures may have been partially responsible, but he had developed a fondness for vacation spas that was to prove lifelong. Cologne and Zurich became favored visiting places.

Nathan Asch's earliest memories derived from this period; he was then less than three years old, he would recall, and his father a rising author of twenty-five:

Through the window and framed by it, there rises the great black gothic spire of the Cologne Cathedral; the interior is elegantly furnished, because my father always felt the need for luxury, but it is also crowded with babies, cribs, a stove, cooking pans, and the babies' toys, because we were all living in one room in a foreign country and were poor. In all this teeming disorder . . . sits my father fearfully angry, while my mother whispers, "Father is working." That is my first memory of him, and it cannot possibly be an accurate one. Still, the picture persists, though later it dissolves into my father sitting in the same position, his nostrils flaring in anger, before other tables. . . . His concentration and drive were so great that it always seemed it would be an overwhelming catastrophe were he to be interrupted; yet interrupt him we did. . . . I wasn't afraid of being spanked by him; he spanked us sometimes, but not unreasonably. . . . Rather, I was almost fascinated by the moment when he would be pulled from his concentration by our noise, and would at first try to disregard it, to remain somehow in his creative world; but we wouldn't let him. . . . [T]orn from his work, he pushed himself back from the table. . . . My father could look more angry than anyone I have ever known; if you remember how Michelangelo's Moses looks, pointing to the Tablets of the Law, and if you can imagine this same Moses wroth at the moment when he caught the Israelites worshipping the golden idol, fire shooting out of his eyes and his nostrils in the overwhelming wrath, you have the image that I have, the memory of my father interrupted at his work. [45]

This scene between father and son would be replayed through the years with but minor variations.

Under similar household conditions, but in Zurich rather than Cologne, Asch wrote *God of Vengeance*.[46] Swiss serenity and lush greenery enabled him, apparently, to focus sharply, in that summer of 1906, on Warsaw's turbulent street life. His *shtetl* tales still leaned to the idyllic. His city stories, however, were growing more realistic and harsh, as he not only absorbed the new social fiction of Gorky and Artzybashev but thought increasingly about the Jewish prostitutes and procurers operating openly in the Warsaw ghetto. In his two major efforts of the next decade, *God of Vengeance* and *Mottke the Thief*, he depicted prostitution's degrading influence on Jewish life and recorded his own hardening view of that life. For its time *God of Vengeance* was a courageous, even foolhardy, confrontation on stage between Jewish religious customs and ghetto prostitution and lesbianism. The only full-length, original Asch drama translated into English,[47] it probes human folly and self-deception in the portly figure of brothel-owner

Yankel Chapchovich and in his pitiful attempt to bargain with God
for his daughter's purity. His failure is quick and crushing, for
divine vengeance, Yankel learns, is not to be escaped nor a sordid
life denied. Yankel is here less a social sinner than an opportunistic
father cherishing a naive dream of filial innocence. Growing aware
that his own deeds have made his dream impossible, he clings more
desperately to illusion, pleading hysterically that God spare his
child. Yet when his failure is clear, he bitterly refuses to play the
hypocrite by covering up his daughter's fall.[48]

Resemblances to George Bernard Shaw's *Mrs. Warren's
Profession* (in which a mother has become rich by operating a
brothel while "protecting" a daughter) are obvious but ultimately
superficial. Both dramas exude moral earnestness, but Asch's play
has the stronger intensity and fervor. Shaw focuses upon
prostitution's social effects and has Mrs. Warren rationalize her
situation and relationship with her daughter. Asch rejects rationalizations as he traces Yankel's awakened sense of guilt and his
naive but singleminded belief in the power of repentance and in a
Torah scroll's amulet potency. Yankel never grasps morality's true
nature, but he does not question man's need for a moral code.
Recognizing that he and his wife have traded too long in human
flesh to save their own souls, he hopes only for better things for
Rivkele, now seventeen, primarily an honorable marriage. Still he
insists she enter such a marriage in purity and innocence, despite
having been raised above a cellar brothel. He hires a scribe to copy
a holy scroll in her name,[49] hoping it will guard her purity against
the family heritage. Placing the scroll in Rivkele's room he declares
God now may inflict upon him any punishment, provided his child
remains unblemished.

It is not to be: the scroll and Yankel's prayers fail to protect
Rivkele from corruption. Sharing her parents' weak flesh, she is
seduced easily by one of her father's prostitutes. Yankel is no Job.
Broken and nearly maddened by defeat, in a final scene crushingly
reminiscent of Greek tragedy, he drags a sobbing Rivkele
downstairs by the hair, thrusts her into the cellar with his
prostitutes, and orders the holy scroll taken from his house. Crying
out bitterly against divine vindictiveness, he charges God with
being as vengeful as any mortal. Yet vengeance here is exacted less
by God than by life, by those inextricable forces man launches
against himself. Yankel is paying the price of his humanity, of his
greedy traffic in human flesh. His little brothel world symbolizes

the larger world's frequent emphasis upon commodity rather than moral responsibility.

Yankel is both purveyor and victim of this materialist code. His attempted division of his world is reminiscent, as Joseph Landis has pointed out, of that of Wemmick the law clerk in Charles Dickens' *Great Expectations*. Wemmick's "business" involves criminals as Yankel's does prostitutes; he builds literally a castle of family devotion and emotional ties, surrounding it with a physical moat against contamination. Yankel, too, attempts a family sanctuary, "a kind of chapel . . . of innocence and learning."[50] But Asch proves both more realistic and idealistic than Dickens. Whereas Wemmick successfully separates his lives, Yankel fails; he is victimized not only by folly and self-delusion but by an uncompromising, childlike integrity that somehow has remained uncontaminated by his profession.

Its admirers have seen *God of Vengeance* as rich in thought and pathos and near-tragic in its depiction of personal suffering. For them its emotional impact overshadows the sordid setting and matter. Indeed, the drama's "sordidness" is what has made it a challenging stage vehicle. The tough dialogue rings true, and the lesbian affection between Rivkele and the prostitute Manke is rendered explicitly but tactfully. (Asch had lifted this situation from one of his earlier stories, "The Beautiful Marie.") Yankel's frantic struggle against disaster evokes sympathy, while his love for his daughter achieves a brief but definite lyricism. Even the symbolism, if apparent, is sharply etched in the lower floor's fleshly weaknesses and the upper apartment's moral strivings.

The play's flaws, however, are equally apparent and even more numerous. Its theme, for instance, has been described, with some validity, as "spurious drama."[51] For despite the admitted emotional impact, the play's action is inadequately motivated; Asch proves too didactic and sentimental to be a superior dramatist. Certainly Yankel is too idealized to be a convincing "uncle" or procurer; like the later Mottke the thief and the general array of Asch "toughs," Yankel is earthy and brutal in a combative encounter where brawn is all. But Asch can not resist imposing upon his tough guys an awakening conscience and an awe of innocence and purity— especially as embodied in a young girl; thinking they have found or nurtured such a paragon, these swaggerers relax their grip on their emotions—or on their enemies—and are toppled.

Asch thus mars his strongest portraits by moralistic twists. He has Yankel attempt the near-impossible: the preservation of his daughter's innocence within the temptational reach of his brothel. Yankel's "combat" with God therefore proves no contest, for a stern God's vengeance hardly is needed to shatter so pitiful a dream. The sheer inevitability of failure reduces Yankel's final lamentations to hollow, self-pitying bombast; if so convinced of a Torah scroll's moral efficacy, he also should have expected God to visit a father's sins upon his child. "I know—you are a mighty God!" cries Yankel.

And you are our God. I, Yankel Chapchovich, have sinned. . . . The sins are mine! Mine! Go ahead and perform a miracle. Send down a fire to consume me on the spot. Open the earth and let me be swallowed up. But protect my child. Send her back to me as pure, as innocent as she was. I know . . . for you everything is possible. Perform a miracle. You are a mighty God, aren't you? And if you don't—you are no God at all. I, Yankel Chapchovich, say to you, you are no God at all. You are vengeful! You are like a man! (106)

Yet even such breast-beating orations, as well as its other flaws, do not prevent *God of Vengeance* from being a stinging indictment of the modern free-wheeling entrepreneur and his "moral schizophrenia": his confused equation of respectability and virtue and his "cherished illusion" that personal and marketplace morality can be kept separate.[52]

Upon completing his play, Asch showed it to Yal Peretz who, taken aback at his protege's temerity, advised him to "burn it." Instead, Asch headed that fall for Berlin to see famed theater director Max Reinhardt and the noted German-Jewish actor Rudolf Schildkraut. Having been deeply moved by the latter's portrayal of Shylock the previous year in Reinhardt's Little Theater, Asch had adapted Yankel Chapchovich to fit Schildkraut.[53] Finding Schildkraut in a Berlin coffeehouse, Asch introduced himself and informed the actor that he had written a play especially for him. Quickly relating the plot, he assured the astonished stage veteran, "If my play is produced in German, only you, and no one else, shall play Yankel." Schildkraut stared at this virtually unknown Polish-Jewish lad, as Asch himself later put it, "as if he were a maniac or simply crazy."[54] Schildkraut was intrigued, however, and Asch soon read the play for Reinhardt, Schildkraut, and a small group of German playwrights and critics. He read in Yiddish, and what the others did not understand Reinhardt, whose parents were from a small Hungarian town, translated for them. Reinhardt liked the play, and Asch left the manuscript with him. But not until four years later did Reinhardt's triumphant German version, with Schildkraut as Yankel, reach the stage. Meantime an immediate Russian production created a flutter of unexpected byplay.

In 1907 the Russian actress W.P. Komisarjevsky (who had starred the previous year in *Times of the Messiah*) decided to produce *God of Vengeance* in St. Petersburg. Upon hearing the news, Asch excitedly made plans to attend opening night; it was a great moment, after all, for a young writer who a half-dozen years before had left little Kutno sporting a long Hasidic coat. But Asch's reception in the Czarist capital was dampening; it consisted of a police summons to show his permit to stay in the city. (The capital then was off-limits to all Jews except merchants of the First Guild.) Having no permit, Asch was ordered to leave St. Petersburg. Crushed and angry at having to miss his play's first performance, Asch retreated to nearby Pskov. The capital's leading Jews pleaded with the police chief, but he was adamant: no permit, no residence. One prominent Jew finally appealed to the Czar's uncle, Prince Constantin Alexandrovitch Romanov. The Prince was a practicing playwright, president of the Playwrights' Club, and a man of liberal views. He bawled out the police chief, and a carriage was dispatched to Pskov; it returned with Asch as the curtain was rising. Waiting at the Komisarjevsky Theater door was a group of cheering Russian students; they lifted the young author to their shoulders and carried him on stage for a standing audience ovation. Asch retold this story for years with unabashed pride.[55]

This Russian staging of *God of Vengeance* proved both exciting and exhilarating. But Reinhardt's Berlin production, in German, despite being withdrawn after only eighteen performances, made Asch's European reputation by winning him his first large non-Yiddish audience. Much of its impact was credited to Rudolf Schildkraut, who caught not only Yankel's violent, deluded nature but also the procurer's "undefiled core of innocence."[56] No one, Asch repeatedly declared, ever equaled him in the role. The play also did well by Schildkraut; *God of Vengeance* was the success of the Berlin season, and he toured Europe with it. Later in America he did Yankel both in German and Yiddish; finally, the talented, somewhat erratic Schildkraut (whose son, Joseph, would win a Hollywood Oscar) used the role to reach Broadway's English-speaking audiences. This Broadway production was closed down by the police and landed its star a fine and a night in jail. In fact, the play's "sordid realism" and "scandalous" theme sparked contro-

versy not only in New York but in Paris and London; not until Rolf
Hochhuth's *The Deputy*, a half-century later, did any serious stage
presentation rival, in Europe or America, its violent public
reaction.

American-Yiddish audiences were especially obstreperous.
Outraged at the "sacrilegious" treatment of a holy *Sefer Torah*, one
New York audience splattered rotten eggs on the stage, and
several Yiddish publications advocated "excommunicating" Asch.
Yet *God of Vengeance* became and remained a standard of the
Yiddish (and Polish, Russian, French, German, and Italian) theater
for many years. Ironically, the play's ultimate acceptance by
Yiddish audiences in America was due largely to the *Jewish Daily
Forward* and its outspoken editor, Abraham Cahan (later Asch's
bitter foe); Cahan attacked eloquently and vociferously, as only he
could, those wishing to kill the play.[57]

Asch harbored a special fondness for this work that established
his international reputation, and he defended it heatedly.
Twenty-four years after acquiring the original manuscript, Max
Reinhardt returned it to Asch to commemorate the author's fiftieth
birthday. Deeply touched, the sentimental Asch declared the
manuscript reminded him "of the flower of my span of life."[58] But in
the 1940's, with the Nazis slaughtering Jews and much of the
Jewish world angered by the untimely appearance of *The Nazarene*
and *The Apostle*, Asch forbade the play's further production. Only
in recent years has it again been mounted for the stage.

Chapter Three

Broader Horizons

The St. Petersburg production of *God of Vengeance* provided Asch with enough money for a trip to the Holy Land. He had decided on a novel about Jesus Christ and wanted local material. Early in 1908 he headed for Palestine, where he was hailed for his tales of Jewish life and feted at a large banquet hosted by Eliezer Ben Yehuda, the noted Hebrew linguist.[1] Warmed by his reception and excited by Biblical sites and reminders, Asch started immediately on his new novel. He also recorded his travel impressions in a series of sketches that blended the land's past and present; these he published three years later as *In the Land of Israel.*[2] Throughout his life Asch retained the perceptions and ideas gleaned now, ideas reenforced by time and subsequent trips. Most significant was his sense of the common core of Judaism and Christianity; the two faiths, he became convinced, were different expressions of the same culture. This idea, hackneyed long before his time, would absorb his thoughts and literally reshape his life. "Walking through the narrow streets of Jerusalem," he recalled years later, "climbing on her hills and walls, I saw in my imagination the things that happened in this holy city, which became a cornerstone of our modern civilization. Since that time I have never thought of Judaism or Christianity separately. For me it is one culture and one civilization, on which all our peace, our security and our freedom are dependent."[3]

Asch continued writing his "Christ" novel on his return to Warsaw, even publishing part of the first chapter. But what he saw in print he did not like; deciding he was not yet equipped to do the novel properly, he put it aside. He would take, in fact, three more Palestine trips and make use of more than thirty years of intermittent reading before publishing *The Nazarene.* When finally he did sit down to write this novel, he reported later, "I found I didn't have to write at all. I merely had to let the story come through me. It was written in my heart and mind, and I had only to keep my pen to paper."[4] Even allowing for his tendency to present himself as an author who wrote with ease, there can be little doubt that its long gestation made *The Nazarene* seem a relatively easy novel for Asch to write, easier anyway than several less controversial ones.

But if now he delayed his Christ novel, his Palestine trip had so aroused his enthusiasm for Biblical materials as to demand immediate expression. Shortly after his return, Asch presented to the Czernowitz Yiddish Language Conference a paper calling for translation into Yiddish of the ancient Hebrew Scriptures and classics. He himself soon contributed a Yiddish rendering of the Book of Ruth,[5] following it during the next few years with several Biblical and post-Biblical dramas. He had developed into a zealous advocate not only of the Bible but of Yiddish itself. Following the conference a testimonial dinner was held for Asch and Yal Peretz in the then Austrian region of Bukovina. There those Jews who considered themselves educated tended to use German. "If you read me in German, and if you read me in Russian," Asch asked the assemblage, "why don't you read me in Yiddish?" Yet, ironically, despite this and other similar pleas, he would often be accused by some critics of downgrading and deprecating the Yiddish tongue.

I   Flesh and the Spirit

Asch must have been reading Freud or other psychoanalysts. His drama heroes at this time are torn between their religious or social obligations and aroused erotic needs. Touched upon in *The Sinner*, these tensions are central to his dramatic spectacle *Sabbatai Zevi*[6] (1908) and the Biblical one-act *Amnon and Tamar* (1909). In the first, Sabbatai Zevi, the seventeenth-century Messianic pretender, and the movement he spawned are used to reenact the eternal struggle between heaven and earth or the spirit and flesh. As had Yankel Chapchovich, the protagonist here challenges the divine law and its moral principles. Asch depicts the complex historic personality that was Sabbatai Zevi as a pietist and ascetic who begins in total devotion to the law but ends a sensual libertine advocating moral laxity and abrogation of the Mosaic code. He credits primarily the erotic Sarah, a beautiful adventuress, with having prevented the self-proclaimed prophet from realizing his Messianic destiny.

Prolonged fasting and prayer have convinced Sabbatai Zevi that he is the long-awaited Messiah. After a symbolic marriage ceremony with the Holy Torah, he announces his divine mission.

Thousands of Jews, harshly abused and aching for deliverance, flock to revere him as God's anointed. Unknown to him, Sarah, a young Ukrainian Jewess, proclaims him her destined mate. By the time she reaches him, her following exceeds his. Sabbatai Zevi accepts her as his prophetess but insists he is bound to the Torah in "holiness and purity." Sarah refuses to be put off; declaring herself his God-appointed wife, she boasts that her passion and appearance have aroused in the people erotic yearnings and a desire to reject the law. She proves prophetic: forced to choose between the Torah's purity and Sarah's beauty, between spirit and appetite, commandment and sin, the people yield to the flesh.

The prophet alone struggles against her blandishments, but finally he too succumbs. Affected by her carnality and strong grip on the masses, he agrees to marry her and to abolish God's laws and rules. Heaven belongs to God, he temporizes, but earth has been given to the God-man—to him, Sabbatai Zevi. Following his lead, his disciples declare the law dead, the forbidden to be permitted, and the restricted to be disclosed. But Sabbatai Zevi learns God is not to be denied: his lust and loss of faith deprive him quickly of strength, courage, and power of speech. He then realizes he had possessed the divine crown and lost it—he had known God's word and forgotten it. Arrested by the Turkish sultan, Sabbatai Zevi meekly converts to Islam. Earthly passion has destroyed his Messianic hopes. But his shame and apostasy have no effect upon the dream of centuries. The curtain descends on a tall old Jew who stands with uplifted arms amid the Jerusalem Temple ruins to proclaim his undying faith in the true Messiah's eventual coming.

Such optimism contrasts sharply with the Messianic views formulated by today's most noted Yiddish novelist, Isaac Bashevis Singer. Asch and Singer both make clear that man is destined always to await—rather than ever receive—the Messiah. (Non-Jewish authors have also probed this concept—most notably Samuel Beckett, in his *Waiting for Godot.*) For Singer this waiting (as developed in *Satan in Goray, The Family Moskat,* and several short tales) seems parochial and self-defeating, too often a mere attempt to escape life's realities. But for Asch Messianic expectations symbolize the faith sustaining the Jew in a world otherwise rendered unbearable. If his corporeal weaknesses prevent the Jew-as-Everyman from actually receiving God's grace in the Messiah's form, he is sustained and ennobled by the hope. The Messiah thus represents to Asch a spiritual and psychological link between God and man. For Singer any Messianic hope is a negative force impoverishing the human spirit; man's faith in God, Singer insists, should strengthen him to cope with his present life on earth—or at least to expect and accept the inevitable defeats.

As serious drama *Sabbatai Zevi* fails. Its few virtues and many shortcomings are those associated with closet drama. Occasional flashes of incisive dialogue and action are overshadowed by melodramatic posturing, verbal bombast, and stilted pageantry. Neither Sabbatai Zevi's inner struggles nor Sarah's compulsions are delineated clearly. Uncertain when to shade realism into surrealism and allegory, Asch tries to enliven the play's flat stretches by spectacle and movement. The singing, dancing, reciting are rather strained, however, and reminiscent of the Renaissance masque, and they have as little dramatic impact. Yet the work is not without its small merits. Sabbatai Zevi is here a nobler figure than is historically conventional. Sincere and somewhat charismatic when convinced of his own purity, he loses confidence and authority by rejecting the Torah for a woman. Having spurned God, he feels the need to renounce Him. On the brink of spiritual and earthly victory, man thus falls victim to his own frail flesh even as had his progenitor Adam. This underlying moral sincerity and concern give to *Sabbatai Zevi* a measured effectiveness not even its rhetorical and structural flaws can destroy.

Eroticism again causes disaster in *Amnon and Tamar*. Derived from 2 Samuel 13, this Biblical one-acter centers on the incestuous love between two of King David's children. Smitten by his half-sister's charms, Amnon schemes to satisfy his lust. Equally infatuated, Tamar accepts eagerly her father's suggestion that she visit her eldest brother. About to consummate their passion, they are interrupted by music signaling a battle's approach. Amnon is immediately on his feet, anxious to lead his company; Tamar protests his leaving but is rejected as a worthless female. After several listless months in her brother Absalom's house, Tamar shows herself there at a sheepshearing feast to which Amnon has been invited. She has awaited this moment and avenges herself by murder and suicide. The playlet lacks an English translation. In Yiddish it achieves, despite the contrived motivation and unpalatable theme, a sensitive, near-Oriental lyricism. Yet in spite of these positive qualities, an English production of *Amnon and Tamar* before 1930 undoubtedly would have precipitated a public

outcry similar to that evoked by *God of Vengeance.* (Much more
notable, of course, is *Tamar,* the updated recasting of the same
Bible events, in free verse, by Robinson Jeffers.)

II   A Visit to America

For Asch 1908 and 1909 were vintage years. A Warsaw
publishing house brought out a volume of his tales and short plays
(1902-1907) entitled *Youth,*[7] and Abraham Cahan, editor of the
Jewish Daily Forward in New York, presented several Asch stories
to his large Yiddish readership. A novelist himself, Cahan later
gained fame for *The Rise of David Levinsky* (1917), his memorable
depiction of East Side Jewish life. He published in the *Forward* the
best (and occasionally the worst) available Yiddish poetry and
fiction; he hoped thereby to improve his readers' aesthetic tastes,
as most had only a rudimentary Hebrew education. Cahan's policy
worked to Asch's advantage before the two came to their bitter
parting. For years the *Forward* serialized Asch's every novel;
Mottke the Thief and *Uncle Moses* alone created for him a large
American following among the paper's quarter-million readers.
Cahan paid his regular contributors a salary: Asch received
seventy-five dollars a week, a substantial income for the time, and
this money went directly to his mother.[8] He also was guaranteed
the largest Yiddish readership available, and *Forward* serialization
of his novels led to their book publication in Yiddish and German.
Until the 1930's, Asch's book sales abroad, in Germany especially,
surpassed his American sales.

His brothers and sisters now moved to America. Asch,
however, was not yet ready to settle in the United States. But in
1909 he visited America for the first time, staying six months, until
summer 1910. Here he wrote *The Compatriot,*[9] a serio-comic
three-act play of Jewish life in the New World. Produced
immediately, it met little success on the New York Yiddish stage,
but it did give Asch his first chance to shape his American
impressions into a literary form.

Asch now also made his first appearance in English translation
with "Through the Wall,"[10] a thin but touching sketch of a beautiful
young girl imprisoned for political activities and of her deepening
loneliness and desperation. Unable to see her, the other prisoners
hear her nervous laughter and light footsteps; feeling her intensely
feminine presence, they find their days less grim. Soon she and the
young man in the adjoining cell carry on a "romance" by their

finger-tappings. A prisoner discovers a gallows outside his window and a pall envelops the prison. Fingers tap the news from cell to cell, and each inmate calmly resigns himself. The young man tries desperately to beat out a message but the girl does not understand. In the morning her wild rappings bring no response, and her lonely sobs are echoed only by a wailing wind. An awkward translation hardly enhances the contrived, sentimental plot, and this slight effort now seems to have been a poor choice to introduce Asch to America's non-Yiddish readers.

His trip resulted also in the inevitable series of travel impressions. Published in the *Forward*, they dwelt on America's scenic phenomena from Niagara Falls to the Grand Canyon. Asch contrasted their natural beauty to the dank clamor of Jewish immigrant-ship life and to ghetto tenements and sweatshops. He thought still in terms of his native Kutno's lush greenery. Realizing more clearly than most observers that the *shtetl* world no longer existed, he was not yet willing to sever his ties to it; nor would he for several years relinquish his self-imposed role of homeless wanderer.

Returning to Europe, Asch published between 1910 and 1914 an astonishing number of tales and short novels. Several proved significant to his creative development, others ephemeral to the point of leaving no more trace than a fleeting reference. One such minor novel was *Earth*,[11] a story of Polish peasant life. More substantial is *America*,[12] a novella often overlooked by commentators who have mistakenly described *Uncle Moses* as Asch's first novel of American life. Asch wrote it soon after returning to Europe, perhaps to express his own inability to cut his European ties and adjust to modern America's bustle and pressures. For *America* relates the sad fate of Yossele (Joey), a sensitive immigrant boy, whose encounter with the alien land proves fatal. In it Asch depicts the rootlessness and traumas experienced by East Europe's Jews torn from childhood soil and transplanted to a hard-driving urban society. Launched in 1881, this immigrant tide crested during the new century's first decade. Asch deals with Jewish immigrants in several later works also, tracing their journeys, settlement, and painful entrance into American life. A subject hardly new to literature, it lent itself to varied treatment. Sholom Aleichem, for instance, portraying this Jewish acculturation in *The Adventures of Mottel the Cantor's Son* (1916), emphasizes primarily the new life's humorous incongruities; Asch, attuned to its more tragic aspects, underlines the newcomers' frenzied efforts to retain in strangeness and adversity their former integrity.

Asch notes their inevitable failure. America is not Warsaw or Kutno; America is America, and the frantic rush across the Atlantic to Ellis Island and from that formidable island to Avenue A can be a pilgrimage evoking terror and emotional havoc. New York's Lower East Side is a tumult of shrieking elevated trains, dark tenements, and grimy sweatshop walls and windows—all illuminated primarily by flashing electric signs. This chaotic world awaits Yossele when he arrives at Ellis Island with his mother, sister, and brothers. His father has come over earlier. For a time he himself is unable to enter. His brothers are sturdy boys intrigued by the new land's challenges. But the bookish Yossele has devoted himself to ancient sages amid *shtetl* quietude. So he, like his mother, had been reluctant to leave for America.

Fate cooperates ironically when Yossele, for minor medical reasons, is refused admission at Ellis Island, that "island of tears," and is returned to his beloved Leshna. Several years later he enters the new land, only to find its size, noise, and confusion, as well as its "dying Jewishness," too much for him. School, street, and even home are strange, hard, frightening. A frail child, he expires not only from a fever but from new pressures and old longings. Yossele's experiences are intended by Asch to exemplify the sufferings of many immigrants during their first years. "In this Jewish child," he writes, underscoring the obvious, "the entire resignation of his people, its meekness under suffering, had a renascence."[13] Immigrant loneliness and pain are stressed again at the novel's end when Yossele's mother, Hannah Leah, returns from her son's funeral to feel that his grave now binds her permanently to the new soil. Death, it seems, provided many newcomers with their strongest link to the golden land.

Sentimental and melodramatic, *America* contains many elements found in Asch's later "American" novels: the painful departures from the old country and fears of the new; the male sense of degradation and loss at being reduced to factory labor, especially needle work; the wrenching displacement of old pieties by new heresies. Satirized, albeit gently, are those who wallow in nostalgia for the "old home"—though all they love are now in the "new"—and the "old" no longer even exists. (When it did, they cursed it unceasingly.) "Columbus" is blamed for all ills, in particular for the widening gap between "greenhorn" elders and their "Yankee" children. In *Uncle Moses, The Mother, East River*, and numerous short tales, Asch expanded and modified these impressions; now, however, he returned to more familiar settings and themes.

III   *Mary:* Novel of a Revolution Lost

Europe's gathering storm attracted Asch to the decade's epic subject—Russia. Convinced that the time's most serious political troubles derived from the abortive 1905 Revolution, he wrote his first novel of the uprising, *Mary* (1911), and three years later, in Paris, completed its sequel, *The Road to One's Self.*[14] In each he tries to indicate the political and social pressures reshaping Diaspora life by tracing the prominent role young Jewish intellectuals played in the early social-reform and revolutionary movements. He portrays their rejection of orthodox upbringing and their reckless plunge into political rebellion, their shocked confusion at the massacres initiated by the 1905 failures, and their final surrender to disillusionment and despair.

Both works are contrived, loosely written polemics. Asch's serious intent and painstaking historical detail are evident, but so is his desire to be "literary and timely."[15] The first novel is of interest for its condensed view of the Jewish political spectrum, depicted more fully by Asch two decades later in *Three Cities*. A conscientious rather than imaginative portrait, *Mary* reveals an author too emotionally involved in the described events to present them objectively. Jewish life in Russia, even under the Czar, had changed drastically in the decade preceding the Revolution. The Ukrainian town in which much of the action occurs, for instance, is no longer a mere *shtetl* but a city in miniature. Asch delineates the changes clearly and, as usual, depicts Jewish life with a lyric eroticism calculated to intrigue and titillate. He also tries hard to bare his characters' inner tensions, but he is only partially successful. Often vigorous and alive in their small intimacies and gestures, they become nebulous and sentimentalized when expanded to symbolize the larger political strife. Asch's personal interest in the day's major issues, as well as his eagerness to include as many of them as possible, spurs him to a cinematic haste. Neither *Mary* nor *The Road to One's Self*, therefore, produces a full-bodied protagonist.

In *Mary*, for instance, the girl so named looms no larger than the other emancipated young Jews who, torn from medieval verities, search for a new code and ideals. Sharing her companions' footloose spirit, she is seen by them as a "gypsy child." Mischa, Mary's cousin, is also a wanderer and idealist.. Torn between Zionism and socialism, he is convinced only of the individual's importance and therefore insists on marrying Rachel, daughter of the physician Lazerovich, after she has been sexually assaulted in a pogrom. Thus Mischa exemplifies his generation's return to their own people as a result of Jewish sufferings and humiliations. So do Maximovich the art critic and Fyodor the editorial writer; both are assimilated Jews who slip easily at first into the St. Petersburg lifestyle. Yet assimilated or not, they soon find even the new Russia has little place for young Jewish progressives. They, like the others, have embraced a revolutionary movement that promises to rid an empire of Czarist oppression. Believing a socialist Russia will liberate its Jews, all these young people sacrifice their careers and willingly endanger lives and freedom. Their awakening is rude and shattering, as a worthless constitution and brutal pogroms reduce their dreams to a cruel mockery. Many lack the will to begin again; other escape into the moral lassitude vividly described in Mikhail Artzybashev's *Sanine*.

Viewing *Mary* as his most important work to date,[16] Asch expected it to evoke a stronger response than had *The Town* or *God of Vengeance*. It caused no more than a slight ripple. But then he was, like so many authors, a notoriously bad judge of his own writings. Certainly a reader today is hard pressed to share his enthusiasm for this novel or its characters; their social ardor and political idealism on occasion do spark Mary, Mischa, Rachel, and the others into life, yet they remain in general rather stiff, indistinct creatures of Asch's craft and convictions rather than muse and spirit. Luckily, he had little time to nurse his disappointment, for now, as Europe grew darker, he turned to the past in search of parallels to current events—and perhaps as personal therapy and escape; this practice he would follow repeatedly through the years. Asch was not seeking light or happy topics; indeed, his subjects now tended to be grim. What he seemed to want was reassurance that mankind (as embodied in the Jews), having survived past holocausts, would weather the present one. Such a thought might help explain why he soon began a long prose poem on the pillaging of Biblical Jerusalem, which he called *The Destruction of the Temple*,[17] and a series of children's tales titled simply *Stories from the Bible*.[18]

IV   A Move to Paris

Life in Poland, in 1912, was growing increasingly uncertain, especially for Jews, so Asch decided to move his family to Paris. Sending the others ahead, he went to pick up his son Nathan in the Polish textile center of Lodz, and then father and son spent a few days in Berlin. For ten-year-old Nathan the interlude proved memorable: it was the first time he could recall being truly alone with his father. "Those two or three days are like a remembered dream. I took my very first ride in an automobile, and dream-like, it was white; I ate pastries the like of which I never knew existed, I can still taste the thin wafer-like chocolate crusts; I saw the Kaiser, or at least I think I did, walking down a street that must have been *Unter den Linden*. My father tipped his hat to him, and the Kaiser tipped his hat to my father. What more could a little boy want— splendid gestures, ineffable sweets, and honor? What more could he get from his father?"[19] What more indeed? In later years these two sensitive beings, father and son, would enjoy few such tranquil moments together. Yet even their stormiest disagreements merely strained, rather than severed, their strong bond.

The Asches adjusted quickly and happily to France. Pre-war Paris was Europe's cultural center and for no people more so than its Jews. To the Latin Quarter and Café d'Harcourt on Boulevard St. Michel came young Jews from Polish, Russian, and Rumanian *shtetlach* and *yeshivas*. They came to be artists, writers, intellectuals, or merely "Europeans," and for some the Asch household, in the fashionable suburb of Chatillon, became a second home. Marc Chagall, Moise Kisling, and Jules Pascin were among the young Jewish artists who left bare attic studios to spend summer Sundays at Chatillon. Asch held court "in a low house . . . with a garden surrounded by a high wall in which were embedded fragments of broken glass that glistened in the sun." Talk of art, literature, and philistinism shifted inevitably to the Jewish small-town life of their youth. Years later many of these visitors spoke with tear-filled eyes of their Sundays at Chatillon.[20]

These two Paris years were pleasant ones. Matilda Asch shopped for Jewish food in the small Paris ghetto, and family visits to the Louvre and Invalides were frequent. Working with few distractions, Asch completed and published a sizable list of works. These reveal a mind filled with simultaneous impressions of several past worlds and of unsettled contemporary Europe. Upon finishing

Stories from the Bible and *Destruction of the Temple*, he wrote three plays and two novels. The two-act *League of the Weak, The Inheritors,* and *Jephthah's Daughter* were the plays, with *The Road to One's Self* and *Reb Shlomo Nagid,* another nostalgic portrait of the fading *shtetl* world, the novels.[21] In *League of the Weak*[22] Asch deals with Polish artistic life and reveals an obvious debt to the fusion of symbol, allegory, and realism found in Leonid Andreyev's Russian stories and plays.[23] A deceived husband here drinks himself to sleep and dreams of uniting society's weak, poor, and rejected into an invisible league headed by himself and the wife of his wife's lover. This rather strained story line is balanced by occasional poignant passages, but the drama overall lacks both the depth and motivation of Andreyev's prototypes or the grace of the Russian's deft, mordant style.

Even less successful is *Jephthah's Daughter.*[24] Another sexually frank scripture-drama, it undoubtedly would have antagonized many had it not remained buried in Yiddish. Based loosely on Judges 11 and 12, it deals with the chaotic period when the Israelites are scattered in Canaan's hills and caves while pagan gods in human guise stalk the earth. Jephthah's area is ruled by Moloch, the bloody Ammonite deity who claims every firstborn; the Hebrew chieftain, however, refuses to acknowledge the god's supremacy or to give him his eldest child. But in no Asch work is man a match for deity (even a deity of low order), and Moloch's victory over Gilead's eccentric judge is swift and total. Not only do Moloch's rays lure Jephthah's daughter to her death, but the youngster goes to her pyre willingly, believing she belongs to the pagan god. Playing fast and free with his Biblical materials, Asch interweaves with characteristic flair and gusto primitive Eastern superstitions and sexual customs. But despite several lyric interludes, setting and plot and characters never become more than painted paste-ups in a grotesque Oriental pageant.

V   The *Shtetl* Fades

Asch rounded out his initial literary phase with *Reb Shlomo Nagid.*[25] During the new century's thirteen years he had moved from province to city, produced tentative sketches of Jewish town-life, shifted from Hebrew to Yiddish, and then won recognition with *The Little Town* and *God of Vengeance.* The latter work had expressed his shocked reaction to Jews caught up in sordid urban currents. But his deeply felt *shtetl* tales dominated this first period, one that he brought to a psychological close in *Reb Shlomo Nagid*. The *shtetl* hardly disappeared from Asch's fiction, but from then on it served as backdrop rather than protagonist. His new novella proved a more mature and varied *Little Town* or "Kola Street" and his hero another enlarged portrait of his father, Moshe Gombiner Asch. The time once more just precedes the author's own generation, when those new ideas soon to shatter the *shtetl* have not yet had full impact.

A glowing household Sabbath opens the narrative, with a birth and a betrothal closing it. Temptations, quarrels, and riots separate these happy events, but all prove momentary trials as the town regains quickly its accustomed serenity. Reb Shlomo dominates and unifies the narrative. His benevolence, piety, and repeated triumphs over "evil thoughts" give him a Biblical patriarch's rich vitality. Chanele, his young wife (an idealized Malka Asch), also is charmingly animated. To gain a comfortable home, she has married, at eighteen, a widower nearly thrice her age and father of seven. Nevertheless, she is devoted to her husband and, being a truly pious Jewish wife, pleases both God and her spouse—the latter by managing his large household after the manner of its original mistress. At tale's end she has had her first child and has won over the most critical reader.

Plot is no more consequential here than in Asch's other *shtetl* tales, but character is more significant, and setting and description still dominate. The Vistula River with its surrounding soil and bounty; the market, synagogue, and street; the patriarch's open house; the Jews and peasants; the day and season—each has its special flavor and effect. Each conveys Asch's delight in man's closeness to nature's forces, a delight surpassed only by the spirit's pleasures—as when the Hasidim welcome their beloved Sabbath:

The Sabbath came at a peaceful gait. The dark night spread over the sky like a black silver shawl spangled with stars. The village was enveloped in somber shadows, all stores were closed, lighted Sabbath candles peered from many windows. Jews were already returning from the synagogue. Reb Shlomo was with his son-in-law, his sons, his servants, and a group of impecunious guests. He walked leisurely, with Sabbath steps, stroked his thick black beard, spreading it over his starched white shirt and his black silk gabardine, and the Jewish spirit was very evident in him. He looked at the poor village Gentiles who idled about in the street and pitied them with all his heart. [26]

Welcomed with near-equal fervor are market days. Peasants haul produce from outlying farms to exchange for money or manufactured articles, with barter and bargaining lasting until dusk.

Free-for-alls are common when Jewish trader and gentile farmer disagree or a farmer gets drunk on new cash. Peasants and traders rush to battle as heads are bashed and blood flows. Soon a merchant elder like Reb Shlomo and several older peasants arrange a truce; culprits are punished on the spot, vodka toasts are exchanged, and both sides agree one God rules over all. Asch's youthful memories lend these events authenticity and a gusty nostalgia. Seemingly, the ten years since *The Little Town* and the darkening war clouds combined to sharpen his appreciation of the past, for he inflates his rustics to heroic proportions and idealizes their homely virtues and setting. He avoids here, as in his earlier pastorals, both the caustic realism of a Mendele or the ironic pity of his friend Abraham Reisen.

Taken together, his early tales lay out not only Asch's sentimental recollections of a lost provincial world but many of the traits and themes that will shape his later works. Frequently pastoral in mood and setting, his stories, plays, and novels to this point often are also, paradoxically, picaresque and kaleidoscopic; if they are peopled by pietists, patriarchs, and saints, they include also his familiar thieves, pimps, and prostitutes, not to mention political activists and religious martyrs. Not only do his characterizations manage, somehow, to be both objective and subjective, but they prove determinedly realistic and hopelessly romantic as well— often all at the same time. To his credit, Asch occasionally juggles these disparate elements with instinct and skill. Yet even his best efforts are flawed, for he fails to plumb convincingly his characters' psyches: the individual portrait-in-depth is not his strong point. Many protagonists are, like Yankel Chapchovich, guilt-ridden, spiritually confused Jews desperate for faith in an ideal or in a God who will purify them and grant them wholeness and inner peace.[27] But too often they are less full-bodied beings than stylized figures whose prime functions are to unify the varied elements of time and place.

Scanning past and present for those moments and events that embody the venerable, peculiar, and quaint in Jewish life, Asch leans instinctively toward the composite group or community portrait. He penetrates more easily the collective spirit than the individual soul.[28] Occasionally his insights prove intuitive and sound, and his characters are jolted into life. But this is more likely in the shorter tales and novels, where details of plot, setting, and history do not accumulate to swamp the little foreground figures. In his mid-length novels (like *Mottke the Thief, Uncle Moses, Salvation*), protagonists are more internally revealed. In his later and broader works, however, Asch is diverted too easily by history, religion, or polemic. As demand for his work grew, Asch was guided often by what he considered his readers' tastes; always prolific, he wrote increasingly for the insatiable maw of newspaper serialization, sacrificing thereby much of his obvious power and craft. By 1914 Asch had proved himself a master storyteller, but one given to settling for work somewhat less than his best.

VI   War and America

World War I loosed a tide of social discontent within the Russian Empire. Much of it focused, predictably, on the hapless Jews. Asch watched in dismay as communities like those he had portrayed so affectionately were burned and their inhabitants slaughtered by covetous peasants, foraging Cossacks, and organized Ukrainian and Russian marauders. His sympathy for the 1905 Revolution, he now felt, was being betrayed by the terrors the revolutionary movement was unleashing not only in Poland and Russia but throughout Europe. Orthodox Jewish life was crumbling under the war's impact, and no new principle of order was emerging to replace it. Polish nationalism, now vigorously renewed, excluded Jews. Communism was proving a ruthless dictatorship, while Zionism, obstructed by British White Papers, seemed merely another false Messianism. Gone was the Messianic anticipation that had gladdened the era into which Asch had been born; Polish Jewry was disoriented and disheartened. If he viewed life generally as a form of pageant, Asch saw clearly now the war's painful realities, especially for East Europe's Jews. Yet he never surrendered completely his faith that present disaster was an apocalyptic promise of future happiness and fulfilment.

Europe was no longer the place to write or to raise a family. Asch had not found the America of 1910 the best of all lands, but obviously it now offered more than did Europe. In 1914, the last year of the great Polish-Jewish migration, Asch transferred his family to New York. His moving, one commentator has observed, "helped swing the Yiddish literary center of gravity from Warsaw to New York."[29] He would remain in the United States for eleven years before returning to Europe for an extended stay, but now no sooner was his family settled than he made his second journey to Palestine. For several months he toured the towns and hills so little changed by the centuries; at every stop he talked to the inhabitants and took copious notes for the novel on Jesus that still occupied his thoughts.

In America the Asches lived their first year in the Bronx, then briefly amid Greenwich Village's bohemiam trappings; after this, Asch rented a house, according to his son Nathan, "on a bare tract of land near a cemetery at about the place where Brooklyn and Coney Island come together." But it was on Staten Island's south side, then still very much in the country, that the Asches took root for a decade. In this "queer, marginal area, inhabited by Italians, emigré white Russians, and strays from Greenwich Village,"[30] the cosmopolitan Asch felt at home, and here his well-traveled children grew to adulthood.

These early years in America were not easy. The war had cut off Asch's European royalties, and while he was known to this country's Yiddish readers, to the English-reading public—Jewish and non-Jewish—his name meant little. And even to Yiddish readers Sholem Asch was a "European" writer. Now on the scene, he soon became a familiar figure wherever New York's Yiddish literati gathered. "When he walked along the streets of the Lower East Side," Nathan Asch would recall, "his name was whispered among the people with a kind of awe."

Was I proud of my father? Yes and no. I liked going with him to one of the cafés on the Lower East Side where the Yiddish writers congregated. A stir could be felt in the place when he appeared, with me following. ("Look who's there . . . and who is the boy? . . . That's his son.") While I, aware that I was being stared at, both arrogantly and modestly kept my gaze averted. Yet I didn't like my father reading Yiddish newspapers on the subway as he rode downtown to the Lower East Side. I was ashamed, as if there were something demeaning about it; just as I didn't like my father and mother, who were both handsome people, and well dressed—my father had his clothes made to order, my mother dressed beautifully in the Paris fashion—starting to talk Yiddish in a place where there were no Jews. There was something terrible about that. (I'm frightened while writing this: almost no one will admit the feeling; yet there it was, I had it.)[31]

Despite his growing fame in the new land, Asch found adjusting to American life difficult; it was too fast, noisy, expensive. Yet he soon developed a deep admiration for American freedom and history, and he acquired, according to his friend novelist Louis Zara, "an insatiable desire for more and more information about the land of his adoption."[32] He previously had seen and written about it as a visitor focusing on its immigrant Jews. Now he experienced acculturation perplexities; these occasionally took the form of literary slips, such as describing a character as a "Yankee colonel from Kentucky." [33]

Asch's adjustment to American life sometimes "embarrassed" his family, according to Nathan Asch, who has already indicated his sensitivity to his parents' foreign ways. "Once I remember being especially humiliated," he has reported.

It was a Sunday in the summer, and we were all traveling in an open streetcar toward Coney Island. I don't remember what started the commotion, whether my father was riding on the step of the car and the conductor wanted him to go inside or whether the argument was over which of the children was to pay half-fare. At any rate, there were words, and my father lost his temper and raised his fist; but the conductor, instead of surrendering, looked very tough and my father, cowed, gave in completely. So I learned that his anger was the anger of a bully; it was a bluff he tried in order to impress his wife and children.

Nathan recorded these youthful reactions many years after the event, with a retrospective awareness that accusing his father of "cowardice" for being reluctant to prolong a public quarrel was "not just." For "when it confined itself to what was his own," Nathan admits,

his family and his Jewish world, my father's anger was genuine and sometimes awe-inspiring. During the First World War, the Jews were being persecuted, displaced by the fighting, robbed of their possessions and driven out of their homes. It seemed then that this was the worst that could possibly happen to human beings, and efforts were being made by the Jews of America to help them. The situation was dramatized by plays in the Yiddish theaters. . . . My father, who was a magnificent speaker, would often at the end of such a play go up on the stage and make an appeal for funds to help the war sufferers. He beat the audience with his anger, he shook it; at the end of one of his passionate orations, the men in the audience flung their wallets on the stage, the women tore off their rings and earrings. [34]

Asch did not confine himself to speechmaking. During the war he had been busy settling his family in America, traveling to the Holy Land, and finishing works started earlier. But as tales of Jewish suffering drifted across the Atlantic, Asch, with characteristic fervor, helped gather funds for the victims' relief, excoriated the oppressors in newspaper articles, and at war's end headed for Europe to report the Jewish plight at first hand.

VII   Miracles and Thieves

Despite these and other distractions, Asch continued writing. But even at his writing table his thoughts were not free of the war. In 1916 he published *A String of Pearls*, [35] a play dealing with Jewish wartime agonies. A Russian military unit enters a Polish town and the commander orders its Jews to provision his troops and then to evacuate within twelve hours. Only the attractive daughter of the patriarchal Reb Melech, the commanding officer decrees, is to remain. As for old Melech, no calamity, not even this one, can shake his belief that God's ways are not to be questioned. But he does tell his daughter to put on her dead grandmother's clothes (including a pearl necklace with secret potion) in the forlorn hope that such garb will lessen her appeal. A strange miracle follows: the orderly who comes to fetch the young girl finds, to his own and the reader's dismay, a wrinkled old woman. This fantastic climax, unfortunately, renders maudlin and artificial what has been a harshly realistic drama.

Imposing melodramatic conclusions on realistic narratives proved habitual with Asch. He liked especially to round-off his works with acts of religious martyrdom or of maidenly virtue saved-by-a-miracle, and in novels like *Sanctification of the Name*, *The Witch of Castile*, and *Salvation*, he developed such episodes fully and even somewhat plausibly. In *The Witch of Castile*, for instance, he carefully prepares the reader to accept both the Roman Jews' choice of martyrdom over apostasy and the "miracle" of his heroine's resemblance to the madonna; the two events appear credible because Asch delineates convincingly the religious beliefs and superstitions involved. But in *A String of Pearls* his swift transforming of the heroine into an old woman, even if viewed metaphorically, remains a forced, sentimental anomaly. He makes matters worse when he closes with a scene of symbolic confusion in which Reb Melech is revealed to be the Messiah and the Polish officer his eternal antagonist, Titus. Apparently Asch hoped thereby to exhort his fellow Jews to purify their spirit and strengthen their faith; yet he could have only baffled and embarrassed them. Final scenes would remain troublesome for him both as playwright and fictionist, and the critic who described this one as "a loose appendage of melodramatic byplay"[36] would be echoed by others through the years.

Asch now completed *Mottke the Thief*, a novel of the Warsaw underworld he had started in Paris before the war. He tried hard in it to recapture the vitality and pathos of his earlier stories, for he needed badly a literary success in America. He had dominated the decade just past as Europe's master talespinner of Jewish lore and legend. But his only novel in English was *America*, and it had made little impression on American readers, Jewish or non-Jewish.

Hence his new novel, he hoped, would garner wide attention and readership—and it did just that. Translated quickly (indeed, too quickly)[37] into English, *Mottke the Thief* made Sholem Asch a household name for America's Jews. If some readers were shocked by the seamy subject matter, others were delighted to find in Jewish fiction characters other than the mournful Talmudist, shuddering pogrom victim, or comic peddler. These fade into background as Asch follows his hard-bitten demi-hero from *shtetl* childhood and provincial escapades (murder included), through a meteoric rise among Warsaw's criminals, to love and final betrayal.

His motives aside, Asch produced here a work more painfully realistic than *The Little Town* or *Reb Shlomo Nagid,* one strongly akin to *God of Vengeance* and to the Warsaw and Lodz sections of the later *Three Cities.* For in his broad but effective portraits of hungry Polish Jews battling for survival, he underscores the similarities between the small town's static but often turbulent squalor and the city's gaudy, grimy existence. Neither muddy backstreet nor ghetto underworld here exudes romance or nostalgia. Certainly the town's threadbare Jewish quarter—with its crowded cobbled streets and damp cellars, its coarse stallkeepers and apprentices, its corrupt constables, arrogant thieves, and pathetic misfits— bears little resemblance to the pastoral bywaters inhabited by Reb Yechezkel Gombiner or Reb·Shlomo Nagid.

The story derives from an old folktale, and the phrase *Mottke ganef* ("Mottke the thief") was a Yiddish colloquialism long before Asch. Here, after a surprisingly humorous beginning (Asch is little given to humor in his fiction), the narrative quickly waxes somber and then grim. This Mottke is an earthy, passionate being unhampered by any complex or civilizing social pressure. A folk figure of "Gargantuan energy,"[38] he could have sprung from any peasant stock; growing up amid poverty, neglect, and hunger, he brawls through life thieving and procuring, guided by his emotions and dreams rather than thoughts. At times Mottke seems little more than a "raffish caricature of Rousseau's natural man."[39] Society, he decides early, is his enemy and life a vicious battleground where only the strong and cunning survive. Scruples and conscience are not for him. The street becomes his arena and pantry where he snatches food from doorways and tables, peddlers and children. Doors slam at his approach amid cries of "the thief!" His mother, Red Slatke, spoils him, and Mottke's elemental attach-

ment to her is tender and touching. Yet when he refuses to go to
school or work, he is beaten—by his father or teacher or work-
master or town constable. Mottke accepts punishment without
whimpering, but he forgets nothing, bides his time, and repays his
enemies twofold.

At seven he is an outcast, at fourteen a skilled thief who goes off
to try the world. His adventures lead him, at sixteen, to a troupe of
vagabond entertainers led by Old Terach, a tumbler and smuggler,
who makes a wrestler of him. Infatuated with Mary the rope
dancer, Mottke discovers she is a prostitute and angrily decides
nothing in life matters but money. He asserts his right to survive at
all costs, but he recognizes that others have the same right. "That's
how things stand," he declares, "and that's how they'll always
stand."[40] Desperate for identity papers, he kills Mary's panderer,
Kanarik, and runs off with her to Warsaw's underworld.

These two hundred pages on Mottke's turbulent youth find
Asch at his best. His prose is crisp, ironic, wryly humorous, and
controlled. Drawn in broad, lusty strokes, Mottke develops clearly
and inevitably. A believable—at times near-admirable—hero or
anti-hero, he is consistently anti-social and tough. Red Slatke and
Blind Leib, his parents; the thief Nussen, Mottke's idol and mentor;
Ephroim Geiger, the town miser hoarding a warehouse of rotting
boots; Moische-Schloime, the synagogue attendant who serves
everyone's jail sentence but is released for the Sabbath; Blind
Pearl, the crooked constable; Burek, the organ-grinder's trick dog;
and the thieving acrobatic troupe—all burst with Rabelaisian vigor.

When Mottke arrives in Warsaw, however, Asch shifts from
realist to moralist, and the narrative grows erratic and unconvincing. Old Warsaw is a dark, tottering maze where anything can be
bought, sold, or exchanged. Mottke has taken on Kanarik's
personality with his passport. Quick-fisted and swaggering, he is
soon the ghetto's most successful pimp. Yet his little world's greed
and ugliness fail to destroy Mottke's romantic fantasies, and he falls
in love with Chanele, a café owner's young daughter. Chastity now
becomes for him (as for Yankel Chapchovich) symbolic of the
highest good. Asch challenges credibility as his cunning, unscrupu-
lous thief is transformed by Chanele's pretty face into a simperingly
virtuous suitor recklessly entrusting his life to people he has every
reason to mistrust. His incredible behavior leads to his rapid
exposure as a murderer.

Mottke's love is pure but unconvincing. Like most Asch heroes, he has a mother fixation: the passive, colorless Chanele reminds him, incongruously enough, of tough, coarse-grained Red Slatke, and in loving her he feels he is reclaiming both his mother and the boyhood he never had. Wanting to be honest with Chanele, he confesses to her his murder of Kanarik. A mere pawn of her greedy parents, she allows him to be exposed to the police: she need merely claim sexual involvement with him to seal her parents' lips. Only the discarded whore Mary comes to help him, but he refuses to be saved: he will not sully the new Mottke so miraculously reborn. Nor can he believe Chanele will betray him when even his criminal enemies have refused. Arrested, his vision of hope and beauty shattered, he goes almost willingly to prison.

Mottke's escapades are heightened just enough to suggest some meaning beyond the simple narrative, but the symbolism is unobtrusive and unimportant. He is totally real and human (if rather thickheadedly romantic), never legendary. As boy and man he fights life and rivals on those terms they tender him; he follows his baser instincts and wins. But the first time he trusts another human being, he is betrayed. Asch seems to be modifying ambiguously (perhaps even subconsciously) his pervasive mother-sweetheart figure. His "bad" (or simply "other") woman is now repeatedly more sexually exciting and courageous than his sentimentalized maternal one. Yet he returns, almost compulsively, to the latter in nearly every novel. Here, love for a "good" woman proves as ruinous for Mottke as it had for Yankel Chapchovich. Danger nurtures these two toughs, and so long as they rely solely on their animal urges they are safe. When they start to yearn for "higher" things and to reject the values of survival for those of convention and respectability, they are destroyed. Asch underlines here—as he had in "Daughter of the Upper Class'—the pitfalls of trying to rise above birth, misfortune, and human frailties. Yet Mottke's fate, Asch makes clear, is not inevitable: the same poverty produces rabbis and scholars.

The maturity of style and thought to be found later in *Three Cities* and *Salvation* is still lacking here. Asch's art and effort barely keep *Mottke the Thief* from mere melodrama. Yet it remains, at least in part, his most vital novel. Mottke emerges as a quasi-picaro who, as he roams Poland living by wits and strength, might have derived from Le Sage. But his character and experiences ultimately are shaped by the tumultuous but tightly bound ethnic world he never leaves. (In turn, he helped shape the behavior and prepare reader acceptance of such later Jewish picaros as Isaac Babel's Benya Krik and Isaac Bashevis Singer's Yasha Mazur.) [41]

In depicting his Jewish and non-Jewish opportunists, Asch is unsparing. "No business is more dependent on mutual trust than the business of living flesh," he writes of some visiting white slavers. "One's word is one's bond, and everybody watches jealously over the honor of the trade."[42] He scores the venality of Chanele's "respectable" parents and the lust and corruption of the Polish commissar and the judge who plot with them to arrest Mottke. Only his whores, pimps, and thieves adhere to an "honor code." They alone evoke his sympathy, and he depicts their joys, sufferings, and sins with tenderness and understanding, and often by a laughter close to tears. Sensually alive, they emerge from window, cellar, and gutter to be personalized by a name or feature. Asch catches their every trait and mannerism as his narrative literally bursts with gestures, sounds, and movements.

He treats people and setting candidly, recognizing the grim seriousness of corruption and crime among Poland's hungry Jews. His moralizing, less obtrusive than in *God of Vengeance*, is overshadowed by the graphic descriptive detail. Inevitably, some Jewish readers, their sensibilities still raw from *God of Vengeance* a decade earlier, found Mottke as unsavory as Yankel Chapchovich, and they subjected Asch to another round of abuse. Indeed, his fondness for the Jew-as-scoundrel moved non-Jewish critics to chide him on occasion. Even sympathetic critics could be less than helpful in noting this trait. Oscar Cargill, for instance, stated that "Asch has never commented on the relative amount of villainy among his people, but he has always found scoundrels enough to counterpoise his better motivated characters, and he has not hesitated to use them. This was one of his special merits as a writer when he was addressing only a Jewish audience. In this sense he is almost as anti-Semitic as Shakespeare."[43] Cargill was being ironic, but even such obvious irony must have offered cold comfort to Asch's more sensitive Jewish readers—or to the author himself.

Chapter Four

After the War

Asch found postwar America bustling and exciting. Living on Staten Island, he was removed somewhat from the city's clamor. Yet his ties to the *Jewish Daily Forward*, then serializing his novels, brought him regularly to that paper's Manhattan offices on East Broadway, where most Yiddish publications huddled closely. There he could observe the teeming East Side streets and tenements and have lunch at the Café Royale, a noisy hangout for Jewish litterateurs on Second Avenue; to join in the heated talk there on books, writing, and politics, one had to have established his intellectual or literary credentials.[1] Tall, confident, and world famous, Asch dominated these gatherings as clearly as he had those in Warsaw.

He was taking increasing interest in Jewish adjustment to the New World—in the immigrants' hopes and struggles, their shifting habits and values. If he appreciated America's promise to her newcomers, he was disturbed by the crushing impact of her complexities on these late arrivals, especially on the not-so-young. He began describing in his fiction their uprooting from a static but cohesive ghetto culture and their pathetic efforts to cope with a sweatshop grind of economic anxieties and social confusions. He pointed up repeatedly the new life's crushing of cherished hopes and its abrasive effects on the natural tensions between greenhorn elders and Yankee children.

I Greenhorns and Yankees

Between 1916 and 1923 Asch revealed in three short novels (*Uncle Moses, Chaim Lederer's Return,* and *Judge Not—*)[2] his dismay at the lessening fear of God among Jews; the prime culprit was American life, with its leveling freedom and material vulgarities. No longer were Jews willing to sacrifice goods and lives for religious faith; the Sabbath had lost its poetry, and God had shrunk to a mere annual Yom Kippur concern. But if these themes aroused his emotions, they hardly fired his imagination. Missing from Asch's wartime and postwar fiction were the verve and exuberance he had exhibited in *Reb Shlomo Nagid* and *Mottke the Thief*. Indeed, he failed to exercise fully either taste or craftsmanship, so rushed was he to supply the *Forward* regularly with fiction installments. Absorbing slowly his American surroundings, he confronted them more with curiosity than intuition. Much taken with the New World's general and external aspects, he impatiently created characters who were little better than conventional types. (Some would reappear more fully realized in his later "American" novels.)

His *Uncle Moses* (1917) exemplifies graphically the melting-pot novel, that exotic sub-genre so popular during the decades of heavy East European immigration. In tracing here the fall from pride and dignity of an arrogant sweatshop owner, Asch develops those plot elements his "American" novels and stories would soon make familiar. A poor young man's energy and driving ambition cause him to run roughshod over others. Success and age, however, arouse in him deep guilt feelings over past acts and engender a desire to make peace with God and man. But punishment must be exacted (in Asch no sinner goes unchastised), so the malefactor's vigor and confidence give way to weakness and uncertainty. A youthful supplanter (here a nephew but often a son) and a destructively beautiful young woman help hasten his fall. (Asch's women, if not maternal figures, inevitably prove martyrs or destroyers.) A compelling if somewhat sentimental tale, *Uncle Moses* is almost unrelievedly depressing. Overshadowing plot and structure are a dozen frightened, blundering humans who are prevented from being better than they are by their harsh lives and weak flesh. Moses Melnik, a onetime butcher's apprentice, is the central figure; after years of poverty in New York, he has a flourishing sweatshop on the Bowery and draws a work force from his native Kusmin. Soon that Polish town's scholars and merchants, cobblers and dandies are sewing garments in his filthy loft, clerking in his store, and living in his tenements. As brutal and arrogant as he is kindly and humorous, Melnik settles squabbles, resolves crises, and regulates lives. Thus the immigrants soon find America to be a "golden land" where all have been rendered equal and where, as one harassed wife points out, "No one has time to pray" (25).

Reluctant to forget the old life, the Kusminites huddle to recall their town's sky and fields, its every stick and corner. "Whenever they met," notes Asch laconically, "they spread Kusmin out on the tables, so to speak, for the only real life they had ever known was the one they had left behind them in their old home" (64). He makes clear that their nostalgia separates the newcomers from American society and renders them vulnerable to exploitation by their new patriarch. Yet not even "Uncle Moses," as he is called, has found happiness in America. Haunting him are memories of poverty and humiliation, of a lost youth and purposeless life. Driven, suspicious, bored, he has absorbed, after years in America, only his new home's trimmings and slang. His ties are to Kusmin, but his workers and relatives hate and fear him. A childless widower nearing fifty, he needs love and loyalty but will trust no one. Only Mascha, a worker's fourteen-year-old daughter, attracts him; her open hostility differs intriguingly from everyone else's fawning deference. Virtually adopting her, Melnik showers Mascha with gifts and directs her education. She awakens dormant desires, and when she is eighteen he forces her to marry him by pressuring her crushed, ambitious parents. The Kusminites may hate him, but he is confident his kindness to Mascha will cause her to love him and bear him children.

Melnik proves another Asch "tough" deprived by love and sentimentality of his vigor, judgment, and courage. Like Yankel Chapchovich and Mottke the thief, he burdens a confused, resentful girl with his dreams of purity and innocence, lavishing upon her his affection and luxuries. But Mascha, wallowing in self-pity, sees herself as a pawn of her greedy parents and sisters and grows increasingly coarse and demanding. So absorbed is Melnik in placating her that he is only half-aware that a growing trade-union movement has undermined his paternalistic structure. When a strike breaks out, Mascha sides with the workers; her help is rejected, but Melnik's power is shattered and his nephew wrests company control from him. His employees, having long feared their patron, now find him a comic figure: the elderly husband doting on an unresponsive young wife. He seems as lost and helpless as they have been since leaving the old country. But Melnik is barely concerned with these events. His wife has borne a son, and he feels his life finally complete; he can accept now even Mascha's indifference. This is true, however, only in the truncated English translation; in the Yiddish version his world explodes tragically. Mascha confesses that the child Melnik cherishes is not his but his nephew's. She then disappears, leaving Melnik to hover haplessly over his first wife's grave. But his fall—the novel's central event—is overshadowed by the evocative details of Jewish immigrant life. Asch again idealizes the *shtetl* past, yet he recognizes that not only is it an age gone but that it was always as much idea as reality; any past, he points oüt, should be cherished only when it becomes meaningful to the present and future. Thus he sympathizes with the young as well as the old, especially with the young people's conviction that they can repay America for their newfound freedom only by continual social unrest and protest.

As he had in *The Little Town* and *Reb Shlomo Nagid*, Asch here depicts provincial-minded Jews dominated by a strong leader. But these earlier novellas had more verve, their little people were more vibrant; enduring the week's travails primarily for the Sabbath's pleasures, they willingly defended their faith with blood and spirit. Describing them enabled Asch to give his lyric tendencies full play. In *Uncle Moses* a sweatshop dreariness mutes the Sabbath's joys and dulls the workers' minds. Asch catches the talk and gestures of shop and home, measures the void between parents and children, and grasps the depth of their mutual anxieties and frustrations. He sums up much of this in a pious immigrant couple's farewell to their family and America on departing for Kusmin to live out their days: "As Uncle Berl and his wife said good-bye they realized for the first time just what their life in America had done to them. They had brought their children to this new country, and America had taken their children away. America had claimed the children for itself. But as for the old couple, as for Berl and Genendel themselves, America spewed them out again, cast them off like worthless, useless bits of flotsam" (72).

Asch may have been thinking of his own parents. Moshe and Malka Asch, who had come to America with their children, chose also to spend their last years in Kutno. Indeed, he based most of this novel's characters on members of the large Asch clan. He would do this increasingly, especially in the later *East River*. Here his accurate descriptions of setting and people, plus his strong empathy with the latter, should have produced a better book. He does soften his moralizing tendencies somewhat, and he even balances out his purple passages and other stylistic lapses with vivid, evocative scenes—such as Mascha and her cousin Charlie's romp at an early-day Coney Island. Nor does he allow his "realism" (the near-*Lolita* theme, for instance) to become sordid or offensive. Yet his attempt to write several varying stories at once creates

inevitably more confusion than clarity, and, as often happens with
Asch, each tale seems more promising than the one he wants to tell.
He intends his hero to be a moving, pitiable figure, but Moses
Melnik never wins the reader's sympathy or complete understanding. The pathos of his early failures and frustrations is as
unconvincing as his later moral transformation. Thus his
misfortunes seem simple justice. Most signficantly, perhaps,
Melnik's struggles with his workers now seem confined to a brief,
closed era in America's history.[3]

Hence *Uncle Moses* proves a rather constricted work that lacks
the range of a *Mottke the Thief* or the intensity of a *God of
Vengeance*. After reading it, one reviewer wondered if America
eventually would bring forth the best in Asch. He finally decided
that it would.[4] Time has revealed otherwise: Asch's Jews-in-
America novels never equaled his better "European" ones. Yet he
did catch in them much of the Jewish migration's joys and stresses,
its assimilative successes and failures. Asch was strongly
responsive to the American-Jewish experience, particularly to its
more painful aspects. But he remained always the concerned
observer rather than involved participant.

II   Cossacks and Martyrs

Asch drove himself hard during the war and postwar years.
After *Uncle Moses*, he published the drama *Who Is the Father?*
(1918) and four collections of his stories and sketches.[5] He also
gathered material for two historical novels, *Sanctification of the
Name* and *The Witch of Castile*, and a drama, *The Dance of Death*.
His interest in Jewish history was intensified by contemporary
events; reports from Europe indicated that Jews caught between
the Russian and German-Austrian armies were being slaughtered
or rendered homeless. Even the war's cessation helped them little;
if anything, peace seemed merely to signal more pogroms.[6] These
disasters, plus a widespread famine, made Asch anxious to see
what remained of the Jewish life he remembered. In 1919 the
American Jewish Relief Committee offered the opportunity: he was
asked to investigate the condition of Lithuania's Jews and to file a
report that would help raise funds for the victims.

Touring Lithuania throughout the summer, he returned home in
September with a detailed account of his observations, much of
which was carried in the *New York Times*. On twenty-four hours
notice, he declared, Russian military authorities had deported all

Jews in the provinces of Kovno and Suwalki. Lithuanian Jewry, long noted for its learning and culture, had been "torn out by the roots" and its members' homes stripped and often leveled. In the large cities he had seen displaced Jewish artisans lining the curbstones; having pawned their tools to feed their families, many had become unemployable. Yet wherever exiles had returned to their homes, their first concern had been to reopen schools and synagogues. Epidemics, pogroms, and hunger had failed to shatter their spirit or faith. Lithuania's Jews, Asch concluded "remind us of that worm which has such vitality in every part of its body that, though severed in twain, each half yet lives on."[7] Asch's report undoubtedly contributed substantially to the campaigns throughout the United States which raised millions for the victims. He also spoke on what he had seen to responsive audiences. His favorite ploy, as Nathan Asch already has reported, was to go on stage after the performance of a Yiddish play to make a stirring plea for funds; deeply sentimental and quickly moved to tears himself, he usually had a similar effect on his audience—once even moving his listeners to throwing money and jewelry on stage.[8]

But primarily he sought to encourage his dispirited readers,[9] both in Europe and America, through his fiction. He began depicting earlier calamities that Jewish faith and courage had turned into spiritual victories. Such "victories" often meant martyrdom, and in his preface to *The Witch of Castile* Asch tried to explain the special fascination Jewish martyrdom and Messianism held for him. In that novel, as well as in such efforts as *A String of Pearls, Sanctification of the Name, The Marranos*, and *The Dance of Death*, he played both historian and prophet to assure his beleaguered coreligionists that they would survive their present sufferings. He saw in the brutal 1918-19 pogroms a repetition of 1648 events, when Cossack hordes had pillaged flourishing Jewish communities in the same districts. In that year the Ukrainian peasants had revolted against their Polish overlords, but unable to reach these absentee landowners they had vented their frustration and rage upon the helpless Jewish minority. By retelling the earlier events and glorifying their martyrs, Asch hoped to comfort the present victims. Then too, he pointed out repeatedly, the Jews had approached annihilation, but their undying faith had guaranteed a saving remnant.

He wanted to depict, therefore, the Jewish view of those tragic days. There was ample precedent: in *Taras Bulba* (1835), Nikolai

Gogol had presented the Cossack side, with Henry Sienkiewicz doing the same for the Poles in his trilogy *With Fire and Sword* (1883), *The Deluge* (1886), and *Pan Michael* (1887-88). Asch knew and used these works to write *Sanctification of the Name* (1919).[10] But a stronger influence on him here was Abraham Friedberg's four-volume Hebrew story-cycle of Jewish history, *Reminiscences of the House of David*,[11] which included many of the memorable seventeenth-century incidents. (In recent years Isaac Bashevis Singer has used the same happenings as backdrop for his *Satan in Goray* and *The Slave*.) Asch's major sources, however, were the old community chronicles of Zlochov, Memirov, and Tulchin, wherein Jewish martyrdom was recorded vividly. Yet despite its grim theme, *Sanctification of the Name* proves a muted prose poem emphasizing peace, spirituality, and courage. Asch conveys the Cossack brutalities with restraint and dignity, describing the pogroms more by effects than direct exposition: a muffled scream or moan, a half-uttered cry, torn holy-book pages fluttering in the wind, a darkly silent house, a candlestick on the doorstep, the retreating staccato of galloping hoofs. The old-chronicle statement Asch borrows as epigraph sums up his approach: "We are ashamed to write down all that the Cossacks and Tatars did unto the Jews, lest we disgrace the species man, which is created in the image of God."

Dividing his narrative into two parts, he dwells first on seventeenth-century Ukrainian Jewish life, and then on the Cossack massacres of the hapless Jews. At first the innkeeper Mendel and his family are the only Jews in Zlochov, deep in the Ukraine's wide steppes. Here Mendel struggles to maintain his Jewishness among the hard-drinking peasants and landowners. For permission to build a synagogue and acquire land for a Jewish cemetery, he even dons a humiliating bearskin and dances before the drunken Polish aristocrats. Synagogue and cemetery attract survivors of pogroms and blood accusations from throughout Poland and the Ukraine, and soon a small Jewish community flourishes in Zlochov. The Jews live quite happily despite their overlord's changeable moods and an everpresent Cossack menace. Shlomo, Mendel's son, marries early and is sent to Lublin's famed Yeshiva, returning at twenty a learned rabbi prepared for communal leadership.

Shlomo's arrival and his love for wife and home enable Asch to fashion another *shtetl* idyl strongly reminiscent of *The Town* and *Reb Shlomo Nagid*. He catches the rustic simplicity of communal meetings, the scholar's position and influence in Jewish life, and the encircled Jews' unyielding faith—weaving these elements into a convincing, if sentimental, montage. He also tries to unravel the secret of Jewish survival, delineating his little group's adaptability to the most demanding circumstances. Surrounded by semi-barbaric peasants, ruled by dissolute Polish nobles, and under constant threat of the rebelling Zaporzhe Cossacks, Zlochov's Jews retain their loyalty to God's law. Asch makes it all living history—except for the legendary note struck by a mysterious little tailor who moves in and out of the lives of Mendel's family and neighbors. He is really a *lamedvovnik*, one of the supposedly thirty-six secret saints whose collective righteousness makes possible the world's continuation despite its wickedness.

Mendel's little community is not destined to last. The narrative darkens as reports reach Zlochov of a Cossack revolt against the Polish overlords. Soon an army of Cossack peasants and Tatars, led by their hetman, Bogdan Chmielnicki, is plundering and annihilating Polish and Jewish communities. Most Jews scatter to the fortified cities, but those in Zlochov want to defend their synagogue. Their rabbi and the ubiquitous tailor, however, command them to flee with the Torah scrolls. They must save their strength, declares the latter ominously, for a higher occasion. Turning for a last look, Mendel sees his beloved synagogue in flames, and it reminds him of the candle one burns for the dead. Asch fashions a stirring evocation of human tragedy and suffering, as he describes graphically the mass flight to Nemirov and the massacre there of its Jews. Mendel and some others escape to Tulchin where, with a cry of "For God and His Torah," they battle the Cossacks to a standstill—only to be betrayed by their Polish allies. The Jews, however, need but bow before the Cross to be spared. Instead, they sing Psalms to Israel's God and chant the *Shema* as under a bright sun the Cossacks slaughter fourteen hundred of them—men, women, and children. Many more are led to the slave markets; yet not one abandons his faith for life or freedom.

Mendel and his wife Yocheved die as they have lived, with pride and dignity. Throughout their difficulties Mendel and his son Shlomo have been concerned that the latter's beautiful wife, Deborah, not be violated. Asch lavishes upon her a welter of physical detail and religious symbolism. One of Deborah's Cossack captors, Yerem, falls in love with her and protects her from harm.

Deeply superstitious, and sensing the girl's religious nature, he declares her "a holy one, a saint" and accepts her claim that a divine spirit shields her from death; had he not seen her in church, on the holy icon? To allay the doubts of his fellow Cossacks, to whom Deborah seems more witch than saint, Yerem reluctantly accedes to her request that he shoot her. Deborah dies believing she will join Shlomo in a better world. (This episode, expanded, becomes the plot of *The Witch of Castile.*) But Shlomo is alive. Ransomed from Turkish slavery, he wanders the world searching for his wife and for some understanding of the catastrophe engulfing his people. At the moment its meaning eludes him, and he is but "one degree removed from doubting" (183). When the holocaust subsides, the Ukraine's surviving Jews gather at the great Lublin fair. Shlomo finds the little tailor there standing before an empty booth. Baffled, he asks the latter what he is selling, to which the little man replies: "I sell faith" (183), the one thing that tragedy and exile have not taken from the Jews.

Asch here strives for a people's pulsations of heart and spirit at cataclysmic moments in its history. Fascinated, as he said, by the theme of sacrificial heroism, he returns repeatedly to the conflict between physical might and moral elevation; the enemy's armed fist, he concludes, merely bestows upon the Jews the more enduring victory, for their repeated willingness to die for Sanctification of the Holy Name renders them spiritually unconquerable.[12] The novel brought Asch new critical and public acclaim, and its descriptions of past Jewish life and culture even made it for some time a popular text in Jewish schools. But in recent years its popularity has faded. A compressed, controlled, and essentially simple tale, it merits more attention than it has received. Asch's lyric intensity here overrides his occasional didactic and cinematic flourishes, and his imaginative recreation of the tragic events gives life and pathos to a significant Jewish epoch.

Yet *Sanctification of the Name* is in some ways a curiously uneven novel. Mendel and his family begin as near-comic characters living in isolation. As their community evolves, they acquire dignity, seriousness, import; story and tone then are greatly altered, with the realism becoming more strongly tinged with fantasy. The leisurely pace and careful descriptive detail soon give way to rapid actions and broad strokes that merely suggest character and motive. Asch may have decided to finish rapidly after originally having a longer work in mind. One who did not like the novel was Abraham Cahan. He cancelled its *Forward* serialization after three installments. When Asch asked why, Cahan told him to write another *Mottke the Thief*—not such foolish old wives' tales as embodied in this work. But the paper's other staffers liked it, and led by their general manager, Baruch Vladek Charney, they organized reader support for the novel's continuance. Cahan acceded to the pressure, but Asch always believed the incident contributed to the later bitterness between them.[13]

The novel had other long-range effects. Its moving depiction of Jewish suffering caused some critics two decades later to expect its author to produce a narrative of the Jewish Holocaust. Asch did deal with German-Jewish life during Hitler's early days in *The War Goes On* (1936), and in *Tales of My People* (1948) he presented a series of stories (dedicated to the six million victims) that described Nazi atrocities. But these critics expected a long novel combining the tragic intensity of *Sanctification of the Name* and the grand scale of *Three Cities*, something close to John Hersey's *The Wall*.[14] That a non-Jew like Hersey should have come the closest to their desired work made Asch's "failure" the more disappointing; when he gave them *The Nazarene* instead of *The Wall*, their disappointment turned vitriolic.

III "Shop Sickness"

Asch also published in 1919 *Chaim Lederer's Return*,[15] another assault on the American middle-class dream. Here an ex-radical and nihilist, having climbed to affluence and position, feels himself spiritually empty and strains to regain his lost ideals. (Asch supposedly based his hero on a contemporary businessman, one Reuben Sadowsky, but he may also have been mindful of Tolstoy's life.) To defeat the poverty that darkened his early life, Chaim Lederer has quashed his socialist values and moral scruples; he has even shared his Jewish employees' evening prayer to wring from them an extra hour of work. Now past sixty, he is impatient for a fresh challenge, for a serious, purposeful life. Relinquishing his shirt business to his son, Lederer determines to recapture those qualities of mind and spirit he had abandoned in his youth.

But his attempts to recapture the past and to enjoy the present prove pathetic. He finds that his early ideals have faded beyond recovery and that mere luxury and travel bore him. As for his shallow, snobbish children, they belong to a new age; also, they resent not only his years of callous behavior toward them but his persistent atheism, which embarrasses them before their socially prominent friends. When time weighs heavily, he revisits his factory, but he now proves a mere nuisance. He grows increasingly bitter and withdrawn. The doctors decide he suffers from a disease spreading in industrial America—"shop sickness," a compulsive need to work far beyond necessity (a Jewish variant, seemingly, of the Puritan ethic). Lederer then decides to renounce his wealth and seek happy obscurity as a factory worker. When his wife refuses to surrender her hard-won luxuries to reembrace the bleak poverty of their youth, Lederer disappears alone. After a perfunctory search for him, his wife and children resume their comfortable lives.

More essay than novel, *Chaim Lederer's Return* has little dialogue and less action. Again expounding his views on Jewish immigrant life, Asch dwells on the tensions between boss and worker and between parents and children. His special target once more is the successful Jewish businessman. For Asch the immigrants-turned-employers are a moral anachronism. He rejects their vaunted altruistic and philanthropic motives to insist that they are merely satisfying a compulsive need for aggressive action: they work because they like to work. "That's what people do," confesses Lederer. "There isn't anything to do except to work, because people don't know how to be idle. . . . Life is just one big shop" (86). Asch's patent disapproval of this work compulsion is ironic, for he himself suffered from the malady to his final moments.

He is ill-served here by a clumsy translation of his rather emotional rhetoric. Until the Nazi massacres, he wrote primarily for a Yiddish-speaking readership conditioned to the broad, expressive gesture and overplayed emotion. Always a direct influence, his audience awareness is nowhere more evident than in this novel; he repeatedly interrupts the narrative (a la Thackeray or Trollope) to address his readers, but with gratuitous moralisms rather than deft wit. In addition, he fails to convince the reader that Lederer, whose life has been a desperate battle against poverty, will embrace it eagerly in his last years merely to fulfil a utopian fantasy of universal brotherhood. Admittedly, Asch's social didacticism and soulful concern for his fellow man are vaguely reminiscent of Tolstoy; yet it is difficult to comprehend how the *New York Times* reviewer could have equated this novel with the Russian's masterful *Death of Ivan Ilych*.[16] If anything, Chaim Lederer seems a near-parody of David Levinsky, whom Abraham

Cahan had introduced two years earlier, and the resemblances between their heroes may have contributed to the growing antagonism between the two novelists. Both Lederer and Levinsky are freethinkers and garment-industry millionaires, and, like their mutual Yankee prototype Silas Lapham, they both remember the old days, old ways, and old miseries. Neither can bring the past into psychic rapport with the present, and each feels his inner identity to be closer to the poor lad he once was than to the affluent manufacturer he has become. But regrets and nostalgia, they find, avail little: there is no return.[17]

IV   Martyrdom, Sex, and Beauty

Asch paused in his writing long enough, in 1920, to become an American citizen, and then he published a stillborn drama, *The Dead Man*.[18] He followed it the next year with *The Witch of Castile*,[19] another historical novella of Jewish martyrdom; expanding an episode from *Sanctification of the Name*, he describes here the troubles of Rome's Jews during the papacy of Paul IV and the Inquisition's burning of a Jewish girl with a madonna-face.

In the sixteenth-century many Jews fleeing Inquisitorial Spain and Portugal have found in Rome a haven for almost two generations. But the Inquisition has been growing stronger in Italy, and its leaders determine to convert the Jews to Christianity. Angered by the Reformation's spreading influence, Pope Paul also vents his rage upon the Roman ghetto's helpless but stubborn inhabitants. His cruelties bring little results: the Jews are no sooner released from the Inquisitorial racks then they chant the Psalms in their cells and refuse baptism. Desperate, Paul condemns them to drowning within the ghetto walls. Temporary succor comes almost miraculously in the person of the beautiful Spanish Jewess Jephta, who so resembles the Virgin that the Romans think Mary has returned to share her people's misery. The truth is more prosaic. A young Venetian painter visiting the ghetto, and struck by the Madonna-like appearance of this youthful Sephardic girl, has painted an altar piece in her likeness; the striking resemblance soon has all Rome astir. The Pope, however, brands Jephta a witch, accuses her of having usurped Mary's face through sorcery, and decides to test by fire whether the peculiar resemblance is witchcraft or incarnation. Jephta dies, as had her father and numerous ancestors, refusing all blandishments to bend her knee to the Cross.

A lifelong antiquarian and art devotee, Asch lavishes historical detail upon Rome's great ghetto. But he readily admits that his narrative embodies little historical fact—other than the 1550 flooding of the ghetto and drowning of a number of Jews. All else stems from his imagination. So concerned is he with the Eternal City's Renaissance grandeur and atmosphere, not to mention Jeptha's startling beauty, that his central theme (none need despair while faith abides in the heart) is overshadowed. Seemingly aware of this imbalance, Asch refers to the novel as an "historical picture"—and as such it is drawn clearly and interestingly.

More signficantly, perhaps, *The Witch of Castile* points up Asch's penchant at this time for the sensual and erotic, qualities as evident in the contemporary *Judge Not*—as in period pieces like *Sabbatai Zevi* and *Sanctification of the Name*. A near-pagan lover of nature and physical beauty, Asch was also an acutely self-conscious Jew who cried out when his people were in pain; thus he often subordinated art to conscience, to the former's detriment. This disharmony between his moral and aesthetic senses created a repeated imbalance in his work. He spoke truest of life's basic joys (for him this meant man's intuitive union with God) when his people were "at once simple and sensual."[20] His delight in nature and beauty he conveyed less with eloquence than shouts of pleasure. His stylistic crudities and "instinctive sensuousness" are reminiscent of Theodore Dreiser, whereas his provincial Jews' fresh, half-expressed reactions to life and setting bring to mind Thomas Hardy's Wessex rustics.

Defensive about his incorrigible romanticism, Asch told one interviewer: "I am a romanticist. But don't confuse me with those who sentimentalize over and falsify reality. . . . I mean that I insist on finding the romance and beauty of life."[21] He meant not only the lyricism inherent in patriarchs walking on the Sabbath to synagogue, but the lyric element in the dreams and desires of his thieves, pimps, and prostitutes. Women posed artistic problems for him, with the most cultivated as sex-driven as any peasant. His younger females prove primarily pleasure objects, with Asch delighting to present them as amorous, seductive nudes. Such appreciation was natural to him, and today his frank voluptousness sounds mild, inoffensive, and indeed, somewhat stilted. His sensuality works better in the Biblical dramas and historical tales, where he could evoke a tribal people's erotic spirit and where ornate dialogue is more suited to the action. Contemporary settings reduce his imagery and language to the quaint and artificial. In *The Road to One's Self*, for instance, Mary steps from bath to admiring lover:

At last she appeared. Her hair was combed upwards, exposing the whole of her high forehead. Her face resembled da Vinci's St. Anne. Her feet, pink with warmth, and quivering from freshness, she put forth as upon the primitives of Cranach. Before her, [trembled] her stomach, full and round, and as if a dewy freshness had breathed upon it. Her two young dove breasts shot out from her as if two big, juicy grapes, and sprang to both sides. From her body oozed the sweetness and dew-covered freshness that lies upon the young, vigorous pine forest in the gray dawn. She smiled joyfully to the youth, and put forth her arms to him. [22]

Jephta "the witch" is described similarly, at every angle and mood, until Asch seems as smitten with her as is her lover Yash. But here Renaissance Rome and ghetto soften the gaucheries of style and image.

Such passages may help explain why neither work was published in English, though Asch's physical intensity, as mentioned, appears now more naive than passionate. Some Yiddish critics and readers objected strenuously to his eroticism; yet Yiddish readers traditionally have accepted a degree of the erotic the American public affected (until recently) to reject. But then most Americans have not had to live in their tenderloin or red light districts and so could afford to be more easily shocked. In the ghettos of the Russian Pale life was open and integrated. The same street housed the rabbi's daughter and the whore, respectable burghers with growing children as well as pimps and thieves. So the Yiddish writer, even more than the Russian, addressed a readership of the lower depths with which he identified. His environment failed to shake his idealism, and he shared with his readers a self-deprecating humor so strong and elemental, often Rabelaisian, that what often appeared to outsiders lapses in taste and morality was viewed within as natural and obvious. [23]

Conscious of this attitude difference, Asch and his translators occasionally softened or omitted in their English versions of his fiction potentially offensive terms, passages, or incidents. Still, he managed repeatedly to outrage both Jewish and non-Jewish sensibilities. For man's adoration of the flesh was to Asch innate and healthy. An attractive woman can turn his rabbis and scholars, merchants and artists, revolutionaries and thieves into aggressive males. When not sexually assertive, his young men are emotionally, even mystically, filial. Only Yechiel the Psalm Jew and Yeshua the Nazarene are not driven by sexual impulse; they are so involved with God as to require no other gratification. But the others exhibit strong sexual-filial drives,[24] and when frustrated or repressed, this drive vigorously reasserts itself. Joel, the "Holy Young Hermit," strives to strengthen his spirit at the body's expense only to find lust endangering his desired holiness. Similarly, several pious elders in different tales are caught with peasant girls, and in "The Red Hat"[25] a married youth avoids the prostitute who strongly attracts him but yields to her completely in his thoughts; he decides a higher power compels one to deeds he neither wishes nor dares. Not inner strength prevents him from surrendering, he sighs, but an outer weakness—a fear for career.

Women are essentially females to Asch: they are born to serve man and his offspring. Once they beget children, his women are dominated by maternal instincts. The few who try to live as independent beings rather than mothers appear anomalous and unworthy. In "Milk" a young mother is impelled by her child's death to find another infant to nurse to relieve her full breasts. In *America*, Hannah Leah considers herself the mother of six, though only four live; leaving for the new land, she bids her dead two a guilty farewell at the cemetery, feeling she is abandoning them. In the same novel a Lithuanian peasant woman turns tigerish to protect and keep her sick children. Equally fierce is the memorable Red Slatke, who battles husband, townspeople, and police to protect her incorrigible Mottke. The latter returns her affection; in Asch, even thieves and vagabonds have strong feelings for their mothers. Yet an ambitious scholar occasionally may prove less than loyal. A widow works herself to the bone in "A Scholar's Mother"[26] to keep her studious Yitzchokel at his books. He soon leaves their humble home, and she finds solace in the thought that he now is too learned to associate with so uncouth and ignorant a woman as she. (Similar rejections recur in *Salvation* and, somewhat modified, in *The Nazarene* and *Mary*.) The painful point is that the selfless, humble mother must withdraw willingly or be shunted aside in the coldly patriarchal world of Jewish piety and learning. If Yitzchokel is ashamed of his mother, it is but a minor factor: he would have been drawn away by the law and learning. Women simply have no place in this world, other than to work and sustain their menfolk.

The sexual and maternal often fuse for Asch to embody the creative and procreative powers of nature and divinity. The earth seems then a bountiful mother-mistress, ever amorous and pregnant, and he exults paganlike when viewing nature giving suck to all life.[27] He relates, in his preface to *Earth*, that he prayed one day and was answered by the vision of a woman naked and barefoot:

Her breasts were full and hidden in the stalks of the field, and her head was adorned with the fruit of the earth, and her shame was covered with the leaves of the fig tree. . . .

Overwhelmed, he asks her identity:

"I am the god thou hast asked for. I am the mother of all creation, the fruition that creates from endlessness to endlessness. . . . For what is man, if not one of my creations, drawing his sustenance from the earth, coming from her and returning to her, in accordance with the years? . . . Other prophets have prophesied in the names of the gods of heaven. Thee I anoint as the prophet of the god of earth." [28]

Uncouth and heavy-limbed, with a peasant's large red hands, she is, for Asch, Eve the mother, embracing and nourishing with love and joy all that lives. Asch worships her with a son's devotion and lover's passion, taking seriously his "appointment" as "prophet of the god of earth."

The Jew in him rebels occasionally at such pagan concepts and stirrings; yet when he thinks of God abstractly he slips into pantheism. God and nature are one, and only through faith and worship can even the most sensitive Jew experience the joyful beauties of God's world. [29] For worship alone opens the Jew's "creative faculties, his understanding of line, of color, of wealth and brilliance of thought." [30] Asch uses several times an incident evidently recalled from his own youthful reflections. Distracted by nature's beauties, a Jewish lad asks his teacher how one praises God when much pleased with nature. The latter laughs: " 'Blockhead! One praises God at bread-breaking during food-taking; but to praise God at the sight of nature? Who ever heard of such a thing?' So he wondered: Nature is beautiful, heaven so lovely, the earth so sweet and good, and such generosity and serenity envelop everything; and need not one praise God for all that?" [31] A stern God of vengeance seems generally alien to Asch; his is a God of love. "God's generosity is everywhere," a rebellious Hasid declares, "at every corner and at every turn; where one moves, there one feels God!" [32]

His pantheistic view of nature is most evident in his peasants. Direct, artless, crude, they live simply, express emotions freely, and accept fate unquestioningly. Asch dwells repeatedly on their elemental passions, crude superstitions, and intense love of the soil. Drafted into the army, the young peasant in "The Peasant and the Land" worries chiefly that his fields will be without a caretaker and plow. "I love the peasants," Asch declared. "Everything is with them as serious and as simple as the earth itself."[33] Both Jews and peasants are of course occasionally exposed to God's wrath, and they witness nature (human nature as well) baring its claws. Yet those who—like Yankel the pimp and Mottke the thief—see only a vengeful God or hostile universe bear personal responsibility for this state of affairs. Even a benevolent Creator, Asch insists, cannot allow human sin to go unpunished.

V   Renunciation, Passion, and Guilt

In 1921 Asch's writings were brought out in twelve volumes, in Yiddish, by a Warsaw publishing house. The event capped two decades of work, and for the occasion Asch headed for Warsaw, where the city's intellectuals warmly welcomed him home. His dramatization of *Mottke the Thief* was then the Yiddish theater's most popular hit, so the year proved a vintage one. As usual, traveling and public appearances hardly slowed his writing; he was planning several new works, including an historical drama on the Sephardic Jews (a group he had dealt with in *The Witch of Castile*) and another novel of contemporary America.

From Warsaw, Asch moved on to Paris[34] for a brief stay, and then he headed back to America. Soon after returning to New York he wrote *The Marranos*,[35] a short play on the settlement in Holland of Spanish and Portuguese Jews; in their previous homes these Jews had been nominal Catholics, while adhering secretly to their fathers' faith. Asch describes their final renunciation of hard-won wealth and position for the Netherlands' religious tolerance. Safe on Dutch soil, however, the newcomers are disappointed to find Holland's Jews a meek and humble lot. A wise rabbi soon persuades them that the Jewish God is not the Inquisition's haughty Lord but a deity of love and peace. Asch conveys with terse vigor the different religious and social viewpoints, yet the play proves fragmentary and fails to develop its intended dramatic impact.

Turning to his own day, Asch produced in *Judge Not*—[36] his most melodramatic novel of American life. He here traces again the disastrous effects of material success upon the Jewish moral fiber. Max Stone is another of his arrogant self-achievers. A bank executive, Stone is also the most assimilated of Asch heroes. His Jewishness is hardly discernible and only briefly alluded to; if he recalls occasionally his East Side childhood, he is beyond Chaim Lederer's nostalgia or Moses Melnik's uncertainties. He shares only their driving ambition and their lack of faith in anything but oneself. One other difference occurs: Stone inadvertently commits a murder and is sentenced to death.

Difficulties with his wife cause Stone to pass up his daughter's birthday party and check into a hotel for a weekend. He befriends an elderly Iowa realtor and his attractive mistress who are in New York on a spree, and the woman makes a strong play for him. That night the old man finds them together and provokes a fight. Stone accidentally kills the old philanderer and is arrested. As he does so often, Asch here intrudes a "moral" issue into his taut narrative and so alters matters as to challenge reader credulity and patience. Mrs. Stone need only testify to their marital problems to get her husband off with a light sentence. But she has a lover and wishes to be rid of Stone. His lawyers plead for permission to expose her infidelity to gain him a new trial. He refuses. His time in prison has enabled him to ponder past misdeeds and to bestir a dormant conscience; he had launched his career, he recalls, with a legal fraud ruining hundreds, and he has treated several women shabbily. These memories supposedly transform this hustling opportunist into a selfless stoic who decides his life has been futile and rapacious and the jury's verdict a just one. Stone spends his last days reflecting on cosmic verities, seeking clemency for a young Negro scorned by the other prisoners, and, inevitably, dreaming of his dead mother—who appears to him elderly but unclad. He literally welcomes execution, having learned, he declares, pity, sympathy, faith—and the inevitability of divine justice.

Asch emphasizes here more strongly than usual those quixotic social forces conditioning human life. He again makes clear that no one is totally blameless or blameful; character and circumstance determine Max Stone's fate, as they have that of Asch's earlier heroes. In fact, Stone seems merely a more sophisticated Mottke; smart, tough, ambitious, he still allows a beautiful woman to destroy him—the only difference being that she is a calculating adulteress rather than a youthful innocent. Stone shares also Mottke's mother fixation, enabling Asch to dwell once more on his omnipresent Oedipal mixture of maternal nature, earth, and sex.

Melodramatic and mawkish, *Judge Not*— exposes Asch's worst literary habits. Beginning and moving briskly until protagonist and dilemma are drawn, the story then slows as Asch asserts his moralizing tendencies. Max Stone's conversion is no more convincing than is that of Mottke the thief or Moses Melnik. Wealthy, influential, harddriving, Stone is an unlikely figure to walk passively to the electric chair—or to be so remorseful for misdeeds American society often condones as to choose death rather than expose a cheating wife. His silence verges on the super-human. Asch again has pushed a protagonist beyond his given character by forcing him to adhere to an imposed moral code.[37]

As a result, not even his effective Dreiserian analysis of capital punishment and jury-trial justice—with its confused jurors, preening lawyers, and circus atmosphere—not to mention Asch's first convincing description of sexual passion, overcomes the inconsistencies of character, contrived prison dialogue, and forced fatalism. Reviewers were quick to point out these flaws, yet most found things in the book to praise; English critic John Mair was even moved to describe *Judge Not*— as "the most polished and perfect of Mr. Asch's novels of Jewish life."[38] One can wonder about Mair's critical powers, but his comment, added to the others, does point up Sholem Asch's flair for writing "good bad fiction"[39] —that is, fiction capable of giving pleasure to people who perceive clearly that it is bad writing.

VI   The *God of Vengeance* Controversy

The sex-and-scandal theme of *Judge Not*—gave little joy to those readers long unhappy with Asch's persistent eroticism, the trait he had first exhibited sixteen years earlier in *God of Vengeance*. In fact that play—thanks in no small part to its erotic elements—had kept the stage almost continuously during the years, with productions throughout Europe; it even had been presented in New York, in Yiddish, by Maurice Schwartz's Yiddish Art Theatre, with almost no public protest. But an English production, as a writer in *The Nation* pointed out, would be another matter. Reviewing the first published English version of *God of Vengeance*,[40] Mary Carolyn Davies wrote, "The play is too revolting in setting and characters to be acceptable on any American stage today, although it has been performed in nearly a dozen Continental countries and has been translated into as many languages."[41] Revolting or not, *God of Vengeance* had proved too reliable at the box-office not to get an English staging. Rudolf Schildkraut, the Yankel of Max Reinhardt's Berlin production, was seeking an English-speaking role to take him to Broadway. In fall 1922, he opened the play at the Greenwich Village Theatre, the playhouse of the Provincetown Players—Eugene O'Neill's old group. His son, Joseph Schildkraut, later recalled that after the opening performance John Barrymore and Marjorie Rambeau pushed through the throng of well-wishers to kneel down, "with tears in their eyes, to kiss Father's hands. The tribute was so sincere and touching that the gesture did not seem at all theatrical."[42]

Others were less appreciative. When the production moved uptown, to the Apollo Theatre on 42nd Street, Jewish and non-Jewish groups exploded in anger. Most disturbing to Jews, now that gentiles were seeing the play, was the housing of a sacred torah scroll in a brothel. Even the normally broadminded Reform rabbinate moved for the play's suppression and seriously considered calling in the police. This decision was made for them: the Society for the Suppression of Vice lodged a formal complaint, denouncing the play as "obscene, indecent, disgusting, and tending to the corruption of the morals of youth."[43] On testimony of two detectives who attended a performance, the producer and eleven cast members (including Sam Jaffe and Morris Carnovsky) were arrested after a Sunday matinee. Producer Harry Weinberger and Schildkraut spent a night in jail. A bitter court battle ensued, and Weinberger and Schildkraut were fined two hundred dollars each.

Asch was not inclined to accept such treatment philosophically. His integrity as a dedicated artist and loyal Jew, he cried, was being challenged unfairly—a cry he would repeat in subsequent years. A formidable group of defenders rallied about him, among them the editors of *The Nation* and *The Outlook*, Abraham Cahan of the *Forward*, lawyer Oswald Garrison Villard, sociologist Harry A. Overstreet, and Dr. Henry Neumann of the Ethical Culture Society. Critics Heywood Broun, Alexander Woollcott, and Burns Mantle praised the play highly. His champions pointed out that if all literary works frankly recognizing immorality's existence were declared illegal, few major achievements would escape condemnation. A guilty verdict could be justified, they argued, only by ignoring Asch's purpose and the play's total effect on the audience.[44]

Despite such outcries, the Appellate Division of the Supreme

Court of New York confirmed the verdict against Weinberger and Schildkraut, and the entire incident contributed substantially to the controversy then raging about salacious plays on the Broadway stage. Those critics, writers, and readers long resentful of Asch's illumination of Jewish life's dark corners (and those merely resentful of his success) now returned to attack his "cheap sensationalism." Inevitably, the controversy stimulated interest in Asch the playwright; his dramas proved increasingly popular with Yiddish theatrical groups, and many of his novels and stories were adapted for the stage. During the 1920's and 30's his plays (originals or adaptations) were in the repertoires of all the New York Yiddish companies. Maurice Schwartz alone staged at least ten different productions based on Asch stories, with most having successful runs.[45] But the basic issue for Asch and his defenders was that the serious literary artist be allowed to interpret life as he sees it without fear of police and prosecution. (Seven years later, in 1930, Asch's son Nathan and his publishers were hauled into court on charges that Nathan's novel *Pay Day* was obscene.)[46]

The furor over *God of Vengeance*, predictably, failed to lessen Asch's literary output. He was then at work on a "Jewish mother" novel, as well as on two shorter works dealing with love and loyalty: "The Wiles of Destiny"[47] and *Joseph: A Shepherd Story in Five Scenes* (1924). The first is a two-scene sketch whose irony and ambiguity cut deeply, if but briefly. The opening presents two fathers haggling over a wedding dowry, with the arrogant groom and his greedy father proudly holding the upper hand. Later, in the bridal chamber, the groom discovers to his horror that his bride has a weak heart. His dreams of a happy future are shattered, but soon his pride and arrogance give way to humility and pity, and he seemingly finds his true self. Asch here makes clear that while haggling and crass materialism may make a wedding, a marriage is joined only when two hearts are opened by trial and sympathy. The other effort, *Joseph*, is a Biblical pastoral drama centering upon Potiphar's lecherous wife and her affection for the virtuous young Hebrew. Asch describes, with rhetorical flourishes, Joseph's entry into Egypt and his striking beauty, piety, and wisdom. He dwells upon Joseph's resistance to the passionate overtures of his master's wife and of her enamored slaves. Asch may have been trying to prove to his critics that he could depict a "chaste" hero, but his penchant for the erotic is much in evidence and undoubtedly this play placated no one.

VII   A Living Legend and His "Jewish Mothers"

In 1924 Asch was again in Warsaw for the publication there of another edition of his collected writings, this time in eighteen volumes. (Coming only three years after the previous one, the new edition indicated how well his books were selling in Europe.) The trip offered him also a welcome escape from the tensions of the *God of Vengeance* trial. In Warsaw, Asch thrust himself into the discussions and debates then engaging Jewish intellectual circles by appearing often at public meetings with improvised "talks" on the different issues. Poland at that time had a strongly organized secular Yiddish school system, and an argument raged (as it had for years) between Yiddishists and Hebraists. Taking a mid-position, Asch expressed his deep sympathies for Palestine and Hebrew, but he rejected the Zionists' extreme Hebraism at the expense of Yiddish culture and education. He thus managed to antagonize both factions.

Yet whatever carping about Asch some Yiddish writers and journalists did in public or private, most were proud of him. Even those hotly debating his eventual place in Yiddish letters considered him one of their own. When in Warsaw he often could be found sitting under his portrait in the large hall of the Yiddish Writers' Club, at 13 Tlomacka Street, surrounded by the city's leading Yiddish writers and editors. At the various PEN congresses he attended he was treated with equal deference by the world's best-known writers. Jews and non-Jews viewed him as a major literary figure.

For most of Warsaw's Jews, however, he was a living legend. He had but to enter a room to attract a gathering, and stories then circulated as to what he had said and done. He seldom disappointed his observers. One morning, wishing to cash some royalty checks, he appeared at the Warsaw office of the Workers' Central Credit Bureau. Seated at an outer desk was a young clerk, Chaim Rozenstein. Three decades later, as a journalist in Australia, Rozenstein would recall clearly the half-hour Asch spent awaiting the bureau director. "Tall, broad and masculine," Asch paced about singing to himself, grimacing as if in conversation, his hair falling boyishly across his forehead. Suddenly he took off his coat and, rather laboredly, got down on the floor and began exercising. Rozenstein could not help smiling at the comical figure cut by

Yiddish literature's "great flag-carrier." Noting the smile, Asch sheepishly confessed he should exercise more. Pointing to his prominent belly, he added: "Some would think I'm pregnant, but I don't know what month."[48] Rozenstein, a physical culturist himself, demonstrated a few exercises, which Asch delightedly repeated. Entering a few minutes later, bureau director Victor Alter was astounded to find his assistant arm-wrestling with the great Sholem Asch. Asch concluded his business with a smiling promise to return for a rematch with Rozenstein. Others encountering Asch garnered equally vivid impressions.

In the 1920's, Asch joined the near-migration of American writers to Europe. Paris was regaining its pre-war serenity, so he decided to return there. World War II, more than a dozen years later, would bring him back to the United States. He then would explain that he had left in 1925 because life in America had proved too expensive and distracting: "There was always an appointment to be kept, a speech to be made, an invitation to accept."[49] But between 1925 and 1939 he frequently recrossed the Atlantic. The Asches took a house in the tree-lined Paris suburb of Bellevue, a short steamer-ride down the Seine. Again settled comfortably in Europe, Asch refocused his attention on life there. He was, for instance, often in Berlin, where he witnessed that city's frantic postwar conditions: inflation and widespread suffering, growing hostility to Jews, the developing conflict between socialism and communism, and Hitler's steady climb to power. He later shaped his Berlin impressions into a bitter narrative, *The War Goes On* (1936), but now he finished *The Mother* (1925), another novel of European Jews transplanted to America.

A loose tracing of the Zlotnick family's shift from Polish *shtetl* to the New York East Side, *The Mother*[50] enabled Asch to deal again with a familiar theme: the differences in human cost between Old World trials met amid friends and flowering countryside and the New World's ugly, impersonal cruelties experienced among strangers and squalor. Yet Asch was not satisfied here merely to recast the immigrant experience; he wanted to reveal the familial and maternal instincts embodied in those gestures and terms deemed peculiarly Jewish. Many writers have dealt with the Jewish mother, but few as extensively and affectionately as did Asch. Yet if she proves the most ubiquitous of his many heroines, only in this novel and in the later *Mary* does she enjoy the central role. There are, in fact, two mothers here—Sarah Rifke Zlotnik and

her daughter Deborah: each repeats, in a different land and in
varied ways, the ancient theme of selfless maternal sacrifice. Sarah
Rifke, with ingenuity and pride, keeps her large family fed,
dressed, and happy. Her husband Ansel, a dreamy incompetent,
contributes little to the household; absurd, bombastic, and
loveable, he is a synagogue "reader" devoted primarily to
cantillating the Book of Esther. Their older children are the
breadwinners; in time one son heads for America and after a painful
wait the family follows. There, in a tenement basement, each
member struggles to shape a new life.

The Zlotnik sons slowly establish themselves and the family's
material worries finally ease. Then Deborah, who has shared from
childhood her mother's burdens, becomes a problem. Befriended by
some young Jewish artists, she falls in love with the sculptor
Haskel Buchholz and goes to share his attic studio. Her illicit
behavior shames her family and helps drive her exhausted mother
to a premature grave. Deborah lavishes her own maternal instincts
on the talented but oafish Buchholz, serving him as mistress,
mother, and model. No sooner does he attain fame then he goes off
with a woman of greater culture and sophistication—to Deborah's
perverse satisfaction. Having fulfilled here her "mission of
motherhood," she returns home to take Sarah Rifke's place.

Asch found that *The Mother* lost more by translation into
English than did any other of his novels; thus he insisted on a
second, "authorized" version seven years after the first appeared.
The new rendering was an improvement, but the book's faults
proved basic. An inherent dichotomy divides the narrative into two
segments, with the author's inevitable sentimental tendencies
more firmly controlled in the first. Its sections on the Zlotniks' life
in Poland and their fight to gain a toehold on New York's tough
East Side have a measured dignity and pathos, as well as a mildly
sardonic humor. Here Asch is no mere lamenter of the
downtrodden but a poised observer whose pity is leavened with
irony. But when, after Sarah Rifke's death, he drops the family to
concentrate on Deborah and Jewish bohemia, he loses his touch. A
successful writer by his twenties, Asch developed early a taste for
expensive homes and hotels, not to mention clothes, paintings, and
books; he was, at best, on the periphery of the shifting groups of
freeswinging, argumentative, politically oriented Yiddish novelists, poets, and journalists. When he sat among them in their
favorite Warsaw or East Side cafés, he remained "the great Asch,"

and even those using the term derisively treated him with respect. Hardly surprising, therefore, that Deborah's coterie of frenetically carefree artists and writers—who have little to say on art or literature—seem contrived, derivative figures. As Asch strains to reestablish his theme of selfless motherhood, his narrative grows increasingly improbable.

Much of the trouble centers on Deborah. A passive, lackluster heroine, she reveals a self-abnegation that is hardly credible. The other principals are equally unconvincing. Meant to epitomize naive, unfettered artistic selfishness, the towering Buchholz seems mere clown and eccentric. Even Sarah Rifke, despite her total dedication to family, lacks the earthy vitality of Asch's other mothers. Both English translations of *The Mother* were greeted harshly by reviewers, some of whom were antagonized by Ludwig Lewisohn's excessively laudatory preface to the second version. Even so, Asch's familiar gusto, sympathy, and descriptive powers are occasionally in evidence. Of added, if extraneous, interest are three "autobiographical" chapters devoted to one "Henoch Lipski," a pious young Hasid turned secularist, because of what they reveal of Asch's adolescent intellectual and religious yearnings. These things do not make *The Mother* a good novel, but they do mitigate its failure.

Chapter Five

Midcareer: More Achievements, More Doubts, More Controversy

Upon completing *The Mother*, Asch turned again to the turmoil in Europe—and was soon embroiled in another controversy; this time it was with some of his fellow Polish Jews-in-exile. In fall 1926 he published in the Warsaw *Today*[1] an open letter to Marshal Joseph Pilsudski, the Polish national hero who had led the fight for his country's independence from Russia. Political events four years earlier had forced Pilsudski to "retire," but now, having overthrown the Witos cabinet, he was again chief of state. Hailing the event, Asch praised the "noble knight" whose sword had "freed the Polish soul." Many Jews agreed: they too viewed Pilsudski as a moderate who had shielded them from the virulent anti-Semitism of the Polish middle classes and peasantry. But those who had found life difficult under the Marshal attacked Asch for his flattery. Later, when the Pilsudski regime revealed its authoritarian tendencies, they renewed their criticism of Asch's political naivete. The entire affair contributed to an even more bitter attack six years later; now it simply formed an ironic link to events that Asch wished to deal with in a new work.

I *Three Cities*

A large novel of revolutionary Russia had long been in his thoughts; it was to be a trilogy entitled "Before the Flood,"[2] he decided, and it would be by far his most ambitious effort to date. He expected to spend at least four years on this work, but it would gain him, he hoped, the stature of a Thomas Mann, a stature that thus far had eluded him. The plot action was to revolve around the cities of St. Petersburg, Warsaw, and Moscow—each of which had been a focal point of revolutionary events and their aftermath. He expected his lifelong concern with European and American city life to prove invaluable, for if the radical movement had affected town, village, and farm, it had literally dominated the city. Asch hardly

87

introduced, at this late date, big-city political life to European literature; numerous writers had dealt with its upper and lower forms. Strongly influenced by Gorky and Artzybashev, he too had depicted in *God of Vengeance* and *Mottke the Thief* the city's seamier aspects. But now, grown more bold and experienced, he determined to catch in human terms Eastern Europe's total epoch of crisis between 1905 and 1920. He had, after all, lived through those years and their events.

He succeeds here to a surprising extent. His *Three Cities* (as the novel is called in English) proves to be a large triptych on the scale of *War and Peace* and *The Brothers Karamazov*. The first of his works to move far beyond *shtetl* and ghetto—though Jews continue to receive most of his attention—it echoes Gogol, Gorky, Tolstoy, and Dostoevsky. It also intersects with many events covered later by Israel Joshua Singer's *The Brothers Ashkenazi* (1936) and Isaac Bashevis Singer's *The Family Moskat* (1950). In it Asch proves as much social historian as imaginative novelist; he details the collapse of the Romanovs, the extravagant stupidities of the Russian upper-classes, the squalor and mounting anger of the empire's workers, the bloody strife of the Red and White armies, and the internecine savageries of the rival socialist factions. But determined also to prove that he has lost none of his flair for nature's imagery, he unfolds this collective decay and turmoil against an evocative backdrop of soil, sky, and clouds.

To tell so large and complex a story, Asch centers on the Russian Pale and its Russian and Polish Jews. His strong ethnic interests apart, Asch finds his fellow Jews sensitive barometers of social change, comprising as they do a wide spectrum of rich and poor, pietists and apostates, Zionists and socialists, Bolsheviks and Mensheviks, even Czarists and patriots. He develops his varied crises through a dozen major characters and a score of minor ones. Diverse, idiosyncratic, often frantic, his little men and women attain a semblance of unity only when fate or history (the orthodox would say God) starts them scurrying to cope with events. They scurry often, for fate, in the guise of the Russian Revolution, cuts across all personal goals and pleasures to involve and render them virtually helpless by a rapid succession of blows. So disordered a world reveals little logic or form, and its cataclysmic happenings swamp mere mortals; inevitably, character and plot soon diminish here, proving of secondary importance to history and description.

As he finished each part of his trilogy, Asch mailed manuscript copies to Warsaw and New York for its immediate newspaper serialization in *Today* and the *Forward*. He thereby gained for *Three Cities* considerable attention on both sides of the Atlantic for several years before its 1933 appearance.

II "Petersburg"

Setting his first section in the years between 1905 and 1914, Asch re-creates luxury-loving prewar Petersburg (as he calls it), with its assimilated upperclass Jews and its Russian aristocrats and officials. In tracing Russia's earlier commercial expansion, he shows that much of this growth has been directed by energetic Jews whose wealth still derives from the land's vast virginal resources. These tea, sugar, and timber kings lead lives far different from those of their poverty-ridden co-religionists. Social position and wealth determine their human relationships, as they play, marry, and intrigue. But they pay heavily for social and economic acceptance in a hostile society governed by corrupt, anti-Semitic functionaries. Believing themselves cosmopolites and idealists, they are in fact committed totally to the established structure, retaining little of their Jewish heritage. Yet they are unable to ignore their suffering brethren, and this reluctant awareness keeps them, in a complex, intangible sense, Jews.

Asch registers the energy and abilities squandered upon idiosyncrasy and whimsical impulse, as well as the desperate futility of lives motivated only by wealth and ostentation. He centers on the celebrated advocate Solomon Halperin and timber king Gabriel Mirkin and their families. The flamboyant Halperin is Russia's most important Jewish lawyer. An irrepressible, vain, posturing liberal, he has amassed a fortune defending unfortunate Jews and lost causes, and shrewdly exploiting his celebrated benevolence. Even members of the powerful anti-Semitic Black Hundred come to him when in trouble. Memorably ironic is the dinner at which Halperin convinces himself and his guests that Petersburg's wealthy Jews are the country's "best Russians." Halperin's wife, Olga, is a voluptuous, self-centered beauty who entertains lavishly her circle of fashionable admirers. Nina, their daughter, is a high-spirited, sensation-seeking charmer who travels with the city's smartest, fastest social set.

Nina is engaged to Zachary Mirkin, her father's young legal assistant and son of the millionaire Gabriel Mirkin. Strongly reminiscent of those sensitive heroes of nineteenth-century European fiction who were toughened or destroyed by harsh realities, Zachary is the narrative's focal point: he is meant to unite the succession of vivid scenes and characters by his direct participation or by his observations and impressions. Lonely, neurotic, self-pitying, and protected from serious work by his father's money, he has ample time to observe Czarist Petersburg's passing parade and to soliloquize with a brooding, perplexed innocence.

Zachary distinctly resembles Jacob Wassermann's Christian Wahnschaffe, Maxim Gorky's Klim Samghin, and especially Tolstoy's introverted, ungainly Pierre Bezuhov;[3] with Pierre he shares a resentment of political authority, an inner turmoil during peace with a degree of emotional stability in war, and, despite great personal wealth, a strong feeling for the masses. If the two differ sharply in social status and personal relationships, each searches desperately for fulfillment and identity. Pierre realizes slowly his estrangement from society; Zachary feels himself an outsider from childhood—that he is without home, family, or fatherland. His mother leaves while he is young and dies without seeing him again. His father raises him as neither Jew nor Christian and with neither love nor hate for Russia. Zachary develops a strong fixation for ripe, confident, large-bosomed women, who respond to his boyish dependency. He soon yearns for Nina's sensual mother—with Asch sparing no Oedipal detail. Unexpectedly consummating his passion, Zachary, driven by shame and guilt, contemplates suicide; lacking the courage to follow through, he flees instead to Warsaw, hoping in its teeming ghetto to find anonymity and a meaning to his life.

But at times he seems more structural device than sharply defined character. Five or six other figures prove more vivid and memorable. Yet all are overshadowed by time and place as Asch defines at length the many social complexities that shape and sustain Czarist Russia. No one here moves forward. Olga Halperin sums up their trifling lives when she says: "We've built up our whole life on words, on beautiful, just, finely-turned words—empty phrases that have no effect" (272). She is, as usual, wrong, yet she is hardly to be blamed, for those few prophets who see that there are to be effects—dire, tragic effects—are being little heeded in Petersburg.

III "Warsaw"

Not surprisingly "Warsaw" is the most "Jewish" of the novel segments, centering as it does on Asch's home ground. With

Tolstoyan passion he describes the city's groups and factions, its political unrest and repression, and its harassed Jews bedeviled by corrupt officials and restrictions.

Weary of his empty Petersburg existence, shamed by his feelings for his fiancée's mother, Zachary has come to Warsaw to find his identity and destiny. He is drawn to the maternal Rachel-Leah Hurvitz, whom he had met in Petersburg and who promises to fulfill his obsessive need for a mother figure. Another of Asch's all-loving Jewish mothers, Rachel-Leah is more aggressive and worldly than her counterparts; her concern embraces not only family and neighbors but a suffering humanity. Solomon Hurvitz, a teacher, has dedicated himself to science, to a free Poland, and to spreading secular knowledge among *yeshiva* students. Like their prototypes—Matilda Asch's family the Spiros—the Hurvitzes make their home a center for radical ideas and politics; they and their friends conspire against the Czar and for a better day. In addition, they help newcomers to Warsaw, and they soon have Zachary embroiled in communal strife and subversive actions. (They also initiate into Warsaw life an unnamed provincial youth who hopes to be a "playwright" and who is helped by "a famous Yiddish writer" (565) revered by the younger generation. Obviously Asch is acknowledging his own debts to his in-laws and to Isaac Leib Peretz.)

Warsaw's revolutionary fervor moves Zachary to sublimate for a time his passion for matrons, while its ghetto forces him to rediscover his Jewishness. Amid Bonipart Street's labyrinthine tenements, courtyards, and workshops he meets Zionists, Marxists, Polish patriots, humanists, and humanitarians; orthodox and radical, cynical and idealistic, they expose a seething ghetto's confusions and pressures. These Jews, barred from soil and factory, are neither peasants nor proletarians: they belong to none of Poland's embattled classes. Harassed and starved, and dependent upon a mix of ingenious, non-productive endeavors, they exist precariously. Most await either Biblical righteousness among men or the great social revolution that promises to all security and plenty. Having departed from their fathers' speech, dress, and beliefs, they search still for a higher will or force. United by classlessness and alienation, most—the young especially—work for the Revolution. Zachary tries to share their lives, but he sees blind dogmatism in every doctrine. Attracted first to Zionism, he soon migrates toward the workers and revolutionaries. After a

fierce struggle to conquer his pride and upbringing, he finds among
these social radicals the acceptance and camaraderie he seeks. He
also finds, as he had in Petersburg, the same widespread human
inability to avoid suspicion, envy, and ambition—or to establish
lasting bonds. Among the hungry even a newcomer's wish to be
kind, he learns, may appear a cruelty.

Yet Jewish inclinations toward brotherhood and socialism stem
here only in part from Czarist persecution; traditional idealism
plays an equal role. This idealism, Asch insists, is inherent in
Judaism. His spokesman for this view is Baruch Chomsky, a
venerable Hasidic leader. Seeing that Zachary doubts man's per-
fectibility or that justice and logic govern the world, Chomsky
argues the converse: man should not imagine there is no justice
simply because he glimpses no sign of it. No, God rules His world
with justice, declares the elder, despite man's limited vision.
"Ultimately justice always conquers" (231). Zachary does recognize
faith's importance, but he also sees its potential dangers—especially in the psychological resemblances between pietists and
communists: many Jewish communists appear merely inverted
Hasids who have shifted their zeal from orthodoxy to socialism,
from Moses to Marx.

Asch is here disciplined and persuasive. He renders vivid and
deeply moving Warsaw's prewar social unrest, political crises, and
human suffering. Both "Petersburg" and "Moscow" reveal literary
debts, primarily to Tolstoy, but "Warsaw"—especially Bonipart
Street's tenements and industrial Lodz's back-courtyards—draws
upon sources indigenous and instinctive in Asch. Where
" 'Petersburg' exhibits power," writes Harry Slochower, " 'Warsaw' exudes warmth and generosity. It has the cohesion of water
particles."[4] These positive qualities override the shattering
horrors of a day in a dehumanizing weaving mill, a First of May
riot, and young David Hurvitz's execution. Even the war that
explodes ending this section enforces, rather than obliterates,
Asch's compassion for Warsaw's struggling Jews and Poles.

IV "Moscow"

War, rebellion, and Bolshevism, in the novel's final portion,
demolish everyone's plans and dreams. All classes and groups are
caught up in a bristling Moscow where gathered Petersburg
aristocrats and Warsaw idealists meet their fates. So entangled
here are good and bad that no one group can lay valid claim to right

or justice. Repeatedly interrupting his narrative with expository or background detail, Asch strives to be the objective artist-historian, to depict in depth the October Revolution and the Bolshevist rise to triumph. But his political views and analysis are essentially those of a liberal now unsympathetic to the Revolution and keenly aware of its flaws. He bears down hard on the inevitable conflicts between any individual cherishing freedom of thought or action and a party discipline demanding blind loyalty. He excoriates the mixed motives and self-seeking of some revolutionary leaders, and he conveys tellingly the frenzied exultation, misery, and chaos of mob rule. He catches also the near-religious ecstasy animating at tense moments both leaders and followers, as well as the altered psychology of certain "comrades" (among them Jews) who change from generous idealists into cruel avengers of capitalist crimes.

The October Revolution finds Zachary in Moscow, where he has come with the younger Hurvitzes who are Red activists. Now a dedicated Bolshevik, he sees the Revolution as the sole champion of the suffering masses. So convinced is Zachary of the Revolution's essential morality that during the streetfighting he overcomes his hatred of violence to command a machine gun squad on a roof above Moscow's Theatre Square. After the Red victory he leads a detachment against the Hotel Metropole where huddle aristocrats and capitalists, including his father and the lawyer Halperin. In scenes bitingly reminiscent of Gogol and Gorky, Asch caricatures the curious offbeats that comprise Russia's "polite society." When bread, flour, and meat give out, the besieged make do with caviar and champagne; only when the sleekly respectful waiters, doormen, and chambermaids are shouldered aside by grimy, menacing figures from the great hotel's cellars and dark corners do the fine ladies and gentlemen realize their old world no longer exists; suddenly desperate and frightened, they begin to bargain for their safety.

Much of Russian humanity wanders through Moscow: former landowners, officers and enlisted men, political opportunists, footloose intellectuals, disenfranchised aristocrats, and enfranchised peasants and laborers. Through this welter of displaced beings walks the Mongolian figure of Nikolai Lenin, dominating the volatile revolutionary factions by sheer intelligence, energy, and will. Only when alone does he suffer doubt and uncertainty, especially before the Brest-Litovsk Treaty. But for Zachary the months following victory bring crushing disillusion; men may make revolutions, he discovers, but each revolution remakes men. His

Bolshevik comrades arouse in him anger and aversion. Long society's underdogs, they are now vindictive, wasteful, and brutal. Most lack even the limited humanity of their bourgeois victims. Nowhere in Moscow does he find the communal spirit of Warsaw's poor. Those unable to twist conscience to party doctrine are rejected as weaklings and renegades. Rejected also is any belief in man's inalienable dignity. "But, Comrade, what is a man?" a Bolshevik leader asks Zachary. "A sausage-skin that can be stuffed with anything. The essential point is, whom does the man serve?" Zachary protests that "A man represents an absolute value . . . [he] is sacred . . . an end in himself." His views soon get him decried as "an anarchist" (827-28).

As the October Revolution hardens into terror and bloodshed, Zachary pities those despised rich now victimized and destitute. Their general tragedy soon becomes personal: his father's sincere efforts to assist the new rulers in behalf of his beloved Russia are rewarded with death, despite Zachary's frantic efforts to save him. Rebelling against party discipline, Zachary returns to Warsaw and to Helene, the older Hurvitz daughter, who throughout the turmoil has been quietly teaching and comforting small children. He has learned much on his pilgrimage through Petersburg, Warsaw, and Moscow, yet he remains uncertain as to what humanitarian activity is right for him.

Some reviewers pounced on Zachary as too weak and vacillating a figure to unite a narrative so teeming with social and human action.[5] These readers missed not only Asch's basic conception of his hero but his central theme: to die is relatively easy, whereas to keep living—to keep hoping and trying—requires courage and endurance. Because Zachary does endure, and without compromising his principles, he embodies hope for himself and for all men. Yet much more vital than the stumbling, uncertain Zachary is his proud, hard-driving father. A wealthy Russified Jew, Gabriel Mirkin thirsts for position, power, and life. Under Red duress he proves courageous and honest, with a Biblical patriarch's regenerative powers. For him Russia symbolizes a social amalgam of Christians and Jews; so long have both peoples lived under oppression, he argues, that their common ideals of freedom and justice should override all differences. Neither personal loss nor abuse lessens his love of Russia. Even a rebellious Zachary recognizes belatedly his father's oaklike strength and dignity.

Asch literally swamps his struggling figures with the flow of historical detail and event. Taking on a character's dimensions is the Revolution itself, as it evolves from verbal abstraction to social cataclysm. Each major phase is viewed and expressed by varied representative individuals: all exemplify Asch's belief in man's potential and his rejection of those dogmas that downgrade man. Any society harboring other ideals, Asch makes clear, courts and merits disaster. Each "city" narrative makes these points. "Petersburg" provides a revealing autopsy of that morally loose, sycophantic prewar capital—despite seeming, as Louis Kronenberger has suggested, "a little old-fashioned, a little derivative from the great Russian masters."[6] "Warsaw" is another matter, proving a powerful, unrivaled portrait of that city's Jews and feverish ghetto. Asch's sympathy for the victimized on all levels imbues this section with compassion and integrity. His detailed flow-chart of neighboring Lodz's daily life and textile mills ranks easily with such mill-and-weaver fiction as Gerhart Hauptmann's drama *The Weavers*, Charles Dickens' *Hard Times*, George Eliot's *Silas Marner*, Abraham Cahan's *The Rise of David Levinsky*, I.J. Singer's *The Brothers Ashkenazi*, and his own later *East River*.

Asch had several times vividly depicted the ghetto, as had others. But "Moscow" is virtually unique in modern fiction. Nowhere else has a novelist described as thoroughly and movingly the "October" Moscow with its inflated hopes and ideals, its crushed dreams and political connivance, and its sheer human misery. The segment rings with Bolshevik, Menshevik, and White Army gunfire, the stormy session of the first Russian Constitutent Assembly, and the "calculated crimes" committed in the name of the proletariat. Only the chronicles of participant Leon Trotsky offer a comparable in-depth view of these happenings. Obviously, Asch cannot make the professional historian's—or even Trotsky's—claim of "historical accuracy"; he was writing not "history" but fiction. Yet life has the unseemly habit of contradicting history and its laws: fact and fiction often merge to become indistinguishable. Perhaps events should have occurred as Asch presents them, for they convey here the depth and complexity of the revolutionary mind—its entangled motives, dreams, and lore. Avoiding glib partisanship, Asch rejects primarily that which is inhumane and unfeeling. If he points up flaws in Communist thinking and behavior, he proves more scornful of the scavenging ragtag White Army for its lack of political ideology or moral discipline. Schoolteacher Solomon Hurvitz's final judgment evokes several decades of shattered hopes and ideals: "We thought," he sighs, "it would all turn out very differently" (898).

Translated immediately into six languages, *Three Cities* was widely acclaimed. The American edition gained special interest from the Washington visit in 1933 of a Jewish commissar, Maxim Litvinov, then Russian foreign minister, whose negotiations with President Roosevelt led to American recognition of Soviet Russia. Asch's first bestseller in England and the United States, *Three Cities* assured the English translation of his later works and their reviews in the important magazines. Louis Kronenberger, in a *New York Times Book Review* lead essay, hailed the novel as "one of the most absorbing . . . vital . . . richly creative works of fiction that has appeared in our day."[7] Other critics, here and abroad, were equally enthusiastic.[8]

Their praise now seems excessive. Asch had learned from his Russian masters how to handle convincingly large, complex themes and events while conveying a strong familiarity with the places and peoples described. But the English version of *Three Cities*, as did that of several other Asch novels, derived from a German translation of the original Yiddish; though Asch's work never depended on "style" in the narrow sense, the effects of this third-hand approach (despite the conscientious, if unimaginative, craftsmanship of Willa and Edwin Muir) are evident. Not that any translation could disguise the structural sprawl, character inconsistencies, and irrelevant philosophizings; yet so vividly conceived are its events and so wide-ranging its moral and social implications that *Three Cities* overcomes all defects to capture rich, momentous segments of both Jewish life and western history. This narrative, wrote Herbert Read, is "yeasty with the very substance of life." He then added that "It would be begging the question to ask whether Sholem Asch is therefore as good a novelist as Tolstoy or Dostoevsky. To me he seems just as good and just as bad."[9] Most novelists would be flattered indeed to be "as bad" as the two Russians. In addition, what Asch failed to provide here in selection, clarity, and rigorous design, he would supply in his next significant novel, *Salvation*, wherein a priest and a rabbi battle not for a multitude but for a single Jewish soul.

V   A Double Jubilee

Despite his public clashes, Asch found the late 1920's to be generally good years for his career and his family. His writing was going well, and his children were grown and leading their own lives, with only his son John, a skilled horticulturalist, still living at home. He and Matilda entertained frequently at their comfortable house near Paris and visited often on the continent. In summer 1929, for instance, they were in Warsaw for the International PEN Congress and then Asch was off on his third trip to Palestine. Yet life was not without dark spots. Germany was in turmoil, and Asch complained in print of not receiving his German royalties. His complaint evoked a satiric open letter from Yiddish writer Moshe Nadir, who recalled visiting Asch's luxurious villa and being impressed by his host's expensive clothes and large collection of art and religious objects. He charged that Asch had not offered a night's lodging to him or their old companion H.D. Nomberg, whose demise Asch had been lamenting in print. Nadir tells Asch repeatedly not to take to heart their friend's death or the loss of his royalties. Nadir will appeal for financial help for Asch, if the latter wishes, to President Coolidge or to other community leaders.[10]

Nadir's pique is understandable. Asch could be abrasive and abrupt with visitors, even old friends. Later he would try to soothe trampled sensibilities, but when preoccupied with his writing or public activities—which was most of the time—he could be oblivious to others' needs or expectations. To a degree he had to be, as an unending line of charities, fund-raisers, and freeloaders made him their target. But if Asch could not escape some public irritations, he also enjoyed many pleasant experiences, both public and private. Nathan Asch, for instance, appeared for a visit in summer 1930, and father and son spent several rare happy weeks together. They made a ritual of taking the train to Paris and then walking the city streets, engaging in playful banter, and usually drifting toward Montparnasse for lunch.[11] Soon separated once more by several thousand miles, they again found communication difficult. Asch did not write English, employing a phonetic English script only when necessary; important matters he wrote in Yiddish. Then Nathan was in the American courts and newspapers on charges that his novel *Pay Day* (1930) was obscene.[12] Some observers were quick to recall that similar legal charges had been leveled seven years earlier at his father's play *God of Vengeance*.

Asch celebrated a double jubilee in fall 1930: his fiftieth birthday and thirtieth year of literary work. He and Matilda headed for Warsaw and Vienna, where public gatherings in his honor had been arranged. In Warsaw the Jewish Socialist Bund[13] urged boycott of his celebration because he had praised the Zionists. Yet Bund members helped pack the hall. Asch rejected the charges, declaring himself a creative artist who belonged to all Jews and who was above partisanship. He insisted on his right to praise both Zionism and the Bundist movement. The front row that evening held Matilda, Asch, his old mother, his brother Jacob, and several other relatives and close friends. Asch rose. "My friends," he declared, "I ask you all to rise to honor my mother, the woman who gave me birth and brought me up. I have her to thank for everything."[14] The crowd gave Malka Asch a standing ovation. Asch's gesture offers insight, perhaps, into his heroes' obsessions with their mothers. A few days later the Yiddish PEN Club held a "literary" evening for Asch in the same hall. But the most impressive gathering was in Vienna. Here Franz Werfel and Stefan Zweig,[15] among others, paid tribute to his work, and almost 300 congratulatory messages were collected. Albert Einstein, Chaim Weitzmann, and Stephen S. Wise were among those extending good wishes.[16]

Asch had so enjoyed his Warsaw visit, however, that he planned to build his permanent home there. He never did. Walking about his chosen site one evening, he fell into a pit; badly shaken, he returned to Paris.[17]

VI   Habits and Foibles

Recently Asch had hired as secretary a young novelist-journalist named Solomon Rosenberg, who was Matilda's second cousin. Rosenberg would later describe his ten years with Asch in a candid but sympathetic portrait titled *Sholem Asch Face to Face*. Asch was now working on *Three Cities*, and Rosenberg was to transcribe in a clear script the master's longhand. The job sounded simple but proved otherwise. Work for Asch had to be done quickly and well. His handwriting was difficult to read, and Rosenburg had to correct his grammar and punctuation; Asch had no patience for technical niceties.[18] Yet Rosenberg was not to change the master's style. After the latter's final revisions, Rosenberg would make two new copies of each chapter, one for the *Forward* in New York and the other for *Today* in Warsaw. He performed his tasks with "great piety," as he considered Asch a major writer. He also grew quite fond of his temperamental employer.

Asch lived and worked in comfort. He dressed expensively and stopped only in luxury hotels. His homes had the prosperous look he needed. His walls held canvases by Corot, Chagall, Levitan, and a drawing by Rembrandt. He collected antiques and furniture with associations, including a table at which Nietzsche had written and a cupboard once Ibsen's. He gathered, in addition to paintings and sculpture, old Hanukah lamps, silver kiddush cups, Hebrew incunabula, and rare books. A true connoisseur, Asch bought several major artists before they had made reputations. Dealers in Nice, Paris, London, and New York offered articles they felt he would want. He liked such things around him when he wrote. In 1932 Asch moved from Bellevue to Nice; there he paced his apartment, and later his villa, puffing contentedly on a cigar and admiring from his windows either the snow-capped Alps or blue Mediterranean. An Italian maid named Rose brought him tea and cookies. His study or "workshop" held his big writing table and an array of books, pictures, and antiques. Wherever he went he searched the nearby libraries and bookstores. Books were a passion. "I require books," he stated, "as I require air."[19] He loved handling them and lined his study with volumes in several languages. One bookcase held his own books in Yiddish, another their various translations, including some in Japanese.

Having completed so exhausting a novel as *Three Cities*, most writers would have rested. Asch had several books in progress. He talked of a lengthy vacation but could never completely lay aside his writing. Ideas, plots, characters crowded his imagination. By summer 1932 he was engrossed in *Salvation*, which would prove one of his finest efforts. His absorption when writing was total. After an early breakfast he wrote nonstop for five hours. His thoughts outstripping his pen, he left out or ran words together, now relying on the faithful Rosenberg to unscramble his prose. Out walking, he jotted ideas in a notebook, and during social evenings he regaled friends with ideas and figures that would appear in his fiction years later. "If I waited for the Muse," he declared, "I would have written very little."[20] On another occasion, he stated: "I do not understand these writers who find inspiration only between eleven and one; when I write I do nothing else."[21] He worked late, slept briefly, then was back writing. He might take a half-hour afternoon nap on the couch in his study. When working well, he was affable—when not, impossible. Caught up in a story, trembling excitedly, he was unapproachable. He identified with his characters as strongly as an actor with a new role. Focusing on Yechiel, his gentle "Psalm Jew," Asch was kindness itself; trying to catch on paper the quick-tempered Pan Wydawski, who liked to loose his dog on visitors, Asch could be as bad-tempered as that irascible noble.

Despite his dislike of intrusions, he was interrupted frequently. Many Jews considered a visit to Nice incomplete without a call on the great Sholem Asch. Periodically he paused to take "atmosphere" trips. He might romanticize a character beyond credibility, but he was a stickler for getting the feel of a scene or setting. Describing in *Salvation* a cabalist Jew who is found frozen, Asch wanted to re-experience a snow scene. At four one morning, toting a heavy suitcase, he boarded a train for a two-week stay in the Alps. Ten that evening he was back: he had felt lonely in the mountains. But the one day enabled him to feel and smell freezing mountain air, to see shadows deepening on snow-covered trees and slopes, to visualize a body freezing into icy rigidity. Now he could put it all into words.

He also visited Poland at this time to observe Hasidic Jews in their familiar setting, to hear the lilt and idiom of their speech, to see again Polish city and country life. He had experienced these things since infancy, but he wanted to sharpen and update his recollections. He even stopped Hasidim on the street to question them about their lives, actions, thoughts. But familiar materials do not guarantee inspiration. Asch spoke off-handedly to interviewers of his literary exertions; he compared fiction writing to writing checks: if one has money in the bank, he was fond of saying, one can write checks easily. [22] His private wrestlings, however, could be painful and shattering. At such times he appealed for reassurance to some friend. Rosenberg once found him tossing and groaning in bed. Frightened, he asked Asch what was wrong. "I can't write," Asch replied. "What do you mean, you can't write? You have written such wonderful works!" "I can't write any more," Asch cried. "It's no good. I'm going to tear up all the pages I've written till now. I'm too old." [23] Asch then was fifty-two. He did not destroy his manuscript; told by Rosenberg that *Salvation* would prove his masterpiece, he resumed work. On another occasion he woke his friend Mayer Mendelsohn in the middle of the night to be convinced his fears of faltering creativity were unfounded.

Despite the obvious self-drama, such incidents help give lie to the legend that Asch was too interested in fame and money to care about his work's quality. Those close to him also testify to its falsity. Asch destroyed all writing he considered below standard, being moved to boast that "What I discard, other Yiddish writers would have made into entire books." [24] Maurice Samuel, the distinguished translator of Asch's most popular novels in English, dismissed such charges of venality as "silly" in view of Asch's "massive conception of himself as an artist." [25] When attacked as mercenary for writing *The Nazarene*, Asch quoted advice Peretz had given him: "If a writer must get money to live on, he had better steal silver spoons than sell his talent cheaply." [26] His self-imposed rule for writing, Asch insisted, was his own amusement. "If I like what I am doing, others will like it. But I must be amused or it is not good." [27] Such views were not those of a mercenary, but of a writer who long harbored expectations of the Nobel Prize.

Another popular legend had it that Asch did not read or study and was unfamiliar with world literature, that his genius was "intuitive" and his talent raw and uncultivated. The truth was more prosaic. Like all creative people, he did depend strongly upon intuition, even to bragging of its importance to him. But he was in fact a voracious reader; seemingly, the varied periods and settings, themes and references of his fiction and non-fiction should have made this clear to anyone. Keen on science and astronomy, he read extensively in both areas. He also knew European literature well, especially the Russian novelists. When living in the United States, he read the major American writers, developing a liking for Ernest Hemingway's work. (His son Nathan took him to meet Hemingway and reported the two men, so different in almost every way, hit it off well.) [28] In addition, Asch read Hebrew, Russian, Polish, German, French, and English. When writing he gathered everything he could find on his subject in these languages, plus Yiddish. Tattered historical pamphlets, religious tracts, Hasidic tales, *midrashim*, and *Musar* books [29] covered his writing table; he absorbed such documents thoroughly, then transmuted their details into fiction. When not writing, he read even more widely. But his idiom of thought and expression was Yiddish. "I am not one of those Jews with many languages at my command," he liked to say. "All my thoughts are in Yiddish and I write in Yiddish." [30]

Asch had his foibles and flaws, but the charge that he was unlettered stemmed from the envy of a few Yiddish writers of his generation who believed his success blocked their recognition as major literary figures. Younger writers, not viewing themselves as rivals, were proud of the recognition Asch had brought to Yiddish writing. Many wrote requesting financial help, literary advice, or recommendations to publishers. Some sent new books for testimonials. Feeling he now occupied Peretz's old role of "patron" to the young, Asch gave endorsements freely, often beyond a new work's merits. Only when the ever-vigilant Rosenberg warned him his commendations were losing value did Asch become discriminating.[31] But older writers were hostile. One even provoked a row with the baffled Asch on Nice's Promenade des Anglais. Hearing that Asch was on the Nobel Prize candidates' list, he swore to prevent him from achieving this honor.[32] Asch never received the Nobel Prize, which he wanted badly. In 1933, the year he was nominated, the recipient was Ivan Bunin, perhaps—rumors had it—due to the prize committee's conviction that a Russian would be a "politically desirable" winner. Asch may not have merited the award; greater writers have been passed over. Yet he seems to have been as deserving as many who have won it. His frustration grew each year, becoming intense after publication of *The Nazarene, The Apostle,* and *Mary.* He had been certain his New Testament trilogy, having attracted so much favorable attention in the Christian world, would impress the prize committee. Many disappointments darkened his final years; his failure to receive the Nobel Prize was one.[33]

VII   Freud, a Medal, and More Controversy

By winter 1933 Asch was well into his next novel, *Salvation;* it was to be his most disciplined work, but his joy of accomplishment was dampened by Hitler's rise to power. At times he was too distraught even to write. Melville Minton, his publisher at Putnam's, arrived from America with glowing news of the reception there accorded *Three Cities.* Asch's gloom persisted as, head bowed, he listened to radio reports of the Reichstag elections and of Hitler's almost immediate persecution of Jews and political opponents. He had to speak out. At a large protest meeting in Nice he attacked the gross distortions about Jews in Alfred Rosenberg's book *The Myth of the Twentieth Century* (1930), following up his speech with an article bitterly denouncing the Nazis. Some of the German-Jewish refugees there urged him to soften its tone. Asch wavered, then refused, mailing the article to Warsaw and New York.[34]

Writing offered at least temporary escape. When he returned to his fiction, he reverted to habit—counterpoising a historical work with a contemporary one. He quickly completed *God's Prisoners*,[35] a short, Freud-oriented study of a sensitive woman's love for a younger man; the theme enabled him to explore again the Oedipal relationship he found so intriguing. Emily Brown, after twenty years with a husband she despises, leaves home and daughter to live on the French Riviera. Falling in love there with Frank Melbourne, an American ten years her junior, she finds herself blocked by sexual inhibitions resulting, in part, from an austere Jewish upbringing. Shattered and frustrated, she confesses pathetically to fearing the "smell of a strange male" and recognizes that her passion is weaker than past values and bonds. "Aren't we like prisoners," she asks, "forged with unbreakable chains to our time and our inescapable environment?" Months of painful indecision culminate for her in an abortive suicide attempt and an abrupt return to New York.

Frank Melbourne strongly resembles Zachary Mirkin. Experiencing first love at twenty-eight, he is as confused and blocked as Emily and readily accepts her rejection of him as inevitable. She seems as much his mother as sweetheart. "I am not only your beloved," she writes in a departing note, "I am your mother who gave you birth. For that reason I am leaving you—because I am afraid I might weaken and kill our love." Such painful dialogue and the fashion-magazine plot are helped little by structural flaws similar, if smaller, to those in *Three Cities:* undue attention to family background and an incessant moralizing that impedes continuity and action. Yet countering these shortcomings are the familiar Asch gifts—sensitivity, insight, and an unabashed concern for life's troubled little people; these qualities somehow lift the novella above the unalloyed vulgarity of straight journalistic fiction. Even Emily's inability to reject a moral code her intellect denies evokes a measure of recognition and sympathy. But all in all the most devoted Asch reader may dismiss the non-appearance in English of *God's Prisoners* as a minor loss.[36]

As for Asch, he was soon entangled in still another imbroglio. When the International PEN held its Eleventh Congress at Dubrovnik, Yugoslavia, in 1933, the moment was sadly historic. Pogroms and book burnings were sweeping Germany, and a generation of German writers was in flight. At the Congress Asch, Ernest Toller, and H.G. Wells, among others, denounced the Nazi terror so bitterly that the hand-picked captive German delegation walked out.[37] About then the Polish Consulate notified Asch it was holding a medal for him. The Polish government, months earlier, had awarded him the order of the *Polonia Restitua* for his numerous moving descriptions of the "Polish landscape." Asch had been pleased to be the first Yiddish writer so honored—and the order's buttonhole rosette, he felt, would be impressive. His critics would carp, but the award was declared to be for literary rather than political reasons.

The world, however, had changed in the months before Warsaw sent the medal. Germany's Jews suddenly were in danger and in Poland anti-Semitism was stirring again. Asch now had serious misgivings about accepting. Many Jews would object to his receiving any honor from Pilsudski. On the other hand, he thought the time for refusal had passed: he should have demurred politely when the medal was offered. To snub the Polish government now might create difficulties for Poland's three million Jews. He decided to accept. The ceremony was brief: an honorary consul, a Frenchman, handed him the medal and Asch expressed brief thanks. Several weeks later David Pinski, president of New York's Yiddish PEN Center, wrote urging the medal's return. Asch hesitated. The same week a message from Aaron Zeitlin, president of Warsaw's PEN Club, warned against the medal's return: the Polish press would respond angrily to so flagrant an insult to the national government. [38]

Asch kept his medal, and his critics berated him for "compromising" his integrity. In America criticism was bitter; one leftist Yiddish theater group, the *Artef*, even staged a satiric one-acter titled *Sholem Gets a Medal*. [39] Asch was never satisfied he had made the right decision, especially as Poland's Jews continued to be mistreated. In 1936 he addressed a letter to the Polish ambassador in France returning his medal as a protest against the persecutions. But he never mailed the letter. [40]

VIII   The Psalm Jews

Despite the troubling reports from Germany and Poland, not to mention the irritations of his own medal dispute, Asch worked during spring 1933 like a man possessed. He was determined to embody in *Salvation* [41] (which he called *The Psalm Jew*) as much of Jewish sanctity as he could; he hoped thereby to emphasize the moral superiority of the Jews to the Nazis. The Ukrainian pogroms (1918-19), he told an interviewer, had moved him to write *Sanctification of the Name;* now the "dastardly attacks of the pseudoscientists in Germany," he declared, were motivating him "to describe a martyrdom not only of the living Jews but also of the Jewish spirit as it was incorporated in Jewish life."[42] Hence he intended the new novel to be not just another historical fiction but a detailed restatement of his own "faith in faith";[43] in it he would reiterate ideas spread through *The Little Town*, *Reb Shlomo Nagid*, "Kola Street," and *Sanctification of the Name*. Not surprisingly, therefore, the harsher aspects of Jewish life that had shaped *God of Vengeance* and *Mottke the Thief* are not to be seen in *Salvation*; instead, its tone and mood echo the wistful elegy to Poland's Hasidic Jews presented by Joseph Opatoshu in his *In Polish Woods* (1921).

To trace a fervent Hasid's half-century search for righteousness, Asch here probes—with compassion, lyricism, and biting humor—the Hasidic world's behavior and piety, its mysticism and spiritual yearnings; in doing so, he also evokes once more the special sounds and textures of larger Poland—its soil, its peoples, its peculiar turmoils. Launched in the eighteenth century, by the venerated Israel Ben Eliezer (known as the *Baal Shem Tov* or "Master of the Good Name"), Hasidism did much to dispel ghetto gloom and despair. It aspired to strengthen the Jewish spirit through simplicity, humanity, and joy despite Europe's violence and terrors; to a considerable extent it succeeded, with its "miracle rabbis" flourishing among Eastern Jews till World War I. But the movement's virtues did not always dominate; indeed, a century of Czarist oppression helped spread misery, corruption, and greed not only among the anxious, ignorant Jewish masses but among the fragmented, competing Hasidic cults. Lettered and unlettered adherents became entangled in a morass of superstition and mysticism. Asch omits no Hasidic shortcoming, but he does try to stress the movement's positive aspects. From its legends and the sayings of its sages (the *Tzaddikim*) he evolves theme and protagonist—the near-saintly Yechiel; the result is a romanticized, idealized view of Hasidic life leavened by irony and realism.

Interweaving fiction, history, and childhood memories, Asch catches a dying world's broad outlines as well as its subtle nuances. (The autobiographical allusions in his later essay "The Guilty Ones"[44] reveal how much detail he borrows from his Kutno boyhood and how closely he identifies with Yechiel.) Jewish life here is isolated and provincial. Those events exciting greater Poland leave untouched the small town on the Vistula River where

Yechiel lives; its life flows about a marketplace of excited, jostling artisans, sellers, and buyers. The neighborhood Poles are sturdy, blond, hard-drinking peasants; a few are priests and even noblemen. The Jews are Hasidim—pale, intense townspeople; some are bustling matrons in ill-fitting wigs, others harried, bearded innkeepers and marketeers. Most devote themselves to prayer, ritual, and theological discussion. For Christians and Jews, confronted daily by poverty and hardship, religion is a passionate matter. But so marred by superstition are both faiths that their basic ethics often are obscured. Intensifying the national confusion caused by the Napoleonic wars are Poland's social and political groups, all of whom are now battling among themselves. Yet if the country's nobles are tattered and isolated, they have remained Poles, Christians, and rulers. They and the peasants compensate for personal degradation by praying and drinking, and by bullying the Jews. Most imposing among them is Pan Wydawski, the lonely, eccentric Count of Topolye. Passionately devoted to Voltaire, the French Revolution, and Napoleon, the Count is eager to establish contact with his peasants, to teach them the meaning of liberty, equality, fraternity. But lifelong barriers of mutual pride and bitterness prove too much; he ends up cursing, whipping, and kicking them. Finding his world crumbling, his properties decaying, and himself an anachronism, the Count puts a showy end to himself. His peasants and Jews, however, have no choice but to endure.

Touching and linking the humble lives of those about him is the simple, warm-spirited Hasidic lad Yechiel (Hebrew for "the living God"). His father and older brother are rigid pietists and followers of the venerated Rabbi Mendele of Kotsk, and in their home no religious detail is ignored. His mother, in traditional fashion, supports the family with a market stall. Yechiel is a disappointment to his father; instead of a talent for learning, he exhibits a zest for God and life. Strong, freckled, fast-moving, he revels in the meadow's sights and sounds. His elders dub him a "savage," but Yechiel, undaunted, helps his mother in the marketplace and falls steadily behind in his studies. He cannot reconcile his passionate conception of God with the cold, angry deity the pietists worship. He is whipped when in the synagogue (the congregation breathless with devotion) he cartwheels, whistles through his teeth, or stands on his hands to count two hundred—all to God's glory.[45] Concerned primarily for others, he even worries whether gentiles share in the hereafter. He dislikes only the "pious wigs"—those smug prigs who demand from God justice rather than love.

Yechiel's father abandons home and family to join his wonder rabbi, and sheer exhaustion soon places his mother in an early grave. Married off to an innkeeper's daughter, Yechiel is again encouraged to study. But he is essentially a mystic and for him the Talmud is too intricate and legalistic: his heart rather than mind expands. Drawn not to scholars but to the meek and lowly, he joins a "psalm fellowship" of workers who meet to study the Psalms (the book of the unlettered poor); soon he becomes the group's leader. So generous and loving is Yechiel to the distressed who belabor him with fears and problems that he gains, reluctantly, the status of rabbi and title of "the Psalm Jew." But to the learned he is merely a crude "miracle" worker.

Asch, as always, is so attuned to every issue's underside that he etches even his most romantic incidents with sharp irony. By the mid-nineteenth century Hasidism was being pressured by the Jewish Enlightenment. Asch conveys rationalism's intrusion into Hasidic mysticism by his deft portrayal of the sincere but aloof Rabbi Mendele of Kotsk. In sharp contrast to Yechiel, Reb Mendele—a devotee of Aristotle, Plato, and Maimonides—considers reason rather than the heart to be man's prime path to God. His court, in its legalism, lack of compassion, and disdain for the masses, exemplifies for Asch the Sadducee approach to religion. So forbidding has Reb Mendele become to his own disciples that by the time Boruch-Moishe, Yechiel's father, dares ask the rabbi for permission to visit his critically ill wife, she is dead.

Yet Yechiel's own climb to personal holiness proves arduous and uncertain. Besieged constantly by the ignorant and needy, who clamor less for God than for gratification of earthly wants, he experiences doubt, failure, and humiliation. No logic, he decides, can answer why the righteous suffer and the evil prosper: one must have absolute confidence that God acts for man's good. Yechiel endures and believes, always sharing his small portion with those who have less. If he slowly absorbs much of the formal knowledge long denied him, he still relies primarily upon the wisdom of heart and spirit. But at times Yechiel's good intentions exceed his wisdom. Early in his career as wonder rabbi he impulsively promises a childless horse dealer that his wife will bear a child within the year. He then is horror-struck at having spoken in God's name. When Reisel, his own young wife, dies in childbirth, Yechiel is convinced of God's displeasure. To expiate his sin Yechiel becomes a wandering beggar, returning only upon learning that his prophecy has been fulfilled: the petitioner has a daughter and in gratitude to his rabbi he has named her Reisel.

Yechiel devotes the next eighteen years to others. Reisel grows to womanhood believing she has cost the rabbi his wife. Her proud parents announce her engagement to a learned Hasid, but she loves a handsome young Pole. On the day she is to be wed in the synagogue, Reisel and her lover ride to a convent to prepare her for conversion and a Christian marriage. While the Jews lament their loss, the Poles celebrate their religious victory. Half-mad with shame, her father begs Rabbi Yechiel to pray for Reisel's death. Stationing the distraught mother outside the convent, Yechiel instructs the father to light a memorial candle for his daughter. He himself prays for the girl's return or death—thereby engaging unknowingly in a spiritual duel with the local Catholic priest. Both pray, at the same time and in identical terms, for the young soul. Before dawn Reisel, unsettled by her mother's forlorn figure outside her window, torn by religious doubts and hallucinations, jumps to the stones below—to die a Jewess. Her father is relieved and the townspeople are reconvinced of their holy rabbi's spiritual powers.

Yechiel alone is assailed by guilt: how dared he pray for the death of a fellow being? "How much evil may a man be allowed to do in order to save a soul?" he asks. "Where is the line to be drawn?" (314). Convinced he has sinned grievously, Yechiel worships God without hope of future reward. Only when (like the Biblical Job) he accepts suffering as the prime means of purifying the Jewish soul does he know peace. "God is to be feared," he declares, "not understood!" (325). Soon after, as a ram's horn closes the Day of Atonement, Yechiel dies. Mourners returning from his funeral find the road barricaded by the builders of Poland's first railroad; their closed world, they realize, is fading. Yet they confidently expect each future generation to produce its own righteous few who—like Rabbi Yechiel—will aspire to holiness and strive to reject evil and cruelty. And each saint, despite a changing world, will continue to suffer the consequences of his own choices.

The most sharply focused and tightly structured of Asch's longer novels, *Salvation* exhibits a rare stylistic felicity—despite an occasional mix of the exalted and pedestrian. If every incident is enlarged by the inevitable details of Jewish town and Hasidic court life, these descriptions provide a logical backing to foreground behavior. Action is swift and pointed, and unified by Yechiel's steady spiritual growth. Asch is not only tracing one man's climb to near holiness, but he is chronicling the desperate strivings of a post-Napoleonic Jewish generation to escape abjectness and despair through Hasidic joy, mysticism, and reverence for life. At times, therefore, Yechiel appears less an individual than a composite of Hasidic ideals.

Hardly a profound thinker or analyst, Asch fails to probe convincingly his hero's deep inner mind. But his romantic-realistic approach does convey the fullness of the Jewish past. An avid, resourceful researcher, he here buries his material's sociological implications in his story's flow,[46] depicting with zest the rigid, vanished little world that was Polish Hasidism. It was a world that lived primarily for its faith. Its prayers, chants, ancient books, its simplified conceptions of God, Messiah, and after-life, its very clothes, food, and daily life are for Asch second nature. He reveals naturally and ironically how its network of precept and superstition worked against itself—how it often made Hasidic religious practices so austere and remote that many adherents were deprived of the very human joys and sympathies Hasidism espoused.[47] (The novel's rare flashes of humor lean to the grim and surly—deriving primarily from acts of the near-mad nobleman Pan Wydawski and his vicious dog.)

By emphasizing that vein of Jewish thought which values faith above form or ritual and which embraces many kinds of believers, Asch is pointing ahead—consciously or not—to his later "Christological" novels and to East River. For like the Hebrew Prophets and like Jesus, Yechiel advocates a compassionate, liberating law while rejecting shallow doctrine and pedants. With Asch such an analogy is not spurious: he always sees these "teachers" as champions of man's moral possibilities and yearnings. Thus Salvation proves a significant prologue to The Nazarene and Yechiel a revealing prototype of Jesus—or Yeshua, as Asch calls him. The novel's publication in Yiddish (as The Psalm Jew) brought Asch his strongest Jewish reviews in years. Much of this critical enthusiasm was in reaction to the dark news from Germany. Israel's light again seemed to be flickering, and Jewish commentators were grateful to Asch for reminding them of their rich, durable heritage. They greeted Salvation as a major achievement and hailed Asch as the most gifted literary defender of Jewish life. His past "errors" were, for the moment, forgotten.

The most laudatory review was by Samuel Niger, then the foremost Yiddish literary critic, who placed *Salvation* at the very summit of Asch's work. He did feel constrained, however, to point out errors in Asch's grammar and sentence structure, even offering examples of how the offending passages should have been written. These comments bothered Asch, who respected Niger's opinions. They also brought an angry retort from Herman (Chaim) Lieberman, a veteran staff member of the *Forward;* attacking Niger for daring to suggest changes in Asch's language, he ridiculed the offered "improvements."[48] Ironically, Niger (whose real name was Samuel Charney) was Asch's close friend and lifelong defender.[49] Lieberman would soon write a vituperative book castigating Asch for his "Christological" novels, a book so bitter it literally helped drive Asch from America.

Chapter 6
The Bad Years

In early autumn 1934 the Asches moved into their newly completed house, three miles outside Nice. Nestled among the lower Alps, surrounded by the beautiful villas of noted writers and actors, of noblemen and millionaires, Villa Shalom boasted an orchard, swimming pool, bowling green, and a veranda where Asch took meals the year round. Fruit trees and flowers lined the entrance corridor on both sides, with clambering vines across the top giving it the appearance of a *chuppa* or wedding canopy. A large terraced garden, divided by a clear stream, covered a small hill and extended into a valley. The house, at Asch's behest, resembled a *Beth Ha-Midrash* ("House of Study"), with the entrance looking like an *ohel* or tabernacle. In front of the house hung two lanterns shaped like Hanukah lamps. Clearly Villa Shalom was not the home of a man harboring doubts about his Jewishness—an accusation soon to be hurled at Asch.

I Troubled Times

Nice was still crowded with refugees from the Russian Revolution. Czarist generals, admirals, aristocrats, and writers were eking out a living by manual labor or by keeping small shops. Displaced Russian Jews also were in evidence. In the streets Asch noted the famed advocate Oscar Grusenberg, who had defended both David Blondes and Mendel Beilis in their blood-libel trials, and Judge Jacob Teitel, the only Jew to have held a judicial post under the Czar. German and Austrian writers too were clustered in and around Nice. Some, like Stefan Zweig, Joseph Roth, and Herman Kesten, were Jews whose books Hitler had burned. A non-Jewish author there was the German dramatist-poet Gerhart Hauptmann, winner of the 1912 Nobel Prize. The Asches were very fond of Hauptmann and on at least one occasion stayed at his San Remo home. Not long after that, Hitler invited Hauptmann to return to Nazi Germany and, to the Asches' shocked dismay, Hauptmann accepted.

Asch's closest friends in Nice were Stefan Zweig[1] and Franz Werfel, both of whom he saw frequently. Earle Balch, Asch's editor at Putnam's, later recalled a drive with Asch and his son John along the Grande Corniche, near the Werfel home. Expressing regret that the Werfels were away, Asch described his friendship for them and related something of their story. Alma Werfel's life had been extraordinary: not only had she shared a celebrated romance with painter-dramatist Oskar Kokoschka, but she had married composer Gustav Mahler, architect Walter Gropius, and finally Franz Werfel. "On account of her distinguished husbands," said Asch, "we call her the Nobel Prize." Balch was startled. "This was so unexpected from Sholem, who was not much given to humor," Balch observes, "that I laughed immoderately. Thinking back, I believe it is the only comparable statement I ever had from him. Usually he was extremely serious, very much engrossed in his writing and his relations with the Jewish community, and not given to blithe commentaries on people. But he was kind and warm in his personal relationships and treasured his friendships."[2] One such friendship was with the Alsatian author René Schickele, then very ill, with whom Asch spent much time playing chess. Yet Asch had a weakness annoying even to his intimates: his near-fawning over people of title and wealth. Once on the Promenade, he left a group of refugees with whom he had been sitting to hasten after a handsome young couple passing by. He soon returned to inform his companions that the young man was a German count. "I didn't know you had so much respect for titles," one companion observed dryly. "He may be a count, but you are Sholem Asch!"[3]

Settled in his new house, Asch started a novel of postwar Germany. His announced intention was to trace in *The War Goes On*[4] Germany's monetary collapse as a prelude to Hitler's rise. Impelled by daily events, totally absorbed in the people and actions he was creating, Asch stopped working only for short walks or drives. Interruption came with a cable from the Jewish Joint Distribution Committee: would he come to America to help raise funds for Europe's Jews? He was finishing the novel's first part and hated to stop. His secretary, Solomon Rosenberg, suggested he tell "the Joint" he would come when his novel was finished. Asch sadly shook his head. "But they need me to get more money to help people. How can I stay in Nice writing books?"[5] Next day he booked passage on the *Conte di Savoia*. Stefan Zweig and musical conductor Arturo Toscanini were fellow passengers, but Asch got most of the attention from reporters when the Italian liner docked in New York, on January 17, 1935. After outlining his present mission and then his new novel, he summed up his view of political conditions. Germany has refrained from moving against her wealthy Jews, he declared, out of fear that if they were driven out the country's financial structure would collapse. "The intellectual people of Germany," he concluded, "are against the Chancellor."[6]

Following a successful speaking tour Asch remained in the United States for some weeks. The New York Art Troupe, wishing to acknowledge his contribution to the Yiddish stage, devoted an evening to dramatized episodes and to readings from his works.[7] Among those honoring him at the Folks Theatre was Abraham Cahan, the *Forward* editor, who would soon lead in his public vilification. Asch enjoyed literary gatherings and exchanging views with other writers. A press photograph taken at a PEN Club dinner in New York showed him conversing with Hilaire Belloc, the French-born English essayist-historian, who had just published *The Hedge and the Horse*. The caption was non-committal,[8] but a reader aware of Asch's mission and of Belloc's loud anti-Semitism might well have wondered what these two could say to each other.

By March Asch was back at work in Nice, and by summer 1935 he had finished *The War Goes On* and was off to Lucerne, Switzerland for the Nineteenth Zionist Congress as a member of the Jewish Agency Council. About this time he saw published in English *In the Beginning*,[9] a slender volume of Bible stories for children he had written years earlier. Intended originally, so Asch claimed, to entertain his son Nathan when a child,[10] the book consists of thirty-five tales derived from Genesis that carry the Biblical narrative from the creation to Jacob's burial. Fashioning a concise, uncluttered prose he might well have employed more often, Asch borrows freely from folklore to enrich the Biblical outline while softening its harsher details and implications. Occasional flashes of humor also have helped this minor effort retain through the years a winning simplicity and vigor. The book's appearance in English must have pleased Asch; very fond of children, he could now look forward to a new generation reading his Bible tales.

He should also have found satisfaction at seeing himself listed in *The New York Times*[11] among the "World's Ten Greatest Living Jews," as selected by fellow author Ludwig Lewisohn. Asch did not make the top grouping of such "first-rank geniuses" as Einstein,

Freud, Bergson, and Buber; still, he was in rather distinguished company in a second echelon that included Chaim Weizmann, Louis D. Brandeis, and Arnold Schoenberg. Despite the good things happening to him, Asch appeared deeply troubled to his friends. Franz Werfel, who accompanied him on a quick trip to London, wrote his wife Friderike that Asch "seems well, but below the surface, like all of us, is a little (or very much) upset; (he) also only wants to work, in order to save himself from life."[12] For Asch at that moment "to work" meant raising more money for Europe's beleaguered Jews and seeing his new novel through the press.

II   Germany In Turmoil

In one sense *The War Goes On* (1936) can be viewed as a sequel to *Three Cities*: at least its events follow chronologically those of the earlier novel. Asch traces here Europe's social upheaval from 1918 through 1923, from the savage civil strife on the Russian border through the bitter German economic and moral collapse that preceded Hitler's rise. He dwells on the desperate strivings of the post-Kaiser generation of Jews to enter a German society that rejects them. So desperate are many Jews that they adopt the ideas and elitism of their most virulent opponents. This action, as Asch makes tragically clear, avails them nothing. He prefaces his narrative with the claim that, as in all his fiction, the material for *The War Goes On* "has been taken from life." But he then adds that he has had "no living person in mind" and that all names and characters stem "from my own imagination." As a standard ploy to prevent lawsuit the statement is understandable; less clear is how this claim relates to such public figures as Adolf Hitler and Hugo Stinnes. Coming as close to allegory as he is ever to go, Asch conveys the tragedy of a nation doing obeisance to an insatiable new god—paper money, a money not worth its printed paper. (The English title, *Calf of Paper*, was more apt than the American, *The War Goes On*.) Germany's inflationary traumas were hardly an untried literary subject by the mid-Thirties, but no novelist had immersed himself in them as deeply as had Asch. Certainly no other would depict with equal clarity and breadth that unhappy land's postwar anguish and despair, a despair that culminated in Nazism. But no matter how involved Asch becomes with historical events and social forces, his prime concern remains people. He interprets history, as always, through numerous posturing, gesticulating individuals who may be strong or weak, modest or pompous but almost always uncertain.

Moralist rather than propagandist, Asch links every public action and private emotion to its social or moral result. He is concerned less with matching political or economic systems than weighing "right against wrong, the hateful against the humane."[13] Having little faith in systems, he has even less in their advocates. If man's better nature is not aroused, and if it is not enabled to prevail, Asch insists, then society is subjected inevitably to cruelty, greed, and ambition. He accuses the Allied leaders of being as meanspirited and shortsighted as the Germans; in basing peace on bayonets and guns rather than on mercy and justice, they have merely replaced old tyrannies with new ones. As always, Asch finds "the people" innocent: the German masses had been duped and led into the war. Yet despite his concern and compassion for his fellows, Asch does see in man an insatiable hunger to be something other than he is. Man's dissatisfaction, his unacceptance of self, not only renders the individual vulnerable to prejudice and hysteria, but too often it causes him to be a perpetrator of false values and mob brutality.

Human flaws are plentiful in a Germany sapped by a rationed diet and crumbling currency. Germans and Jews grow desperate as the nation's rich natural resources, as well as its science, technology, and labor power, are reduced to paper symbols and documents. With the long-inviolable mark now a joke (thousands will not buy a beer or sausage), profiteers and speculators run rampant, mad doctrines gain adherents, and greedy political factions shatter German order and morality.[14] Frightened by the Russian Revolution, chauvinists, militarists, and monarchists align themselves against socialists and communists. The Junker military remnants—preferring French occupation to domination by their own workers—murder Red leaders in the streets, while conveniently ignoring the increasingly active rightists. Between left and right are the drained, vacillating Social Democrats. Supposedly in power, the Weimar Republicans are at the mercy of powerful industrialists and speculators—like the ominous "man with the black beard," Herr Hugo Stinnes. These manipulators usher in the new standards, the new enthusiasm, the new religion, and the new man of the future: Adolf Hitler. No German remains unscarred by these forces the times have set loose. Some battle more determinedly than others, but for everyone struggle ultimately proves vain and pitiful. Most affected are the poor and the Jews, both of whom are subject to the whims of the numerous self-appointed leaders and patriots.

As in *Three Cities*, Asch portrays wealthy Jews striving to assimilate into a hostile society. Sparing neither Jews nor their enemies, he entwines the lives of two Ukrainian Jews, Aron and Misha Judkewitch, with those of the German-Jewish banking family of Bodenheimer—and to a lesser extent with the von Stickers and Spinners. Aron Judkewitch seems the novel's major figure as a fast-paced opening chapter presents not only pillaging armies in the Ukrainian town of Drobka, but also a pogrom, hidden money, and a bandit leader's pregnant mistress. From this confusion steps the opportunistic Aron, gripping money derived from playing both sides of the Russian Revolution. His brother Misha, a dedicated Bolshevik, accepts his comrades' murder of his parents, but he determines to shoot his brother for profiteering. Aron escapes to become a successful manipulator on the Danzig stock exchange. There excited money speculators have thrust the German mark into a downward spiral. But a demented world continues to buy marks, and Aron happily supplies them. Most traders count on things getting better; he banks on disaster and proves right. He harbors no faith in paper money or in permanence of any sort; nothing exists, as he sees it, except the present moment, which the individual has to seize to survive. Believing in nothing, "not even in the . . . omnipotent Money-God" (20), Aron converts his currency into tangible properties. But he realizes even these have little value, that all possessions are speculative illusions deriving worth only from the beholding eye. Needing idols to bow and scrape before, men have devised money to supply that need.

Falling in love with the modest wife of a pious Hasidic Jew, Aron forces the inept husband to give her up. Driven from Danzig by the advancing Soviets, Aron heads for Berlin, where he has developed an interest in the venerable Bodenheimer banking house. Vivid and melodramatic to this point, the story takes a new turn as Aron plunges again into speculation on the mark, shrewdly using the spreading inflation to wrest control of the foundering Bodenheimer bank. Rarely in fiction, writes Milton Rugoff, has a character personified so completely, "in terms of the mere printed symbol, the mere paper of money, as Aron Judkewitch."[15] Yet his goals are not despicable: he wishes only to place the bank on a sound basis and through it to establish himself socially and lead a quiet, decent life. He fails. His wife despises him for being impotent

and resents his having deprived her of the child she has surrendered to her first husband. She degenerates quickly, bringing him
little happiness. Nor do success and wealth win him social acceptance. To the Bodenheimers and their compeers Judkewitch (his
name is symbolic) is an uncouth, interloping "Eastern" Jew who
gambles on the mark's depreciation and gobbles up all that is
rightfully theirs. He represents the shattering of their culture,
security, and happiness.

Aron also loses his author's sympathy and interest, as Asch
turns to the Bodenheimer brothers and their families. Near-stereo-
types of the respected Jews of a German community, they are the
sons of a trusted banking house established by their grandfather
and made powerful by an imperious father. Loyal German
citizens—with a strong taste for Aryan women—they reject
baptism for themselves but not for their children. Their personalities and acts reveal Asch's ambiguity toward German Jewry: his
grudging admiration for their abilities, intelligence, and drive—his
resentment of their snobbery, assimilationism, and disdain of East
Europe's Jews.

Of the three brothers only Max, the dignified, inept head of the
family and holder of an Iron Cross (Second Class), sportsman and
man of fashion, has remained in the family profession. After years
of unimaginative effort, he can no longer cope with the new profiteers. In the best German banking tradition Max sacrifices his
family's every possession to salvage its "good name." So imbued
with Prussian convention and propriety is he that rather than
watch a vulgar Ukrainian Jew like Judkewitch take over the business, he fires a bullet from his army revolver through his own
brain. But the most satiric portrait is that of Dr. Heinrich Bodenheimer, the family scholar. A sensitive intellectual "gifted with
Jewish irony and sensibility," he hides these qualities behind a
Prussian manner and appearance. A respected journalist special-
izing in labor and capital, Heinrich can write feelingly of universal
love and humanity. Snobbish, opportunistic, and paradoxical, he is
disdainful of his fellow Jews but has renounced an academic career
rather than be baptized. A fearless analyst of God, he advocates a
synthesis of "the Roman body and the Christian soul" (103).
Heinrich is also something of a buffoon, making a fool of himself by
supporting a vulgar anti-Semitic actress who refuses to be his
mistress, insults him publicly, and carries on openly with men "of
pure Aryan race." Still she exemplifies for him the finest qualities

of the "superior" Nordic type—a theory to which he devotes his energies. Only tragedy forces upon him the falsity of the life and values he has struggled so to defend. Indeed, Asch's mocking portrayal of this highly intellectualized Jew for whom Judaism is "superfluous" and Christianity the world's "highest moral power" (103) should have been enough to invalidate the apostasy charges his critics soon were to level at him.

Adolf Bodenheimer, the youngest brother, is viewed by his family as an unstable eccentric. An unmarried, unworldly but perceptive art critic and collector, he prefers paintings—especially those of the French expressionists—to business, politics, and people. These disturb his inner harmony, force him to seek refuge among his Corots and Cezannes, until his nephew Hans and the youth's sweetheart, Lotte von Sticker, come to him for help. Startled to discover people may be more important than paintings, Adolf sells his precious collection for these "two living master-pieces." Most carefully drawn is Max Bodenheimer's gentle, uncertain son, Hans, a living example of German Jewry's confused attempts at assimilation. His parents had baptized Hans as a child to spare him the ignominy of being a Jew. But baptism, wealth, and Teutonic features, as well as his mother's respected German family, fail to compensate for his "inferior" blood. To the bigots Hans is neither Jew nor gentile, but he, a serious and sensitive idealist, feels tied to both Jewish and Christian traditions.

Hans falls in love with golden-haired Lotte von Sticker, daughter of a bigoted Junker and sister to a swaggering embryonic Nazi. Following violent scenes, the lovers are thrown out of their houses. Only eighteen, Lotte lacks parental consent for church or civil ceremony. Uncle Adolf offers assistance, but Lotte's brother, Wolfgang, finding his sister carrying her Jewish lover's child, shoots her fatally in the belly. Her cold, silent father, Robert von Sticker, is a Goethe scholar impoverished by the inflation; without a farewell, he fulfills his daily obligations, arranges his "second-class funeral," puts his manuscripts in order and—like Max Bodenheimer—fires a bullet through his brain. Aron Judkewitch, too, discovers his paper fortune gone and his life a mockery. Only his brother Misha, now an important Soviet delegate to Germany, has benefited from Europe's turmoil.

These private tragedies unfold in a Berlin that flaunts a frenetic, decadent night life while its confused masses starve and its speculators allow potatoes to rot and margarine to go rancid.

Those persons the plummeting mark has not driven to suicide develop a hostility to "Americans and Jews." Amid the confusion Germany's postwar young long for moral direction and discipline, but they are instead crushed by the hatreds born of shame and hunger. Gaining prestige is a new breed of rabble clustering about an Austrian prophet of death, one Adolf Hitler. These include Martin Konrad Schreier, a posturing beer-hall orator and early advocate of Aryan superiority; Adolf Klemens Hintze, a government postman paid in worthless paper and bloated by food substitutes; Albert Spinner, long a loyal Social Democrat and unionist but moved by hunger to listen to Nazi promises. Their crushed collective ego awaits a demagogue. Their pathos is that of a proud people reduced by defeat and privation to degradation and confusion. When Adolf Hitler appears, shouting and ranting in beer cellars, he seems wound on a mechanical spring, a virtual *Golem* or wooden monster whose arms wave while his mouth opens and closes, spewing hatred. Europe's guns may be silent, its men no longer marching, and its dead mouldering in their graves, Asch points out, but its war goes on.

He is protesting angrily the human failure to rise above self-interest and partisanship. If he portrays feelingly the helpless sufferings of both Germans and Jews, he insists (as he had in *Three Cities*) that the Jew—do here what he will—can not escape his role of victim: he is damned whether or not he takes political sides. In the process Asch reveals again that his literary strengths and weaknesses both derive from his moral vision—from his deep compassion and sense of outrage. When he describes his victims' desperate acts and maneuvers, his prose proves spare and rapid, his narrative clear and linear. In vivid, if painful, detail he traces the conditions causing the disciplined but increasingly perplexed and truculent Germans to nurse delusions of grandeur and to fall helplessly into Hitler's hands. Their hatred for the Jews he attributes to the Teutonic rejection of the Christian ethic. But if Asch detests the incipient fascists of the right, he is also bitingly critical of the Social Democrats and communists for their assaults on the struggling Weimar Republic. He is especially ironic with the leftist Jewish speakers for thundering against the system and principle that had given their fathers and themselves "what share they had of the good things of life—the dastardly principle of democracy" (362).

In dealing with these and his other suggested social factors,

Asch appears logical and convincing. But when he probes his characters' thoughts and motives, he reduces them too often to generalized types or to mere spokesmen. (If this novel's "moral note . . . is vibrant," wrote Louis Kronenberger, "the human note is shrill.")[16] Overshadowed by events, his people seem borrowed Prussian-German figures—down to the bullet-in-the-brain suicides: the stolid, dignified banker, the brilliant but ineffective intellectual, the strongwilled matriarch, the deferential wives, the son of mixed-blood, the proud Junker, the young fascist. Asch renders their plight with wisdom and sympathy, yet by the 1930's these were all familiar to fiction. In addition, *The War Goes On* is, even for Asch, a highly discursive effort, and its early chapters on Aron Judkewitch, for all their verve and interest, seem almost irrelevant as he fades from prominence. Asch even stops characters in mid-motion to insert social detail or to sermonize. Thus young Hans speaks for the author as well as himself when he rejects cynicism and despair to insist that each generation must wage anew the battle for individual freedom.

As usual, his historical flourishes find Asch at his descriptive best. Especially effective are his depictions of the Danzig financiers in frenzied action or the machinations of the Dutch food speculators; Berlin striving frantically to rival Paris in elegance and in the gay vices (moving Asch to a rare bitterness); Hitler haranguing a Munich beer-cellar audience; or, a huge crowd of German workers gorging on sausage and cider as they degenerate into a gross, carousing mob. Yet these and similar passages, despite their vigor and passion, detract from the novelist's prime obligation to convey history and setting through his individual characters' thoughts, emotions, acts. Asch can, when he chooses, do precisely that, and in a kaleidoscope of memorable protraits and scenes he does so with stunning effect: the sensitive, idealistic Hans being publicly embarrassed by his professor and assaulted by his fellow students; the cultured, decorous Bodenheimers gobbling food and whipped cream against the growing food shortage; Berlin's posturing parlor Marxists, having grown wealthy on the labor of others, loudly championing the "masses" against the Social Democrats; a hungry postman by turns blackmailing and fawning on a Jewish butcher, while silently swearing revenge against all Jews and aliens.[17]

Such scenes not only personify vividly a nation's spreading moral decay, but they render intrusive and irrelevant Asch's repeated digressions into past German-Jewish relations. Yet only toward the end does the narrative grow thin and forced, as if a tiring Asch were hurrying to conclude. Four decades later *The War Goes On*, despite its flaws, remains a perceptive portrait of a troubled era.

III   Bright Spot in a Dark World

Having completed this long, complex novel, Asch was not able to relax and savor its favorable reception. Europe was growing darker. In July 1936 Spain was wracked by civil war and Poland and Germany by increasing attacks on Jews and others. For Asch the one bright spot was Palestine, where he saw reemerging the ancient Jewish state. Three decades earlier he had published, as *In the Land of Israel*, a thin volume of impressions garnered in the Middle East, and since then he had several times returned to the Holy Land. He now determined to base a novel on recent events there. He started *Song of the Valley*[18] as a sequel to *The War Goes On*. In the earlier novel Aron Judkewitch had a sister, Libka, who turned from Bolshevism to Zionism; Asch planned to transform Libka into a man—Jossel Judkewitch, an idealistic pioneer in Palestine who differs sharply from his speculator brother.[19] But he soon changed his mind: Aron is not mentioned, while Jossel is accompanied to Palestine by an older brother, Chaim, an equally dedicated *chalutz* or pioneer.

Needing a new look at the locale, Asch made his fourth visit to the Holy Land; if, as always, he was deeply stirred by the rich Biblical past, he was even more excited by the reclaiming of Israel's soil, roads, and shrines. He thought again of the Jesus novel he had started thirty years earlier. But as he mused on ancient Rome's destruction of Temple and land, and heard the daily reports from Germany and Poland, he experienced old fears. "Won't it happen again?" he asked. "If we build a Jewish land, won't it happen again?"[20] Yet the achievements of the *chalutzim* reassured him; he was especially impressed by the vigor and courage of the *kibbutzniks* at En-Harod, with whom he soon developed close ties and who would remain fiercely loyal to him during the later years of controversy. Deciding to model his characters after his acquaintances at En-Harod, he hastened back to Nice to resume writing. What he produced, in *Song of the Valley* (1939), was less a novel than a series of interrelated sketches, a paean to seventy young "Muscovites" who painfully reclaim an infested swampland at the foot of Mount Gilboa in the Jezreel Valley. Of diverse backgrounds, these young people are linked only by their zeal to transform the barren valley into a lush, self-sufficient community. City-bred, inexperienced, and lacking shelter, adequate tools, or food, they hurl themselves joyfully into their seemingly impossible tasks.

His people, always real for Asch, here seemed even more so for being modeled after close friends. One Sunday afternoon, working on his chapter "The Emek Demands Its First Sacrifice," he announced sadly that "I've buried Judkewitch." [21] He was despondent for the rest of the day. Yet no character develops into a major figure: Asch's prime interest is the collective achievement. In addition, his people now seem all too familiar. Berl Chaimowitsch is the stern, dedicated but beloved leader. The maternal, strong-willed Sarah longs for the green outdoors but feeds and nurses the entire group. Small, sickly Jossel Judkewitch, sustained only by courage and will, is the first to give his life for the colony. Equally recognizable are Mendel Schwarz, the scarred ex-revolutionary terrorist; the few pale and shirking intellectuals; and the powerful, inarticulate ex-sailor Meyer Burlak, who finds in the frightened Hannah an earthy, large-bosomed mate with an unhappy past. These offer few surprises in word or deed. Asch even includes the inevitable Arab (here the woman Fatima) despised by her own people, who devotes herself to the newcomers. Still this familiarity may be less Asch's fault than that of later writers of "Israel novels"; after all, Song of the Valley was an early effort to transmute the new Israel into fiction.

In keeping with his material, Asch tries for an uncluttered colloquial prose. Sentimental, occasionally even maudlin, he still manages a hardheaded recital of the difficulties encountered. Arab-Jewish hostilities flare, but they are not the major obstacles. Harsher opposition comes from within the Jewish community; many who preceded the pioneers to Palestine now want only a transplanted European life—with Jews employing other Jews or Arabs to work for them. But the toughest opponents for the settlers are the land, nature, and their own inexperience. The battle is basic, grim. The stagnant valley has defeated two earlier groups, swallowing up even their graves. A sudden storm obliterates weeks of backbreaking toil, while heat, dirt, flies, and malarial fevers take heavy toll. From adobe huts scattered along the mountain's bare sides, the native Arabs are disdainful of the strangers' mad persistence. Undaunted, these raw pilgrims dredge their swamp and battle the elements and fevers while filling the valley with songs, dances, and shouts of "Long live Israel!" A few dissidents do rebel and leave—enabling Asch to express his distaste for those who have lost contact with the ancestral soil. The more religious settlers are disturbed by the near-pagan welcome given the bull ("Samson the hero") sent them for their cows, but nationalism quickly overrides orthodoxy.

Asch cannot restrain his obvious pleasure at the change from writing of dispossessed, passive, wandering Jews. Several characters do still resemble the nervous, introverted ghetto dwellers they had been; yet they too evolve rapidly into calm, determined farmers driven by an old dream—to reestablish their ancient kinship with the land. They are, they feel, a people reborn, a people sharing "a sense of oneness—*one* past, *one* future, *one* destiny, *one* hope" (136). As for this land, so familiar and so alien, it will, despite ten centuries of neglect, flow again with milk and honey. The politically minded see even more: an Israel that will serve as model for a new universal social order. Within a season the settlers purify the water, plant a tree nursery, produce a crop, and establish a settlement. Even the dead Jossel is "replaced" when the colony's first baby is named after him. Encouraged by this group's success, another pioneer band soon settles nearby.

If, over all, *Song of the Valley* seems little more than a fragmentary outline of life in Palestine following World War I, it does suggest the larger historical and emotional drama involved. Asch wrote surprisingly little additional fiction about this new state that would be his final home, confining himself to two brief sketches, "A Peculiar Gift"[22] and "Eretz Israel."[23] The first is set also within the shadow of Mount Gilboa, where Reb Noah, an ex-drygoods merchant from Poland, joyfully tills the soil. Under a blazing sun, Reb Noah rhapsodizes to a visitor about the land and its history, and reveals how he had won the friendship of his Arab neighbors. Rejecting knife and revolver, he had armed himself with a Turkish fez and his six-year-old son. No Arab, declares Reb Noah, attacks a father accompanied by a young son, for "the Arabs are Semites, and Semites are merciful."

Thinly disguised as "the visitor," Asch enters the story to muse that Reb Noah's self-proclaimed "gift for Palestine" slumbers in all Jews. This slight, sentimental tale is almost redeemed by the author's whimsical humor and by his surprising knack for punning—gifts only rarely seen in his work. Even less effective is

"Eretz Israel," a hurried little parable set after World War II, when arrivals to Palestine had to penetrate the British naval blockade. A waiting group of young Sabras (native-born Palestinian Jews) are disappointed when a refugee ship's lifeboat unloads only a dying old man and a child. The old man thanks God for having allowed him to live long enough to deliver the child to the Jewish homeland. The waiting youths, who have been grumbling over risking their lives for so little, quickly realize these newcomers symbolize Israel's past and future.

As he approached sixty, Asch must have given thought to his own past and future. His past had often been stormy, but his future, he may have mused, should be more calm. He could not have known the bitterness, hostility, and turbulence soon to envelop him.

IV   Charges Old and New

In winter 1937 Asch was talking increasingly of primitive Christianity and the novel on Jesus he had wanted to write for three decades. It was now taking shape in his mind. Quickly finishing *Song of the Valley*, he immersed himself finally in *The Man from Nazareth*, [24] as he called his new work. By the fall he had completed the first part, despite general and personal irritations. The 1930's had filled Asch, as it had all men of goodwill, with a deepening horror at the growing Jewish catastrophe. Polish Jewry's plight especially caused him to withdraw literally into the past, into—as Nathan Asch would put it—

that queer moment in Western history two thousand years ago when the Jews had split; and . . . [my father] started accounting for the split, explaining it from the Jewish point of view, began to retell the Christ story as it appeared to those whom, though they were of good will, Christ was leaving. . . . I am trying to suggest only that he saved himself much misery when he stopped writing about the Jews of Poland just before they were wiped out completely, as he retreated from the present into a past that one cannot be sure even existed actually, but which is imperishable, ineradicable for that very reason. [25]

On the personal level Asch was again under sustained attack—this time from a number of Yiddish writers. Their most persistent charge was the old one: he did not write grammatically. To this, Solomon Rosenberg, a former proofreader in Warsaw for several Yiddish publishing houses, replied that among the attackers were some whose own grammar required correction. Finally Samuel Niger, the leading Yiddish literary critic, who earlier had himself criticized Asch's grammar, spoke up; "these attacks on Asch are going too far," he protested, "and are getting to be quite crazy."[26] Unhearing, the attackers voiced another complaint: Asch's translated books bore no indication of having been written in Yiddish. Unable to remain silent, Asch published, in the Warsaw *Today*,[27] a calm, detailed reply. He dismissed as ridiculous the charge that his books did not state they were translations from the Yiddish. He always spoke of himself as a Jew and a Yiddish writer, he declared, and each fact was as well known as that John Galsworthy and H.G. Wells wrote in English. Further, he had insisted always on using his Jewish name, Sholem, so that when an American publisher had wanted to alter it to S. Asch, he had shifted to Putnam's—where all his books were published as by Sholem Asch.

He rejected also the charge that while in Palestine he had deprecated Yiddish to praise Hebrew. He had stressed repeatedly, he declared, the value of both in Jewish life. Indeed, he had acquired much of his Jewish knowledge by his ability to read and use Hebrew. His love for both tongues had even caused him difficulty, for at one time, he recalled, the Hebraists had been furious at him and at famed poet Nachman Bialik for insisting that Jews should not divide into opposing camps of Hebrew-users and Yiddish-users. Then Asch turned to his alleged grammatical errors.

If I have the choice of observing all the strict rules of the Yiddish grammarians, or of expressing myself freely, and painting my scenes and my people as I see them, I will not hesitate to sacrifice the grammar. If the Yiddish of the philologists is right, then my Yiddish is Turkish. But my feeling is that the language of the philologists has departed from the natural speech of the people. I learned my Yiddish from my mother, and I say that what she speaks is true Yiddish, good Yiddish. The words my mother used are holy tongue to me.[28]

Despite his bravado, Asch was deeply hurt by the constant carping at him and his work. He was even moved to boast that, as the Yiddish writers did not want him as one of them, he would write in another language. But this was mere pique: he could write only in Yiddish.

In April 1937 Asch again interrupted his writing for another American tour to raise money for Europe's distressed Jews. The stateside reporters found him, as always, ready with a dramatic statement. Germany's "fascist agitation" and the Polish government's "lax attitude," he charged, were causing "the utter impoverishment" of three million Polish Jews. Poland's "young government" was running a grave risk. "During the Russian regime there was no repect for law on the part of the people of Poland. Now, through the beatings and hatred of Jews, there is a new disrespect for law and order, which endangers the government of Poland itself and the life of the Polish nation. Moves against the Jews are moves against the government."[29] Such happenings were sobering, but he tried hard to enjoy himself while in New York; he attended the fortieth-anniversary celebration of the *Jewish Daily Forward*, and then went over to the Jewish Theological Seminary of America to receive the degree of Doctor of Hebrew Letters. Despite these happy events he returned to Europe, in July, in a black mood. The New York Yiddish critics had treated him roughly for his published defense against their attacks. Abraham Cahan had aggravated matters by insisting that it was undignified for a writer of Asch's stature to squabble with critics. Asch vented his anger on his household, firing Solomon Rosenberg one day and rehiring him the next with a salary increase.[30] Somewhat calmed, he took Matilda to their favorite Austrian vacation spot at Bad Gastein.

They were back in Nice in the autumn, and Asch worked on *The Man from Nazareth* through winter and spring 1938, finishing the novel's first two sections. The ominous reports of Jewish sufferings in Germany and Poland grew more persistent—as had the personal attacks on him since his honoring by the Jewish Theological Seminary. In the summer his mother died. His somber mental state was revealed by several short stories he wrote at this time. Two attracted considerable attention—"Stalin's Dream," a powerful attack upon the communist dictatorship, and the lengthy "De Profundis,"[31] which centers on Stash Grabski, a lonely young Polish anti-Semite who kills a Jewish neighbor in whose house he had played as a child. Soon stricken with remorse, Stash befriends his victim's widow and children and later is killed defending them from his former comrades. (Bernard Malamud may well have found here the basic plot for his novel *The Assistant*.)

For Asch 1938 continued to prove a bad year. Informed he needed minor surgery, he discussed with Matilda a spring visit to Vienna, in whose doctors he had great confidence. But in March Hitler invaded Austria and Asch decided to have his operation in New York. Then came a letter from Abraham Cahan. Asch had sent the first section of his new novel to the Warsaw *Today* and to the *Forward*. Cahan's response was a near-ultimatum: Asch should destroy what he had completed and write no more of this Jesus story. Furious, Asch raged about his house for days. How dare Ab Cahan dictate to him! Asch might on occasion solicit advice, but he flared at any undue pressure. Their confrontation was serious. Cahan had been publishing stories by Asch since 1908 and had serialized almost all his novels; in effect, he had established Asch in America, and the latter had proved his most popular contributor. But Cahan was not easy to please. As powerful in Yiddish letters, in his dual role of editor and writer, as had been his friend William Dean Howells in English, he considered himself the final authority on things Yiddish. He often issued literary decrees to the leading Yiddish prose stylists, many of whom were dependent on the *Forward* for their livelihood. Years before, he had angered Asch by labeling as "rubbish" the highly popular *Sanctification of the Name* and, without warning, had stopped its serialization.[32] Only pressure from his staff and readers had caused Cahan to resume its publication.

Now he accused Asch of having "gone off the rails" with a novel that was too "Christian" for his tastes. When the latter did publish *The Nazarene*, Cahan, with the enormous influence and prestige of the *Forward* at his disposal, launched a campaign of vilification against author and novel, devoting two years of his life to the task; he even wrote a book, *Sholem Asch's New Way*,[33] expressing his angry disapproval. Equally disheartening to Asch was the news from Warsaw. Editor Szitnicki of *Today* wrote that he could not at that moment publish the opening chapters of *The Nazarene* in Catholic Poland; the authorities likely would consider them blasphemous and close down the paper. They had suspended only recently the Polish daily *Opinion*, also published by *Today*, for running Joseph Klausner's *Life of Jesus*.[34] As he sat working on the final chapters, Asch must have pondered the ironic predicament posed by his novel: reviled in America for being too "Christian," it was being rejected in Poland for being "anti-Christian."

By spring 1938 the darkening war clouds cast a shadow over even the sunny Riviera, where refugees from Germany arrived daily. But these newcomers did not convey fully the impending horror and tragedy; they were mostly the wealthy who had escaped with many possessions and who were able to reestablish themselves quickly in France. Asch pushed the Nazis from his mind

with thoughts of first-century Nazareth and of Jerusalem with its
Roman legions. Walking with the faithful Rosenberg along the
Mediterranean coastline or toward the Alps, he felt himself
communing directly with old Palestine's Jews and Romans. So fully
and clearly were people and events "coming back" that Asch could
not resist a near-smug expansiveness. "You know," he declared, "I
am blessed with intuition. I sense more than I know. I find myself
groping in the dark, but I get there in the end. Intuition is the holy
spirit for the writer." [35] Few thoughtful critics would quarrel with
his conclusion, but his boast tended to be misleading; certainly
Asch had his share of intuition, but he hardly relied on it alone: he
now was reading diligently through a three-decade accumulation,
in five languages, of background studies and documents.

V   Back in America

In May, Matilda and Asch left for America on a tightly planned
schedule. After his operation they would visit with their children
and relatives and return to Nice by October. Asch had also an
"official" reason for the trip: he was to confer in the United States
with fellow members of the Jewish Joint Distribution Committee
about finding a haven for Central Europe's Jews. "We have to take
out 150,000 Jews from Central Europe each year for five years," he
told the New York reporters who met the French liner *Normandie*.
"If that can be done the Jewish question can be settled. As long as
Hitler lasts in power so will the Jewish question in Central Europe
last, unless this emigration be accomplished. Palestine could take
from 40,000 to 50,000 Jews each year if the laws were changed and
a Jewish state established." [36] Despite his thorough knowledge of
conditions in Europe, Asch could not imagine the Nazis would
slaughter not 750,000 Jews but six million. In this miscalculation he
had plenty of company.

By September Asch was straining to resume work on his novel,
so he wrote his son John to prepare the villa for his and Matilda's
return. But on September 30 the radio carried news of the Munich
pact signed by Chamberlain, Daladier, Mussolini, and Hitler. Asch
was deeply disturbed, and his relatives and friends, cautioning him
that war was imminent, urged him not to leave. Sadly, Asch agreed
to give up his beautiful Villa Shalom, with its incomparable view of
Alps and Mediterranean, and to settle in the United States. He
telegraphed John to ship furniture, books, paintings, and
everything else moveable. Then, having been forced so unexpect-

edly to remain, Asch presented himself to interviewers as having arrived at a carefully reasoned decision.

In fact, at each press encounter he grew more expansive and didactic. He had returned, he told John K. Hutchens of the *Herald Tribune*, to live out his remaining years in America. Yes, New York was now "an easier town" than thirteen years ago when he had moved to France. The "high cost of living and . . . the terrific tempo of American life, particularly in New York," had caused him to leave in 1925. "Such pressure makes it difficult for the creative impulse to survive. Now I have come back to the country of my adoption because it has become a center of world literature." [37] But for young writers life in America remained difficult. "Every book is expected to be a success," he stated on another occasion. "The poets, especially, don't get a chance. The real writer needs a lot of patience, a lot of imagination." He should not be rushed. Asch continued the theme with Robert van Gelder of the *New York Times:* "The difficulty of the young writer in America is that in this country every one must earn a living. It is demanded; starvation is not allowed. He who serves his apprenticeship in Paris, for example, may starve if he pleases. He may starve and work. Who cares? His hunger is his own affair. But over here it is necessary to learn quickly—or earn a living by some other means. Starvation is against the American principle." [38]

Asch was not to live out his days in the United States; he would leave fifteen years later under a critical barrage, disappointed and nearly crushed. But now he was no sooner settled than he headed for London and discussions on free Jewish immigration to Palestine. "Dr. Asch"—as the *New York Times* now referred to him because of his honorary degree—and his fellow delegates (Rabbi Stephen Wise and lawyer Robert Szold) [39] could have saved themselves the trip; they and the Jewish Agency for Palestine representative could reach no agreement with the representatives of the British and Arab groups. But Asch was soon deeply involved in personal troubles. For despite the numerous interruptions, he had finished *The Nazarene* by late spring and had sent the manuscript to the respected Maurice Samuel for translation into English.

With the war, Asch's life had entered a new phase. Pondering his future, he must have had many dark thoughts. He was almost sixty in a country that only half-remembered him. Europe was sealed-off, his royalties there were stopped, and his Yiddish readership was disappearing with its physical landmarks. The *shtetl* was obliterated. Poland, Russia, indeed Germany, would never be the same. American readers knew him primarily as the novelist-historian of a Europe now gone. On the other hand, despite moments of depression and self-doubt, Asch had supreme confidence in his own abilities; now, despite definite misgivings, he was relying heavily on *The Nazarene* to win him a new and wider readership. But he was too experienced an appraiser of his Jewish audience not to realize that the novel would rub many readers the wrong way, especially in so troubled a time. He had antagonized many fellow Jews before, with his views on circumcision, his play *God of Vengeance,* and his acceptance of a medal from the hated Pilsudski. Yet he failed to foresee the shock, the distaste, the virulence his Biblical novels would evoke. Certainly he did not realize how completely he would lose his near-legendary reputation as a Jewish leader. For he proved totally unprepared for the avalanche of hostility, even hatred, that engulfed him for writing a "Christianizing" or "missionary" book, one designed, his critics cried, to lure Jews from their traditional faith.

Asch's problem, at least in part, was that he viewed *The Nazarene* with eyes and thoughts very different from those of his critics; for him, the novel was, as he put it, not merely "the main product of my life-work" but a prolonged expression of "the Jewish-Christian idea."[40] He hoped, rather naively, that by pointing up Christianity's Jewish background, or the common heritage of Christian and Jew, to contribute to a future of better understanding, one in which past injustices and bitterness would be forgotten. He wanted to reconcile, not unite, the two faiths and cultures. For Asch considered Jesus himself to be, despite the sins committed in his name against Jews down the centuries, the finest emanation of the Jewish spirit;[41] he was, in Asch's eyes, a great Jewish saint whose martyrdom had been turned into a weapon against his own people by their enemies.[42] "Jesus Christ is to me," the novelist declared, "the outstanding personality of all time, all history, both as Son of God and Son of Man."[43] As the novel and its author's supporting statements sent shock waves through the Jewish community, many of its self-appointed defenders derided Asch as a shoddy opportunist and turncoat taking mercenary advantage of his people's tragic plight.

Of these charges he was innocent; whatever his faults of timing and taste, he was neither turncoat nor opportunist. He had long been intrigued by the essential Jewishness of the earliest

Christians. In 1909, following his first Palestine visit, Asch had visualized in reverent terms Mary's journey from Bethlehem to Jerusalem. But he was bothered even then by the thought of Jews and Christians reading "the same Psalms in two languages to two Gods." He had hoped that both peoples some day could feel they worshipped the same God. Years later he confessed that he had become "infected with the Jesus legend while in Jerusalem. (I hope my pious readers won't stone me because of this.)"[44] Now, torn emotionally by the Nazi persecutions of Jews, he convinced himself that he could restore Jesus to the Jewish tradition, without dispossessing the Christians. He would reclaim this "martyr in Israel," long banished by the exigencies of faith and dogma, who had died on the cross for sanctification of the Holy Name; he would explain how Jesus' martyrdom had been misused through the centuries by enemies of the Jews to punish and degrade them. "I want to show in this book," he stated, "how far Christianity has departed from the original Christian faith, which was almost the same as the Jewish faith."[45]

Asch was aware that he had charted himself a dangerous course; certainly he knew that Jesus' fate had induced, as Philip Rahv has put it, "a kind of traumatic neurosis in the Orthodox Jewish mind."[46] But his novel, he was convinced, would be recognized and welcomed as "an act of mediation" between the two faiths. So confident was he of his novel's eventual acceptance by Jews and non-Jews alike that he determined also to reestablish the reputation of Judas Iscariot—the "devoted" disciple who believed so literally and impatiently in his master's Messiahship that he delivered Jesus to the Romans to force and resolve the crisis. To accomplish these ends, Asch decided, he would have to accept much of the New Testament's miracles and mysticism; yet he saw no reason why he should not still be able to depict Jesus as a pious Jew. Typically, he submerged himself so deeply in his major character that Yeshua ben Joseph fused in his imagination with Yechiel, his beloved "Psalm Jew." The result was that *Salvation*, as Samuel Niger has pointed out, came to seem "nothing else but an introduction to *The Nazarene*, "whereas the latter appeared" the realization, the completion and crowning of *Salvation*."[47]

VI   Yeshua of Nazareth

If Asch began writing his narrative with a definite idea of what he wanted to say, he was much less certain of how best to say it. At first he planned to call his book "The Man Who Was There," to emphasize its reincarnation theme. He even wrote a long introduction on that subject, which he soon dropped, but he did retain reincarnation as a plot device by which to compare Judaism's past and present. He decided finally on three dissimilar narrators to relate his tale: the Roman military commander Cornelius, the disciple Judas Iscariot, and the Torah student Jochanan. To interlock their narratives he then added a variant of the Wandering Jew (that scoffer condemned to roam the centuries). His narrative structure determined, Asch set out to re-create Jesus' tumultuous world by, as Ralph Thompson later put it, "a highly dramatic compound of history and pseudo-history, earnest and erudite."[48] The resultant novel is a lengthy, reverent, and somehow plausible retelling of the life of Jesus from maturity to entombment.

Any outline reduces *The Nazarene* to the near-fantastic. Yet the reader soon accepts not only the awkward shifts between present and past but those details most challenging to credibility. All elements fall into the basic storyline of the chief storyteller, a young unnamed Jewish scholar in pre-Hitler Warsaw. He is hired by Pan Viadomsky, an elderly anti-Semitic Orientalist, to translate a yellowed secret manuscript. A confused mix of savant and charlatan, Viadomsky tells his young assistant a strange tale of having lived a previous life; he is, Viadomsky asserts, a reincarnation of that Cornelius who, as lieutenant to Pontius Pilate, witnessed the incredible events linked to the Wonder Rabbi of Galilee. Not only had he "been there," but he, Viadomsky-Cornelius, bears the mental anguish of sins committed against this strange Yeshua of Nazareth. The first to suspect the rabbi's threat to Rome, Cornelius had aroused Pilate's fears. He had arrested Yeshua (Jesus) and had forced the crafty high priest Kaifa (Caiaphas) to the hasty night trial, condemnation, and surrendering of the prisoner to Roman execution. Then he, Cornelius, had directed Yeshua's punishment—torturing him unnecessarily before death. For this latter act the Nazarene had laid upon him "the curse of being," thereby sentencing him to live through the centuries in one body after another until he should merit forgiveness.

Now, as the irascible Viadomsky, he is driven by guilty memories. Yet how could he, a proud centurion, he cries, have given credence to the "divine mission" of another of those despised little Jews crowding Jerusalem's narrow streets and alleyways? Had not city and Temple overflowed with self-proclaimed prophets? Here in modern Warsaw he labors to recall those momentous events as he had experienced them. He longs only to expiate his guilt by presenting to the world Yeshua of Nazareth as he knew him, feared and grudgingly respected him, and finally destroyed him. As always, a city's teeming life ignites Asch's descriptive powers. Through the skeptical, pagan sensibilities of the arrogant Cornelius, Asch reproduces in rich, sensory detail the Jerusalem of two millennia ago, when it was the meeting place of Oriental, Hebrew, and Roman cultures. Moving through the upper-city palaces, towers, and gardens, Cornelius watches the Sadducee aristocrats and priests desport in Hellenic elegance. He walks the Temple courts then resounding with the learned discourse of rabbis and disciples and the shouts of jostling farmers and merchants, beggars and pilgrims. He wanders the lower city's crowded marts and crooked alleys where the hungry and diseased subsist on discarded filth. From this human refuse, drained by the Roman and the Jewish priesthood's tax collectors, come those who seek solace in religious ecstasy, a later life, and a Messianic deliverer.[49]

Slowly, Cornelius becomes aware of the Jews' rigid laws and their learned debates, their strong bonds and bitter feuds, and especially their belief that at any feast the Messiah may appear to liberate them from Rome. Their successive revolts having failed, the despairing masses are turning increasingly to ultimate ideas and last things—and to the Messiah. In Galilee, a region noted primarily for impoverished, unlettered fishermen and laborers, Cornelius encounters the lean, white-robed miracle rabbi of Nazareth, one Yeshua ben Joseph, a carpenter's son, who is attracting a following among the fishermen. In his teachings, Rabbi Yeshua rejects those traditions and laws he considers no longer relevant. To many Jews he seems the savior who can free Israel. But he shatters his followers by declaring he will know much suffering before fulfilling his mission.

Cornelius hears the rabbi's Sermon on the Mount, sees him heal the sick, and observes his effect on the adoring poor. Even scribes and scholars are impressed. For if the rabbi unnerves them by stating, "You cannot pour new wine into old bottles," he is quick to insist that he has come not to "destroy the Law and the prophets, but to fulfill them. . . . Sooner shall the heavens and the earth pass away than one jot or tittle of the Law." True, his method differs from theirs; his goal, however, appears the same: to love God and one's neighbor. Cornelius observes also the escapades of Bar Abba

(Barrabbas), the daring guerrilla leader who challenges both priests and Rome, and he decides (as would Pilate) that this burly Joppa fisherman's physical violence is nothing compared to the gentle rabbi's insidious preachings. One with such power to arouse the masses, thinks Cornelius, is no harmless dreamer. Indeed, the cynical legionary comes himself within a hair of yielding to the rabbi's magic. Something beyond the Roman's comprehension hovers over this strange carpenter. Yes, this unknown preacher threatens mighty Rome.

Interrupting his story, Viadomsky-Cornelius, in his Warsaw apartment, displays an ancient manuscript in a Samaritan script; it was written and buried, he declares, by Judah Ish-Kiriot in a tomb-cave outside Sepphoris. The astounded young Jewish narrator finds it to be indeed a fragment of a fifth, or "lost," Gospel according to Judas Iscariot, with additional sayings and doings of Rabbi Yeshua. Some events and statements he finds to be familiar borrowings from the four Gospels; other happenings are "new." Asch makes them all sound "authentic," as he has Judah fashion a rapturous prose poem, in New Testament-like terms, of his master's life. Included is an account by a baffled Miriam (Mary) of her son's birth among shepherds, his simple childhood, and his increasingly strange ways. Treating the wondrous aspects of Yeshua's life with restraint (in contrast to his later approach in *Mary*), Asch hints at and implies the miracles rather than making a direct claim for them. Striving for a Biblical tone and rhythm, he traces movingly Yeshua's spiritual development, his wanderings and teachings, and his growing fame. If his prose slips occasionally into a lushness of phrase or image, Asch manages mostly to control the measured cadences and idiomatic archaisms of these 200 pages that bring Yeshua to Jerusalem's gates.[50] (Translator Maurice Samuel merits at least partial credit here.)

Accepting essentially the Jesus of the Gospels, Asch does not hesitate to include not only sermon and parable but revelation, vision, and legend. Both Jews and Christians, he reasons, accept, after all, such phenomena as part of their faith. Nor does he balk at inventing non-Biblical characters, at providing Jesus with brothers and sisters, or at making basic changes in Biblical plot. His primary change involves shifting responsibility for Jesus' death from Pharisees to Sadducees and Romans. He also evaluates Jesus psychologically, socially, and politically; Asch sees him as a sensitive youth who feels so keenly his people's need for the

Messiah that he becomes convinced God has chosen him to be their
redeemer. "He sought the justice of God among men and found it
not," Miriam tells Judah. "And I perceived that with each injustice
he loseth the blood of his heart." Forsaking his carpenter's bench,
Yeshua goes from village to village preaching and healing; in each
he ignores the mockers and answers his questioners with
suggestive scriptural phrases. Followers flock to him and his fame
spreads "like an ointment through the land" (207). His championing
of the poor and rejected stirs hostility in the wealthy Sadducees
and a fear of insurrection in the Romans. He debates the Pharisees,
yet he attracts many of their rabbis by his interpretation of the law
and use of parable; even his preachings of the Resurrection and the
Messiah's coming seem to them derived from the exegeses of their
beloved sage, Rabbi Hillel.

Only in his last days does Yeshua refer to himself as the Messiah. For most of the narrative he differs little from the other rabbis; they too perform miracles, have disciples, weave parables. He
differs in degree rather than kind. The poor idolize him, and the
scholars, albeit grudgingly, admire him.[51] But the masses grow
increasingly restless with Messianic anticipation as tales spread of
his deeds and words. Finally he declares himself the awaited
Redeemer, and with his disciples he proceeds to Jerusalem. To
fulfill the prophet Zechariah's prediction, the Galilean enters riding
upon an ass, thus attracting a horde of eager "salvation" seekers. In
the city he courts arrest and execution as a rebel and blasphemer.
Learned Jews come seeking a sign that he is their Messiah; failing
to receive it, they refuse to follow him. Rabbi Nicodemon, who
embodies that tolerance and vision Asch considers basic to
Judaism, tries to protect Yeshua from Romans and Sadducees. Yet
Nicodemon concludes—as have Jews through the centuries—that
Yeshua's doctrine is valid only for non-Jews, "for those that are
born without the spirit, or for such as would deny the spirit."
Yeshua has been sent, states this Pharisee rabbi, to bring solace to
the nations by moving them close to the One God's "great light"
(592). For the suffering Jews, however, the Messiah's advent still
lies in the future.

The novel here takes its strangest twist. Viadomsky's unnamed
assistant (and Asch's prime narrator), who has remained skeptical
of his employer's tales, is now engulfed by events. Under
Viadomsky's promptings, this modern young scholar becomes
convinced that two thousand years earlier he had been one

Jochanan, pupil to Rabbi Nicodemon and a witness to the Nazarene's last days. His memory thus stirred, "Jochanan" begins describing Yeshua's entry into Jerusalem, his saving of Miriam of Migdal (Mary Magdalene) from stoning, and his driving the money changers from the Temple. Jochanan also observes the Last Seder, overhears Judah's decision to hasten the redemption, and witnesses that disciple's kiss of betrayal, collapse into madness, and suicide. He even hears Nicodemon's eloquent defense of the Nazarene and his denunciation of the Sanhedrin trial as contrary to Torah. Jochanan agonizes with the Nazarene as the latter is stripped and crowned with thorns and humiliated by the legionaries. He then follows the Galilean's struggles under the heavy cross to Golgotha. As the latter suffers on the cross, Jochanan looks vainly to the heavens for intervention. The Nazarene's final agonies and words are relayed by Rufus, Jochanan's fellow student, who soon will join the "Messianist" sect. Finally, the reader is returned to the present, as the Jew-hating Viadomsky dies while clasping the hand of his Jewish assistant.

Yeshua's death is viewed by Asch as the final consequence of the interaction between the Galilean's personal wish for martyrdom and Rome's punitive, imperious behavior. Guilt lies with Pontius Pilate, Asch insists, and not with the Jews. Pilate, whom the Gospels portray as wishing to save Yeshua's life, here seeks his death. Even Kaifa the High Priest so fears this enigmatic teacher that he refuses to arrest him until forced by Roman command. The Jews, a few priests excepted, strive to save the condemned rabbi, and they hope to the end for a sign or act destroying the oppressor. Young Jochanan sums up the Jewish attitude: "We had thought that now, now, the measure of his suffering had been filled, now the salvation was at hand, now he would lift his head, and his enemies would be utterly destroyed. Our hunger had filled our hearts: Let it happen now! . . . But the moment had passed, the miracle had not burst upon us. There only stood before us a tormented and beaten Jew, and at his side his hangman, Pilate" (671).

Crucial here is Judah Ish-Kiriot's confused act of loyalty. An impatient enthusiast obsessed with the Messiah's advent, he presses Yeshua as to his identity. "Judah," the rabbi replies, "I am only he who sitteth in thy heart. I am faith. I dwell in each heart in that measure in which the heart can hold me" (319). But Judah's heart and dreams are closer to earth than to sublimity; unable to contain his eagerness for the redemption, he betrays his beloved leader, hoping thereby to compel him to assert his divinity.

VII   "The Gospel According to St. Sholem"

Asch was striving here for nothing less than the reconciling of Jewish and Christian "differences." He literally expected that this novel, as well as others he now planned, would cause Jews and Christians to recognize their common religious roots and to experience a renewed "family feeling." Reminded of this historic kinship, Christians of goodwill, he hoped, would be moved to protest past and present cruelties to Jews. "Christian civilization is stained with blood," he declared, "and of that blood not a little came from the veins of my forefathers." Yet that very blood was a common heritage, and the true follower of the Jewish prophet known as Jesus Christ had his "equal share" in Israel's God. His most earnest desire, Asch insisted, was to gain full recognition for this indissoluble bond and for the Jewish contribution to Christian "faith, culture, civilization."[52]

He chose to achieve this end by emphasizing repeatedly the essential "Jewishness" of Jesus' ethical principles. Had Asch's Jewish critics, therefore, read his "Christ" novels more carefully, they might have charged him not with being an apostate but, more validly, with being a proselytizer who wished all men to be spiritual Semites. Placing Jesus-Yeshua within the tradition of the Prophets, Asch presents him as both a prophet in Israel and the Christ of the gentiles. Here Yeshua's last words are not from the 22nd Psalm: "My God, my God, why hast thou forsaken me?"; instead, they derive from Judaism's central prayer, the *Shema:* "Hear, O Israel, the Lord our God the Lord is One." As Ernest Sutherland Bates stated it, Asch "goes to extreme limits in claiming Jesus of Nazareth for the Jews."[53] Thus complaints against him more logically should have come from Christians disturbed by his "Judaizing" than from Jews. "Nothing could be more characteristically Yiddish or more imperative in its way," perceived Alfred Kazin at the time, "than this Gospel according to Chaver Sholem." Much of the novel's "dramatic intensity," Kazin pointed out, derives from "an emotion frankly and almost excitedly patriotic. . . . Yeshua here takes his place in the Hebraic martyrology, a Jew betrayed by Judah Ish-Kiriot. And not the first Jew to perish on the cross."[54]

Asch's Nazarene is superhuman rather than divine—a warm, forlorn, strangely gifted Jew who loves his people and their God.

Developed more fully than in the Gospels, and tied more specifically to his day's social and political turmoil, Jesus still resembles strongly his traditional image. His movements, from early soul-searching to crucifixion and burial, are enlarged and infused with his humanness. Basically neither a rebel nor a founder of a new religion, he is a righteous Jew who adheres to the Mosaic code and its prophetic ideals—*as he interprets these ideals.* "Jesus did not come to tear asunder the society he lived in," said Asch. "On the contrary, he came to strengthen, to secure, and to extend it. Jesus was not a Christian; he was a Jew."[55] Indeed, when stripped of ascribed miracles, he here strongly resembles Asch's ideal, archetypal Jew, as exemplified by Yechiel (his Psalm Jew) and by his later fictionalized Moses and Second Isaiah. Some critics have protested that Asch depicts Moses and this Isaiah as direct prototypes of Jesus; their unhappiness is understandable, but they misinterpret Asch's premise. He never suggests that Judaism is to be replaced, but that Christianity, having evolved from Judaism's prophetic tradition, is linked to its mother faith by irrevocable ties. The reader must remind himself frequently that this Rabbi Yeshua of Nazareth is he whom centuries of Jews have viewed as the source and cause of their sufferings. ("The Gospel according to St. Sholem," scoffed a Jewish critic who lacked Kazin's sympathy for "Chaver" Sholem's view of Jesus.)[56]

Ever mindful of his hero's Jewishness, Asch never forgets his own. "I have the utmost reverence for the authors of the New Testament," he stated. "As a Jew, I believe with all my heart that many chapters and parables were written in the holy spirit."[57] He cannot accept, however, the New Testament whole. "Yet, what other authority," he asked, "had I to work with? What greater book? But there are details impossible, in scholarship, to accept. As an example, the statement that after Pontius Pilate had passed sentence he washed his hands, as a way of showing that he was purifying himself of the deed. Tell me, would Hitler rend his garments to show grief? No. And neither would Pilate wash his hands to purify his soul. The act is utterly Jewish."[58] Hence Asch has Rabbi Nicodemon, not Pilate, wash his hands and then declare the Jews innocent of Yeshua's murder.

An enthusiastic student of the past rather than a penetrating scholar, Asch here brings to bear three decades of preparation,[59] weaving into his dialogues Talmudic and Midrashic references that add historic and religious resonance. His mood or tone is, for the most part, sober, subdued, devoid of dramatic flourishes; lacking is the soft pastoralism of, say, George Moore's Biblical novel *The Brook Kerith*, or the hardboiled modernism of Ernest Hemingway's Christ sketch "Today Is Friday." Yet men and cities, tradition and lore, spirit and flesh fuse imaginatively and compellingly. At his best when chronicling city life, Asch can etch, with an equally sharp, "detached passion," [60] Sidon's sexual degenerates and mutilated slaves or Jerusalem's tumultuous pilgrims at Passover. Numerous figures step forth to contribute to the pervading sense of historic crisis: [61] the fervent desert ascetic Jochanan the Baptist; the wealthy, devout Joseph of Arimathea, faithful even after his master's death; the deformed slave Phillipus of Gederah, who turns from Hellenic ideals of beauty and harmony to Judaism's turbulent uncertainties. Especially challenging to the imagination, however, are the two Miriams: the remorseful prostitute and the devoted, long-suffering mother. Sentimentalized, even idealized, the two women retain their humanity—as do Peter and the other disciples, who also reveal Asch's fluent portrait skills. Fleshed out in rich, vivid detail, all convey Jewish suffering and aspirations under Roman oppression. Most intriguing is the tall, bearded Nazarene himself, whether preaching in Aramaic under a fig tree, or in tender converse with his mother; whether condemned of blasphemy before the Sanhedrin Court, or lashed and tortured at Golgotha. Thanks to them all, this cosmic drama generally unfolds without seeming overly "precious or violent." [62]

The novel, however, hardly lacks faults; most distracting are the time-and-action shifts between modern Warsaw and first-century Palestine. But if distracting and basically unnecessary, the shifts may have their positive aspects; perhaps, as Albert Van Nostrand suggests, they do amplify the original story's conflicting elements, perpetuate the old religious dilemmas, and create the illusion of a continuum in which "nothing is resolved, but everything is realized." [63] Yet even when such justification is accepted, the chronological superstructure seems cumbersome and irrelevant; except for that, the novel compares favorably with such adroitly varied multiple narrations as Robert Browning's *The Ring and the Book* or Lawrence Durrell's *Alexandria Quartet*. Asch had set himself the formidable task of paralleling the style and content of the Gospels. Despite clear limitations and discordances, he met the challenge with deep commitment and considerable imagination, ingenuity, and force.

Chapter 7

The War Against Sholem Asch

Asch and Matilda, at the urging of their physician, Dr. Isidore Tunick, spent part of the summer of 1939 at Lake George, New York. Milton Tunick, the doctor's son, now a Manhattan attorney, recalls that Asch liked to be rowed about the lake while reading his new novel's English page proofs. Occasionally he would ask Milton, then a youth, the meaning of an English word. He also prevailed upon the boy to accompany him to the county clerk to get a fishing "button" or license. When Asch caught his first fish, a small perch, he ran to show it to "Magda," who nodded approvingly and agreed the lake was "the most beautiful place in the world." But Asch's restless energy required more than fishing. He roamed the area's antique shops and arranged for English lessons and driving instructions; he even bought a jalopy and then rented a pasture in which to practice driving. Somehow these latter activities did not mix; he soon complained that a good driving practice meant inevitably a poor English lesson, whereas a satisfying English exercise usually promised a bad driving session. [1]

I   Bad Taste or Bad Timing

The happy summer closed with the appearance of *The Nazarene* and a whirlwind of abuse far surpassing anything Asch, or virtually any other writer in twentieth-century America, had experienced. Journalists, rabbis, and luncheon lecturers dredged from the past every alleged breach of tradition and taste to hurl at "the apostate Sholem Asch." The invective was much harsher than that aimed at such Jewish authors as Claude G. Montefiore, Chaim Zhitlowsky, Joseph Klausner, or Martin Buber for their reappraisals of "Jesus the Jew" [2] —or even at Sigmund Freud for his radical theories about Moses. In retrospect, Asch's major crime seems to have been bad taste or, more precisely, bad timing. Today, Jewish commentators and scholars like Maurice Eisendrath, Joel Carmichael, David Flusser, Samuel Sandmel, and Hugh Schonfield, among others, can publish their varied views of Jesus, Judaism, and Christianity without generating more than well-mannered discussion or debate. Indeed, a historian like Nahum Glatzer can address a large Jewish congregation in Los Angeles on "how Jesus related to the Jewish expectation for a Messianic peace on earth"[3] and be warmly received. In short, were *The Nazarene* now to make its initial appearance, it would stir little more than a slight grumble from even the most parochial Jewish critics.

But Asch had chosen the worst of possible moments. The year of *The Nazarene* was 1939; Hitler was at the summit of his power and "Christians" again were slaughtering Jews. And Sholem Asch, the revered Jewish author and champion of his people, picked this time to publish a book presenting Jesus Christ not only as a rabbi but as the Jewish Messiah. Indeed, his fellow Jews had been looking "toward their greatest writer," as Harry Golden later put it, for a book—but hardly one on Jesus; they were looking to Asch, explained Golden, "to make concrete the horror out of this tragedy, a literature fit to stand with the records accumulated by Justices Jackson and Parker and Attorney General Biddle at the Nuremberg Trials. Asch did not do it. Instead he was trying to build a ghost bridge between Christians and Jews."[4]

Many readers could only ask why Asch had published such a novel at that sensitive time. He had several reasons. One was that he badly needed a literary success in America. More significantly, however, the plight of Europe's Jews had convinced him that the Jew-gentile clash was again not mere history but part of the present. What better time then to bridge the gap between peoples and faiths? But Asch was too early: not for two decades would a meaningful ecumenical movement evolve. At that moment the Nazis and the war had the world's Jews in turmoil. Christian readers might applaud *The Nazarene*, Christian professors of theology and philosophy might write Asch laudatory letters and reviews, and Yale's Sterling Library might request and receive his holograph Yiddish manuscripts;[5] the Christian world might do as it pleased—even recognize Asch, as one Jewish commentator put it, as "a gigantic one-man good will committee."[6] But for Jews the novel built neither bridges nor "good will" toward Christians. Instead, rumors circulated of Asch's imminent conversion to Christianity. Nor were all non-Jews favorably impressed by *The Nazarene;* some Christian spokesmen even denounced it as a thinly disguised attempt to exonerate the Jews of their guilt in the Crucifixion. Many liberals (Jews and non-Jews) scorned it as too orthodox, while some orthodox found it too liberal.

Nevertheless, two million Americans may have read *The Nazarene* in the two years following publication. An exceptional record for any novel, this was especially so for another fictionalized life of Jesus—one translated from the Yiddish and using the familiar devices of reincarnation and "secret" manuscripts. Asch had infused into this oft-told tale imagination, dedication, craftsmanship. But other novelists had done as much. Admittedly, *The Nazarene* did offer the novelty of having been written by the best known of Jewish writers, who had depicted Jesus with reverence and in keeping with the Gospels.[7] Yet this hardly seems an adequate explanation for its popularity. Whatever the cause, his novel's immediate success stung many of Asch's Yiddish literary colleagues into jealous hostility and bitterness.

Their anger had its ironies, especially their charges of his disloyalty, opportunism, and apostasy. For despite his shortcomings as man and writer, Asch had devoted his life to religious ideas and issues. His writings testify to his near-obsession with his Jewishness and his fellow Jews—their history, their destiny, and their relationship to God. Literally or metaphorically, Sholem Asch was both a "God-intoxicated" man and a "professional Jew." Undoubtedly, those now attacking him included individuals outraged by what they considered his flaunting of their sensibilities. But the acknowledged leaders were free-thinking socialist journalists, such as Abraham Cahan and Herman (Chaim) Lieberman, who had long before proudly rejected Judaism's God and parochial trappings. Lieberman, it will be recalled, had defended Asch's literary style against the strictures of the Yiddish critic Samuel Niger, who considered himself Asch's personal friend. Now Lieberman viewed Asch and his work differently. Spurred on by Abraham Cahan, his employer, Lieberman later published a lengthy, shrilly vicious diatribe entitled *The Christianity of Sholem Asch: An Appraisal from the Jewish Viewpoint.*[8]

Relying heavily on distortions, misquotes, and non-sequiturs, Lieberman repeatedly descends in his book to a tasteless, irrelevant assault on Christian thought and practices. Labeling *The Nazarene* "a work of apostasy," he charges that it "may lure away ignorant Jewish children into worshipping foreign gods. Let the Christians crown Asch as a new apostle. To Jews he is but a desecrator, a misleader and seducer, a traitor to all that is most precious and holy, a corrupter of the house of Israel, an incendiary of the Holy Temple."[9] Appearing in 1953, Lieberman's book inflicted significant public and psychic damage on Asch. But the earlier, more telling attack was that of Abraham Cahan. The fiery little editor had been Asch's first and most vocal advocate in America. He had defended *God of Vengeance* against its deriders and had published in the *Forward* most of Asch's novels. But his enthusiasm for Asch had cooled through the years, and there had been trouble when he had pressured Asch to scrap *Sanctification of the Name*. Now he led the attack on Asch, encouraging others, like Lieberman, to do the same.

Cahan launched, literally, a "war" against Asch.[10] His open, vociferous hostility generated much ill feeling toward Asch, and himself. Cahan's motives were complex and ignoble. If sincerely indignant about the theme and tone of *The Nazarene*, he was also jealous of its wide acceptance by non-Jews. He had tried years earlier to become an "American" writer, with novels in English of Jewish immigrant life. His *Yekel* (1896) and especially *The Rise of David Levinsky* (1917) had been praised by critics like William Dean Howells, Hamlin Garland, and Lincoln Steffens. But the American reading public had proved indifferent, and Cahan had to return to Yiddish journalism. Not surprisingly, therefore, Asch's success as an "American" novelist rankled. When he learned that Asch was writing a novel about Jesus, Cahan had advised him[11] not to touch so dangerous a subject and had refused to publish in the *Forward* the chapters sent him.

Cahan's warnings were not without merit. Those numerous Jewish writers before Asch who had tried to "bridge the gap" between Judaism and Christianity had received little thanks from the Jewish community. Even Asch's attempt to reclaim a "Jewish Jesus" was not new. Earlier Jewish scholars and writers had made similar efforts, and many American and German rabbis had expressed comparable views. But generally the Jewish public had ignored them. What mattered, apparently, was the identity of the writer or speaker. This was made evident when the highly respected Rabbi Stephen S. Wise, in January 1925, declared from his rented Carnegie Hall pulpit: "Jesus was human. Jesus was a Jew. Jesus was not a Christian."[12] Christian leaders, far from being offended, hailed Wise's statement as "the first sign of Jewish reconciliation with Jesus." Jewish spokesmen, however, responded with anger; they accused the rabbi not only of turning "apostate" himself, but of directing "the younger generation to the baptismal font." Wise was forced to play the penitent before a convocation of orthodox leaders.[13] "The conclusion seems inescapable, writes Samuel Sandmel, commenting on the incident, "that the uproar was caused not so much by what Wise had said, but who it was saying it, and at what juncture."[14] Rabbi Wise quickly reclaimed his popularity, if not with all religious leaders, at least with the Jewish public.

Sholem Asch did not fare as well. The historical moment in 1939 was more grim than it had been fourteen years earlier, and Wise had not antagonized Abraham Cahan; the tempestuous little editor had become obsessed with *The Nazarene,* and his savage attacks on Asch went beyond literary propriety.[15] For two years Cahan scanned Judaica for arguments to use in *Sholem Asch's New Way,* his small Yiddish book against Asch. He there confessed to being an unrepentant socialist. "I am not religious," he wrote. "I am a complete freethinker. I respect the traditions of our people, however. And the attitudes of us Jewish freethinkers towards such a line of thought as that of Sholem Asch were precisely the same as the attitudes of the religious Jews to it."[16] So he was moved to belabor Asch for, as he saw it, grossly distorting the Jewish tradition to have it conform to Christian dogma about Jesus. Asch had thereby done the Jews and their martyrs a great disservice. In addition, Cahan insisted, Asch expected his novel to garner Protestant approval and readers.

This last charge was partially true. Asch needed a financially successful novel. He also wanted the Nobel Prize, and the story of Jesus seemed of enough substance and import to win the requisite critical attention and approval. But his choice was hardly mere expediency. He had started a novel of Jesus thirty years earlier, stopping then only because he felt unprepared. He recorded later his impressions of the first Palestine trip that had inspired his subject and theme: "Walking through the narrow streets of Jerusalem, climbing on her hills and walls," he recalled, "I saw in my imagination the things that happened in this holy city, which became a cornerstone of our modern civilization. Since that time I have never thought of Judaism of Christianity separately. For me it is one culture and one civilization on which all our peace, our security and our freedom are dependent."[17]

Acutely aware he was dealing with Christianity's most vital story and figure, Asch tried to infuse his novel with humanity and significance. Several Jewish reviewers accused him of altering his manuscript after completion to make it more acceptable to Christians. Earle Balch, then vice-president of Putnam's and Asch's editor there, dismisses this claim as "utter nonsense."

One bit of evidence that was brought forward was the fact that "The Nazarene" was submitted in unbound form to many religious leaders before publication. This is true, but the book had already been entirely printed. The unbound copies were a quick and inexpensive way of bringing it to the attention of a great many people who might make the book a subject of their sermons, and thus spread the gospel of its quality. It was indeed sent to many Protestant ministers, but also to many Catholic preachers, and to a great many Jewish rabbis. No changes were suggested by any of these people, and none were made.[18]

When Asch published *The Apostle* (1943) and *Mary* (1949), the charge that he was currying Christian favor was repeated. Many people, in addition, were annoyed that whereas his Biblical novels were not quite history, biography, or, strictly speaking, mere fiction, they somehow resembled each discipline and even combined all three. To make matters worse, his narratives appealed to those readers and reviewers who had made bestsellers of *Quo Vadis* and *Ben-Hur* and who now were doing the same for *The Robe, The Big Fisherman,* and *The Silver Chalice.* Indeed, some critics, especially in Yiddish journalistic circles, seem to have been angered more by the impressive public acceptance and royalties that Asch gained from his "Christological" novels than by anything he said in them.

Yet most critics were genuinely interested in his handling of the subject matter. Some argued that as an artist Asch was entitled to treat his materials as imaginatively as he wished. "To actuality," Lionel Trilling has pointed out on another occasion, "the novel owes nothing, although to reality it gives total allegiance: so runs the prescript of criticism."[19] But "Biblical" fiction, several commentators here insisted, makes special claims on Jewish and Christian sensibilities, especially when the author has enjoyed for decades— as had Asch—the role of a spokesman for his people. And with each scriptural narrative he rekindled this debate on his motives and method. But now, several decades later, it appears unfair to fault a writer for wishing to attract readers—provided he does not violate his artistic integrity and purpose. On this point, Asch was without sin: he had violated neither conscience nor integrity. His "Jesus" novels merely extended and expanded ideas, themes, and sentiments embedded in his most "Jewish" narratives.

II   Old Wine in New Bottles

Few readers in 1939, however, were prepared to relate *The Nazarene* to Asch's earlier fiction. Yet those doing so should have found little that was truly new. Self-sacrifice for God, embodied in an idealized Jew (often a rabbi or teacher), had been his motivating theme for a quarter-century. Equally significant had been his insistence on the spiritual affinity of all who worship Israel's deity. Even as early as *The Little Town* and "Kola Street," he had stressed the unity of purpose linking not only Judaism and Christianity but the differing factions within each fold. In each story he expresses also his preference for the advocates of a law's spirit rather than letter, as well as his disdain for scholarly legalists who feel superior to their strong-backed, ill-educated brethren. Reb Daavidle in *The Little Town* offers example; he foreshadows by gentle dedication both Yechiel and Yeshua, but his strong sympathy for the unlettered poor angers his affluent congregants into displacing him as town rabbi. In this very "Jewish" tale Asch underlines, if ironically at times, the religious interplay of *shtetl* Jews and Christians; when Friday grows dark, for instance, and Sabbath candles appear in windows, Christians head for church and Jews walk to synagogue. The cantor's call of "Come O beloved!" accompanies the church bell so that "the singing and the ringing mingle" to become "a single prayer to a single God" (*Tales of My People*, p. 100).

Two decades later in *The Mother* (then in *Salvation, The War Goes On,* and *East River*), Asch was still emphasizing Jewish and Christian ties. Thinly disguised as young Henoch Lipski, Asch reexamines in *The Mother* his own adolescent religious doubts and questions—drawing upon the same personal memories he would recount later in *Salvation* and in several autobiographical essays. "Why did God create Gentiles and Jews?" Henoch wonders. "If He is omnipotent, why does He not order matters so that every one will believe in Him? But if He does not do that, why are the Gentiles to blame that they are Gentiles?" (42-43). Extraneous to his novel's plot, the "Henoch" chapter enables Asch to work out ideas later central to *Salvation* and *The Nazarene.* The devout Henoch may grow into a socialist and Yechiel into a holy man or *tzaddik*, but the latter repeats Henoch's question and thereby points ahead to Yeshua of Nazareth. "What are these nations of the Gentiles?" ponders Yechiel. "There is no creature breathing that is not made by God, and so they are also a part of God's creation. Why do they not all acknowledge His name? Why do we not see the fulfillment of our New Year's prayer that all might make a covenant together to do His will wholeheartedly?" (*Salvation*, p. 316). Like the Rabbi of Nazareth, Yechiel approaches God through His law's spirit or intent rather than letter. Both draw their followers from the oppressed and their strength from Psalms (the book of the unlettered), and both value the personal deed over the public ceremony; in fact, Yechiel's final message seems a direct gloss on Yeshua's Sermon on the Mount. Especially striking are the physical similarities of the two teachers' final moments: each dons a white caftan and amid lamenting disciples awaits death with a "shining countenance."

So obsessed was Asch with the complex ambiguities of Jewish-Christian bonds that he kept returning to them in his contemporary novels as well as Biblical ones, in his last narratives as well as earliest ones, and in his essays as well as fiction. In *The War Goes On*, for instance, young Hans Bodenheimer learns early that being baptized does not free him of his Jewish heritage. But it is his cynical secularist uncle, Dr. Heinrich Bodenheimer, who expresses most succinctly the Aschean view of the Jewish Messianic dilemma: "I often think how really extraordinary it is that the Jews, who brought the message of salvation to the heathen world, should themselves reject it. . . . They were terrified of realizing their own Messianic idea lest it might kill all human hope. . . . Even if their Messiah were to appear now to the Jews . . . they would wrest his message from him and preserve it against a day that will never come, a day beyond Time. . . . That is the permanent quality of the Jewish character: always to seek and never to find" (*War Goes On*, pp. 241-42).

Asch's attempts to point up similarities in thought and belief between Jews and Christians now seem forced and sentimental. Yet he was writing fiction, not history or philosophy, and here the distinction is not an idle one. Proud, sensitive, vain, Asch was not an easy target for his critics. No living author, after all, could match his list of Yiddish literary "classics." If occasionally he had portrayed the Jew as thief or intriguer, he had repeatedly extolled Jewish warmth and virtues. His bitterest opponents did not know what to make of a writer so seemingly ambiguous in thought and deed, one who for several decades had been a living legend to Europe's Jews. Refusing to accept harsh criticism philosophically or quietly, Asch defended himself in articles, interviews, and in several long, impassioned essays. Repeatedly he declared himself a Jew devoted to his people's welfare. "In everything that I have done," he argued, in "everything that I wrote in the book, in the interviews that I gave, I have aimed at one thing: to help the Jews in their present dire circumstances. Never before have the Jews been so isolated in the world. They have no defenders, and are surrounded by enemies. My only aim was to create friends for them. I do not take back one word that I have written in *The Nazarene* or said in interviews." [20]

He demanded the artist's right to exercise his imagination, ability, and conscience. Choosing a public pose of naiveté, he described himself repeatedly as a fiction writer, a teller of tales, and a poet (what the Germans call a *dichter*). "I am not a theologian," he argued. "I am not trying to reform my own or any other religion. I am a writer, a Jewish writer, who has all his life tried to understand the Jewish spirit." [21] And he did express revulsion at Christian cruelty as readily as respect for Christian idealism. But despite his obvious sincerity, Asch often did little to help his cause. His "explanations" of his position, especially those formulated in English, tended to confuse the issues and to spur on his enemies. The most flagrant example was an injudiciously worded interview, in 1944, with Frank S. Mead of *The Christian Herald.* Asch here gave free flow to his feelings and tongue:

I couldn't help writing on Jesus. Since I first met him he has held my mind and heart. I grew up, you know, on the border of Poland and Russia, which was not exactly the finest place in the world for a Jew to sit down and write a life of Jesus Christ. Yet even through these years the hope of doing just that fascinated me. For Jesus Christ is to me the outstanding personality of all time, all history, both as Son of God and as Son of Man. Everything he ever said or did has value for us today and that is something you can say of no other man, dead or alive. There is no easy middle ground to stroll upon. You either accept Jesus or reject him. You can analyze Mohammed and . . . Buddha, but don't try it with him. You either accept or you reject. . . . [22]

Some readers interpreted this statement to mean that Asch recognized Jesus as the Messiah, that he had embraced—at least tacitly—Christianity, and that he advocated solving the "Jewish problem" by dissolution. (Somewhat similar charges had been leveled against Israel Zangwill for his play *The Melting Pot.*) Asch's phraseology annoyed even his friends. But to embrace Christianity or to dissolve Judaism was far from his mind. Recognizing the good in Christianity, he never subscribed to its theology nor advocated its dogmas. "It is not my purpose," he wrote, "to . . . [dispute] with anyone or to offer an apologia for my own faith." The two faiths were hardly in competition. "There is no necessity either," he added, "for the one side to diminish the role of the other—there is glory for all—in the development of the moral values of mankind, or to maneuver for strategic advantage in the history of religion. Let them stand firm upon their own ground" (*What I Believe*, pp. 101-102).

If Asch was no apostate, neither was he as naive as some critics claimed. "I do not believe that by trading a few dogmas in our faiths," he declared flatly, "we shall reach a better understanding between Jews and Christians" (*What I Believe*, p. 101). A true reconciliation of the two peoples, as he saw it, meant essentially stronger sympathy and more good will between them; he found very painful, therefore, the charge of *meshumed*, or apostate. "I have never done anything in my life," he complained to an interviewer,

to justify the rumor that I have left the Jewish religion. . . . I believe that, if it is possible to come not only to an understanding but to a spiritual kinship between Jews and Christians, it will be accomplished . . . only through religion—because, if you have accepted Christianity, you have also accepted the whole tradition in which the Messianic idea is rooted.

This is the Old Testament. By accepting the Old Testament you become the spiritual children of the Hebrew patriarchs—Abraham, Isaac and Jacob—and the Hebrew prophets become your prophets as well as ours.[23]

III   Attackers and Defenders

As unfair as the apostasy charge was the claim that Sholem Asch was, at the least, an unwitting *missionary*. Not a single Jew is known to have converted because of his novels—nor a non-Jew moved to an anti-Jewish act. Abraham Cahan's assaults on Asch "for Judaism's sake," therefore, were unwarranted, and many among Cahan's acquaintances and staff abhorred his behavior. But no one dared defend Asch before this contentious little man who for a half-century dominated Yiddish journalism in America.

Asch suffered keenly from Cahan's attacks. Melech Epstein, the veteran journalist who knew both men, has described an early 1941 encounter with Asch; talking like "a deeply wounded man," the latter could not conceal his concern that Cahan was isolating him. "Cahan will not drive me away from Jewish life and literature,"

Asch several times repeated.[24] But for a time it looked as though Cahan might: thanks to his influence, every Yiddish newspaper but one closed its pages to Asch. The exception, ironically, was the *Freiheit*, a communist paper Asch had always disliked. In 1943 he began placing his fiction in its pages so as not to be cut off from his Yiddish readership. Both he and the paper's editors issued statements that neither was responsible for the other's views. Their relationship lasted less than three years, but a decade later Asch would be called before the McCarthy Committee because of this communist "connection." Asch outlived Cahan by six years, but he felt to the end the animosity stirred by Cahan and the *Forward*. At his death no Yiddish cultural organization (the Bund labor group excepted) dared call a memorial meeting to honor one of the major Yiddish novelists of his time.

Yet Asch was not without Jewish defenders; the most prestigious was Yiddish critic Samuel Niger, who viewed *The Nazarene* as "Asch's highest achievement." Much support, however, came from younger American-Jewish critics like Philip Rahv, Clifton Fadiman, Alfred Kazin, and Louis Zara. Defending a novelist's right to express himself as he wished, they branded the disloyalty-apostasy charges as not merely irrelevant but pernicious and parochial. "It is understandable," Louis Zara later wrote, "that our rabbis should look askance upon any new treatment of the Christ story. But it is regrettable that any Jewish leaders should become dogmatic on an artist's right to create from his brain and from his knowledge of history." Asch was writing fiction, after all, not theology. "No one challenges the right of free criticism here," Zara argued; "the question is, may a Jewish artist ever dare to touch such material, or is it 'verboten' to him because he was born a Jew?" [25]

Some Yiddish critics were later to echo these ideas. Writing in the *Day-Jewish Journal* after Asch's death, Shlomo Bickel admitted that *The Nazarene*, *The Apostle*, and *Mary* were not to his taste. Yet from matters of taste, he pointed out, "to accusations of apostasy and betrayal of one's people, such as have been made against Asch, there is indeed a great distance, as great as the distance between disinterested discussion of art and theological inquisition." Historian Solomon Grayzel, editor of the Jewish Publication Society, also came to his defense. "Harsh critics" have exaggerated Asch's guilt, declared Grayzel, "for he had done no more than carry to its logical conclusion an attitude prevalent in wide circles of contemporary Jewish life. . . . There was nothing new in presenting a sympathetic view of Jesus of Nazareth; it had been done often enough by Jewish scholars and novelists." [26]

Admittedly, Asch carried his literary sympathy for Jesus further than did most of the others. But that was hardly his major error, for his critics were fully aware he was saying nothing not implicit in the writings of numerous Jewish authors. Asch's crime lay in his bad timing—and his popularity; unable to forgive his success with non-Jewish readers, his enemies wielded the Hitler massacres as a club to belabor him. Asch was essentially a romantic writer—and one not strong in judgment, tact, or delicacy. Milton Hindus very rightly points out that he was blessed more with imagination than judgment. "In Platonic language," Hindus states, Asch "emphasized the *One* at the expense of the *Many*, though in his own mind he was merely mediating between them." [27] His commitment to the Messiah concept made him more sympathetic to the Jewish mystical tradition than to the rational one. He could write feelingly, therefore, about an obvious charlatan like Sabbatai Zevi while unable to accept the rationalism of Maimonides, whom he found hostile to Messianism. Maimonides finally included the Messiah in his principles of faith, Asch charged, only because the Jewish masses found little meaning in a religious existence devoid of such hope. And the Jewish masses were Asch's chosen audience.

But if he rejected in his writings a rationalistic approach in favor of an imaginative and emotional view of God and man, he was hardly the unlearned, unthinking primitive some have made him. His stance was conscious, deliberate, and shrewdly formulated. "Instead of acting as instructor to the perplexed," Hindus has charged, "Asch, in the confusion of unanalyzed feelings about his own heritage, succeeded . . . only in perplexing the instructed." [28] This is misleading. Asch's feelings were not "unanalyzed," and he knew more of Jewish history and thought than most of his journalist critics. He chose the approach he felt to be right for him, fully aware of the risks he ran. In addition, he opted repeatedly to say or do the unpopular thing, feeling he could not remain silent when an issue had to be raised, a question answered, a cause fought. Asch's judgment often led him astray, but his sincerity was never forced, his intention never mean-spirited, and his courage never lacking.

IV   America the Beautiful

With the hubbub over *The Nazarene* at its peak, the Asches again settled in America. The novel's wide sale (about 250,000 copies the first year) made their situation comfortable, and Sholem and Matilda bought a home in Stamford, Connecticut, on Sky Meadow Drive. His declared intention now was to remain in America and "to create something American."[29] He began by lending his extensive collection of Jewish art and ceremonial objects to the Jewish Theological Seminary in New York. America had changed for the better during his absence, he told interviewers; New York, for instance, was a much "slower town" than in 1925. Later, at a literary forum at the Hotel Astor, he congratulated his adopted country for having become the world's literary center.[30]

Life in Connecticut proved pleasant. Asch practiced his new hobby of fishing and his old one of flying homing pigeons—the latter with his friend Samuel Wise, who owned a paint store on Pacific Street. Several afternoons a week he checked the nearby Stamford Book Store to make certain his books were on display. Reassured, he would sit there for hours in a chair reserved for him by the front window, reading and gazing out at passers-by as the afternoon sun filtered through. Asch never bought a book, reports Charles Hinton, then the store's manager, but "he was a true conversation piece."[31] The news from Europe continued bad, but the turmoil did bring some old friends within temporary reach. A few gathered in his home on November 1, 1940 to celebrate his sixtieth birthday. Franz and Alma Werfel were there, as was Asch's editor at Putnam's, Earle Balch, who recalls clearly that "memorable evening." Matilda prepared "a Jewish dinner appropriate to the occasion . . . and Sholem presided at a little religious ceremony at the table." Franz Werfel proved "small, eager, full of enchanting observations and humor; the famed Alma "was still, though far from young, a fascinating woman."[32] Asch reminisced about the glittering dinner party the Werfels had thrown for his fiftieth birthday—at which they had feted, on gold plates, Vienna's most brilliant intellectuals and musical people. The contrast between that opulent occasion and the present modest gathering struck them all. During the intervening decade the Werfels had barely eluded the Nazis in France; as a result, Franz, when in Lourdes, had vowed that if he survived he would dedicate a story to St. Bernadette.

Asch never stopped writing, but after publishing *The Nazarene* he felt the need to slacken his pace temporarily and do some "catching up." He had been living in the past for so long, he told an interviewer, "in the Temples and roads of Jerusalem, studying and writing and rewriting," that the past seemed more real than the present. He did not say so, but time was taking its toll on him—as were his critics, his work, and the war. Reporter Robert van Gelder described Asch at sixty as "a well-fed-appearing man, with tired, red-glazed eyes, an unusual capacity for quick enthusiasms, [and] a manner that seems to reflect a deep and extraordinary kindness."[33] The war was for him a deeply painful event, being yet another challenge to his persistent hope that a decent world could be forged from past tragedies.

Yet if it scattered many families, the war did assemble the Asches briefly. Nathan Asch and his second wife were living in upstate New York, at Saratoga Springs. Alone, or with Matilda, Asch would descend periodically on the Springs for a European-style "rest cure." Mixing generosity and unthinking selfishness, despotic benevolence and family feelings, his father, Nathan later recalled, would disrupt his living pattern:

While he was visiting in Saratoga I would cease to be myself and become exclusively my father's son. It was nothing he demanded or even suggested; but he was so overwhelming, he so much took for granted that the world turned only around him, that I accepted it, or played along with it. He was always friendly and relaxed at those times and even concerned about me in my penurious state. Once he said to me, "If I were in your place, I wouldn't accept it. I'd raise such a scandal!" I never stopped wondering what he meant by that. Raise a scandal with whom? With myself for not writing more salable stories? With the publishers and magazines for not buying them? With him for daring to flaunt his riches, his ease before me?

Ruth Asch Shaffer and her daughter had been evacuated from London to the United States. Moses Asch and John Asch were also living in the New York area. Nathan is unsparing (of himself as well as his father) in recounting his impressions of a rare family gathering:

At a dinner he gave for us all at a New York hotel, I saw him as he must have been seeing himself: the patriarch with his sons and their wives and their children. . . . I dislike the patriarchal concept: it goes back to a tradition I was never part of; and my father's benign mien, his complacency and self-satisfaction, were not, I felt, justified. I blamed myself for not basking in the rays of his beneficence, for not sitting, so to speak, at his feet. I was glad when the dinner was over. But I did approve when, on the night before I went off to camp, he gave C. and me some money and told us to go night-clubbing. It was what I would have done in his place. [34]

The war sharpened Asch's appreciation of America, moving him to express repeatedly his admiration for her institutions and history. In a piece for the *American Mercury* titled "I Adopt an American Ancestor," he praises Connecticut's hardy settlers and declares that the local colonial church's tall, white spire holds for him none of the fears evoked by the Gothic church towers in his native Kutno. The little prayer house arouses only "a deep reverence for the early settlers who built her." Wandering about a half-hidden old cemetery, he spots a tiny, worn American flag planted near the gravestone of one Elias Ferrison, a veteran of Valley Forge and the French Revolution. The sight awakens in Asch a passion for America's Revolutionary heroes, a passion, it seems to him, "only an immigrant and a stranger enamored of freedom can feel in quite the way that I do." [35] His search of local church documents yields a rich find: a laconic, hostile biography of Elias Ferrison by an unsympathetic descendant. The biographer proves to be a Congregational minister of the Civil War period who disapproved of his surprisingly radical Minute Man ancestor.

Elias had returned from the war with a crippled leg and the passionate conviction that the Revolution had been fought to free not merely Americans but all peoples. America was not settled, he had insisted, solely for those who found themselves on her territory, but for all who believed in her ideals. Visiting his hero's grave, Asch visualizes the old soldier nursing his lame leg by the fireplace and thinking of the battles in which he had fought. "He was thinking also of me; yes, of me and of generations to come—distressed and persecuted at the hands of tyrants—for whom he had prepared a refuge. Who, indeed, has need of this refuge more than I—I who am a Jew, born in Poland under the regime of the Tsars—in triple bondage? I am enjoying the blessings which this dead hero has bestowed on me. . . . Long, long ago, Elias Ferrison adopted me as a son. Today I adopt him as an ancestor." [36]

Asch subtitled his effort "A Fable," to indicate, perhaps, that Elias Ferrison sprang from his imagination rather than musty archives. Real or imagined, the old soldier symbolizes Asch's need to place his Judeo-Christian "message" in an American context. "Why cannot a bridge be thrown between the two faiths?" he asks in his essay "The Guilty Ones," a bridge that "could not possibly have been built in the Old World; there were too many painful memories . . . and evil deeds." No, God has chosen America "to fulfill the new religious mission entrusted to its hands."[37] He often repeated this idea, occasionally adding a personal note: "Since I came to America I sought an opportunity to express the gratitude in my heart for all that I have seen in America. I believe that I made my contribution to the American ideal through my efforts to foster greater understanding between Jew and Christian through an appreciation of their common religious heritage."[38]

Even a dozen years later, when persistent criticism from some quarters caused him to move abroad, he retained his admiration for this "American ideal" and for a United States that had embraced so generously countless numbers of his fellow Jews.

V   Still Another Defense

Soon immersed in *The Apostle,* his sequel to *The Nazarene,* Asch was, as usual, thinking of still other novels. One taking shape in his mind would center, not surprisingly, on America's "common religious heritage" and on the tribulations of intermarriage; he planned to rely heavily here on the experiences of his brothers and sisters and their families. But he was not yet ready to commit himself. "I am not thinking of a novel," he informed an interviewer shortly after publishing *The Nazarene.* "No, I am thinking of the East River. I do not sit down and decide that now I must do a novel, but only think of a subject. And then, if a novel is there for me, it evolves." He would not complete *East River* until 1946, but he evidently already had the basic plot. For he now added, rather injudiciously, that "In Europe wealthy Jews mingle with wealthy gentiles, but the masses of the Jewish people keep and are kept strictly to themselves. Here, it seems to me, that situation is reversed, for the masses mingle and intermarriages are frequent. I think this is a healthy condition."[39] He was thinking primarily of the good relations between America's Jews and Christians, but this seeming affirmation of intermarriage quickly prompted his vigilant critics to renew their assaults.

Had Asch been thickskinned, cynical, or calculating, he might have shrugged off these attacks, or even reveled in their boosts to his book sales. Instead, he suffered, protested, proclaimed his innocence and good intentions, and, when he could no longer restrain himself, wrote *What I Believe*[40] —a prolonged expression of his personal faith and a general lament for man's finer moral and humanistic values. Only occasionally do personal anger and in-jury seep through his essay's moderate, carefully modulated tone. Tracing the rise of modern atheism, Asch reiterates his unshakable faith in God and his own familiar desire to help bridge the gap between Jew and Christian. He also tries to connect his unfinished novel on Paul to *The Nazarene* by emphasizing the essential Jewishness of Jesus and Paul (whom he compares to Moses) and by linking them to the Hebrew Patriarchs. His historical interpretations here not only fill out the backgrounds of *The Nazarene* and *The Apostle*, but they point ahead to his novels on Moses and Second Isaiah. Through Jesus, Asch states, Paul "wedded" the gentiles to Israel's God and to Judaism. "I know only too well," he writes, "that the match was marred by much quarreling. . . . And yet, however bitter the quarrel became, the marriage has not been broken off. It cannot be "(*What I Believe*, pp. 121-22). So when men speak of Christian civilization, "I, a Jew, feel myself a part of it. Its course has been devious, its inadequacies are many; its record is stained with blood, and of that blood not a little came from the veins of my forefathers. For all that, its spirit was drawn from the sources which feed my soul" (135-36). Israel's God, as well as her prophetic faith and spiritual values, he insists, provides Christian and Jew with a common, irrevocable base.

Moving to the present, Asch assails not only Bolshevism and Nazism but his own generation's indifference, shortsightedness, and impotent "arteriosclerotic liberalism"; these imposed on the young of the 1920's and 30's "a world disfigured by injustice and steeped in bitterness. . . . What wonder, then, that the youth laid hold of the life-line of Communism and Nazism, only to be drowned in the seas of their hatred?" (186). The resultant animosities, persecutions, and wars have made it impossible for all Europeans to attain equality. In America alone is true freedom possible. The Mayflower settlers, Roger Williams, the Declaration of Inde-pendence formulators—these had viewed all men as equal before God and had given history its best chance of solving the world's old spiritual ills. Only America, with a freedom resting "on the creator and not on the creature" (180), could produce "a new Amos" in Abraham Lincoln.

Having thus unburdened himself, Asch returned to *The Apostle*. But then, amid the lingering furor over *The Nazarene*, as well as over his injudicious public statements and impassioned polemics, he had an unexpected mishap: his home caught fire.

Sparks from an open fireplace set the chimney on fire and smoke filled the house. Asch fought the blaze with a garden hose until neighbors arrived to help; then he climbed to the roof to direct their efforts and, being overcome by the smoke, was nearly asphyxiated. He was helped to safety by a laundress in his employ, Rube Delasce, and revived by the Stamford police.[41] Clearly, for Asch 1941 was not a vintage year.

VI   No Holocaust Novel

In addition to his personal problems, he was tormented by the Nazi obliteration of East Europe's Jews. He expressed his angry horror in articles and stories strongly reminiscent of his earlier *Sanctification of the Name*, in which Jewish victims met death with an unrelenting faith in God. Aware of his anguish, his friends urged Asch to write a novel of the Holocaust; not only would such a work prove therapeutic, they argued, but it might mollify those angered by his "Christological" novels. Instead Asch moved from Jesus to Paul, in the second volume of a trilogy he now hoped would bring him his long-desired Nobel Prize. The first century also provided some escape from the painful news reports. Yet he could hardly ignore what was happening to his beloved Polish Jews. His short writings make this clear. But immersing himself totally in Europe's horrors was more than he could face. Helen Grace Carlisle, then a Stamford neighbor, recalls a visit from the Asches during the winter of 1942-43, when accounts of the destruction of the Warsaw ghetto were just coming through. During the evening Asch began outlining, in highly emotional terms, a story forming in his mind: an old Jew, newly arrested by the Nazis, can not refrain from chanting his Sabbath prayers and is murdered "with a look of astonishment in his eyes."[42] Not able to contain his feelings, Asch hurried home to put the story on paper, calling it "Exalted and Hallowed"—the opening words of the Hebrew prayer for the dead.[43] That winter Asch's "sadness," notes Mrs. Carlisle, "grew heavier and heavier."

He continued doggedly on *The Apostle* through those terrible days, but from time to time, unable to stand his own silence, he would collect several newspaper items on Nazi atrocities and produce an article or story expressing his sorrow. He does not know, he declared in one such article, "In the Valley of Death," what else to do about the horrors perpetrated in his native Poland except to write about them. After outlining the Nazi efficiency in mass murder, he describes the obliteration of three Jewish institutions he had visited in the past—an orphanage, a sanatorium for consumptive children, and a religious school for young girls. When the girls at the school were ordered to prepare for a sexual visit by German soldiers, Asch states, all ninety-three—and their teachers—took poison. He later fictionalized this incident in "A Child Leads the Way," but here he concludes bitterly: "Never would Hitler have dared to select one people for annihilation had not the road been prepared for him by all kinds and degrees of anti-Semites. . . . All who have prepared this ground of hatred toward the Jews and other races are exactly as responsible for the bestial slaughter of the Jews in Poland, and others, as Hitler and his clique."[44]

Deeply fond of children, Asch was pained by thoughts of their suffering and murder. Of his fifteen or so "Holocaust" stories ("Tales from the Shadow of Death"[45] he called them), about half center on the young. Several of these stories ("A Child Leads the Way," "Jewish Eyes," and "The Duty to Live") are based on actual incidents and prove effective. The others, however, are marred by a Mother Rachel fixation; in these a Biblical figure ("Mother Rachel" or a Prophet or Jesus) visits the victim—literally, or in a vision. Sentiment then replaces "facts," straight narrative degenerates into bathos, and a potentially moving experience is transformed into quasi-scriptural melodrama. In "Christ in the Ghetto," for instance, Jesus descends from the cross to don the garments and prayer shawl of a rabbi the Nazis have murdered at the church altar. Then taking on the countenance of the fallen rabbi, he decides to head off a Polish mob bent on attacking the ghetto. In "The Carnival Legend," set in an earlier period, Jesus again climbs down from his cross, on the eastern wall of St. Peter's in Rome, this time to take his place among eight elderly Jews forced to run a lengthy course for the merriment of the carnival crowds. On this day the jeering Romans are reduced to stunned confusion when one runner reveals himself to be the Jew of Nazareth. Bathos is somewhat lessened in "The Duty to Live," in which a group of nuns save two Jewish children from the Nazis and encourage them to retain their Jewishness. Like "Christ in the Ghetto" and "The Carnival Legend," this tale too is weakened by mawkish language and imagery, yet it persists in the memory.

VII   Abraham's Children

His short stories had been appearing in English for over 30 years, but only when *The Nazarene* made Asch a controversial, best-selling "American" author did Putnam's bring out a collection of them. His *Children of Abraham* (1942) consists of 29 stories that cover about as many years of composition. Oppression, suffering, ecstatic vision, and courage provide their matter, texture, and plot. Extended and supported by Asch's familiar body of legend and folklore, the tales range from medieval Rome, through varied Russian and Polish ghettos, to New York's skyscrapers or tenements and Hitler's Germany. Together they reveal Asch's rich imagination and basic humanity, his knowledge and sensitivity, and his pride in Jewish resistance to crushing pressures. Their themes are familiar: past and present sufferings for God's holy name; tensions between saintly rabbis and their more worldly congregants—as well as between parents and children; the sanctity of marital love; the reawakening Jewish love for the soil, and Jewish immigrants caught and held in America's sweatshops.

The quality, not surprisingly, is uneven. Several tales are simple evocations of mood and sentiment, their substance revealed by such titles as "The Song of Hunger," "My Father's Greatcoat," and "The Footsteps." These permit Asch to indulge his taste for apocalyptic imagery. In "The Song of Hunger," for instance, some near-starved children feed on fantasy to describe their visions of food or to recount their families' tricks for making the hungry days pass. Other stories dwell on a single element or trait: a mother's loneliness, a man's bad luck, a girl's rebellion against custom, a Jew reunited with his land, or helpless Jews and peasants bound by a common poverty. A few sketches merely express an idea—hunger, pain, piety, nostalgia, death.

Several tales prove memorable, but even these owe something to the slighter ones preceding them. The separate titles and plots flow into a loose but surprisingly integrated narrative of cumulative power that exceeds easily the actual sum of its parts. The people are equally varied: an old man in New York, an innkeeper in Poland, a farmer in Lithuania, a young girl in Warsaw. All are Jews—serious, suffering, patient, religious, and torn. Ranging from the intensely provincial to the totally cosmopolitan, they index Asch's talents, weaknesses, and preoccupations. Many are from Asch's native Polish *shtetlach* and are caught up in the diverse currents of exodus and migration that Jews have experienced through the centuries.

But worldly sufferings, Asch makes clear, never justify relinquishing one's Jewishness, much less one's faith in God. He underscores again his aversion to apostasy and apostates—a reaction exacerbated undoubtedly by the accusations repeatedly aimed at him. In "The Last Jew," "The Heritage," "White Roses," and "Fathers-in-Law," he lays bare—without anger or comment—the pathos, irony, and emotional confusions that result when ancient customs and beliefs are confronted by modern temptations and rewards. But his sympathy and respect are reserved clearly and primarily for those God-intoxicated idealists and dreamers who refuse to compromise their faith or group loyalty. Nearly every tale, in fact, reaffirms the eventual triumph of those who live by the spirit; as earthly hope fades, these turn their eyes to heaven. "Such is the way of Jews," declares the "White Roses" narrator, "if they are not quarreling with their God, they are lonesome for Him."

Total consecration to God is the theme of "The Boy Saint," the volume's longest, most carefully wrought tale. Here Asch explores again the potential spiritual rapport between Judaism and Christianity in the person of Joel, an ascetic youth who strongly resembles not only Yechiel but Jesus and St. Francis, as well as I.J. Singer's Yoshe Kalb. Very different from the guileless Joel is Stash Grabski, the young Polish anti-Semite of "De Profundis." As discussed earlier, this novella traces in Tolstoyan terms its confused protagonist's moral regeneration. Yet in these stories victims as well as perpetrators may bear guilt. In "Heil, Hitler!," for instance, a distinguished Jewish professor, who had previously been tormented by the Nazis, confesses that fear had caused him to shout "Heil, Hitler!" Such "cowardice," he now feels, has deprived him of the right to hate. But not guilt alone evokes humility and shame: poverty often produces similar emotions. In "A Letter to America" a needy congregation's once-proud elders, their gabardines reduced to tatters, swallow their pride to write of their plight to fellow-townsmen now living in America.

Asch displays repeatedly his strong sense of tradition, his appreciation for that which is finely aged or time-encrusted; on occasion this awe of the past moves him to disparage the new, to identify it with the raw, glittering, and tawdry. At the same time, he is slightly embarrassed by this attitude; thus he can use Old Neufeld, the antiquarian in "Dust to Dust," to mock gently his own love of antiques—at least to see his lifelong obsession with old objects in ironic perspective. For Neufeld prefers starving with his genuine antiques to making a living with machine-made imitations. Indeed, many characters here yearn for the past, for a religious fervor now gone, for an age when life was simpler, closer to the soil and seemingly to God. This nostalgia grips as strongly those in New York as those in the old country, the young as well as the old.

Much more autobiographical than "Dust to Dust" is "Young Years," a long, meandering remembrance of Asch's first months in Warsaw. Thinly disguised as the narrator Simon, Asch wanders repeatedly from a feeble story line to recall again those difficult early months when, as an ambitious novice writer and an idealistic advocate of the Jewish Enlightenment, he went knocking on the doors of the leading Jewish writers and editors. He limns fondly several noted rationalists who then were making the new knowledge available to the young. But his most eloquent passages deal with those often brilliant but generally threadbare young disciples of intellectual freedom who, like himself, hurried from the provinces in their Hasidic gabardines to Warsaw, Vilna, Kiev, Odessa, and other great cities to work for a better world. That their hopes and efforts ended in frustrations, revolutions, and wars made their idealism, in Asch's eyes anyway, the more poignant. Not all the stories in *Children of Abraham*, however, are laments; several, like "The Lucky Touch" and "From the Beyond," exude the laughter of a people forced to find joy in life's trifles.

The many years of composition represented by these stories perhaps rendered their uneven quality inevitable. Yet collectively they overcome, at least in part, many problems of calendar, place, and idiosyncrasy. Their world is the Diaspora, their thematic links are Jewish tragedy and pride—a proud people's demand for identity and dignity—as well as the desperate tenacity of an ancient faith. But these elements, as Sholem Asch was keenly aware, derive essentially from man's communality; thus they render the world of Abraham's children first human and only then Jewish.

Chapter 8

Brothers and Enemies

Asch published *The Apostle*,[1] in 1943, amid dispatches from Europe describing the Nazi massacres of Jews. He knew full well the book would be excitedly and, in some Jewish quarters, bitterly received. If anything, he fomented controversy by also bringing out that year a Yiddish version of *The Nazarene*. (He had needed almost four years to find a Yiddish publisher for it.) His new book, like its predecessor, was (with its 800 pages and 375,000 words) in the grandiose "heroic" novel tradition. Based on the life of Paul, it represented Asch's attempt not only to trace Christianity's birth and growth but to reveal the Christian debt to Judaism. For him, Christianity was the culmination of Jewish thought, with its rituals and concepts rooted in Jewish ideas and practices. Many had already misread his intent, but for him his New Testament trilogy was literally a religious task: he meant each volume to be both a paean to Israel and an act of spiritual "reconciliation."[2]

As he expected, the Yiddish press proved vitriolic but the American public generally receptive. Newspaper reviewers praised the new novel, clergymen hailed it from the pulpit, and bookstore managers reported good sales—with the Book-of-the-Month Club distributing a "dividend" edition. These successes, however, failed to ease Asch's bitterness at being cut off from Jewish groups where he had long been hailed as a leader. Now their spokesmen assailed him as an apostate. To make matters worse, American literary circles failed to welcome him. Asch's "latest excursion" had increased his sales, Oscar Cargill sympathized, but it had not decreased his isolation. "He is still an immigré [*sic*] writer, a man without a country—only now there are Jews and Christians who have got him mixed up with Mephistopheles."[3]

I Paul and the Jews

But if wounded by his critics, Asch refused to defer to them; in fact, he was here more bluntly outspoken than in *The Nazarene*. Turning again to Christian beginnings, he drew this time not only

162

from the Acts of the Apostles, Paul's Epistles, and Josephus, but from such contemporary scholars as Joseph Klausner, Claude G. Montefiore, Moses Hadas, and George Foot Moore—all of whom had stressed the ties between Christianity and Israel. In addition, Asch dropped his previous reincarnation, flash-back, and story-within-story devices for a straight narrative of Paul's life.

His stance in the novel is that of an oral storyteller who links almost every descriptive detail to a historical comment; he thereby keeps the reader aware of encountering both history and fiction. Avoiding direct acceptance of the miraculous (or Jesus' divinity), Asch follows the Biblical outline, telescoping, rearranging, expanding the traditional materials. Where the record is sketchy or silent, he elaborates and extends it; he suggests new motives for familiar figures, develops secondary characters into vivid personalities, and stretches brief scriptural references into dramatic episodes. He clearly relishes his ability "to clothe with flesh a dead world" [4] and to recapture those tremors of decay that toppled an empire. Asch is convinced that spiritual energy flows easily into any void created by physical or moral exhaustion; thus he dwells on bodily and ethical weaknesses, describes with zealous anger the decadent Mediterranean world against which Jew and Christian protested, and lingers obsessively over the splendors, depravities, and squalor of exotic fleshpots like Antioch, Corinth, Ephesus, and Nero's Rome. In each he catalogues the idolatrous cults with their lustful, bloody rites and festivals. One reviewer described the novel as "a dark master-painting of a writhing pagan world, with even a reminder of the vastness of Dante and Doré in the scope of its canvas." [5]

Whatever its merits, his descriptive virtuosity repeatedly makes heavy reading, and Asch wishes to spare the reader none of his hero's experiences, good or bad. Admittedly, the Paul of Acts and the Epistles is a complex being, much more so than the Gospel Jesus, whose personality (at least in literary terms) appears simple, direct, and nobly, if pathetically, human and unified. But Paul is an epileptic visionary who identifies himself proudly as of the stock of Israel (the tribe of Benjamin), as a Hebrew of the Hebrews, and—as touching the law—a Pharisee. At first he denies the Nazarene and persecutes his followers, only to become the new faith's major theorist and apostle. More than any other figure, therefore, the scriptural Paul embodies the conflicting forces that gathered about the living Jesus and that multiplied rapidly after his death.

Asch tries valiantly to fathom this strange, paradoxical zealot, even interrupting his narrative to "pray" for guidance in the task: "O Father in heaven, Thou Who probest the souls of man, open a little ray of light for me . . . that I may see . . . the forces that wage war for the possession of a man's soul" (149). His Paul, like the New Testament original, proves a tortured, often unsympathetic fanatic for whom life divides into yea or nay; for him any life devoid of faith or God is a mere sequence of meaningless torments. Stubborn, irascible, overbearing, he lacks the warmth of his friend Joseph bar Naba (Barnabas) or of fellow apostle Simon bar Jonah (Peter). Paul's obvious talents and courage are flawed by epilepsy, malaria, a drooping eyelid, and an exacerbated sense of guilt; convinced he has been "cursed" with divine election, he views his life as a prolonged "sacrifice" for God's cause.

The early narrative is lively and varied. Seven weeks after the Crucifixion, the Nazarene's disciples in Jerusalem disseminate the Teacher's words. New converts are mostly Jews—either poor and uneducated or rich Greek-speaking merchants; their customs and attitudes, more flexible than those of the orthodox, render both groups open to new religious ideas. Among those drawn to the Messianists is the learned Reb Istephan (Stephen); one offended by the new faith is young Saul of Tarsus, a Temple student of the great Rabbi Gamaliel. A Pharisee and Nazarite, Saul longs for the Messiah who will cleanse the world of moral depravity. Yet he fears this new division in Israel and denounces these Galilean blasphemers who give the name of God's "Anointed" to one crucified and buried—one who then supposedly "rose" from the dead like some Canaanite or Babylonian deity.

His zeal aroused, Saul assists in the stoning of Istephan and, encouraged by the High Priests, leads in the persecution of Jerusalem's Messianic Jews. Hearing that Damascus has become a seedbed of the new movement, he heads there—only to be stricken blind on the road and to experience then a confusing vision of this "New Messiah" (who appears before him in prayer shawl and phylacteries). His blindness is cured in Damascus by a Messianist who declares that Saul is fated to be the Nazarene's apostle. Siding with those who consider Saul of Tarsus the true founder of Christianity, Asch traces his hero's painful formulating of the Messianic doctrine, his slow realization that no reconciling of orthodox Jews and New Messianists is possible, and that a new church can emerge only outside the Jewish fold.

At the same time, his New Testament readings have convinced Asch that in thought and behavior Saul remains a Jew and Pharisee who does not want to separate himself from Israel. But the forces he has set in motion cause this division. In addition, he is a Greek in lifestyle and a Roman citizen; thus no one label describes or explains him. Zealot and mystic, philosopher and missionary, he is a driven being who accepts any sacrifice or humiliation to pursue God's truth. Retreating into the wilderness for three years of meditation and self-purgation, he emerges determined to remove, by faith in the Messiah, the barriers between Greek and Jew. Adopting the Greek name of Paul, he roams Asia Minor forming congregations of gentiles eager to share the Jewish God and of Jews who find the rabbinic laws burdensome. He declares invalid both circumcision and the dietary laws. "He is not a Jew who is such outwardly," Paul argues, "but he is a Jew that is one inwardly, circumcised in the heart and the spirit, not in the letter" (552). Tense, blunt, domineering, deeply versed in Mosaic law and Greek lore, he is torn between old allegiances and new mission. "The Messiah sent us forth to be a light to gentiles," Peter admonishes him, "but thou . . . settest fire to the House of Israel." Paul flashes anger. "I say there cannot be one God for the Jews and another for the gentiles: there is but one God. Likewise . . . there is but one Messiah" (485-86).

Asch struggles to fuse Saul the Jew and Paul the Greek, but the figure that emerges conveys less a sense of fusion than of a man being ground between millstones. The conflicting emotions and thoughts tearing at his hero, however, do enable Asch to capsulize the larger discordances separating the new and old faiths. For despite his tendencies to oversimplify and sentimentalize, he still recognizes their deep, complex differences. Yet he is happier describing the bonds that survive: how numerous new Christians remain loyal Jews, keeping synagogue traditions and praying in the Temple; how the synagogue not only protects and nourishes the new teachings but provides the audiences for Paul and the other Christian preachers. But Paul is not to be confined. He soon moves beyond the Judaic tradition, beyond the religious boundaries drawn by Peter and the other disciples, and, most significantly, beyond the limits of Asch's bountiful sympathy. One God and one congregation for Jews and gentiles, Paul declares, with the Torah replaced by the Messiah. His pronouncements spark quarrels and tumult among friends and foes alike; not only does Israel reject his teachings, but even the Jewish Messianists view them as a call to false worship. Indeed, the Jerusalem church elders, led by Yeshua's brother, Jacob ben Joseph (James), guard zealously their group's devotion to traditional Judaism. They are dismayed by Paul's turn to the gentiles and his gradual insistence that his converts be free of Jewish ritual. When he brings uncircumcised newcomers into the Temple courts, the Sadducean priests (his former allies) threaten arrest. Having antagonized virtually everyone, and not wishing to increase Jerusalem's turmoil, Paul falls back on his Roman citizenship to demand a trial in Rome before Caesar.

Asch expands on Paul's Rome sojourn. After nearly five years in and out of prison there, Paul is cleared by Roman authorities of religious charges and leaves to tour the young congregations in Asia Minor that his followers have been nurturing. At this late point he still flaunts his pride in his Jewish heritage; he is not a rebel, he declares, but a loyal son of the true tradition who is striving to bring the world's nations to Mount Zion. He has said nothing but that stated by Moses and the Prophets, "that the Messiah will suffer . . . be the first to rise from the dead, and . . . be a light to Israel and . . . the gentiles" (600). But when the Jewish Messianists scorn all gentile converts as strangers who would usurp their inheritance, Paul grows defiant. "The whole law is fulfilled in this word," he asserts, that "thou shalt love thy neighbor as thyself" (495). To fulfil this dictum, he even intervenes when trouble flares between Christians and orthodox Jews. His influence proves limited, however, especially with the sophisticated or educated (Jewish or gentile), because he refuses to transform the Messiah into a philosophical concept, symbol, or "Logos" for them; the Messiah, he insists, is the very "flesh and blood of faith for . . . the universal redemption" (679). The Jews reject his views, and Paul is left with the sad knowledge that future generations will see him as having "thrust a wedge between Israel and the world."

The novel's ironic conclusion centers on Nero's destruction of his city. Blame is placed on the Christians, with Jews sharing Christian sufferings: the Romans see no differences among those who worship Israel's God, refuse to bow to Caesar, die reciting the *Shema*, and receive Jewish burial. Arrested as a leader of the arsonists, Paul finds Peter in the prison, and the two old apostles go together to die. Convinced he has kept the ancient faith, Paul

expires crying out—not to the Messiah for whom he is dying—but
to Israel's God. At the Sabbath worship following the executions,
an old rabbi has the last word. Rome's sword conquers for a time,
he declares, but Jerusalem's spirit "conquers for ever!" (804).

Asch then appends—in the manner of early Jewish religious
writers—a coda[6] thanking God for enabling him to complete his
chronicle of Israel's "merit": "I thank Thee and praise Thee, Lord of
the world, that Thou hast given me the strength to withstand all
temptations and overcome all obstacles, those of my own making
and those made by others, and to complete the two works, The
Nazarene and The Apostle, which are one work; so that I might set
forth in them the merit of Israel, whom Thou hast elected to bring
the light of the faith to the nations of the world, for Thy glory and
out of Thy love of mankind" (804). If intended to placate his critics,
the coda failed; most of them dismissed his highly subjective re-
creatings of Jesus and Paul as a stumbling block and a foolishness.

II   Paul as Jew and Gentile

Admittedly The Apostle, either as tract or novel, does pose
problems; the most serious stem from Asch's waverings between
modern and traditional viewpoints. Avoiding direct discussion of
some critical Biblical points, he renders sharp verdicts on others.
He depicts, for instance, Luke gathering materials for his Gospel,
Paul writing the Epistle to the Hebrews and the Second Epistle to
Timothy, and he implies that the disciple John is author of the
Fourth Gospel. He accepts the Protestant claim that "the Lord's
brethren" are the younger children of Joseph and Mary, but he
shares the Catholic view of Peter as the chief apostle. He insists
also that Jews and Christians share the same Messianic
ideal—thereby underlining his misconception that every faithful
Jew or Christian is a literal adventist.

Nor does Asch resolve fully Paul's Jewishness: his own
intrudes. Being "lovingly and homogeneously Jewish," as Alfred
Kazin aptly puts it, Asch fails "to penetrate Christianity's inner
life."[7] He makes Paul as Jewish as he had Jesus, also bearing down
hard on the Judaic elements in the apostolic church while de-
emphasizing the influences of the mystery cults. At the same time,
he tries not to antagonize his gentile readers; the results are
confusing. Asch is not a subtle writer, nor is his rhetoric always
precise. When not exaggerating Judaism's ennobling qualities, or
its importance to Christianity, he is causing its adherents to seem

overly narrow and unenlightened. Still, he could have more validly been charged by Christians with Judaizing Christianity than the reverse. But he published *The Apostle* precisely when Jewish sensibilities had been rubbed raw by the Nazi slaughter, so that Jewish anger was much greater than Christian. Some Catholic reviewers, however, quickly expressed their unhappiness with aspects of his plot and characters.

The displeasure of both Jew and Christian is easily understood. For despite the obvious effort and emotion Asch put into his narrative, *The Apostle*, like all the longer Asch novels, proves a mix of good and bad art. Edward Wagenknecht categorized it well; *The Apostle*, he wrote, is as much less "intellectual" than Thomas Mann's *Joseph* novels as it is more intellectual than Lloyd Douglas's *The Robe*.[8] If a well-intentioned, at times even lofty, message of spiritual brotherhood, the novel derives its basic relevance from its author's fondness for historical data, for the panorama of ancient splendor and corruption. Major and minor New Testament figures are fleshed out with appreciation and insight, with the women—as always—the more vivid. But his Christians are rivaled, even surpassed, by such redoubtable pagans as Caligula, Nero, and Seneca. All attain a degree of life. Memorable scenes are numerous: the stoning of Stephen; the sufferings of the slave workers and the struggles of the Messianists in Alexandria, Antioch, Ephesus, and Corinth; Nero's orgies; Paul calming fellow passengers on a foundering ship, as well as his debating with Seneca; the condemned Christians singing and praying in the Circus Maximus.

These external scenes are enriched by Asch's reverence for man's inner needs and by his awareness of Christianity's impact on history. Yet such positive qualities are nearly overshadowed by negative ones—like the needless theological hairsplittings, the interminable sermons and discussions, and the pompous dialogues that almost crush not merely character and plot but pace and style. Repeatedly, lucid, controlled passages give way to pseudo-spiritual slush. Pagan excesses are here less seductive than in *The Nazarene*, but Nero's cruelties are the sadistic equal of anything in the earlier novel. Nor are the psychological subtleties or the ironic humor that sustain Mann's complex *Joseph* narratives evident here. Shaped more by religiosity and emotion than by analysis and thought, *The Apostle* apparently did appeal to those readers whose tastes fell between Mann and Douglas. But today Asch's approach appears so dated as to bother both skeptic and believer. For despite his awareness of contemporary Biblical studies, he ignores them; instead, he relates Paul's story as would an eyewitness oblivious to the insights of recent archeology and anthropology.

The Biblical Paul would challenge any novelist. His letters reveal a tortured "saintly demon"[9] capable of shattering men's minds and imposing on them his personal vision. This Paul proves too elusive, complex, and Christian for Asch to grasp. Not that the latter fails to try; he strives valiantly to balance in his hero what is mystical and rational, legendary and historical. But the figure that emerges is so obsessed and opinionated, so ambiguous in thought and behavior that his convictions appear repeatedly to derive from aberration rather than belief or reason. In addition, Asch's thesis was impossible. He wanted nothing less than to reconcile two religions that for two thousand years had been diverging—theologically, socially, emotionally. But no fictional recasting, no matter how well intentioned, could sweep away the accumulated bitterness and differences.

Not surprisingly, *The Apostle* drew a mixed critical reaction. Oscar Cargill, a longtime Asch admirer, found it "somewhat labored and dull,"[10] whereas Clifton Fadiman saw the novel as "an act of faith, truly apostolic in its humility and simplicity." It is impossible, Fadiman wrote, "not to admire the reverent spirit that produced it and its greater companion book, *The Nazarene*."[11] But whatever his literary success or failure here, Asch's prime error was poor judgment. Jewish anguish at the slaughter of the six million by a "Christian" nation, to the seeming indifference of other Christians, was at its peak. For a writer, or for anyone else, to appoint himself at that moment the reconciler of Jews to their "spiritual brothers" was sheer effrontery; that he was the celebrated (and controversial) Sholem Asch only made matters worse. The valid charge, then, for his critics to have leveled at Asch was hardly of apostasy—he was Jewish to his marrow—but, as with *The Nazarene*, of exhibiting abominable timing and taste.

III   Another Reply and Explanation

Ironically, Asch's career in America, despite the verbal assaults from Abraham Cahan and other Yiddish journalists, was at its crest. His books were selling well and gaining the approval of critics like Oscar Cargill, Clifton Fadiman, and Alfred Kazin. In fact, in those emotion-charged World War II days, when Nazi atrocities were daily more evident, some reviewers—as they had a decade earlier—began fanning Asch's hopes for the Nobel Prize by raising the issue. Clifton Fadiman, reviewing *The Apostle* in *The New Yorker*, suggested that the Swedes, as an act of political defiance and symbolism, encourage the Nobel Committee to award to Asch the 1943 literature prize. "If there ever was a symbol of everything they [the Nazis] hate, it is Sholem Asch," declared Fadiman, "and that is one of several good reasons for conferring upon him the Nobel Prize."[12] Today, few critics would advocate awarding a literary prize for political reasons—or, conversely, that it be denied for such reasons. Yet Earle Balch, Asch's editor, became convinced, after conversations in Stockholm with two committee members, that he detected, as he put it, "a degree of anti-Semitism there. I know that one member I talked to was in frequent correspondence with Hitler."[13]

Also working against Asch was his lack of strong support from the academic community. When literary historian A.A. Roback, in 1938, approached a Harvard senior professor of English about Asch as a Nobel candidate, this noted scholar claimed never to have heard the name.[14] Such incidents, for there were others, irritated Asch, as he was eager for recognition by college and university people. He had a strong regard, therefore, for Yale's librarians, who several years earlier had requested the holograph manuscript of *The Nazarene;* now, to his gratification, they asked that he deposit at Yale his other manuscripts and books.[15] He was so delighted when a library grant from philanthropist Louis M. Rabinowitz, in 1945, made the donation feasible that to his own available manuscript drafts and notes he added some collected rare Jewish volumes and documents. He then used the formal donation ceremony to express his love of books, of Yale, and of America. "The leaves of my manuscripts represent the days of my life," he stated, "for I had no other life outside of my work." Yale University he viewed as his "second spiritual home" because of the Hebrew tradition early leaders, like Ezra Stiles, had implanted there. He was especially pleased, he added, to have his collection go not to a Jewish but "a general American" institution . Certainly America's Jews should use the ancient learning to build Jewish institutions in the new homeland, Asch explained, but they should also see that their culture is worthily represented in the "general temples of knowledge." Only then would the Jewish contribution to civilization be appreciated. As for himself, he hoped future generations would link his name to those who had established "the tradition of the Hebrew book at the Library of Yale."[16]

Pleasurable occasions, like this one provided by the Yale library, were rare for Asch during these troubled years. But he appeared to be bearing up well. His friend Louis Zara described Asch, then in his sixties, as still of tall, dignified bearing, with "iron gray hair and mustache" and a nature both "warm and earnest." He has "a passionate love for simple people," said Zara. "But his mien is a melancholy one, resulting from that deep sense of *Weltschmerz* which has been the burden and torment of all Jewish prophets and poets. . . . One gazes at him and realizes that this is a painfully honest man, one who speaks freely because his heart will not let him do otherwise."[17] Much more than *Weltschmerz*, of course, was bothering Asch. When the allegations of his "Christian leanings" did not diminish, he tried again to reply. He was no more pro-Christian, he argued in interviews, than Rembrandt had been pro-Jewish in painting rabbis, Michelangelo in sculpting Moses and David, or Thomas Mann in penning his *Joseph* novels. Never had he preached Christianity to the Jews or to anyone else. On the other hand, he had not, in his frequent artistic descriptions of Jewish religious strivings, he pointed out, advocated Hasidism or urged Jews "to visit rabbis and believe in saints."[18] Thus his record and conscience on both counts were clear.

Finding his replies drowned out by the familiar "apostate" charges, Asch felt compelled to write yet another "explanatory" history of Jewish-Christian relations. He had published "The Guilty Ones" and *What I Believe* before the full, shocking exposures of the German slaughter of Jews, but even then he had asked how Christians could reconcile their evil acts with their belief in a suffering Christ. "With a wrath chastened by grief," Lewis Mumford wrote, Asch had enumerated the wrongs "done to the Jews, with the passive consent of Christians, if not with their active connivance."[19] Now, in *One Destiny: An Epistle to the Christians*,[20] he asked not only Christians but the Jewish Holocaust survivors to recall their common religious heritage; both groups must realize anew, he declared, that no peace is possible for either until the two halves of their faith are again joined, spiritually if not structurally.

Lapsing repeatedly into a pseudo-mystical jargon, Asch here plays the prophetic apostle who sees visions rather than facts, drama rather than reality. If he rejects the actual union of synagogue and church, he also ignores the ideological differences posed by the Trinity, Original Sin, and Christ's divinity; instead, he insists upon the common religious character and values derived from Old Testament concepts of the Messiah, redemption, and salvation. Jesus merely had "expanded" Judaism and his actions should have moved Jews to share his ethics, Asch states, whereas Christians have no choice theologically but to accept Israel's God. More bothersome than this glossing over of Jewish-Christian differences, however, is Asch's dismissal of other faiths. His spiritually united world has no room, seemingly, for Hindus, Moslems, or Buddhists, as the Jewish-Christian idea alone contains "the possibility of salvation for our tortured world."[21]

Few Jewish critics were impressed by Asch's thesis. One reviewer conveyed their general reaction by observing, with mock relief, that at least Asch's effort was titled "One Destiny" and not "One Faith."[22] Asch himself, seemingly aware that his "fraternal" argument was weak, attempted to explain why so many Christians, past and present, had rejected both Israel's God and Jesus' ethics to spew hatred at Jews. But in tracing the causes of this hatred, he ignores all psychological, economic, or political factors to revive the medieval concept of the Antichrist; then he cites anti-Semitism as the major weapon wielded by this son of Satan to destroy Jesus' teachings—with Adolf Hitler merely "the last link" in a lengthy chain of Satanic evil. Entangled in this chain is the Church itself. Adopting the role of "chastising rod," the Church, Asch insists, invented a Judas and an Ahasuerus to cut off Israel from all productive labor and to drive her behind ghetto walls, thereby robbing her of every human right.

If the Church is thus guilty, no one is free of complicity in crimes against the Jews; all are accomplices, for instance, in the recent Holocaust, especially the German nation. Every German man, woman, and child, Asch declares, "is infected [with] . . . the disease of bestiality and blood lust." For this all forty million "will bear forever the mark of Cain." But the entire Christian world must carry "the accessory guilt" (*One Destiny*, pp. 33, 35). Having leveled his charges, Asch relents slightly. Neither past nor present Jewbaiters, he states, should be considered genuine "Christians." Italian, French, Belgian, and Dutch Christians, among others in Nazi-occupied Europe, had risked their lives to help Jews. Catholic priests and nuns had tried to save Jewish children. Pope Pius XII himself had provided example during the war by protecting five thousand Jews. Each Christian's attitude toward Jews, therefore, registers validly his true spirituality.

Yet only America, Asch concludes, provides an adequate haven for the Jewish remnant's physical and spiritual regeneration. Only America, the healthiest nation in a sick world, recognizes the Jewish gift to civilization and the "single nature . . . of the Jewish-Christian man" (85). It alone extends hope for this unhappy world by the potential it offers for renewal of the Jewish-Christian ethic.

IV   The Ikes and the Mikes

In his articles and essays Asch generally reflected the ideas of his fiction-in-progress. He now planned several more Biblical novels based on concepts he felt were common to Jews and Christians. Before turning full attention to them, however, he completed, in 1946, *East River*,[23] a novel he had been writing for seven years. Placing his "fraternal" theories in the New York that precedes World War I, he fashions here another parable of love and religious differences. But if obviously sincere, *East River* evokes, unfortunately, too many recollections of *Street Scene* and *Abie's Irish Rose*, as Asch depicts again his idealized Jews and Christians whose gropings for a common God not only unite them but connect them to all who would share in the search. Four decades earlier, in *The Town*, he had described prayers of synagogue and church that blended in the air while ascending to one God, and through the years he had restated this idea in short and long fiction. Here he insists that Jew and Christian can live not merely under one sky but one roof.

Theme, issues, and setting, therefore, are vintage Asch. Inter-marriage and religious tensions; poverty and bigotry; character compromise and reform; disputes, greed, and competition in the garment industry—all contribute to the "yeasty stew"[24] of immigrant struggle. Despite his reliance upon the familiar, however, Asch reaches for more than he can grasp, and only the slightest of narrative lines links his welter of editorial comments, social detail, and swarm of characters. Events range from an amusing rooftop roundup of mating pigeons to a vivid re-creation of the infamous Triangle Shirtwaist factory fire.[25] Individual portraits are, as always, varied, sentimental, and lively. Reaching back for scenic touches to memories of his 1911 visit to America, Asch draws even more heavily on the American experiences of his brothers and sisters and their children; people and incidents are so thinly disguised that Asch family folklore easily identifies each figure.[26]

He confines his human polyglot to East 48th Street, from First

Avenue to the East River. There, at river's edge, prior to the appearance of fashionable apartments and sleek parkway, cluster colonies of overworked, insecure orthodox Jews and Catholic Irish (the "Ikes and the Mikes"), nostalgic Poles and exuberant Italians. There small groups of pious Jews rock ceaselessly in synagogues and prayerhouses, united by the vision of the Golden Land (the *Goldene Medina*) behind their closed eyes. On the sidewalks, amid the shrieking gramophones and flaring kerosene torches, pushcart peddlers hawk wares and children scamper. All are "Tammany's children," as among them move opportunistic political flunkies resolving differences, providing jobs, and even enforcing a measured decorum. Asch is keenly aware that an unsympathetic observer (a Henry James or Henry Adams) would find 48th Street a Babel of the jargons and customs of "superfluous" human fragments who, driven from Europe's slums, have brought to America's melting pot little literature, culture, or wealth. Such an observer would discern few significant differences among the ghetto dwellers. Yet if melting in the same pot, each group does retain its differences and distance, its dreams and delusions. Ground down by poverty, entrapped in dark tenements and dirty streets, and locked into airless sweatshops, the newcomers cling stubbornly to old habits, old memories, and fading hopes.

Using speech and squabbles to expose his characters' fears and gropings, Asch blends three strains persistent in his fiction: the earthy Jewish folktale redolent of tears, nostalgia, and eccentricities; a visionary idealism beyond sect and schism; and an impassioned indignation at the exploitation of poor Jews by greedy co-religionists. His concern for the poor and their problems is deep and unshakable, but his "solutions" seem too often no more than a benevolent paternalism. Downgrading other misunderstandings between Jews and Catholics, Asch stresses the religious ones, and he concludes that both groups must look no longer to Europe's past but to America's promise of a "religion of love." Concocting a loose amalgam of Isaiah, Plato, and Thomas Jefferson, Asch argues that his new religion will not only unify Jews and Christians, but it will bring together bosses and workers by ending sweatshops and strikes. Acting out Asch's theories are the devout grocer Moshe Wolf Davidowsky, his wife Deborah, and his sons Nathan and Irving. Committed to God and man, Moshe Wolf, a near-bankrupt, feeds gentile and Jew. Refusing to question his fathers' dogmas and rituals, he tries to transmit his beliefs to his sons. He views suffering as a sacred trial and is reluctant to complain of the blows that benumb him. Still he is shattered when Nathan is crippled by polio and Irving marries the daughter of a drunken, Jew-hating Catholic neighbor; in a vain attempt to erase Irving from his memory, he even says *Kaddish* [27] for his younger son.

Moshe Wolf's sons enable Asch again to confront traditional Judaism with modern industrialism. (He had covered much the same ground in *Uncle Moses* and *Chaim Lederer's Return.*) Here the insatiate young garment industry engulfs the East Side, reducing its hapless immigrants to sweated, underpaid, seasonal labor. To outmaneuver the growing unions, the manufacturers develop a pernicious system of "take-home bundles"; these are sewed on ceaselessly in their tenement rooms by non-union men, women, and children, many of whom suffer from the "proletarian sickness," tuberculosis. Leading the manufacturers is the hard-driving Irving, who had decided even as a child to escape 48th Street. At eighteen, he set up his own garment factory and soon after married Mary McCarthy, his chief model and designer. Now eager to share his new wealth with his family, he is rejected: his father cannot accept his marriage, and his brother Nathan disdains him as an exploiter of the poor. Nathan also loved Mary, but he had decided his paralysis made marriage impossible. After long wallowing in self-pity, he is bullied back to usefulness by a tough-talking doctor. He then becomes a union writer and lecturer and helps to organize the garment workers. But when his partial recovery moves him to assert a belief in God, he loses his socialist followers and his job.

Generally not given to symbolizing, Asch here hints at Nathan Davidowsky's Messiah-like qualities. (Jewish lore links the Messiah to King David, whose court prophet was Nathan.) Indeed, Nathan proves more saint and auctorial voice than activist; his conclusions echo those of Asch. Only faith in God, he declares repeatedly, makes possible social justice or true brotherhood—yet each has been vitiated by the suspicion existing not merely between Jews and Christians but among the differing Christian sects. Neither Jew nor Christian views God's mercy as encompassing everyone. "How strange it is," Nathan thinks, "that I, created by God, can conceive of a universal salvation, whereas God—according to the conception of the religious sects—lacks the tolerance to offer salvation to all men" (125).

But if a saint and sufferer, Nathan is no Myshkin; his saintly "contradictions"[28] and sufferings—instead of thwarting him and others—prove temporary and productive. After various non-scarifying complications, all events slowly jell and move (thanks primarily to Nathan's selfless example) to happy conclusion. Conversely, Father McKee, Mary's priest, precipitates much of the difficulty; pronouncing her marriage invalid, he so frightens the devout girl with hellfire that she breaks up her home. Yet this priest, Asch insists, awakens in Mary a concern for others that wins her father-in-law's respect. Irving, who has disregarded religion, ethics, and workers, also changes; he reconciles with wife, father, and brother, revamps his sweatshop, and signs with the union. Nathan regains his union job, and Moshe Wolf, forsaking his narrowness, not only accepts his Christian daughter in-law and baptized grandson but finds new meaning in the Passover with them at table. After a Sabbath of Hasidic reading and commentary, Moshe Wolfe, his mind filled with visions of the saintly *Tzadikim*, dies peacefully.

In *East River* Asch parades his literary vices. Melodramatic, sentimental, and didactic at his best, he here mixes—and loosely—realism and near-fantasy, authentic insight and trite gesture. Always the leisurely talespinner, he now literally savors narration's sheer detail and process. Reluctant to think through his ideas, he reduces complex issues to easy generalities. Anxious to wring from Jewish ritual and taboo a religious "love of mankind," he attacks Jewish "apartness." But his indiscriminate fraternalism, extended logically, suggests obliteration not merely of orthodoxy's parochial concepts but the total East European (and even East Side) Jewish life he loved. The anonymous reviewer in *The New Yorker* may have been unduly curt in dismissing *East River* as a work "of integrity, completely sincere and heavy as lead,"[29] but he was not far from his mark. Neither was critic Harold Rosenberg, who confessed how difficult he found evaluating a novel that mingles "meditation and bathos . . . descriptive talent and theatrical 'corn' . . . social concern and contempt, partly conscious, for . . . reader and . . . fiction."[30]

Yet no Asch novel is easily dismissed. Even this lumbering, humorless chronicle disentangles more clearly and vividly than any other fictive effort (not excepting Cahan's *The Rise of David Levinsky*) the ambiguous reactions of several Jewish generations to socialism, Russia, and America. No novelist has caught more convincingly the tenement sounds and gestures of immigrant life, the machinations and infighting of the garment unions and employers, or the disintegrative pressures of the new land. Certainly no writer within recollection has conveyed more feelingly (unless the younger Asch) the workers' terror of such terms as "slack season" and "fired," nor the ways their new bosses used these fears. If Asch loves and sentimentalizes his Jews, he also sees their warts and foibles. If pained by the Church's bigotry, he appreciates its goodness and service: a devout Catholic would be hard put to describe more reverently the troubled Mary kneeling for solace, with her tiny son, before the Virgin. If he can not resist larding his sharp physical details with needless moralizing, neither can he avoid catching recurrent flashes of human dignity and truth. Impassioned and concerned, Asch gropes beyond externals for qualities raising man above the animal. Lapses in taste and judgment detract here repeatedly from his stature as artist but not from his worth as a feeling, perceptive human observer.

V   More Tales of His People

By 1946 life began to brighten somewhat for Asch, a fact that seemed to anger his critics. Displeased with *The Nazarene* and *The Apostle*, they were no happier with *East River*. Metro-Goldwyn-Mayer helped them little by paying heavily for screen rights[31] to the new novel, which shortly thereafter won Asch the Anisfield-Wolf Award for his handling of "racial relations."[32] Then Asch published two literary reminders, in Yiddish, that most of his fiction embodies a deep concern for Jewish ritual and custom: the first was *The Burning Bush*[33] —a volume of earlier ghetto stories, while the second was a two-volume compilation of such "Selected Works"[34] as "The Town," *Reb Shlomo Nagid*, and *Song of the Valley*.

Asch still resisted the pressure from friends and foes to write a "Holocaust" novel, a chore he found unbearable. But as he did wish to commemorate Poland's obliterated Jewish life, he brought together (in English this time) his early novella "The Town" and ten short stories he had written before, during, and after the Nazi slaughter. Titling them *Tales of My People*,[35] he dedicated them to "the Memory of the Jewish Children of Poland." Most of the tales have been discussed above. Several reveal the moral strength of Jews confronted by the Nazi horror; others are vignettes of Jews in America or Israel. Despite gusts of sentiment and moralizing, the stories catch the faith and dreams, the stubbornness and ironic humor that sustained beleaguered Jews through those troubled years.

Yet the dominant figure is less the Jew-as-victim than as wanderer or perennial refugee; torn between old beliefs and a changing world, the semi-acculturated Jew barely retains "a vague spiritual wholeness."[36] Valuing ceremony and inner life above time and place, he shrugs off danger with the expectation that God is watching. His inner tensions, however, pervade these eleven tales. So does an identical folk mood, with stylistic and tonal similarities outweighing differences between the earlier and later stories. In "The Town" Asch established the pattern: its nostalgic evocation of a static Polish riverbank *shtetl,* with its uncritical acceptance of ancient dogmas, its spare yet zestful cohesive life amid hostility and oppression, its Hasidic intimacy with God and awe of the dead, provided basic plot elements for the stories that follow.

In Asch's fiction even harsh events seldom appear grim. Many acts prove here more romantic than realistic, more didactic than dramatic. His eagerness to tailor a story to a moral point or exotic custom often drains his characters of individuality and reduces his narrative to a bare sketch. For instance, "Tricked," "The Dowry," and "A Divorce" are mere suggestive or skeletal additions to Asch's list of marital tales. The first two hinge on a surprise: in "Tricked,"[37] the bride confesses belatedly to a weak heart; in the other, a prideful groom and his father find the promised "dowry" is the bride's young orphaned sisters. Undaunted, the spoiled young scholar accepts his new responsibilities. The third tale, "A Divorce," has a loving husband and wife forced apart by law because they are childless; their plight enables Asch to attack again blind adherence to the law's letter rather than spirit.

His other seven stories probe Jewish bewilderment at a world gone mad. The idea that God may *not* be watching his embattled creatures was for many readers a theological commonplace, but for Asch it represented a sharp departure: never before had he hinted at a lack of heavenly concern. Not that Asch's Jews here doubt God's existence, but they fail to understand His allowing their senseless slaughter. Even the Nazi outrages can not make Asch go further. Yet he emphasizes anew the Jewish will to survive every bestial horror. In one death camp women prisoners even recognize the garments of loved ones. But people become used to anything, he writes; their ability to adjust is unlimited. In these women the will "to endure . . . had already overcome . . . every emotion that might have endangered their survival" ("Jewish Eyes," *Tales of My People,* p. 229).

Considering his sensitivity to the loss of the six million and his sentimental proclivities, Asch's lapses in emotional control are hardly surprising. Like all Yiddish writers, he feels caught between an old world a long time dying and a new one only dimly emerging. The interim too often confuses him, frightens him into needless moralizing and sentimentality—as in stories like "The Finger," "Mama," or "Jewish Eyes." In the last, the female stormtrooper leader, a woman who sleeps on mats of human hair and has lampshades of human skin, does not understand why the Americans are so upset by her gold-framed earrings. "They're only Jewish eyes," she informs the invaders. His point made, Asch can not resist spoiling a good story by moving from realism to bathos: the young victim's eyes are delivered to her in heaven by a dead G.I. Effective in different ways, the tale's reality and fantasy segments fail to become one. Yet even Asch's inferior stories, when brought together as here, still create a memorable folk ambience. His empathy and compassion for all men, including the most vile, transform these thin tales of Jewish travail into haunting comments on human vulnerabilitiy, comments that linger in and disturb the memory.

VI   "Miriam," Mother of Jesus

Many disgruntled Jewish readers were somewhat appeased by the "Jewishness" of *Tales of My People*, as well as that of *The Burning Bush* and of the "Selected Works" volumes. They found disquieting, however, the news that the heroine of Asch's forthcoming novel was to be "Miriam," the mother of Jesus. When *Mary* [38] appeared, in 1949, their worst fears were realized; many Jews found it the most "Christian" of his novels. But for Asch *Mary* formed with *The Nazarene* and *The Apostle* a two-thousand-page re-creation of early Jewish-Christian life that could crown his career as artist and prophet by bringing him the Nobel Prize. Even more compelling was his lifelong desire to reconcile Jacob and Esau. In *One Destiny* he had pointed to the Holocaust as proof that only when Jew and Christian recognized their common concern for morality and justice could the world be saved. Repeating this theme in "The Guilty Ones," he had argued there for a "bridge" of ideas and ideals between the faiths.

His exemplary intentions, however, engendered neither good fiction nor public approval. By war's end the personal attacks on him had lessened, but *Mary* bestirred old enemies and brought new ones. His "ecumenical" Jesus and Paul had pleased a few Jews and numerous Christians; here his Mary and Jesus angered many in both faiths. Asch's basic problem was his own Jewishness, his conviction that Jesus Christ derived from Jewish Messianic yearnings; that without synagogue audiences Paul could not have preached of the "Risen Lord"; that a devoutly Jewish childhood prepared Jesus for his cosmic role.[39]

Asch's Jesus is not the dying-and-ascending figure of Catholic liturgy and imagery; neither is he the wistful, aloof prophet untouched by the Higher Criticism, nor the benign culture hero of Renan or Emerson. He is the Rabbi Yeshua ben Joseph, a militantly devout Jew among Jews whom Christianity has expropriated from Israel. As such, he is neither "the first Jew nor the last," Alfred Kazin has pointed out, "to suffer for representing God not only as a person, but as an idea of human excellence."[40] In this guise he had haunted Asch for three decades; thus despite Jewish reluctance to accept as their own one in whose name so much Jewish blood had been spilled, Asch was determined to restore Jesus to Israel. He failed pathetically. Catholics were hardly impressed by a synagogue Christ. Among Protestants only the middle-class, church-social goers identified with this Rabbi Yeshua; to them he seemed a prophet spiritually larger, deeper than the protagonist of Lloyd Douglas's The Robe or of Frank Slaughter's The Crown and the Cross. Indeed, Yeshua did not seem to these Protestants very different, despite his synagogue background, from the Synoptic Gospels' hero—who also embodied the best Jewish and humanistic values.

These bookclub Christians provided the chief readership for the new novel. But Mary, intended by Asch to be both "prelude and postlude"[41] to his Jewish-Christian trilogy, turns out a thrice-told tale. Augmenting, altering, even contradicting many of his earlier impressions and conclusions, he here argues again that the Gospels exist primarily to reveal Israel's spiritual gift to the nations and its ties to Christianity.[42] More pastoral and lyric than The Nazarene or The Apostle, this novel is the least convincing of the three: its message seems extraneous, its ideas more obviously slanted. On the other hand, plot and setting are simpler than earlier, with no complicated Wandering Jew structure or minutely described Jerusalem riots or revolts. Its tone is the familar one of respectful piety, but its events lean more on miracle, as Yeshua's "divinity" is unabashedly asserted.

As for Mary, who is so little known historically, Asch freely extemporizes her biography. Yet her character and life posed serious challenges for him. Striving for a Jewish-Catholic-Protestant Mary who would appeal to all, he created a Mary who, like his Jesus, antagonized many of each faith. Most of the writings on Mary have been by Catholics, and these, according to his editor, Earle Balch,[43] had a strong influence on his thinking. Viewing her, in terms of the Messianic events, as the prime link between earth and heaven, Asch enlarged her role beyond the point acceptable to most Protestants. But Catholics disliked his attributing other children to her, and many Jews agreed with an angry Maurice Samuel, his longtime translator, that Asch, in his eagerness to plant Christian roots in Jewish history, had succumbed to Mariolatry;[44] he had erred also, they believed, in depicting Jesus as having "freed" some Jews of the Mosaic laws. Asch rejected such criticisms. God's choice of a Jewish mother for the Christian Messiah (and of the devout Joseph as earthly father), he argued, underscored the Christian debt to Judaism. And, admittedly, his Mary is a tender, frequently perceptive and intuitive portrait; his sympathy for her is unqualified, his attitude reverential. Not surprisingly, she emerges (the miraculous birth aside) a traditional Jewish mother obsessed with protecting her child. Only when her defenses are overcome do the fated events unfold.

Here narration proves as thorny as characterization. In *The Nazarene* Asch was given a universal figure without parallel; Jesus' actions and teachings, his disciples and enemies lent themselves to historical, as well as imaginative, probing and analysis. But Mary is significant primarily as the mother of this vital figure. Dramatically, her life is a reflected one, with her joys and pains those of spectator. Relying upon Scripture, especially Luke, Asch adapts every detail related to her. The Gospels had served him well previously by providing a lifeline for an adult Jesus and Paul. For Mary they offered little guidance, causing Asch to "enlarge" more than before, to dip more deeply not only into his imagination but into Catholic tradition and folklore. The result, as one reviewer put it, is "a careful, reverent sugar-sweet assembly of Apocrypha."[45] Most effective are the early events, those closest to Mary: the Annunciation, her betrothal to Joseph, the Bethlehem journey and starlit birth in the stable—as well as family life in a carpenter's cottage. With simple cadences and rich, sensuous images, Asch evokes a Nazareth nestling amid Galilee's valleys;

knowingly and sympathetically he presents the inhabitants' customs, dress, and foods, their skills and burdens, their tensions and hopes, and, above all, their reluctance to acknowledge a simple townsman as the awaited Messiah.

Galilean life emerges as stark, precarious, and vibrant, but Asch is concerned less with historical accuracy than with his heroine's character. To him she is not "Mary" but "Miriam,"[46] and the modest cottage she shares with her mother, the pious widow Hannah, is a haven for all who enter. Like many young women of the House of David, Miriam yearns to bear Israel's Messiah. A gentle, devout girl, she prays constantly for deliverance from this proud delusion. Preparing to introduce his "miracles," Asch hedges them about with psychological rationalizations. If he grants, for instance, that Jesus is conceived by the Holy Ghost upon a young virgin, he suggests that her feverish devotions cause her to see visions and hear voices; these same devotions move God to select her to bear His anointed one. Hence Miriam's prayers produce both psychological and divine results. Then shortly before her marriage to Joseph ben Jacob, Miriam has an angelic visitor who voices the Annunciation: She will bear a son conceived by the Holy Spirit to be called Yeshua, and "he shall reign over the House of Jacob forever, and of his kingdom there shall be no end . . ." (39). Thus Asch moves freely between the "real" and fanciful, the given and imagined. He may draw deeply, therefore, from Jewish occult lore (as when he describes Satan's efforts to prevent Yeshua's birth); or, he may exercise his imagination to expand a traditional scene—a memorable instance being that in which Miriam sings the Magnificat in the mountain retreat of Elisheva (Elizabeth) and the mute Zachariah. When she "magnifies" the Lord, the cave seems charged with the supernatural. Her listeners scarcely move. An exultant Zachariah alone dares break the ensuing silence; tearing the curtain from the cave entrance, he "bellows to the mountains the inhuman cry of the dumb. It faded, inarticulate and echo-borne, from range to range—the first annunciation to the world of the Messiah's coming" (78-79).

Neither father—that is, neither Zachariah nor Joseph—proves a dominant figure. For Asch, feminine nature is nearer to creation and truth than is the masculine, and in his fiction no relationship is more strongly asserted than that of mother and son. Beside this elementary bond the male, as lover or father, wanders timid and directionless. Joseph offers example. Of the Davidic line, he is still a gentle, humble man who defers to wife and "son" in all matters, and who, like so many among the poor, awaits the savior foretold by Isaiah. This savior will deliver Israel from her captors, promulgate a new law, and establish a new convenant between God and humanity. "Salvation is for all," rich or poor, learned or ignorant, Joseph declares, "or for none" (144). Dismayed at the ugly gossip about Miriam before their marriage, he bears silently the humiliation of his strange parenthood. Unable to understand Miriam's joy in her conception, he refuses to question her. When God does reveal the divine plan, Joseph asks only: "How shall I thank Thee . . . that Thou hast found me worthy to be a guardian to her?" (54). Feeling himself outside the sacred mystery, he strains to fulfill his "obligation" by helping Yeshua through the formative years. But Joseph here, as in the Bible, fails to emerge fully from history's shadows.

He is overshadowed again by his wife, her son, and the divine events. Wishing to center upon Miriam, Asch enmeshes her in her son's life and probes endlessly her reactions to his unfolding destiny. Yet inevitably Yeshua, in his growing self-awareness, usurps the narrative. Recognizing his mother's compassion for all that lives, he foresees she will prove man's intermediary with God, for not even the Lord can prevail against her tears. Miriam calls him *tinoki* ("little one"), dresses him in spotless white linen, and sets him apart from his brothers and sister—the children she bears Joseph;[47] their natural births contrast for her the "unfathomable character" of her firstborn.

Moving through Yeshua's uncharted childhood, Asch is hardpressed to depict convincingly the Messiah-to-be as both human and divine, as Son of God and schoolboy, playmate, brother. He tries to trace the youth's first stirrings of "uniqueness,"[48] to imagine Yeshua's early, scarcely conscious tapping of his awesome powers. But he decides that it is the boy's insatiable curiosity and charismatic personality that primarily distinguish him from his compeers. At first, mother and child here are as one. At thirteen, however, Yeshua senses his Messiahship and the problems begin for Joseph's family. Recalling Yeshua's strange birth, his townsmen now resent his questioning of the Law, his quixotic tales and parables, his improvising on the Prophets, and (galling in a carpenter's son) his immaculate linen garb. A few perceive the man to come, but most foretell a tragic end. Even his brothers are discomfited by Yeshua's Messianic intimations. Miriam defends him. "Your ways are the ways of the quest, of groping in darkness," she tells her younger sons. "His is the way of the unerring guide" (387).

His "way" causes Yeshua to discover quickly a world in pain. He sees a sacked city's pitiful remnants, slaves shackled and bullied until they drop, and ruthless tax collectors bleeding the poor. He rejects Satan's blandishments in the wilderness and witnesses the depraved rites of Baal and Astarte; in Jerusalem, he observes the high priesthood collaborating with Rome, the senseless Temple sacrifices, and the Holy City's pitiful outcasts. Despite all, Yeshua rejects the view that all men sin and merit punishment; yet each encounter leaves its mark on him. In time Miriam's courage fails and she refuses to grant Yeshua "permission" to begin his ministry. If her son partakes of the divine, she cries, she is but flesh and blood, and she will not surrender him. Only after Mother Rachel (in a vision) accuses her of blocking man's redemption does Miriam free Yeshua for his mission.

To this point, most of the actions belong to Yeshua rather than Miriam; these lead Asch back across ground covered in *The Nazarene* or *The Apostle* and tempt him to augment and modify his earlier materials. But Yeshua's later movements are filtered through his mother, causing the narrative to resemble, as Milton Rugoff suggests, a play whose main action occurs offstage—with one player, not the major one, acting her role at center stage.[49] Climactic scenes are reported indirectly, in fragmented, impressionistic passages. Yet these elliptical sketches repeatedly prove as effective as the earlier detailed portraits. Again, Miriam, her role thus enlarged, is present at critical moments, with or without scriptural sanction; Asch even brings her to Gethsemane to see the arrest—as well as, of course, to Calvary to witness the final agonies. Conquering her revulsion, Miriam climbs the crest to meet her son's gaze and to cry, "Tinoki, tinoki, tinoki!" In reply, Yeshua moans, "Emi" (Mother) and dies. Miriam rallies her son's scattered followers, and when, in the final scene, Yeshua reappears to his grieving apostles, she is the first to see him.

VII   A New Storm

Protestant clergymen led in praising the new novel, with some popular reviewers close behind. Edmund Fuller, for instance, hailed the entire Asch trilogy as "an epic work in the grand tradition" that was equaled among Biblical re-creations only by

Thomas Mann's *Joseph* tetralogy.[50] A cooler appraisal, however, may well find *Mary* to be often lucid, tender, and even touching, but it should also recognize signs of the author's fatigue and flagging interest. The final sections in particular offer evidence of a writer too long with one subject. After developing in detail Yeshua's boyhood, Asch, rather than continue to create new events, skips to scenes he has described in the previous novels. He also reveals his waning inspiration by relying unduly on dreams or "visions"—all of which are clumsily set forth in a maudlin, over-ripe prose. Thus he can take Miriam and Yeshua through a meticulously observed Sabbath, only to dissolve the realism into a painfully gauche "vision" wherein Miriam is confronted by Old Testament figures.[51] Too often, in fact, Asch's fatigue is compounded by his sentimental anxiety to link Jewish and Christian traditions.

Such lapses not only trace a lessening auctorial discipline and control, but they help to explain Jewish distaste for *Mary*. Jewish hostility toward Asch, somewhat diminished during the war, now flared anew. Mere months before *Mary* appeared Asch had published, as preface to *Tales of My People*, his moving dedication to Hitler's victims. The flames, he there wrote, could destroy only the Jew's "physical substance," not his "spiritual essence."[52] But in the clamor that greeted *Mary*, reviewers and public wits chose to ignore his Holocaust tales and sentiments. Sholem Asch lamenting martyred Jews was hardly news; his fictionalizing the mother of Jesus was. Speakers on all levels again had an easy target. Even entertainer George Jessel, a professed longtime Asch admirer, won a laugh from his audience at Hollywood's Temple Israel by claiming that had he not known *Mary* to be by the author of "Mottke Gonif and other great folk tales," he would have guessed it produced "by order of a Spanish Inquisitor in the fifteenth century who stood behind Reb Asch [sic] and guided his quill."[53] Asch, a man of large ego who relished recognition and praise, bled from such criticism.

Critical reaction in Britain and Israel was, as with his earlier novels, calmer than in America, where Asch again received several punishing blows. Most painful, perhaps, was the open break with Maurice Samuel, who had refused to translate *Mary*. Between them there had long been what Samuel termed "a tug of war." Asch repeatedly had been annoyed at the praise garnered by Samuel for the success of his novels in English. Samuel, for his part, had been displeased with their financial arrangements and the difficulties posed by what he considered Asch's stylistic crudities. "I wanted certain passages changed," he later admitted, "because I couldn't translate them and make them sound real. Sometimes I got my way, sometimes not. At one point I refused to translate . . . [*Mary*] and he had it done by someone else. . . . I argued with him on artistic grounds, but he wouldn't yield, and here our divergence was so wide that I gave it up. I thought *The Nazarene* and . . . [*The Apostle*] were good books, but *Mary*, besides being sloppily constructed, went off into a kind of Mariolatry that I couldn't stand."[54] Earlier, in a 1948 letter to Asch, Samuel had spelled out his disappointment in the new manuscript.

It baffles me that you should consider the book a contribution to better understanding between Jews and Christians. I am painfully certain that the Book, if published as it stands, will do two things, increase anti-Jewish feeling and bring your name into disrepute. I don't want to see either of these things done. . . . In *The Nazarene* and *The Apostle* you took the more or less neutral stand that Jesus came for the gentiles, not for the Jews. In this book you say flatly that Jesus came to liberate the Jews from the "rabbis and scholars." In the earlier books you were rooted in the developing Jewish traditions. But in *Mary* you make it appear that the Jewish law and ethics become petrified after Moses. [55]

Deeply hurt by what he felt to be Samuel's misreading of his intent, Asch refused to alter his approach.

To his credit, Samuel, despite their differences, continued to defend Asch against the accusations of apostasy and greed. "Those who charged Asch with apostasy," he later wrote in his autobiography, "usually added that in his New Testament novels he had also sinned for money; he had deliberately descended from his natural level. . . . To one who knew Asch personally, the charge is silly. . . . He had a massive conception of himself as an artist, and developed a deep grievance as year after year went by without bringing him the Nobel Prize. To him his New Testament novels were more than literary masterpieces; they were a Messianic attempt to reconcile Jewry and Christendom."[56] The two soon made peace, and Samuel then translated Asch's *Moses* (1951) and *Passage in the Night* (1953).

Obviously, Asch's fiction must stand or fall on its merits. That poor judgment and taste, and even worse timing, flawed much of it hardly need again be argued. But special external factors did intensify Asch's literary shortcomings. His excessive moralizing and sentimentality, for instance, may be blamed, at least in part, on his Yiddish readership in America; it was a readership typified by those who looked to the *Jewish Daily Forward* for their fiction and who expected a tug at the heart. For years Asch catered unabashedly to these readers, with a subsequent loss in subtlety of style and tone. Even when this readership was denied him, he could not forgo old habits. In addition, he was a man of strong will and convictions who resented bitterly the attitude many gentiles and Jews, especially the latter, took toward his New Testament novels. "The Jews want it both ways," he once flared angrily. "They refuse to hear the story of Jesus yet boast that Jesus was a Jew."[57] Thus he refused to alter his style in any way that could be interpreted as a concession to his critics. He was also saddened, as Maurice Samuel realized, by the annihilation of his Yiddish readership in Europe, especially of his beloved Polish Jews. "He wrote his later works with a deliberate view to translation," Samuel noted, "knowing he would have few Yiddish readers, and therefore such style as he had deteriorated."[58]

Another likely contributor to his weakness for purple prose was his feeling of writing increasingly for an undiscriminating bookclub audience. Earle Balch, the Putnam editor who helped prepare for English publication several of his translated manuscripts, has recalled the novelist's dissatisfaction with the final chapters of *Mary*. Asch even tried to rework these chapters in his "somewhat inadequate English," then giving them to Balch for a final polish. The two were struggling to remove the inconsistencies between *Mary* and *The Nazarene* when Asch handed Balch a completely new treatment of the Crucifixion; the editor was dismayed to find the originally restrained description now marked by "blood and color and purple passages." Had Asch been looking, Balch asked, at a reproduction of El Greco's "Crucifixion"? He had. Tactfully, Balch hinted that the new version seemed too emotional, too highly colored. "Schmaltz, eh?" laughed Asch, and returned to his first version.[59]

Asch failed to eliminate enough "schmaltz" to save *Mary* from being one of his lesser works, but he was never guilty of an old charge his critics now leveled again—that he submitted before publication his "Jesus books" to Christian clergymen for their suggested changes. Earle Balch has denied the allegation, and Maurice Samuel, who was perhaps in an even better position to know (at least for *The Nazarene* and *The Apostle*), also discredits this claim: "As he could have done this only after I had made the translations, and as I didn't see any changes in my translation, I know the statement to be a lie."[60] Yet this unjust slur, like so many others, is occasionally still heard.

Chapter 9
On The Move Again

In 1950 Sholem Asch turned seventy. His best work was behind him, and so were the "Christological" novels that his critics claimed had marked his departure from Jewish thought and life. To prove such allegations false, Asch determined to confine himself in his last years to Jewish subjects and figures. He soon had three novels in progress—and they would turn out to be his last. Almost complete was one on the lawgiver Moses that he had been writing for several years. In rough draft was a contemporary story of a hard-driving tycoon torn by guilt for a youthful misdeed. In outline was a narrative on the most elusive of Old Testament prophets, the Second Isaiah. Each novel continued a familiar theme, and each, Asch hoped, would help disprove the charges of his apostasy. But an even more compelling motive behind his renewed concern with Jewishness was the lingering pain at loss of his primary readership—his beloved Polish Jews, as well as those of Rumania, Hungary, Russia, Lithuania, Latvia, and Austria. Their slaughter had blunted his spirit. Too wracked to undertake a Holocaust novel, he nevertheless could not, as already seen, leave the tragedy alone; in tale, sketch, and essay he returned to the horror. Only years after his death would novelists, in particular Andre Schwartz-Bart and Elie Wiesel, manage to equal his anguished reactions to the Nazi death camps.

But he was heartened in this dark period by a newly restored edition of *Salvation*,[1] his novel of Hasidic life that most critics considered his finest work. Perhaps he hoped *Salvation* would combine with his new novels to reclaim many affronted Jewish readers; if so, he must have written his last works with added urgency and haste. He also must have garnered some satisfaction from the public recognition of his seventieth birthday. The New York press, for instance, marked the occasion with several interviews, and in one John K. Hutchens described Asch as still "vigorous looking, with grey-white hair, a lined, strong face, and a vibrant voice."[2] But he looked better than he felt, especially as he considered these last years to have been "poisoned" by the

188

unceasing attacks, professional and personal, from self-appointed Jewish arbiters. Always eager to present his side, he responded quickly to reporters' questions about Jewish hostility, the recurrent rumors of his apostasy, and the claim that his forthcoming novel was a belated grasp for Jewish favor.

The charges were all falsely based, he replied. His plans for *Moses*—like those for *The Nazarene, The Apostle,* and *Mary*— dated back to his 1906 Palestine trip. Even then Moses, as did Jesus, challenged his imagination; these two teachers together, he felt, had created "the Judaic-Christian idea" which has so influenced the present world.[3] Indeed his belief in the "common roots" of the two faiths stemmed from his earliest reflections. "I have never thought of Judaism and Christianity separately," he stated. "For me it is one culture and one civilization, on which all our peace, our security and our freedom are dependent." Yet he was, he made clear, no apostate; never had he done anything to justify the rumor that he had left the Jewish religion. "I am a Jewish writer, a writer of the Jewish spirit." If he was also a "religious" writer, he added, it was in the same sense that Rembrandt and El Greco were religious artists.[4]

Having had his public say, Asch returned to Connecticut to complete his new novel and to help Matilda with plans for a new home in Florida.

I The Move to Miami Beach

Deciding to spend their last years in a warm clime, the Asches sold the Stamford house in 1951 and moved to Miami Beach. Awaiting them was a two-cottage home, built to their design, that sat on one of the man-made islands reached via the causeway linking city and beach. Their furniture, books, and paintings, their religious and art objects, had forced them to add a seafront "cottage" and large study to the small house originally planned. Asch even had a private dock, where he would sit, fishingpole in hand, and be viewed from the cruising excursion boats. Tourists gaped as megaphoned guides enumerated the literary accomplishments of the renowned Sholem Asch. But Sholem and Matilda, as they gazed through their large windows at the lush lawn and flowers, at the sunbathed trees and blue-green bay, and at night at the Biscayne Islands skyline, must have mused on the distance they had travelled from Kutno and Warsaw.

Amid this casual ease Asch completed *Moses* and began

collecting material on the 1925-26 Florida land boom to use in *A Passage in the Night* (which he called "Grossman and Son"). Under the Florida sun he relaxed somewhat, even adding some occasional golf to his leisurely fishing efforts. Reporters found him the familiar, expansive international man of letters who was as always eager to voice appreciation of his adopted country and its gifts. "Freedom is like health," he told one interviewer, "you do not appreciate it till it is gone. Here in America the young people take it as a matter of course. But we, who are old, who have lived under the Czars, who have seen our friends and families destroyed at Buchenwald or tortured by the Communists, we never take it for granted. In America every breath you draw is a breath of freedom. In how many countries today can that be said?"[5] Such comments, although sincere, were for the public record; in private, he lamented bitterly the hostility that had followed him even to relaxed Miami. Not that the resort city lacked Asch admirers; these stared at him in restaurants, stopped him in street and store for autographs or to introduce their children. One fellow even rushed over to kiss the great man's hand.[6] Some wished to reminisce with Asch about Poland and the old days and ways; for them his Mottke the Thief, Reb Shlomo Nagid, and Yechiel the Psalm Jew were cherished friends. Such pleasant encounters were reassuring, but the tirades from local Jewish papers and pulpits cut deeply. Most painful was an abortive attempt by "Yiddish-speaking extremists" to assault him on the street. Asch declined to file charges,[7] but suddenly Miami seemed menacing and remote.

No longer young, their children and grandchildren scattered, Sholem and Matilda, despite a wide circle of Miami acquaintances, felt lonely. Letters, a phone call, and telegraphed fare to California brought son Nathan for a warm reunion, cozy morning coffee talks, and relished moments of "profound understanding."[8] But old tensions and resentments surfaced quickly. Nathan Asch had struggled for years to make it as a writer; a respected companion of Hemingway, Josephine Herbst, Robert McAlmon, and Morley Callaghan,[9] he could not repress resentment at his parents' luxury and comfort; nor could he accept his father's treating him, at fifty, like a child. "Perhaps it was confronting both these elements," he later recalled, "that got my visit off to a bad start. My father, after greeting me tenderly, took me for a ride with him in his new automobile, and passing a golf course, said, 'Wait for me.' He then disappeared to play a few holes of golf, while I, who had just travelled thousands of miles to see him, sat waiting in the car."

Soon their disputes, essentially trivial but frequent, culminated in a bitter exchange:

At that moment my father came in. On his face was all the anger I had come to know through the years. . . . "You hate me," he said. "You have always hated me." "You're talking nonsense," I replied. "You know that I don't hate you, or I wouldn't have come all the way out here. Only you have been acting very strange—treating me as if I were a child. I am wondering why you asked me to come.". . . . "I don't want my friends to think you've suddenly run off," my father continued. "You'll have to stay here, and we'll both have to control ourselves, until the day of your flight."
I didn't like that. . . . I was disappointed. The image of my father crumbled a little: he was less. But we got along better after that. [10]

Later Sholem Asch would declare that no writer can possibly tell the truth about the relations between people.

II   Moses, a Fallible Prophet

As Asch settled into his new home, his latest novel came off the press. But this time even those who expected his every Biblical narrative to attack the Jewish tradition found they had little to fear: *Moses* [11] neither enhanced nor diminished the tradition. Several reviewers then dismissed it as a belated attempt to placate Jewish readers.[12] The charge was unfair, for if Asch did hope the book would win back some former admirers, he in no way repudiated those views that had won him his enemies. He again made clear his dislike of those practices that derived from the Mosaic letter rather than spirit. Still he did wish to emphasize Judaism's positive aspects; in fact, he here expressed anew his obsessive conviction that the Jews remained, as a Catholic reviewer observed, "the channel for redemption to the world."[13]

But the most parochial readers, Jews or Christians, should have found in *Moses* nothing heretical or scandalous: Jesus is not mentioned, not even in the visionary promises of a redeemer-king. Some traditionalists may have been annoyed by the schizophrenic Moses confronting them; eager to imbue his hero with the luster of the ages, Asch had borrowed qualities from a mélange of mythic and legendary figures. Other readers probably resented Asch's felt need to rationalize the Pentateuch's more "primitive" aspects and to square God and Moses with modern anthropology and archeology. (He had been stung several times by past criticism for having ignored such findings.) Many Christians and Jews also must have found tiresome here his attempts, yet again, to bridge the

many gaps between their faiths. Yet Asch, to his credit, saw in the
Exodus an epic (even mythic) tale that refused reduction to idle
memory or dated history. Man's need to wrest—with God's
help—freedom and order from fate, nature, and other men
remained, he realized, a theme rich in symbol and allusion.

He tries to enclose his narrative in a double frame—that of
the religious novel and his personal view of history. His reach, as
usual, exceeds his grasp, and his hero emerges blurred, fuzzy-
edged, remote. But Asch can place partial blame on intractable
material: the Biblical Moses is a bare, stylized, lore-encrusted
figure who at life's end proves as inscrutable as in youth. His few
personal traits flash too briefly to make humanizing him easy. An
indomitable seeker of justice, an exalted prophet and shrewd
legalist, he remains a fallible creature of anger and humility,
impatience and perseverance, tenderness and harsh decision. Great
deeds and intense sufferings can not render him a Son of God or
Redeemer in the Christian sense.[14] When his followers—long
enslaved and then intimidated by wilderness and freedom—back-
slide into rebellion and idolatry, Moses laments his thankless task
of mediator between a jealous God and stiffnecked people. Asch
seeks for his Moses the human touches that the Bible chroniclers
thought extraneous, and he does fashion—but only at times—an
admirable, falcon-eyed hero intent upon hammering a slave rabble
into a nation.

Asch may intend, as some critics charged, to impress his Jewish
readers, but if so he still reveals no desire to minimize Hebrew
failings;[15] nor does his shift from New to Old Testament change his
style or method. Paraphrasing and amplifying the broad narrative
line from Exodus through Deuteronomy, he speculates on much
that the Bible compresses: Egyptian religious practices, Hebrew
family life, and the slowly forged spirituality separating the
wanderers from pagan neighbors. Abraham had pledged the
Hebrews to a God visible in His works; Moses has them reject
tribal vagaries for a divine law by which their offspring and those of
other nations will live for centuries. Belaboring this point, Asch
selects, explains, and condenses the Old Testament legal codes, to
emphasize, as always, the law's spirit rather than letter. Indeed,
his denigrating of legalist or priestly attitudes toward worship
moves him to his sharpest deviation from Scripture. Exodus,
Leviticus, and Numbers present the Jewish priesthood as a
sacramental body consecrated at God's command to enforce

worship and ritual. Nothing in those books suggests that the laws of diet and sacrifice result from the pressures of self-serving priests. Nor does the Moses-Aaron relationship posit, except by extension and hindsight, the inevitable clash of priest and prophet, of tradition and ethics. Yet Asch makes ritual and sacrifice mere priestly devices, concessions wrung from a reluctant Moses by an ambitious Aaron, aided by a superstitious, semi-barbaric tribal horde.

Asch gropes for abiding meanings behind his parochial images. But the shaping into convincing fiction of the rich myth and legend embedded in the scriptural narrative, as well as in the folk compilations like the *Haggadah* and *Midrash*, is beyond him; he knows and uses these collections, but he can not approximate their poetic irony and folk humor, their grasp of human absurdity and glory. He lacks the imaginative instinct for the interplay of inner and outer realities that enables Thomas Mann to fashion serious literature from the Joseph lore. To compensate, Asch tries to link legend and history by dating, localizing, and "documenting" his events; in the process he repeatedly cleans up, tones down, and explains away bothersome miracles and incidents. All this "modernizing" is aimed, apparently, at a postulated sophisticated reader who accepts only miracles made rational or logical. To underline his every moral point, Asch not only intrudes in his own voice but he has Moses speak endlessly. Still, his depiction of the timeless encounter of Creator and created diminishes neither the divine presence nor the human cry for a close, almost familial, intimacy. Here righteousness not love is, quite accurately, the Hebrew's prime motive force; thus evil and evildoers are punished quickly and without apology. Much more time, suffering, and wisdom will be needed, Asch makes clear, before nomadic shepherds can accept a God of love.

Asch fails again, however, to grasp the implications of his ideas; his rejection, for instance, of communal acts guarded by ritual, taboo, and punishment could have deprived Judaism (or any religion) of all but the most rudimentary symbolic forms. Yet weak logic is hardly his sole fault. Amid a confused ambience of pagan sex and naive piety, he mingles realism, miracle, and fantasy, in a misguided effort to conciliate the devout who read the Bible as history and the skeptical who view it as myth. The Old Testament does hold simultaneous overlays of history and allegory, of the rational and supernatural, of the late and primitive. But so vividly and freely did these elements exist in the minds of Bible chroniclers that they flow into narrative unity; in Asch they remain visible, disparate, and obvious—with all motives expressed in block letters of ambition, jealousy, envy, and revenge.

Compounding these faults is his style, never an Asch strong point. Straining for a stately rhetoric, he achieves a stuffily reverential prose reminiscent of bad organ music and dull religious tracts. Even his more vigorous images are buried under a relentless flow of adjective and metaphor dredged from a simplistic reduction of history to pageants and mob scenes. Yet, as always, dismissing even a bad Asch novel is difficult. Leslie Fiedler, after pinpointing lapses of style and taste in *Moses*, declares that "it may be taken as tribute to the power of the Biblical story over a writer who has some real relation to it that Asch manages to survive purely literary objections."[16] Fiedler's response is understandable, but a greater familiarity with Asch's fiction would have lessened his surprise: every Asch novel somehow "survives purely literary objections." Each, like *Moses*, proves enough better than the sum of its flaws to engender some critical retraction or qualification. Also, as Fiedler suggests, neither bogus solemnity nor posturing figures can obscure the ancient tale's appeal—an appeal here reinforced by Asch's impassioned conviction, repeated endlessly, that the price of redemption and of love of God and neighbor is a high one and one to be paid by each generation.

Several other positive qualities merit mention. Ignoring dates and data on occasion, Asch, with Talmudic zeal, then delves into textual exegesis to strike an inner symbol or meaning. In addition, his harassed tribesmen, stumbling en masse under desert sun and in sandblown darkness, convey both sweep and force. And if the cumulative physical detail proves tiring, it also forms a pointed, suggestive backdrop for people and events. To judge by newspaper reviews and booksales, many readers found in the lengthy travail of Moses and his followers some trace of reverential shudder or catharsis. So if at times he trivializes the Exodus—its language, mood, and spirit—Asch still manages to "bootleg" into the reader's unconscious, as Fiedler puts it, a measure of "archetypal resonance."[17]

III   Guilt and Old Age

Asch completed his next novel despite personal hurts and his growing discontent with life in America. The setting of *A Passage in the Night*[18] is modern, but its axiom is pseudo-Biblical: God forgives a man's sins against Him but not those against another person; the victim alone can do that. Published in 1953, the same year as Saul Bellow's *The Adventures of Augie March*, Asch's novel, with its echoes of William Dean Howells' *The Rise of Silas Lapham* and Theodore Dreiser's "The Old Neighborhood," seems decades older. Critic Maxwell Geismar who, incredibly, disliked *Augie March* and admired *A Passage in the Night*, described the latter as a "realistic" novel possessing the "wisdom and perspective of long experience"; it was, he claimed, "almost Dreiserian in tone and content."[19] Had he meant by "Dreiserian" an indulged liking for chance, sentiment, and melodrama, Geismar would have been close to the truth.

Asch borrows a figure he had worn thin in *Uncle Moses* and *Chaim Lederer's Return*, as well as in several other narratives: the driving, morally confused entrepreneur displaced in old age by a son or young kinsman. The reader is stirred not only to symbol-mongering thoughts of Fisher King and Osiris-Horus and Oedipus, of King Lear and Père Goriot, but to suspicions of Freudian sublimations—by a fading author confronted by an ambitious novelist son. Asch does not allow these mythic possibilities clear expression, and he could counter the "Freudian" insinuation by pointing out that he had used the father-son struggle when still a young writer. Yet his stubborn reiterating of this plot idea makes it temptingly suggestive, and at first it works well for him here. As always, Asch is at his best in time past. By flashbacks he retraces effectively his elderly hero's climb to success and slackening devotion to God and Torah. His approach also enables him to describe again a greenhorn generation's thrust into American life and to reintroduce his familiar panoply of East Side streets, shops, and pushcarts—with their ethnic mix of Jews and Catholics. But now he augments these groups with a slight sprinkle of New England Protestants. Yet whether in New York or Florida or Connecticut, Asch's befuddled little people grope anew for moral and social verities to replace discarded earlier ones.

Four Grossman generations move through this family chronicle. Shamaya Grossman, the zealot patriarch, dies early. His obsession was with God, whereas his son Isaac offers worship only to ambition. Success as a hotel tycoon comes early to Isaac, but with few joys. His wife and son and their stylish friends render him a stranger in his own lavish home and reduce him to a comic pretense of being better, richer, more aristocratic than he feels. He resists only their constant pressure to reject his early life and values. Thus time present finds Isaac Grossman an aging widower who clings to his past by contributing to radical causes and visiting the old neighborhood synagogue. Recalling his father's warning that the thief who fails to repay his victim merits divine punishment, Grossman grows convinced that his soul is in pawn to a man from whom in youth he had stolen. Desperate for a small sum to launch his business career, he had failed to return twenty-seven dollars lost by Yan Kovalsky, a forlorn little Polish drunkard. The deed has soured his life. He has since wounded scores of others in his push to success, but Grossman gives them no thought: they tried to do the same to him. Only the lost Kovalsky weighs on his conscience.

Penance for Grossman proves difficult. Opportunists seize on his guilt feelings to bilk and blackmail him, while his son and family friends, convinced Kovalsky never existed, accuse him of hallucinating. And if the victim were real? "Everyone . . . has a Kovalsky," declares one friend, "to whom we can't make restitution." Forget him. Grossman cannot forget, so the family hires psychiatrists who use his mental depression to place him in a sanatorium. There he ponders a paradox: his lifelong cravings for power had brought success, recognition, dignity; his single impulse toward remorse and atonement has led to shame, dislocation, disappointment. His commitment strikes him as a just punishment.

Asch is taxed to stretch his parable beyond the small theft at its center. Tolstoy or Dostoevsky would have shaped this peccadillo into a morality play redolent of guilt and atonement. Lacking their disciplined intellect or style, Asch fails to infuse either characters or plot with adequate substance and subtlety. Still his thesis, if simplistic, seems fair: moral indulgence leads to suffering; moral strength, penitence, and good works alone offer redemption and peace. But what credibility he has managed to sustain deteriorates when he rejects modern psychiatric practices for a glib pop-Freudian pseudo-religion he calls "spiritual psychotherapy." Armed with this tortured mélange of diagnosis and treatment, he dismisses all medical men as benighted latterday priests who consider only themselves proper guides for the psyche's dark journey. Misinterpreting Grossman's personality and needs, they force him to suffer and languish until an intuitive rabbi (a veritable teacher saint), called in by the hero's idealistic grandson, helps the old man exorcise his ghost and win vindication.

Interestingly enough, Grossman's "hunger for integrity,"[20] repeatedly voiced, and his concern about personal enemies and unfulfilled goals hint again at authorial yearnings. But Asch does not permit even these hints to become specific. Nor has he allowed the years to alter his code hero: Isaac Grossman is but one more ruthless Asch activist humbled by age, a delayed conscience, and the inevitable mother complex (fed here by a selfless secretary). Equally familiar are his tiresome moralists (rabbis, grandchildren, gentile wives, storekeeper-Talmudists) and especially his grasping opportunists (doctors, lawyers, sons, businessmen) who lack not merely scruples but sense. Yet, if not examined closely, the story often moves briskly. Not only is America's confused absorption of its Jewish immigrants depicted sensitively, but so is its erratic assimilation of its Polish newcomers. In addition, Asch is given here to numerous balanced moments between polar figures—father and son, rabbi and priest, physician and patient, lawyer and client. If contrived, some confrontations still achieve dramatic resonance. But even these small encounters generally aim at reemphasizing the need for Jewish-Christian unity. Finally, Asch sounds a rare personal political note: through Lazar Grossman, Isaac's son, Asch evaluates the 1930's Depression to reveal himself a Roosevelt New Dealer.

IV   Driven from America

In 1945, when presenting his books at Yale, Asch extolled an America that twice had provided him "a safe nest."[21] No longer would this country, he then declared, be merely a temporary home for him or his children and grandchildren. Yet for Asch himself it proved just that. The war and the Nazi crematoria had stirred in him yearnings for Israel, the Jewish homeland, while here the unrelenting personal attacks literally drove him from the country. Abraham Cahan, for instance, not only refused to publish his work in the *Forward* but convinced other Yiddish newspapers to boycott him. Only the *Morning Freiheit*, a Marxist paper, offered him space, and when he accepted some Yiddish journalists then castigated him as a Communist sympathizer. The most bitter criticism was in an article by Alexander Mukdoiny, whom Asch years before had angered by refusing to recommend him to the *Forward;* he had explained then that the theater-and-book reviewing chores Mukdoiny coveted were handled by Abraham

Cahan himself. Mukdoiny's article later followed Asch to Israel. Of
more immediate concern to the novelist in the early 1950's was
Senator Joseph McCarthy, then hitting his stride as Chairman of
the House Committee on Un-American Activities. Several times
McCarthy summoned Asch, who for decades had attacked Marxism
in fiction and essay, to discuss his *Freiheit* connection. "Somewhere
I had to be printed," Asch declared repeatedly. "After all, I'm a
Yiddish writer. And when the *Morning Freiheit* opened her pages
for me, I accepted. After all, America was at that time allied with
the Communists against Nazism. But after the war, when the
relations between East and West became sharper, I stopped
writing for the *Freiheit*." [22]

The Yiddish newspaper boycott and the McCarthy hearings, the
Jewish press-and-pulpit hostility, the appearance of English of
Herman (Chaim) Lieberman's hostile book, and the attempted
street assault in Miami Beach all took their toll. In fall 1953 the
sturdy, reliable Matilda, complaining suddenly of ill health, sailed
for Nice, with Asch soon following. At New York's Gotham Hotel,
prior to boarding the *Queen Elizabeth*, he told reporters he would
stay abroad until his wife felt better. No, he did not intend to surrender his American citizenship or to settle abroad. "That doesn't
mean," he smiled, "that I have to come back to Miami Beach. That's
not America." [23] He neglected to mention that he had been sending
letters to Israel, inquiring of friends and officials about possible
public reaction to his settling there. Yet at several less public gatherings he had admitted, and rather dramatically, that his move was
indeed permanent. "I am returning to England with a broken
heart," he then declared. "Intolerance among my own race has been
too much of a handicap for me to work." This parting sally did not
go unchallenged; indeed four years later, at Asch's death, Jewish
journalists were still replying to it. [24]

For the next three years, from winter 1953 to winter 1956, the
Asches divided their time among Nice, London, and Israel. A
testimonial dinner for him in Tel Aviv in 1954 convinced Asch he
should move there. Matilda, however, was not enthusiastic.
Missing her children and grandchildren, she suggested they return
to America. Refusing, Asch assured her that they would visit in the
States more often, and shortly thereafter they did come to New
York for the publication of his next novel, *The Prophet*. [25] He met
there with Solomon Rosenberg, his former secretary, to whom he
confided his bitterness at those still accusing him of apostasy.
During their ten years together, Rosenberg later recalled, he had

never heard Asch comment adversely on his critics; now, unable to contain himself, Asch referred to them as "carrion." Their slanders, Rosenberg claimed, hastened Asch's death.[26]

Asch marked his seventy-fifth birthday as he had so many others, with a press conference to launch a new novel. To reporters gathered at the Harvard Club he appeared, despite a heavy cold, as sound as ever. One observer was reminded of Albert Einstein, three others of an Old Testament patriarch or prophet.[27] Was he now, with his "Messianic pentology"[28] out of the way, thinking of retiring? No, he replied, but he was living once again more in Biblical times than in the present. Then, warming to the occasion, he added that, seemingly, a period had closed in his life, because for the first time in a half-century he had no story in mind. "There's a great emptiness, and I'll have to wait for something to come along. But there is nothing I can do but wait."[29] This was mere rhetoric, with Asch indulging in his familiar role-playing for the press. He may also have been reacting to charges that his recent writings were too facile and too hastily done. He hardly lacked ideas for future books, having revealed to Solomon Rosenberg his plans for novels on Rabbi Akiba, the Warsaw ghetto, Israel, and most immediately Jacob and Rachel.[30]

When his questioners shifted to his stubborn reiteration of Jewish-Christian ties, Asch replied that he had worked always for the "comfort" of Jews and considered himself "a very good Jew." He had refused, however, to be denied the joy of creating from Judaism's "rich spiritual heritage."[31] Yes, some "good people" have opposed him, but the interviewers should keep in mind that Jews have experienced "terrible tragedy" and are naturally concerned about continuity. He had always known he would have to pay a high price for his views; still not a day passed that he did not receive letters from young Jews asking him to stay with his convictions. "I am not a strong man," he said, "but I believe that no power could make me not write what I want to."[32] He then confronted the charge cutting deepest—that he had left Judaism; he dismissed this as vicious nonsense. "I am a Jewish writer who wants to serve humanity by bringing Jews and Christians together—not by abolishing their individual religions or by having each accept the other's religion, but by showing Christian and Jew alike the sources of their common spiritual inheritance." After all, to accept Christianity is to accept that whole Old Testament tradition in which the Messianic idea is rooted. As for his critics, literary and personal, Asch took the long view. "I am not Socrates," he declared, "or Jesus or even Spinoza. But just as Greece could not judge Socrates, this generation cannot judge me."[33]

V   A Prophet in Israel

The gathered reporters were sympathetic, but how, asked one, did Asch explain his treatment of Bible literature—for instance, his acceptance of the miraculous? "People sometimes ask me," Asch responded, " 'Do you really believe in miracles?' The miracles are what make the Bible. You have to take the Book as it is, or leave it. I would have no right to write a book about Moses, say, without Moses' miracles." His own religious views, he added, should not be an issue. "I'm a religious writer of course. But Titian was not a religious man, and yet he painted the miracles. Rembrandt was not a religious man, and yet he painted religious pictures. An artist draws the whole of his subject."[34]

His new novel? No, it had not proved difficult. The primary material, he pointed out, had come from Isaiah 40 to 55, a Scripture segment in which allusions and style differ from that book's earlier and later sections. These sixteen chapters, Asch might have added, are attributed by scholars to an unknown prophet of the Exile they term Deutero or Second Isaiah. Jews see him as a gentle comforter who in a sorrowful hour brought hope of redemption; Christians accept him as a harbinger of Christ and as the shadowy poet-lyrist of Handel's *Messiah*. His calls for Jerusalem's redemption and his foretelling of a redeemer who would bear "good tidings," "publish peace," and be "wounded for our transgressions" have made him for many, as for Asch, a major link between Old and New Testaments. To Asch, this Isaiah is a clear prototype of Jesus, one falling midway in time and spirit between the Ten Commandments and Christian teachings. About this near-mythic figure Asch weaves a series of visions,[35] and in them he sprinkles phraseology and imagery from Second Isaiah, plus bits from Micah, Ezekiel, Daniel, Nahum, and Psalms. Without mentioning Jesus, Asch alludes repeatedly to the long-awaited Messiah. Stubborn to the core, he still hoped, after so many disappointments, to convince critics of both faiths that his Messianic ideas were valid.

These ideas were not without some historical logic. In their extreme form—that is, in their most fervent Messianic yearnings— some aspects of Judaism (Hasidism provides example) did approach the Christological. A point in time when Jewish and Christian

Messianism nearly coalesced occurred in seventeenth-century Eastern Europe; this juncture has provided theme and setting for various literary efforts, among them *Satan in Goray* by Isaac Bashevis Singer. This novel, written twenty years earlier but appearing in English at the same time as *The Prophet*, reveals a different approach both to prophetic Messianism and Jewish-Christian bonds.[36] If Asch gleans Jewish writings for hints of such links, Singer plays them down; Christian influences upon the Messianic delusions of the latter's rustic Jews, while visible, are not central but internal and subtle. Differences also extend to language and style. Singer's spare, sinewy prose varies pointedly from Asch's overwrought diction and images. Asch leaves little here to the imagination, wringing from his backdrop the garish values of an oldtime film spectacular; not only does he revel in the sensuality of Babylon's royal feasts and in the sexual writhings of its competing religious cults, but he insists on cataloging its intricate network of palaces and markets, slave workshops and pillories, as well as an endless array of trades, artifacts, and practices.

Nor does his plot offer many surprises. When, at a Babylonian feast, Jerusalem's sacred Temple vessels are profaned, a disembodied hand inscribes strange words on the wall. The aged Judean seer Daniel is summoned and prophesies doom for the pagan king and country. Thus Judah's exiles, he declares, should give thought to returning to their own land. Many greet his warning with mixed feelings. A new generation of Jewish merchants and traders, flourishing and smug, now considers Babylon the Promised Land; most farmers agree, preferring Babylon's fertile soil to Judah's rocks. As for the Judean young people, they find little appeal in a God who reputedly punishes the smallest transgression. Few exiles, therefore, are willing to return.

Suddenly a new voice is heard. A strange young mystic, with a name borrowed from the revered Isaiah, appears to declare that God expects Israel to help all nations prepare for "true redemption." His Yahweh is no God of vengeance but a shepherd aiding stumbling lambs. "I have chosen thee," the prophet quotes, "and not cast thee away." Salvation and redemption are near. "I have raised up one from the North, and he shall come." His listeners are confused. Does the prophet refer to Cyrus the Persian who advances upon Babylon promising freedom to all nations? Swaying and trembling, Isaiah continues:

> Behold my servant . . .
> Mine elect, in whom my soul delighteth;
> I have put my spirit upon him;
> He shall being forth judgment to the gentiles. . . .
> He shall not fail nor be discouraged, till he
>   have set judgment in the earth. . . .

Shall the Lord's instrument be a stranger, a gentile? Impossible, argue the elders; this Isaiah must mean the Messiah, the anointed one!

They are right. Cyrus is for the prophet a mere instrument that can take Israel but a short way toward the One God; only the Messiah, appearing when all men are prepared to receive him, will complete the task. Yet the Persian, by his amazing conquests and generous promises, does move Isaiah to declare him a divine agent. Thus the prophet is crushed and confused when Cyrus proves as blind as Judah's oppressors, Sennacherib and Nebuchadnezzar: upon Babylon's fall the Persian proclaims not Yahweh but Bel Merodach the true God. He then reduces the Jews to scrambling factions by favoring their return to Jerusalem.[37]

A major struggle follows, between the wealthy merchants and those aged survivors who cherish memories of the Temple and of promises by the prophets Jeremiah and Ezekiel of a return. When the wealthy spokesmen revile Isaiah for having "misled" them about Cyrus, he accepts their abuse as deserved, and he refuses to eat or drink. He soon approaches, at least temporarily, Messiah status himself: Babylon's Jewish trade leaders—like the later Sadducees—plot to try this "rebel" in secret before handing him over to the government. But the religious elders shatter the conspiracy by declaring Isaiah to be in the tradition of Israel's Great Prophets. The vindicated prophet now strikes a different, dire note: the return means new suffering. Redemption will come, he states, only after a "man of sorrows" serves as humanity's scapegoat. Yet contrary to expectations, he warns, this Suffering Servant will redeem not Israel alone but all nations, and not physically but spiritually. Isaiah's words produce turmoil, but finally the dreams of prophet and exiles coalesce into the long-awaited return to Zion. As the first caravans prepare, Isaiah dies; his last thoughts are on the Davidic Messiah destined to lead all men from sin to goodness and faith.

At times this ancient hero appears pressed by a modern

one—Asch himself, who apparently found much in the plight of the beleaguered seer with which he could identify. Certainly his own decision to settle in Israel sharpened his satire of those Jews reluctant to leave the Diaspora for the Promised Land. Also, the descriptions of the abuse heaped upon Isaiah appear to have been triggered by authorial needs that novelist Meyer Levin has described as "masochistic." Asch lingers repeatedly in his fiction, Levin aptly points out, "upon details of torture when the victims are characters with whom he appears to identify."[38] The harsh reactions of some critics to his writings had stirred in Asch a strong self-pity, plus a sympathy for such "unappreciated" modern prophets as Theodor Herzl, Chaim Weizmann—and Sholem Asch. Just months before his death, for instance, he chose to republish "The Stranger," a story he had written years before of a simple but eloquent Jew who wanders into a small town where for years he remains a forlorn figure; then he inexplicably converts to Christianity, becomes a priest, and rises quickly to bishop. The crude peasants, moved by the stranger's preachings, cease their habitual drunkenness and extend the Jews kindness rather than abuse. After years of peace the stranger staggers into the synagogue, recites the "Hear, O Israel," and dies. On the story's reappearance Asch confided to friends that he had explained here the "idea and motive" behind his so-called "Christian" books, but, he lamented, no one, on either occasion, had grasped his point.[39]

Similar examples of self-justification and self-pity are evident in *The Prophet;* equally evident is Asch's easy altering of history and tradition to support his polemics. He disregards, for example, the fact that a suffering Messiah atoning for mankind's sins departs clearly from Old Testament prophecy; indeed, `he deviates from both Jewish and Christian traditions to support his "common redeemer" idea. He does so by culling the Bible for those passages that, like Isaiah 53, describe the "Righteous Servant" as an unappreciated herald who suffers for others in lonely dignity and sorrow. "Despised and rejected of men," the awaited one is

> . . . a man of sorrows. . . .
> Surely he hath borne our griefs
> And carried our sorrows;
> Yet we did esteem him stricken,
> Smitten of God and afflicted.
> But he was wounded for our transgressions. . . .
> And with his stripes we are healed. . . .
> And Jehovah has laid on him the inquity of us all. . . .

The possibility that Asch also saw here at least fleeting parallels to his own experience requires no great stretch of imagination. On the other hand, he chose to ignore the embarrassing fact that Christian exegetes do not read into these lines any recall of a Jewish past; they view these and similar allusions as foreshadowings of Jesus' coming. For Jews, such statements are parables on those Hebrew transgressions that caused their fathers' banishment to Babylon— as well as indications of the conditions for redemption.[40] Finally, Asch slights the fact that Jewish Messianism, as a coherent movement or even concept, came much after the Exile and its prophets.[41]

His stretching of these theological and historical points, however justified artistically, made it difficult for some Jewish and Christian critics to read *The Prophet* solely as a literary offering. They resented what they considered Asch's reaching "beyond interpretation" to create "an apocryphal document"[42] that mixed his own thoughts and words with the prophet's God-given ones. Several critics also declared his characters to be more modern than Biblical. Their sentiments obviously bothered Asch, but they hardly deterred him; he had argued repeatedly, and with cogency, that he wrote fiction, not Scripture, and that an artist reshapes his materials to achieve imaginative, not literal, truth. As for his Biblical Hebrews strongly resembling their descendants, he cheerfully agreed. "There are those who seek to know contemporary Jews in the light of the Bible," he had once stated, "but I seek to know the Bible in the light of the Jews of today. If Abraham is not the shrewd Jew of the Ghetto, what is he?"[43] Indeed, his critics would have done better here to accuse him of bad writing and an inadequate respect for his craft. They might have charged haste and impatience, as when he points half his tale toward Babylon's fall and then dismisses the final event in a few lines. Even more serious is Asch's late discovery that his characters and actions lack adequate thrust or movement for a novel; to sustain his skeletal plot he substitutes prolixity for the Bible's prime literary virtue, compression.

Several earlier Asch plays and novels had been salvaged by an engaging hero. But this lonely, sorrowing Isaiah is never connected to pagan temple or court, so that the plot's two segments read, as one critic has suggested, "as if pages from one book, meant for a different audience, had been misbound with another."[44] Too detached and saintly to exhibit flesh and sinew, Isaiah proves no "eloquent, God-intoxicated psalm-singer," wrote a *Time* reviewer, but "a bearded positive thinker doling out pep talks to the dispirited." [45] Such a barb may now seem glib, but Asch's self-parody and his recycling of ideas and characters from his earlier works do make of *The Prophet* a concocted, formula effort far removed in quality from *Salvation, Three Cities,* and *Mottke the Thief,* or even from *The Apostle* and *The Nazarene.* The English version is helped little by a too literal rendering of the original Yiddish, which was marred by clumsy constructions and grammatical errors. Sorely missed is Maurice Samuel's deft touch.

If Asch realized the quality loss in his last three novels, he never said so. At seventy-five, after a half-century of near nonstop writing, he gave no thought to quitting. Instead, he began a long-planned novel on Jacob and Rachel. His hopes were especially high for this book; after all, he would be writing most of it in Israel, its natural setting.

Chapter 10
Israel—The Last Days

In spring 1955, orthodox Jews in the Tel Aviv suburb of Bat Yam distributed placards harshly criticizing their mayor for offering asylum to the "apostate" and "missionary" Sholem Asch. Shortly thereafter, Herman (Chaim) Lieberman, Asch's old nemesis, appeared to deliver an impassioned diatribe against the author. Reports of these events reached Asch in Nice. "Such attacks against me," he wrote to Mayor David Ben-Ari, "are very damaging to my wife and make her ill."[1] They both had wanted the Israel move very much, he added, but now they were undecided. Ben-Ari responded with convincing reassurances, and the following February the Asches arrived at their small new house on Arzoloff Street. Settling in, Asch hired as secretary an experienced writer, Itzak Panner, whose published journal now provides the most detailed, if somewhat disjointed, record[2] of his employer's brief sojourn in Israel.

Asch at seventy-six still cut an imposing figure. "Tall, majestic, and aristocratic with his mane of white hair," Panner recalls, "Asch caught the attention even of those who did not know who he was" (14). During his first weeks in Israel, Asch was visibly nervous, feeling, he later confessed, as if the ground were "mined." Might not his townsmen, he asked repeatedly, burn down his house or even assault him on the street? Such acts were highly unlikely, his new friends responded, but they did admit that some local orthodox Jews had urged an "unofficial boycott" against him. These few were survivors of the religious group who, thirty-five years earlier, had established Bat Yam; they alone opposed his residence in their "holy community." The town majority, Mayor Ben-Ari insisted, were delighted to have him there. Most residents now were late arrivals from Poland and Eastern Europe; Holocaust survivors, they identified strongly with his *shtetl* characters and tales.

I Tensions in Bat Yam

Yet Ben-Ari, a seasoned official, had been aware his invitation would cause difficulties; these had surfaced quickly when local zealots opposed his action and "friendly liberals" cautioned against involving the community in a troublesome adventure. But for David Ben-Ari, who hailed from the Polish *shtetl* of Plonsk, as well as for Israel's other Eastern Jews, Sholem Asch was the beloved re-creator of the Kutnos and Plonsks of their youth—a Yiddish-speaking world of which nothing remained. For *that* Asch Bat Yam had to have a place. When a tearful Asch lamented that "My Polish Jews don't exist anymore, and there's no one now to take my side" (23), Ben-Ari felt that as a representative of those lost millions he had to defend their chronicler. And he succeeded. A shrewd strategist, the mayor enlisted support from an official in the ministry of religious affairs and then warned the leader of the most vocal opposition group that he would be held personally responsible for any mishap to Asch. Additional help came from Asch's hometowners in the Kutno (Landsmen) Society, whose chairman, Aaron Elberg, was also the local leader of the militant Irgun unit. Needless to say, Asch experienced no physical assault. Ironically, other Asch defenders were the Yiddish press and Yiddish writers—two groups whose American counterparts had been his most vociferous opponents.[3] The "Asch boycott" in Israel, Itzak Panner has stated, was "an imported article, an artificial ice that began to melt very quickly. A little later this was true even in the orthodox circles" (17).

Some bitterness, however, did persist. Invited to a large student program, for instance, a smiling Asch stepped forward at its conclusion to congratulate a teacher. The latter, from an orthodox school, turned his back. Asch was left standing, with hand extended, before a gaping crowd of students, parents, and teachers. Stunned, his face flushed with anger and humiliation, he remained motionless for a few moments and then walked slowly off. "Listen, Mr. Mayor," he complained to Ben-Ari, "maybe I won't live long enough to see it, but you will, when all these will regret that they have caused me so much pain for no good reason" (67). Such slights proved rare, as most Israelis accepted Asch in friendly, even prideful, fashion. His weathered face and public friendliness, his soft-spoken, Polish-accented Yiddish, his ability to speak Hebrew (if awkwardly), and perhaps even his doorpost *mezuzah*[4] —these hardly added up to an apostate or missionary.

Still his fear of assault lingered, and on March 13, 1957 his composure again was shattered when an Israeli terrorist assassinated Dr. Rudolf E. Kastner, formerly a Jewish communal leader in Hungary; after the war Jewish survivors had accused Kastner of cooperating with the Nazis to help his own friends and relatives to escape. A bitter libel trial had resulted in Kastner's acquittal.[5] His death renewed Asch's fears. "Kastner is innocent!" he declared, "I'm nearly positive that he is innocent. But even if he is guilty, this does not make the attack any less a crime. These terrorists are a great peril to our young democracy—a real misfortune" (89).

His misgivings, while understandable, proved needless, as organized opposition to his presence soon disappeared; exaggerated tales of public hostility, however, spread abroad. One story was picked up by Jewish newspapers in England, America, and even in Israel. Supposedly, Asch had gone on Yom Kippur to Tiferet Zvi Synagogue in Tel Aviv, where he had sought, and been refused, an *aliyah* (the honor of being "called up" to the reading of Torah). When the story appeared the synagogue president, a Mr. Raziel, dismissed it as insulting and false. The congregation members had invited Asch, he stated, to be their honored guest.

We were very happy to have the great privilege of seeing Sholem Asch wrapped in his *tallith* in the seat of honor we had given him in our synagogue. The whole Yom Kippur day and the preceding Kol Nidre night Asch was sunk deep in prayer.

The day after Yom Kippur we were astounded to read that we had refused Asch an *aliyah*, under pressure from worshippers in our synagogue. . . . We did not give Sholem Asch an *aliyah* because it is our regular practice on the High Holy Days to give *aliyahs* only to our regular congregants, and not to occasional visitors or exalted guests who happen to be there that day. It is a complete invention to say that any question of giving Sholem Asch an *aliyah* or not giving him an *aliyah* even arose with us.[6]

But the story proved too good to die, and it became part of the legend of Israel's rejection of Asch. Even "objective" commentators repeated it,[7] as they did other distorted accounts of undying hostility toward him by religious Israelis, who supposedly created scenes whenever he appeared in their synagogues. No one even tried to explain why, if the stories were true, the sensitive Asch would repeatedly subject himself to public insult.

Yet despite the slurs, lies, and occasional slight, Asch and Matilda adjusted quickly to their new community. Bat Yam, with its tree-lined streets and its houses half-concealed by shrubs and gardens, must have reminded them of Kutno. When their four-room cottage proved too small, they began planning an addition. They had left many possessions and books in London, but they still felt cramped by their furniture and art objects. "The entire house," observes Panner, "was one museum of valuable art, paintings, and unusual antiques" (33). Asch hardly helped matters by keeping his two massive writing tables in his usual disorder; to find any item, he had to rummage through letters, manuscript pages, pictures, and books. But he professed, for the first time in years, to be happy and at peace.

II "Hero" of the Sinai Campaign

In Nice and London he had worked hard on his new novel, *Jacob and Rachel*, but he had been slowed by the move to Israel. No sooner was he settled there then he experienced another, truly explosive, interruption: the Sinai Campaign. The fighting stirred in Asch memories of the Holocaust and disturbed him deeply; he felt his new country to be in great peril. "The world is against us," he lamented, "they may destroy us" (25). Anyone holding an American passport was urged by the American embassy to return to the United States, and many people did. But Asch, although frightened, determined to stay. When he later published an article praising Israel's young military heroes, he was hailed as a patriot by the press and radio. His every comment received wide coverage, and with each interview his rhetoric soared higher. "With the heroes of Israel in the deserts of Sinai," he rhapsodized over the radio, "were all the generations of the Jewish people. And with those who fell there were all the Jewish sacrifices of all the diasporas. . . . I believe completely that . . . the creation of the state, after the destruction of European Jewry, was a miracle of God. I also believe in the future of Israel, that no human evil will ever succeed against her" (34-35).

A writers' group soon after that gave him a testimonial dinner, at which several spokesmen praised him anew for not running away; one speaker even read aloud the "Sinai" chapter from his *Moses*. Deeply moved, Asch declared that he hardly merited "a pinch on the cheek" for staying. "Our children," he added, "have done a great deal more. We ought to bow our heads before them. . . . We are used to the world having pity for us, being sorry for us. It's good for the world to be occasionally angry at us" (35). For Asch the evening was most gratifying; after so many turbulent years in America, he literally savored this "acceptance" by his new countrymen. He could not know, of course, that his days now were numbered. After the dinner he, Matilda, and several friends went to a cafe, where he began to feel sick and had to be taken home. In the morning he was at his desk, but he had suffered a mild stroke: the first warning that he was seriously ill.

The next months brought good and bad moments. Jakov Pott (Jacob Pat), a *Forward* staffer, wrote from New York to compliment him on his support of the Sinai action, as well as on his reception at the Writers' Club. Greatly pleased, Asch saw the letter as "the first dove of peace" from his self-declared enemies. His renewed popularity made him good copy and caused Moishe Grossman, editor of the monthly *Haimish* ("Homelike"), to print Alexander Mukdoiny's old article attacking him; in this piece, Mukdoiny criticizes Asch for having published in the Communist *Freiheit* and accuses him of being selfish toward other writers, of "never giving but always taking." To keep matters stirred, Grossman featured in his next issue a defense of Asch, by the poet Rechuda Potash. Asch found this cold comfort; he could not understand why anyone should dig up such old, discredited charges. But Grossman found reader interest high and followed these articles with others. On each occasion Asch, extending his long arms, would ask, "What do they want of me?" (103). He looked, notes Panner, like a helpless elephant trying to rid himself of attacking flies: No more such articles, Asch ordered, were to be brought him. "They have written about me bad and good," he cried. "I have had enough" (40).

Asch himself only rarely spoke negatively of those who were embittering his last years. Panner once mentioned the harsh criticism evoked by his "Christian" books; Asch replied that he would not mind such attacks as much if he could feel his critics to be sincere in their concern for the Jewish community. "But their fight against me is a personal one. The main motive is simple hatred and envy" (48). Neither praise nor criticism, however, or even increasing signs of failing health, altered his work habits. When the Sinai turmoil subsided, Asch busied himself with *Jacob and Rachel* and turned over to Panner several early chapters for copying. After some initial difficulty with his employer's handwriting, syntax, and orthography, Panner requested permission to make needed mechanical and grammatical changes. Asch proved amenable; they could reach agreement always, he assured Panner, without "consulting the rabbi." He was right, and soon the two worked smoothly together.

Asch's temperament had changed little with age. He still acted the overgrown child—impulsive, capricious, completely uninhibited, and alternately gentle and crude. Matilda felt compelled to explain her husband, now seventy-six, to new acquaintances; he was an artist, she would state, and thus given to moods and whims. He could leave an invited visitor without a murmur to return to his study. On the street he might ignore a friendly greeting or, with a quick handshake, walk off from a companion because of a sudden idea he wanted to write down. Yet those who came to know him, says Panner (echoing his predecessor, Solomon Rosenberg), realized that Asch intended no insult; he was merely self-absorbed. Certainly he was catholic in his slights, seldom discriminating between the ordinary and famous. Several times he turned from his door prominent, but uninvited, visitors who had come to pay their respects. He had some cause, beset as he was by requests to appear at numerous affairs honoring local writers and poets. Not only was his work interrupted, complained Asch, but he now lacked the strength for speechmaking. When he and Matilda did socialize, they exercised their lifelong preference for the wealthy and socially important.

Asch was reluctant to extend friendship, especially to fellow writers, as so many had turned on him. Yet he did gather a few literary intimates: Eleazer Pines (of the Yiddish magazine *The Golden Chain*), Samuel Katz (his Hebrew publisher), D. Sivan (his Hebrew translator), and Arthur Saul Super (his English translator). He accepted a new acquaintance cautiously. Inscribing for Panner a copy of *The Nazarene*, then newly rendered into Hebrew, Asch wrote: "To Itzak Panner, my colleague—in the hope that he will become my friend—Sholem Asch" (31). Only when assured of Panner's loyalty did he confide in him.

His suspicions extended beyond those close to him. Despite his public praise of Israel's young people, for instance, Asch harbored strong reservations about this strange generation. He even rejected the idea of following up his *Song of the Valley* with a realistic novel of contemporary Israel because he felt he would have to describe her youths negatively. "Our Sabras remind me," he told Panner, "of the first generation of Jewish Sabras in America in the beginning of the century. . . . The old Jewish culture and tradition remained alien to them. And to the English culture they did not completely reach. So they remained spiritually poor. The second generation took roots, however, in the English culture." Israel's youngsters, he continued, are also "empty of any Jewishness" or of the Diaspora's "rich, thousand-year Jewish culture." Nor has "a new Israeli tradition" yet evolved for them; thus their generation is left "spiritually poor" (36-37). He felt his views confirmed when, on the beach, he was struck by a ball and received no apology; angered, he declared Israel's young to be neither Jews nor gentiles: lacking spiritual awareness, they are interested only in sports, cheap films, sex, and physical pleasures (134).

Occasionally he commented similarly on Israel's older generation; its members also, he complained, had divorced themselves from East Europe's rich Jewish culture by rejecting Yiddish and virtually everything it represented (148). As for Israel's literary tradition, it had not yet developed to where it could strengthen native writers; hence he admired only those authors, like S.Y. Agnon, who had immigrated there. He considered Agnon "a great Jewish writer" (37); although he wrote in Hebrew, Agnon was from Eastern Europe (Galicia), and most of his fiction was set there. Also he, like Asch, relied heavily on Biblical and Talmudic materials. Among the others writing in Hebrew, Asch saw no one of stature—certainly no one to rival a storyteller like Zalman Shneour or poets like Nachman Bialik or Saul Tchernichovski.[8] He was equally unimpressed by Israeli reading tastes. When young readers responded well to the Hebrew version of *The Nazarene*, Asch, greatly pleased, hoped that his *Song of the Valley* would also find a receptive audience; he wanted to reaffirm in this new country his standing as a major novelist. He had it translated into Hebrew and then began frequenting Tel Aviv's bookstores to check sales figures and to autograph copies. When it sold poorly, he was crushed, unable to understand why Israelis were not buying a novel glorifying their achievement. Maybe, he asked resentfully, they wanted another *Nazarene*?

Only at En-Harod did *Song of the Valley* stir interest. This *kibbutz* in the Valley of Jezreel had provided Asch, thirty-five years earlier, with his narrative's locale and characters, and the novel's reissue gave the *kibbutzniks* double cause to celebrate their *Shavuoth* holiday. Some pioneers were still alive, and they invited Asch to the festivities to thank him again for his depiction of their victory over swamp and valley. Asch had barely altered their identities, and to them and their children he was one of their own. Whenever he was in Israel he came first to En-Harod, and if the *kibbutzniks* understood his Ashkenazi Hebrew no better than he followed their Sabra pronunciation, it mattered little. A thousand people now jammed the auditorium to applaud him. Children brought him flowers and baskets of the first *Shavuoth* "fruits"— honey, dates, citrus fruits, and vegetables; officials extended greetings, and a speaker displayed the carefully preserved novel manuscript that Asch had given the *kibbutz*. Another speaker read from the section describing the settlement's start. After touring the *kibbutz's* latest improvements, Asch and his party left in an auto laden with gifts.

As pleasing as was this reception, Asch was moved equally by another incident linked to *Song of the Valley*. After World War II he had received from a concentration-camp survivor a tattered copy of the novel. The sender wrote that in the camp of several hundred Jews this had been the sole Yiddish book. Passing it secretly from hand to hand, the prisoners had prayed they might survive to go to that holy land described by Asch. Only a few had survived, but these had preserved the book that they felt had helped them fight off despair (154). Asch treasured both the letter and the soiled and torn volume.

III   An Unfinished Novel

Asch enjoyed talking about writing and about writers he had known. His comments, usually devoid of rancor or envy, were direct and candid. "There are writers who are teachers," he would say, "and . . . writers who are only writers. Sholom Aleichem was only a writer. I also am only a writer. Peretz was a teacher. I was one of his pupils." He owed Peretz a great deal, Asch would add; Peretz, after all, had convinced him to become a Yiddish, rather than a Hebrew, writer. Yet Peretz had liked only his novella *The Town*. "Everything that I wrote after that he did not like. If I had listened to him, I would not have gotten out of the *shtetl*. Peretz advised me to burn my play *God of Vengeance*. Instead, I took the drama to [Max] Reinhardt" (43). Asch's rejection of the "teacher" [9] label seems ironic, since he had spent years trying to "teach" Jews and Christians to cherish their "common" religious heritage. But "teacher" translates into Hebrew as "rabbi," one who functions as "master" or "leader" more than "writer," and Asch, a loner, wanted about him neither disciples nor literary atmosphere. "I'm not a 'rabbi' like Peretz," (107) he would say. The few Israeli-Yiddish writers who now came to him received a guarded reception. He could not remember their names, and if uninvited they were turned away.

In any event, his new novel was absorbing his waning energies. Groping for a fresh approach to the Jacob and Rachel story, he read and reread not only the Bible, Talmud, *Haggadah*, and *Midrash*, but volumes of history and archeology in German, English, and Hebrew. Fascinated by the Dead Sea Scrolls, he devoured everything he could find on the old Orient and on the modern digs in Babylonia and Mesopotamia, especially on the excavations at Ur. In addition to the major sources, he relied upon lesser folk compilations, interweaving their tales with those of the *Midrash*. Soon he was describing for guests ancient Ur's streets and people, its laws and customs. His characters now seemed familiar neighbors. Rachel had informed Jacob, Asch declared, that Laban wanted to substitute Leah for her on the wedding night. "So Jacob and Rachel agreed on signals enabling him to recognize if it were Rachel entering the dark tent. But Rachel, moved by pity for her ugly sister, gave to Leah all those signs that she and Jacob had agreed upon. Thus she sacrificed herself for her sister." Asch insisted that he had not made up this story; thumbing through an old Yiddish compilation of Biblical folktales for women (known as the *Tz'enah u-Re'enah*),[10] he pointed out where Rachel had shared her "secrets" with Leah. On these secrets, he added, "my novel is based" (42).

But he could not decide how important to make his women. When Panner brought the recopied second chapter, Asch began crossing out passages dealing with Jacob's concubines, Bilhah and Zilpah, whom he depicts as Rachel and Leah's half-sisters—Laban's daughters by a concubine. He had developed at length each sister's character and longings, as well as the bickerings among the four. "I don't want to devote so much attention to the women," he now explained. When Panner protested that these and other omitted passages were relevant, Asch smilingly replied there would be enough left. He often practiced such literary "masochism," he explained, to avoid repeating himself. Ironically, he failed to realize to what extent he had made needless repetition a trait of his later writings, especially when he dealt with a favorite character. Rachel, for instance, had moved through his earlier novels and stories as a symbolic spirit; now he determined to render her an earthbound woman competing with her sisters for their husband's affection. But he quickly reverted to his mystical view of her as the spiritual mother and prime consoler of all Jacob's descendants. "Rachel crying for her children" was for Asch so meaningful a phrase that he could portray her only as closer to heaven than earth.

Here, as elsewhere, his ideas about women seem compounded equally of awe and veneration, naiveté and disdain. But then he had cause to be smug, even patronizing; he had been extremely fortunate in his own women: his mother, wife, and daughter had always doted on him and catered to his whims. He remained his mother's darling long after he had won world renown, while his wife served him selflessly for over a half-century as adviser, business manager, private secretary, press agent, and bodyguard. If Asch often made her the prime target of his piques and complaints, he was fully aware of her devotion and returned it. Several of his most sympathetic fictional women were modeled after her, notably Rachel-Leah Hurvitz in *Three Cities* and Rose Rosenberg, the totally committed secretary in *A Passage in the Night*. As concerned about Matilda's health as she was about his, he often quieted visitors with a whispered, "My wife doesn't feel well. She's sleeping."

She knew thoroughly his every novel, short story, and article, not to mention his every virtue and vice. Certainly no one was more aware that his actions too often approached those of a pampered child accustomed to realizing his slightest whim. Impulsive, impatient, captious, he flared angrily one moment, laughed playfully the next. Adjusting to every shift, Matilda could be gentle or stern, maternal or coy. Running fingers through his thick grey hair, she would exclaim, "wool, pure wool" (165). Her " 'Shulimshe, I beg you' had the power of a liontamer," reports Itzak Panner, who often witnessed her magic, "a liontamer who with hypnotic glance forces the wild lion to lie down quietly at her feet" (163).

She was her Sholem's buffer against intrusion, distress, or hostility; friends, relatives, reporters had to win her approval before approaching the master. Unable to prevent quarrels between Asch and his sons, she made certain all three remained devoted to him. She distinguished instinctively between sincere and calculated friendships offered her husband, and between honest and dishonest criticism. Her vigil was total. The least slight to him drew her immediate ire, and she missed nothing. Journalists requesting interviews found she knew whether they had written favorably of Asch; if not, they were refused admission. During the interview she sat by to block, quietly but firmly, any question she considered "political," by which she meant controversial. Controversy she had experienced enough.

IV   The Stroke

Despite interruptions, Asch had written six chapters of *Jacob and Rachel* by January 1957, and he decided to take a short rest because of "fatigue." He was much sicker than he realized. Panner found the last pages inaccurately arranged, the sentences garbled, and character and place names confused. Reluctant to frighten Asch, Panner said nothing, but he decided to put Chapter Six aside for a time. The very next morning, a Sunday, he learned that his employer had suffered a stroke and was in the hospital. Saturday evening the Asches and the Ben-Aris had celebrated Hanukah with wine, potato pancakes, and an exchange of gifts. Asch had led the singing, but in the morning he had been rushed to the hospital. On the way to the ambulance he had opened his eyes to see Charlie Ben-Ari, aged nine, standing nearby. "Chaimke," said Asch weakly, "pray for me," then again closed his eyes.

With her husband down, Matilda, who had become pale and sickly in her later years, found new strength. When not at the hospital she answered queries from friends, editors, and reporters, assuring all that her husband's illness was "nothing," that in a few days he would be fine. She had tried to keep his attack quiet, but the news was flashed round the world. The first telegrams were from the four Asch children. No, they need not come, Matilda assured them, their father was doing well. But Ruth Shaffer flew in from London anyway, confident her presence would help both parents. A blond, smiling woman, then in her forties, she immediately lessened the tension in the suddenly somber Asch home. Able to read her father's books in Yiddish as easily as in English, she considered him a great artist; as for Asch, he idolized his "Rutke."

He returned home after two weeks, with a private nurse and under doctors' orders to rest. Sitting dull-eyed in a large chair, Asch asked Panner repeatedly about the *Jacob and Rachel* manuscript. But his thoughts that February quickly shifted to the sanctions with which Dwight Eisenhower and John Foster Dulles were threatening Israel because of the Sinai Campaign. He would go to America, he kept saying, and by radio and television open that nation's eyes to the validity of Israel's action. Soon he was pacing the garden, the worried Matilda trailing behind. He was straining to resume work, but not on his novel; instead, he had a new thought: he would republish in Yiddish every story and article about Palestine he had written through the years, plus novels like *The Town, Sanctification of the Name, The Witch of Castile,* and *Salvation*; these, he hoped, would reenforce in Israel his standing as a major Yiddish novelist. Setting Panner to clipping from books and newspapers the Palestine items, he himself began revising and even rewriting entire pages. Despite his doctor's warnings, he spent hours at his desk, while a helpless Matilda, knowing that stopping him was impossible, watched silently.

Yet when the first volume was ready for publication, Asch killed the project by willfully demanding an advance from his publisher—in direct violation of their agreement. Quickly realizing his error, he wrote a long apologetic letter, but to no avail. Finding no other publishing house interested in so formidable a venture, he resumed his novel, trying so zealously to regain time lost that he frightened his wife and daughter. The work seemed to improve his health and mental state. Starting before dawn, his thick notebook of reading notes beside him, he would work all day. He refused to relinquish even small pleasures and followed each prescribed medicine or juice with cognac and a cigar. By March his headaches were gone, and he was boasting that his strong natural constitution had conquered his illness. An observer might have thought him as sound as before his stroke, but his health remained precarious; his doctor would not permit him in the street alone, or to drive or to bathe in the ocean—all activities Asch missed. For several months he was restricted to a daily walk to the beach, accompanied usually by Itzak Panner.

His novel was not shaping up as expected. By Chapter Nine he was intrigued more by the secondary Abraham and Sarah than by his hero and heroine. Steadily expanding the parental roles, he complained that Abraham had not been explored properly by modern writers because they knew so little of his first years and early milieu; this was a major lack, he argued, for Abraham had founded not merely a new culture but a new civilization. What was it in Ur, asked Asch, that had moved him to reject Nimrod's idols and thereby force the first confrontation of monotheism and paganism? And what urges motivated the beautiful Sarah, of whom even less was known? Unlike his ethereal Rachel, Asch's Sarah was a sensual beauty whose every anatomical point evoked his zestful description; only when older did she accept her matriarchal role. By then Asch had five chapters devoted solely to her and Abraham, so he laid aside his previous ones for a new "beginning" novel on them. He would make little progress on this fragment, but its five chapters do reveal his awareness of Thomas Mann's adroit use of Freudian insights in the *Joseph* novels; they reveal also Asch's inability to achieve a similar complexity of thought and meaning.

By spring 1957, he and Matilda had decided to visit London that June and to return in the fall to add the needed wing to their house. Asch would leave some manuscript with Panner and then send more from London. He plunged immediately into his construction project. As he walked about his property with the architect, discussing the work plans, Matilda stood at a distance, reports Panner, "watching with a sad smile" (116). Asch was fending off death with future projects. In addition to his house expansion and new literary efforts, he talked of organizing a loan association and a free library for Bat Yam's new Polish immigrants. So when did he have time, he would ask, even to write a will? Yet he fooled no one, not even himself. He did have a will and he was thinking of death. Bat Yam, he assured Mayor Ben-Ari, would "not lose anything" by his presence. "Everything I invest in here will remain for the city" (168). Even cherished items, like a small Torah scroll salvaged from the Nazis and an antique brass lamp from an old synagogue, were to be given to the synagogue planned by the immigrants. He hoped to be buried in Bat Yam and, in the custom of medieval Jewish scholars, to have the top of his writing table form part of his casket (169). He would get neither wish.

But now his forthcoming trip engrossed him, as did the enlarging of his house and property. Wanting to plant fruit and pine trees, he decided to buy an adjoining land parcel; when complications developed, he angrily blamed the red tape on his being Sholem Asch. Everyone, he insisted, liked to take advantage of him. After numerous legal difficulties, and after selling his auto to raise money, he placed a deposit of three thousand pounds on the neighboring strip. He would plant the new trees there, he stated, on his return from London.

V   The Last Trip

As departure time approached, Asch and Matilda worked feverishly; their paintings were taken down and sent to the Tel Aviv Museum for exhibit; their heavy luggage was shipped ahead, the furniture covered, and needed writing materials and source books packed. Now referring to his unfinished novel as *Abraham and Sarah,* Asch handed Panner a reworked chapter for copying and told him to forget *Jacob and Rachel* for the present. Their mutual concern should be the narrative of Abraham and his wife. Even as the hired car arrived to take him and Matilda to the airport, Asch kept instructing Panner on the copying and mailing of chapters. He would send additional manuscript from London. They wished each other good health, and Asch kept waving until his auto turned the corner.

Panner never saw Asch again, but he did receive two letters from him. The first (dated June 27, 1957) declared that the flight to England had been spoiled by the loss of the bag containing his and Matilda's shoes. The envelope contained also the first seven chapters of *Jacob and Rachel*—with no mention of *Abraham and Sarah* and no explicit acknowledgment that Asch had switched back to his original theme. There was only an ambiguous reference to a "Chapter Twelve," on which he was working. Now he was waiting impatiently, Asch wrote, to hear that this material had arrived safely. Shortly thereafter, Panner received the second letter (dated July 6); it contained the *Abraham and Sarah* segment, completely revised and expanded to seven chapters. He had been working day and night, explained Asch, and he was sorry that Panner had been working "for no good reason." As a secretary, however, the latter would have to "learn an axiom in writing: as long as the manuscript is not in print, the writer has the right to rework it. A manuscript is not a book. You should not wonder that I keep changing it. This is my manner of writing. To help me, you have to follow my procedure. . . . You can see how much work I put into a book. So forget everything that you copied; that will all be lost" (160-61).

He intended to rework again, declared Asch, all the material written and recopied thus far. The earlier seven chapters, he felt, needed only slight revision, but the other seven, those dealing with Abraham and Sarah, were now very different from the version Panner had copied. He was reverting to his original plan, so he would use these as the opening chapters of *Jacob and Rachel.* Panner was to make three copies of all the revised material and mail one set to London. And if all continued to go well, Asch soon would send to Bat Yam a third group of seven chapters. He hoped to finish the book very soon. So certain, it seems, was Asch of completing the novel that summer that he neglected even to add his customary, "If God will help" (161).

On July 10, as he sat at his desk, writing with one hand while holding his throbbing head with the other, Sholem Asch became very ill. He died the same day. Perhaps, in his last moments, he realized that he was going; if so, he may have recalled the words he had God speak to Moses when He refused the lawgiver's plea to have his life extended. He had, God replied, made man the gracious gift of death.

Usually death softens the most bitter controversies. So it was with Sholem Asch. A few diehard utterances were heard; one commentator even saw in the novelist's death and burial outside his beloved Holy Land "the finger of a higher destiny"; Asch, he argued, "had not yet earned . . . [the] reward" of resting in that sacred soil.[11] But most Jewish journalists and spokesmen paid him a last warm tribute—and then proceeded to forget him. The comments of S. Dingoll, in the Yiddish daily *The Day*, were typical: "He contributed to our literature much that is rich and lovely. Against that Asch we have sinned more than he sinned against us. All the stories that were spread about his apostasy were lies." Even the *Forward*, which under Abraham Cahan had spurred the attacks on Asch for his "Christianizing" books, carried a memorial article. "Sholem Asch had a great dream," wrote Abraham Menes, a regular contributor. "It is in fact the dream of us all, of our finest thinkers. Asch sought a way of approach between Jews and their neighbors. This is surely the desire of us all. Asch loved the Shtetl, the Jew of the Shtetl, and the non-Jews of the Shtetl."[12] Hillel Rogoff, Cahan's successor as *Forward* editor, also wrote favorably of a dead Asch in the same columns where so often the living one had been excoriated.

In England, where reactions to Asch had always been more positive than in America, the eulogies were even stronger. An editorialist for the generally conservative *London Jewish Chronicle*, obviously feeling that he spoke for most of England's Jews, pulled out all stops: "Not only Yiddish literature, but the whole world of humane letters is deprived of a giant figure in the death of Sholem Asch. The attacks that were made upon him by some theological partisans were really a tribute to his ability to stimulate discussion about those fundamental issues which will confront all thinking men and women in these times. It may well be that we have said farewell to the last great Yiddish writer of all time."[13]

The tributes would have pleased and saddened Asch. Had these writers defended him while he lived, they would have brightened those last years darkened by savage assaults upon his character and work. Outraged and broken, he had written the faithful Solomon Rosenberg: "I shall be grateful all my life to everybody who helps to destroy the terrible apostasy libel against me." Rosenberg and Itzak Panner were close to Asch during periods of stress, and both have testified that he never quarreled with an honest critical opinion, no matter how negative. But the distortions of his personal and literary motives evoked an impassioned self-defense:

I have said and I say it again that I have no other ambition than those which are purely literary and artistic. I am no religious reformer. (I feel very comfortable with the Prophets, with all the holy Jewish spirits, up to the builders of Chassidism, who satisfy all my religious thirsts.) Nor am I a scientist. . . . The only ambition in my life is to demand for the Jews the full credit for the contribution of the Jewish spirit to the world treasure of faith, culture, civilization. . . . I do not choose the themes that inspire me. . . . I don't go looking for my inspirations. They come looking for me. If you like, call it the holy spirit. I don't believe you can write books without the holy spirit.

I don't feel at all guilty against anyone, because I follow my artistic aspirations, even when they lead me into fields which Jews have not been accustomed to tread. . . . Who will forbid me to give expression to the great artistic vision that dominates me when I see what the Jewish spirit has created? [14]

Neither his pleas nor the disclaimers of close acquaintances have erased his false image as a deceiver and misleader of his fellow Jews. "Because Asch's portraits of Jesus, Paul, and Mary were warmly sympathetic," stated Maurice Samuel, who knew Asch and his work so well, "he was widely and stupidly accused of seeking to convert Jews to Christianity, from which it follows that he was himself a secret convert, a sort of undercover agent for the Church. This malicious invention still comes up during question periods of my lectures. As it happened, Asch was Jewish through and through; apostasy was as remote from him, with his make-up and attachments, as from an orthodox Jew."[15] Even so responsible a critic as Irving Howe, a half-dozen years after Asch's death, could write: "The Jews never fooled Sholem [sic] Aleichem. Peretz, I think, was sometimes deceived by the culture of the east European Jews, and Sholem Asch tried to deceive it at the end of his career."[16] Thus do misconceptions linger.

Undoubtedly Asch contributed, directly and indirectly, to the confused reactions to his work and personality. He was not an easy man to know or understand. The most poignant expression, perhaps, of the mixed thoughts and feelings he engendered is that recorded by Nathan Asch shortly before his own death: "I had loved my father and hated him and had also been completely alienated from him—that is, I had tried to think differently from him and do things as he would not have done them, and sometimes had been proud of him, and sometimes had been both at the same time."[17] Asch considered himself a devoted father, and, in his fashion, he was. Most of his conscious life, however, was devoted to his writing and to his wife. His children, especially his sons, had to content themselves with what was left.

VI   Sholem Asch—Writer

Asch thought of himself as essentially a storyteller; hence he felt entitled to any narrative device that would help him reach a wide readership. When the Nazis obliterated much of that readership, he grew increasingly concerned as to how his stories would fare in translation. He even tried to help the translators by "explaining" the Yiddish terms in his narratives.[18] Indeed he loved to explain, to describe and convince, for despite his desire to entertain, he was an unabashed propagandist and evangelist; his chosen mission was to underscore the "common heritage" of ideas and traditions underlying Judaism and Christianity. To many of both faiths this task seemed pointless. Asch did not agree—for him the past was a vital source of contemporary values. "I have taken it upon myself," he declared, "to awaken certain ancient memories, to point to ancient moral values which are charged with the power of salvation for us and our days." If his reading of history was both idealistic and simplistic, Asch still was no innocent. An astute observer of people and events, he traveled and read widely. Painfully aware of the centuries of blood and bitterness between Jew and Christian, he hoped for their spiritual and moral rapprochement. Neither was he a coward nor hypocrite; he never hesitated to voice his convictions or to point a blaming finger at those abusing their fellow men—and particularly at those mistreating his beloved Jews.

Asch hardly excelled as a stylist, but his verbal shortcomings, though real enough, have been greatly exaggerated. His writings reveal considerable stylistic unity, even in translation; admittedly, the unity is of uneven quality. Driven by a hyperactive imagination, Asch wrote in haste and with a lack of patience for the precise term, nuance, or syntax. Spontaneity and ebullience shaped his prose more than did reasoned, controlled expression. [19]

(Theodore Dreiser [20] offers an interesting parallel here.) He was satisfied to catch the idea, feeling, mood, to evoke the responsive tear or smile. Given to the broad stroke, he frequently omitted a character's features or hair color for the general image or effect. He also paid little heed to the flow or rhythms of his prose; Germanic elements often rendered his Yiddish sentences so clumsy that few of them parsed easily. Even his better translators were not able to conceal these flaws. Certainly he lacked the verbal clarity and precision of contemporaries like Isaac Leib Peretz, Joseph Opatoshu, Israel Joshua Singer, or Isaac Bashevis Singer.

Most of his fiction appeared first in Yiddish newspapers and periodicals; this does not excuse, but it does help explain his episodic plots and overwrought figures. To cover lapses of imagination or feeling, he mastered those rhetorical devices often associated with the Yiddish theater's inferior productions or melodramas. He would inflate his characters' emotions into a gushing sentiment that evoked his readers' tears. These readers waited as anxiously for the next Asch installment in the Warsaw *Today* or New York *Forward* as readers of Dickens (an Asch favorite) did the next segment in the death of Little Nell. His hasty "installment" writing was as responsible for his defective style as was his incorrigible romanticism.

These traits are even more evident in Asch's plays, where his characters project emotion by gesture, rant, and threat. His inability to modulate his style to stage proportions, to convey nuance and suggestion, render his dramas inferior to his fiction. Much blame here must rest with the raw, uncertain state of Yiddish drama and its unsophisticated audiences; together these produced an exuberance that ignored a stage's limitations. Yiddish drama, as Johann Smertenko has pointed out, had no Jonson, Dryden, or Racine to urge and practice restraint and discipline.[21] And Asch was no Shakespeare to transcend fads and pressures. He was best as novelist; he needed the novel's length and flexibility to fashion character, mood, and setting. Both long and short fiction inevitably included his detailed descriptions of place, cultural habits, and especially nature. So proud was he of his depictions of sky, soil, and stream that he would introduce or prolong them needlessly. Yet Asch's verbal crudities seem as innate and innocent as his love of nature. His meanings, although not always simple, are generally intelligible, while his nervous, sonorous phrases construct and sustain a strong mood. So deeply personal is his involvement with mood, theme, and character that even his most didactic passages are charged with intensity and vigor.

Asch never doubted he was writing serious literature, and much of his fiction does rate careful consideration. But a good deal is diminished by coarse, sentimental sermonizing. Asch is "too substantial" to be ignored, Milton Hindus points out, "yet his lapses in style and structure . . . vitiate . . . his aesthetic effect and make the sensitive reader hesitate to take his work seriously." Hindus's evaluation is only partly valid, as is his claim that Asch lacked "a true religious understanding,"[22] that he confused the truly spiritual with its external trappings. Admittedly, Asch's teeming imagination and descriptive skills frequently caused him to externalize what should have been his characters' deepest thoughts and feelings; he succumbed often to the blandishments of nostalgia, eroticism, and pageantry. A poor critic of his own writing, he valued most those works evoking pleasant memories; when revising, for instance, *Song of the Valley*, a minor novel but one that had made him a folk hero to Israel's *kibbutzniks*, he declared it his "greatest creation." Highly emotional, he was easily moved to tears. Slightly malicious jokes circulated among Yiddish journalists about his public crying when reading to audiences from his works or when appealing for funds for Europe's troubled Jews. Even alone in his study he choked up when writing something sad or laughed aloud when creating a humorous incident.

Many distinguished writers, however, have found merit in Asch's prose. "If Asch could write clearly and grammatically," Isaac Bashevis Singer has stated, "he would lose his rugged strength. He is the great artist he is because he can't be bothered with all the small niceties."[23] Reminded that he had needlessly repeated a word in a sentence, Asch shruggingly replied, "You don't have to be so fastidious with Yiddish." Some critics interpreted this and similar statements as expressions of his disdain for his mother tongue. But he meant only to compliment the Yiddish idiom's strength and flexibility. He was paraphrasing the Talmudic comment that "The jug is not as important as its contents." On another occasion, as already noted, he declared: "If I have the choice of observing all the strict rules of the Yiddish grammarians, or of expressing myself freely, and painting my scenes and my people as I see them, I will not hesitate to sacrifice the grammar."[24]

Repeated criticism, however, rendered Asch sensitive, and one interviewer's casual reference to style even stirred his anger. "Did Shakespeare think of style?" he flared. "Did Whitman? No, only the academicians, who come after, choose the most obvious motif of a thousand manners and call it style."[25] But despite his protests, he remained alert to the possibilities of varied expression and sought always new narrative modes. Recognizing that his early lyricism had derived from a rhetorical innocence and unself-consciousness, he strove repeatedly to recapture that element of simplicity. He tried every prose form, revealing a keen eye for detail—social, political, and religious. Missing little, Asch reverenced even less; his every comment has a slight ironic edge. Painfully aware of a dwindling Yiddish readership, he wrote increasingly for his translators, seeing himself in his later years as a "universal artist," rather than merely a Yiddish one.[26] His novels and stories then grew longer and slower paced, with every aspect described for the uninformed reader. The last novels in particular bore the heavy impress of the serial writer: narrative scenes sandwiched between historical descriptions and philosophical commentaries, or interrupted by authorial asides reminiscent of Thackeray or Trollope.

Yet whatever his faults, Asch never lacked readers. Some reviewers have credited his popularity in translation, especially in English, to gifted translators[27] like Maurice Samuel or Willa and Edwin Muir. And certainly these and other gifted interpreters often did improve his novels and stories. But Asch's fiction proved immensely popular in varied languages and countries, and through the years his translators were many and of differing talents. In the total view, therefore, his literary virtues and vices are seen clearly—and as his own. Maurice Samuel, the most notable of Asch's English translators, has spoken to this point. "As the sales of [Asch's] books soared," recalled Samuel, "one after another, into the hundreds of thousands, the rumor got about that he owed everything to my genius as editor-translator. There was no truth in it, but the rumormongers were nearly all Yiddish writers with their own standards of evaluation and modes of reasonings."[28]

What Asch needed was a tough-minded editor, a Maxwell Perkins or Edward Aswell, to cut from his fiction those passages weakened by haste or by lapses of judgment and taste. In short, he needed someone to bring out the best in his work and to restrict the worst. He was not blessed with such an editor, although Earle Balch of Putnam's did extend valuable advice on several novels.

Asch refused to accept strong guidance; assistance in grammar and syntax he took willingly, but beyond that he was difficult to move. Success, after all, had come easily and early. How did one convince an author who by age thirty had won international recognition that he failed too often to write up to his potential but pandered to his worst instincts. He never felt his intentions to be anything but high, or that he was compromising his skills. As a result, stylistic deficiencies have diminished his reputation, as they have that of Theodore Dreiser and Sinclair Lewis, among others. For modern literature has been evaluated, especially in America, in terms primarily of style and imagination. From Hemingway and Faulkner to Saul Bellow and Ralph Ellison, today's most valued writers, as Alfred Kazin points out, are those whose writings are strongly secured by style.[29] A Flaubert obsessed with language purity or a Joyce attuned to every poetic nuance ranks higher with critics at present than do those of "comprehensive vision" like Balzac or Dickens—or, for that matter, Dreiser, Lewis, Wolfe, Steinbeck, or Asch. In the fiction chronicles of the latter group, powerful effects derive less from the conscious exertion of style than from the vast, often awkward, accumulation of detail.

Of course Asch posed for his readers problems extending beyond a mere clumsiness of style. He baffled and frustrated critics by refusing to adhere to any one literary method or approach. Within the same short story, and almost certainly in a novel, he might employ such varied narrative modes as historical documentation and folklore, scientific rationalism and scriptural myth, social polemic and (albeit rarely) symbolism or allegory. His works, therefore, proved difficult to categorize. Also, many reviewers, clerical and lay, frequently viewed as literary heresy any "fictionalizing" of Biblical materials. Thomas Mann and Nikos Kazantzakis, among others, have suffered from this attitude, and Asch's talents were clearly of a lower order than those of Mann. Serious critics generally have placed Asch's Bible novels on a level equidistant between Mann's *Joseph* novels and Lloyd Douglas's *The Robe*, a level resting squarely, states Milton Hindus, in that "no-man's land between the popular kitsch of the best-seller lists and a qualitative literature of serious intent."[30] As generalizations go, this one may be fair enough, but, again, Asch repeatedly proved a better artist than his itemized faults would indicate. His moral seriousness and sincerity, plus his strong historical sense, gave to his fiction a basic authenticity that sentiment and melodrama could diminish but not blot out. Few writers have understood their fellow Jews, past and present, as well as he, or matched his grasp of their religious and cultural traditions. His knowledge, his sense of *knowing*, shielded even his most hackneyed plots and characters from total distortion or travesty.

Asch ranged widely in his fiction, concentrating on the Diaspora's major geographic centers—Poland, Russia, Germany, America, and Palestine. He moved as freely in time, with tales and novels placed in Biblical, Talmudic, Medieval, Renaissance, and modern settings. Critics attacked him from many vantage points and for numerous reasons, but not one critic of consequence had the *chutzpah* to deny his grasp of social history or the varied nuances of time and place. His Biblical Jerusalem, Medieval Rome, Polish *shtetl*, Warsaw underworld, or New York sweatshop often proved more vital and convincing than the gesticulating little people he placed in them. Over all, however, Asch saw his fellow Jews clearly and whole, and no one criticized them more candidly or tellingly. Yet his commitment to them and their destiny was total. No Jew, no matter how culpable, Asch insisted, was beyond hope.

Several themes recur in his fiction to make this point. The most pervasive one (derived from Hebrew literature) is that redemption is possible for anyone capable of compassion for another human being—and especially for the harassed Jew. Nearly as prevalent here is Asch's concern with Jews whose vacillations between their fathers' religious beliefs and their society's secular mores continually test their personal worth and values. Asch himself does not vacillate; he can conceive of no higher good than a universal community in which all men are bound by a common faith in the divine and by the recognition that all are God's fallible creatures and burden. In his pages, therefore, Pharisees, Sadducees, and Zealots, Hasidim and Cossacks, thieves and tycoons, peasants and priests, Zionists and Socialists, Poles and Russians, Bolsheviks and Mensheviks, Irish-Americans and Italian-Americans are marked more by similarities than differences.

All pulsate and swarm with energy. What Asch describes, he makes his own: textile factory or lush fields, ghetto or church, *shtetl* or city. Unraveling customs, habits, and attitudes, he catches his scurrying figures' gestures and sounds, their very shapes and substance. Too often, however, he will borrow representative types from dusty books and newspapers rather than create living individuals from observation or experience. He also

likes to idealize or romanticize his people, but then he is just as fond
of castigating or satirizing them. And if they are frequently
infuriating caricatures, they are only rarely lifeless. No writer has
depicted more effectively the rich variety of European Jewish life,
the traumas of migration, or the mixed joys of the American
"greenhorn."

Asch was torn by images of the Jew-as-opportunist or criminal
and the Jew-as-saint. He relished the idea of the tough Jewish
hustler grabbing every chance to survive in a hostile world. But he
also felt compelled to offer a counter figure—that of the visionary
reformer revitalizing man's moral values and spiritual dreams.
Indeed, Asch so loved the Jew in every guise that he subordinated
taste and judgment to emotion in portraying him. As a result, his
good Jews and bad Jews often are hard to distinguish: with
different luck and circumstance, the thieving Mottke, for instance,
would have proved as virtuous as the saintly Yechiel. Both blend
into Asch's archetypal Jew who, with minor variations, reappears
as Moses or Deutero-Isaiah, Jesus or Paul, or a score of lesser
figures.

Asch has been rightfully termed both "a pagan poet" sensitive
to the joys of nature and flesh and "a passionate Jew" who cried out
when his people experienced pain. But primarily he was a moralist
who placed conscience before imagination[31] and who never allowed
his admiration for the vibrant rascal to impede virtue's triumph
over evil. Yet even when moralizing slowed his narrative, his prose
conveyed an emotional, even lyric, intensity. At his best as a
chronicler of the senses, Asch was one of the first Yiddish writers
to dwell on the tangled ties of the sacred and the sensuous or
sensual—on even the most religious Jew's hunger for physical as
well as spiritual beauty. He brought to Yiddish fiction a new love of
soil, sky, and water, and an unabashed fondness for the female
body. His appreciation often lacked precise—or even fluid—
expression, but it exuded a joyous, near-pagan elation. His *Earth*, a
short novel unavailable in English, offers numerous examples:
setting his mood and tone in the preface, he personifies Mother
Earth (as noted earlier) as an erotic goddess with a peasant's heavy
limbs and breasts: " . . . When I opened my eyes, I saw a woman
standing before me . . . naked and barefoot. Her breasts were full
and hidden in the stalks of the field, and her head was adorned with
the fruit of the earth, and her shame was covered with leaves of the
fig tree. . . . "[32]

No gap existed for Asch between nature and God; nature, he felt, could exemplify with equal clarity the divine will or pure physical joy. "Not only the heavens declare God's glories," he wrote. "God's deeds are also written on the tablets of the earth, in the movements of the wind through the bare fields, and in the colors which twinkle on the surface."[33] His most vigorous characters are those who feel themselves at one not only with their Maker but with an abundant, vital order of seasons, grasses, and creatures. Hence his Polish peasants, as tightly bound to the soil as are his *shtetl* Jews and pioneer Zionists, are presented sympathetically. "I love the peasants," Asch stated. "Everything with them is as serious—as serious and simple—as the earth itself."[34] And for him the earth bestows its blessings on all who rely upon it, whether uncouth *muzhik* or Jewish rustic. He raised this conviction repeatedly into self-conscious metaphor, as in *Song of the Valley* where he dealt with Jews who had gathered from scattered lands to rejuvenate Palestine's sands and swamps.

In fact, Asch's major figures generally appear ingenuous creatures who turn saints or sinners, intellectuals or peddlers by force of fate or circumstance. And those who function on an intuitive, unaffected level—like Yechiel the artless "Psalm Jew" or Joel "the boy saint"—exhibit life at its quickest. Their innocence and love of God and man invest them with a holy aura. But even his more earthy seekers, like Mottke the thief or Yankel the whoremaster, are essentially guileless, bemused innocents adrift in a world that eludes understanding. Disturbed and confused, each feels compelled by deep, irrational yearnings to act against judgment and conscience.

Few Asch males are not dominated by their sexuality. Yechiel is one of the exceptions, for so strongly does he love God and humanity that he exhibits few other emotional needs. Yet he marries the first girl offered him and remains devoted until her death; thereafter he abnegates sex, dedicating himself to righteousness and charity. Most others, however, are governed by the flesh. Age and position make little difference. Rabbi or patriarch, scholar or merchant, revolutionist or thief—each is turned by an attractive female into an aggressive male. If thwarted or repressed, each courts disaster. When not being sexually aggressive, nearly every Asch boy-man harbors a compulsion to grope for the maternal bosom, aching as strongly for the mother's caress as the lover's embrace. Haskel Buchholz turns from his youthful sweetheart to an older, more exciting mother-mistress. Zachary Mirkin finds his two prospective mothers-in-law more sexually appealing than their daughters. (His first fiancée marries his father.) Max Stone, condemned to die after a fight over a slut, approaches execution with near-erotic dreams of his dead mother.

For Asch sexual passion and the seductive nude are unabashed delights; he enjoys catching his more voluptuous women in suggestive poses and moods. His Tamar is not the Bible's demure maiden ravished by a lustful half-brother, but an erotic oriental deftly arousing her lover's passion and then killing him when he proves more soldier than lover. Of the same amorous blood is the carnal prophetess Sarah, who hails the pretender Sabbatai Zevi as the Messiah but lusts for his body. Lottie von Sticker blithely disregards ominous Nazi threats to give herself joyfully to her Jewish lover. Deborah Zlotnik defies convention and family to become mistress, model, and mother to the lumbering sculptor Haskel Buchholz, and then gives him to another who she feels can do more for him. Yet even the lustiest woman—sophisticate or peasant—having begotten a child, is dominated by maternal feelings. Red Zlatke, Sarah Rifke Zlotkin, Rachel-Leah Hurvitz are the most vivid figures. But all his women reveal a fierce, protective passion for their children, for whom they willingly suffer hunger or death; their zeal is so primal as to exceed the rational. When occasionally one, like Emily Brown or Olga Halperin, attempts to live more as woman than mother, she appears anomalous and unworthy. When not mothering their men, Asch's females, the young ones especially, are expected to provide a male sexual pleasure; even the shyest virgin is to fulfill joyously the divine dictate to be "fruitful and multiply."

Lacking depth and subtlety, Asch relied heavily on imaginative sweep and detail and on a strong historical sense. He sought always new subjects and settings, new knowledge and insights. Appreciative of good scholarship, he absorbed as much as he could to help explain the climes, peoples, and lifestyles he included in his fiction. His mental and physical vigor flagged little until his last years; if he began then to repeat himself, he still presented an astonishing variety of topics, plots, and characters, from ancient past to his own day. Few writers have matched his literary range, diversity, and bulk. An output running to about fifty novels and plays (perhaps two hundred volumes in all editions and translations) merits at least limited critical attention and respect; if he wrote no genuine masterpiece, he did produce a half-dozen novels of some quality and in *God of Vengeance* at least one play that has been finding new readers and audiences for more than a half-century.

Most critics would agree with Louis Zara that Asch's best work was that of his "early Jewish period" and that when he "became a worldling he moved on to a stage where the applause was louder but where the audience no longer was truly his."[35] Still, his *Three Cities* trilogy, *The Apostle*, and even *The War Goes On* are arguable exceptions. His major weaknesses were his mawkish probings of psychological relationships and his penchant for the melodramatic. But the lyric fervor with which he depicted his old-country rustics and saints, peasants and thieves often carried over into his modern city narratives and his Bible tales. The most exotic or cynical of his characters are richly human; they reveal at least flashes of simple, even crude, but elementally fresh, motives and emotions.

Asch did not lack courage. He risked career and reputation to depict as deeply Jewish beings such tradition-and-emotion-charged figures as Jesus, Mary, and Paul. The Jewish author best known to non-Jews, he was the first Yiddish writer to win international acceptance and to help gain for Yiddish fiction its proper place in European and American letters. Thanks primarily to his success, the classic triumvirate of Mendele, Peretz, and Sholom Aleichem received their much-deserved critical and public recognition; he also helped create appreciative readerships for younger novelists like Israel Joshua Singer and Isaac Bashevis Singer. Much-maligned and undervalued in life, Sholem Asch, as man and artist, merits—if not accolades—at least respectful attention from present readers and critics.

Notes and References

CHAPTER 1

1. See Solomon Rosenberg, *Face to Face with Sholem Asch* (Miami: Aber, 1958), p. 144. Only the Yiddish version of this important source of Asch memorabilia has been published, and copies are difficult to find. All textual references to this work, therefore, are to the TS pages of the English translation by Joseph Leftwich, in the hope that Leftwich's rendering will in time find the publisher it merits.

2. Nathan Asch, "My Father and I," *Commentary,* 39 (January 1965), 55.

3. David Lifson, "Sholem Asch," *The Yiddish Theatre in America* (New York: Thomas Yoseloff, 1965), p. 90.

4. Quoted in Herbert S. Gorman, "Yiddish Literature and the Case of Sholom Asch," *Bookman,* 57 (June 1923), 395.

5. Introduction to *The God of Vengeance,* in *The Dybbuk and Other Great Yiddish Plays,* ed. Joseph C. Landis (New York: Bantam, 1966), p. 70.

6. The comment was occasioned by Asch's reactions to a private reading and discussion of his play *Prestige* in Chadotov's home. Chadotov also reports several other emotional—but joyful—Asch reactions to plays in which he appeared. Deeply moved by the performance, Asch would rush to Chadotov's dressing room, tears streaming from his eyes, and embrace and applaud the actor and all involved in the play. But after seeing his friend perform in a stage version of Dostoevsky's *Crime and Punishment,* Asch was nearly beside himself. "He came in sad, quiet, and dejected," Chadotov recalls. "Suddenly, he threw himself on me and began to shake and hit me with his fists, yelling: 'Nikolai, Dostoevsky is a genius, tremendously great. And you are a devil.' He hurled himself on the couch, face down, crying like a baby. I tried to calm him." (Nikolai

N. Chadotov, *Near and Far* [Moscow and Leningrad, 1962], pp. 209-11. Quoted, in Yiddish, in Chazkel Nadel, "The Popularity of Sholem Asch," *The Soviet Homeland*, 8 [February 1968], 138-39.)

7. Asch's approach to the novel, as Alfred Kazin has pointed out, is not the contemporary, or even the modern, one. His is "closer to Richardson than to Joyce" and falls "naturally into the panoramic." This older tradition has produced "solid monuments in fiction," states Kazin, but too often it seems "empirical and coarse." For in it "nothing is merely suggested, and everything is fully described; the settings are elaborate, characters make their entrances as if to begin a recitative aria, and communication is through oratory." ("Neither Jew Nor Greek," *New Republic*, 1 November 1943, p. 627.)

8. "Sholem Asch: Still Immigrant and Alien," *College English*, 12 (November 1950), 67.

9. Charles E. Shulman, "Sholem Asch," *What It Means to Be a Jew* (New York: Crown, 1960), 63.

10. See Shulman, p. 65.

11. See Landis, p. 70.

12. Quoted in Joseph Leftwich, ed., "Foreword to the Revised Edition," *Yisroel: The First Jewish Omnibus* (New York: Thomas Yoseloff, 1963), pp. 17-18.

13. Asch always recognized November 1 as his birthdate, but his birth certificate listed January 1. His mother, however, claimed he was born four days after Passover, which would place his day of birth in the spring. (See, in Yiddish, Solomon Rosenberg, "Sholem Asch, His Son and His Critics," *Free Worker's Voice* [*Freie Arbeiter Stimme*], 1 August 1965, n. pag.)

Early in his career Asch spelled his given name "Shalom," "Scholem," or "Sholom," and occasionally he omitted the "c" from Asch. Kutno has been spelled "Kutnia" and "Koutno."

14. Sholem Asch, "Dedicatory Foreword: One of Six Million," *From Many Countries: The Collected Short Stories of Sholem*

Asch, trans. Maurice Samuel and Meyer Levin (London: Macdonald, 1958), p. ix.

15. "A Word About My Collection of Jewish Books," *Catalogue of Hebrew and Yiddish Manuscripts and Books from the Library of Sholem Asch*, compiled by Leon Nemoy (New Haven: Yale Library, 1945), p. vii.

16. Quoted in Rochelle Girson, "The Author: Sholem Asch," *Saturday Review of Literature*, 8 October 1949, p. 20.

17. Quoted in Beatrice Washburn, "Sholem Asch Writes Novels by Hand in Old World Aura," *Miami Herald*, 1 February 1953, p. 17-E.

18. Girson, p. 20. The proper spelling of the Yiddish word is *stroz;* it means literally "doorman" but was used to mean "janitor," not "porter."

19. See Rosenberg, *Face to Face*, p. 1.

20. Rev. of *Moses* in *Time*, 1 October 1951, p. 104.

21. "Kola Street," in *A Treasury of Yiddish Stories*, ed. Irving Howe and Eliezer Greenberg (New York: Meridian, 1958), pp. 260-61. All textual references are to this translation by Norbert Guterman.

22. *Salvation*, trans. Willa and Edwin Muir (New York: Putnam's, 1951), pp. 20-21. All textual references are to this second or revised edition. (See below, Chapter Five, note 41.) For Asch's vivid description of the Sabbath's arrival in a typical *shtetl*, see *Salvation*, p. 32.

23. Girson, p. 20. In a recent article on the Vistula River community of Kazimierz, journalist S.L. Shneiderman presented that town as the "backdrop" for many Asch novels and stories, especially for *The Little Town* and *Salvation*. He also repeats several undocumented and undated anecdotes popular there dealing with the youthful Asch. The first involves his supposed "affair with the beautiful and wealthy Stefanie Feuerstein." The second has Asch, attired in "satin gaberdine and fur-edged cap," on

horseback, trotting "around the synagogue . . . while people were entering it for Sabbath services. They threw stones at him, shouting furiously: 'Apostate! Apostate!' " Perhaps Shneiderman best sums up his own approach here when he confesses that "Scholars have never been able to unravel myth from fact in the historical fabric of Kazimierz." See S.L. Shneiderman, "Homage to Kazimierz," *Midstream*, 21 (April 1975), 23-25.

24. Sholem Asch, "The Guilty Ones," *Atlantic Monthly*, 166 (December 1940), 713-14.

25. "The Guilty Ones," p. 714.

26. Sholem Asch, "I Adopt an Ancestor: A Fable," *American Mercury*, 56 (January 1943), 47.

27. "The Guilty Ones," p. 714.

28. Girson, p. 20.

29. Asch attributed his liking for German literature to the "delicate romanticism" bequeathed him by his mother and the "self-confidence and . . . healthy aggressiveness" passed on by his father. (See Samuel Niger, "Sholem Asch," *Columbia Dictionary of Modern Literature*, ed. Horatio Smith [New York: Columbia U. Press, 1947], p. 34.)

30. See A.A. Roback, *The Story of Yiddish Literature* (New York: Yiddish Scientific Institute, 1940), p. 219.

31. Quoted (in Yiddish) in JK-Sh, "Sholem Asch," *Biographical Dictionary of Modern Yiddish Literature* (New York: Congress for Jewish Culture, 1956), I, 183.

32. JK-Sh, p. 184.

33. Asch had acquired enough Polish to read Prus (1845-1912) in the original, and he was strongly impressed by the latter's exposing in his novels the bigotry, pride-of-class, and greed rampant in nineteenth-century Poland.

34. Asch's memoir (in Yiddish) on Peretz appeared in the May 1950 issue of *The Future (Zukunft)*; see JK-Sh, p. 184.

35. In Yiddish, "The Hasidic Hat!" is *Dos Shtreiml* and "Bontche the Silent" is *Bontche Shveig*.

CHAPTER TWO

1. Quoted in Jacob S. Minkin, *The Shaping of the Modern Mind: The Life and Thought of the Great Jewish Philosophers* (New York: Thomas Yoseloff, 1963), p. 360.

2. See Fred Goldberg, "Translator's Introduction," *My Memoirs: Isaac Leib Peretz* (New York: Citadel Press, 1964), p. 13. Asch was attracted in particular to Nomberg and Reisen, both relative newcomers like himself. In their company, Asch later claimed, he shared hunger and want—and that he even "lived in dark and dank holes and came in contact with human need." Even careful critics, like Samuel Niger and Charles Madison, have accepted this claim unchallenged. (See, for instance, Madison's *Yiddish Literature: Its Scope and Major Writers* [New York: Frederick Ungar, 1968], p. 222.) But Asch, who repeatedly rearranged autobiographical details, here seems to have romanticized his early hardships; admittedly, Warsaw's ghetto offered him ample "contact" with human need, but his doting parents would hardly have allowed him to experience hunger, or even discomfort.

3. Quoted in Minkin, p. 360.

4. Quoted in Johan J. Smertenko, "Sholem Asch," *The Nation*, 14 February 1923, p. 180.

5. "Little Moses" *(Moishele)* appeared in issue No. 48 (2 November 1900) and "The Grandfather" and "The Hanukah Lamp" in No. 50 (16 November 1900) of *The Jew (Der Yud)*. In 1901, the same magazine published Asch's "Messengers," "The First Seder Night," "Money Makes A Man Respectable," "Mottele," "On the Bank of the Weisel," and "A Gift to Our Poets." (See Nachman Meisel, *Sholem Asch to His Twenty-Fifth Year of Creation* [Warsaw: B. Klezkin, 1926], pp. 5-6. In Yiddish.) *The Post, The People's Times,*

and *Today* are translated titles for *Ha-Doar, Die Folks-Zeitung,* and *Heint.*

6. In later years Asch, who was again revising his biographical data for a reporter, informed his interviewer that he had met Matilda when he came to Warsaw "to study in the Rabbinical College under . . . [her] father. She was away from home teaching at the time." (See Washburn, p. 17-E.) He had, of course, come to Warsaw solely to pursue a career as a writer.

7. Moses Asch is a folklorist who has been associated in recent years with Folkway Records and *Scholastic Magazine;* John Asch is a botanist. Both live in New York. Ruth Asch Shaffer and her family have made their home in London for many years.

8. The pen name of Sholem Jacob Abramovich (1836-1917).

9. The pen name of Sholem Rabinovich (1859-1916).

10. Lewis Browne, "Is Yiddish Literature Dying?" *The Nation,* 2 May 1923, pp. 513-14.

11. See Howard Morley Sachar, *The Course of Modern Jewish History* (1958; rpt. New York: World, 1963), p. 218.

12. Smertenko, p. 180.

13. See John Cournos, "Three Novelists: Asch, Singer and Schneour," *Menorah Journal,* 25 (Winter 1937), 83-84.

14. *In a Shlechter Tseit* (Warsaw: Progress Publishing Company, 1903). "*In An Evil Time* was written in sadness and trouble," declared critic Bal Makhshoves, "when you want to cry more often than laugh. When the bit of hope becomes immersed in a sea of sadness and anguish. Each sketch . . . leaves a deep sadness in the reader's heart." (See [in Yiddish] Isidor Eliashev, "New Talent," *Selected Works* [New York, 1953], I, 133-37; see also Meisel, pp. 6-7.)

15. See Sarah Goldberg, "Sholem Asch: A Romantic Realist," *B'nai B'rith Magazine,* 41 (June 1927), 389.

16. Quoted in Madison, *Yiddish Literature*, p. 230.

17. *The Little Town (Der Shtetl)* appeared originally in *The Friend (Der Freint)*; the following year (1905) it was published in Minsk as a book.

18. "Sholem Asch: Still Immigrant and Alien," p. 68.

19. "Sholem Asch," *Poet Lore*, 46 (Winter 1940), 304.

20. Sol Liptzin, "Sholem Asch," *The Flowering of Yiddish Literature* (New York: Thomas Yoseloff, 1963), p. 178.

21. See Charles A. Madison, "Scholom Asch," *Poet Lore*, 34 (Winter 1923), 527-28.

22. Quoted in Madison, *Yiddish Literature*, p. 223.

23. *The Little Town*, in Asch's *Tales of My People*, trans. Meyer Levin (New York: Putnam, 1948), p. 85. All textual references are to this translation.

24. *The Little Town*, p. 122.

25. Howe and Greenberg, p. 79.

26. The original title is *Die Yatische Tochter*. (*Yat* is slang for a respected or distinguished Jew.)

27. See Madison (1923), p. 528.

28. See Cournos, p. 82. In another instance, Cournos reported that Asch had "expressed a predilection for Dickens and the 'prophetic' school of novelists, with Tolstoy as its chief protagonist and confessed to both having been factors in his creative development. This Dickensian element is strong in all of Mr. Asch's early fiction; and, indeed, there is still a strong dose of it in the earliest story of the present collection" (*Uncle Moses*). (John Cournos, "From the Yiddish," *New York Times Book Review*, 2 October 1938, p. 21.)

29. See the headnote to "Through the Wall—A Sketch by Scholem

Asch," *Current Literature*, 49 (October 1910), 461-63.

30. Quoted in Louis Zara, "Sholem Asch; a Titan Among Us," *Chicago Jewish Forum*, 1 (Winter 1942-43), 11.

31. Originally titled "The Fellow and the Child," it is included, as "Abandoned," in *Great Short Stories of the World*, ed. Barrett H. Clark and Maxim Lieber (New York: McBride, 1928), pp. 740-43.

32. Quoted in Madison, *Yiddish Literature*, p. 223. Second in importance only to *God of Vengeance* among Asch's dramas, *The Return* merits detailed comment. Its first title was *He Went and He Came Back* and was so published in Hebrew translation in the magazine *The Messenger* (*Hashaloich*) in 1904 and then in the original Yiddish in Peretz's *The Yiddish Library* (*De Yiddishe Bibliotek*), Nos. 3 and 4 (1904). In December 1904 the Polish writer Stanislav Witketitsh translated the play into Polish, and the Cracow Polish Theater then produced it and met with considerable success. This was no mean accomplishment for a Jewish playwright in Poland. (Later that year the Cracow company did well with Asch's one-act *The Liar*.) In 1909 *The Return* was published in Warsaw in book form as *Mit der Strum*, or *Downstream*. It was produced for the first time in the United States by the New York Neighborhood Playhouse, in the 1915-16 season, and in the 1919-20 theatrical season by Jacob Ben Ami's Jewish Art Theatre.

33. See Isaac Goldberg, *The Drama of Transition* (Cincinnati: Stewart & Kidd, 1922), p. 374.

34. "Winter: A Drama in One Act," in *Six Plays of the Yiddish Theatre*, ed. Isaac Goldberg (Boston: J.W. Luce, 1916), pp. 124-49. It was published originally, in 1906, in the Yiddish magazine *The New Way* (*Der Neier Veg*), the organ of the Socialist Territorialists in Vilna. Most of Asch's early tales and sketches, however, were being brought out by Kultur, a publishing house in Minsk.

35. Originally titled *Gleben*, this was the first work Asch completed in America.

36. Included in *Six Plays of the Yiddish Theatre*, pp. 151-75.

37. *Times of the Messiah (Moshiakhs Tsaytn)* was first published as *In the Time of the Messiah, a Tragedy in Three Acts;* it later came out as *A Dream of My People (A Cholem fun Mein Folk).* A still later edition was titled *A Play of the Times in Three Acts* (Vilna, 1906; 2nd ed., Vilna, 1907). On February 12, 1906 it was produced in St. Petersburg as *The Return to Zion,* starring the prominent actress Komisarjevsky in the part of Justine. On July 15, 1906 it was produced on the Polish stage in Warsaw.

38. Quoted in Madison, *Yiddish Literature,* pp. 224-25; I have slightly altered the punctuation.

39. Its original title was *Yichus.*

40. See "Sholem Asch," *Encyclopedia Britannica,* 14th ed., XXIII, 892.

41. See Rosenberg, *Face to Face,* pp. 12-13; see also Nathan Asch, p. 56.

42. *Momenten* (Warsaw: Progress Publishing House, 1908).

43. Information in a letter from Solomon Rosenberg to Ben Siegel, 27 January 1966.

44. Quoted in Madison, *Yiddish Literature,* p. 227.

45. "My Father and I," p. 55.

46. *Got fun Nekomeh* (Vilna: Zukunft Publishing House, 1907).

47. All textual references are to the most recent English translation, that by Joseph Landis. (See above, Chapter One, note 5.) Also in English is *Sabbatai Zevi,* but it is more spectacle than drama. Asch wrote fifteen plays in the decade preceding World War I and six more in the years that followed. Also, several of his novels (*Mottke, Salvation, Three Cities*) were adapted for the Yiddish theater. Yet not one of these plays has been translated into English.

48. See Landis, p. 71.

49. The holy scroll's traditional importance in Judaism cannot be overestimated. Such a scroll consists of the Old Testament's first five books, carefully transcribed on vellum. The task takes a highly skilled scribe years and is therefore expensive. To a religious Jew the sponsoring of a scroll is an act of consecration; when completed, the scroll is presented to a synagogue or temple in an individual's name.

50. Landis, p. 72.

51. Madison (1940), p. 308; see also Madison (1941), p. 24, and his *Yiddish Literature*, p. 225.

52. See Landis, p. 71.

53. See Landis, p. 72.

54. Quoted in Itzak Panner, *Sholem Asch in His Final Home* (Tel Aviv: I.L. Peretz, Library 1958), p. 44. (In Yiddish only—*Scholem Asch In Sayn Letzter Heym.*)

55. See Rosenberg, *Face to Face, pp. 6-7.*

56. Landis, p. 72.

57. See Panner, p. 8.

58. "A Word About My Library," p. xv.

CHAPTER THREE

1. Compiler of the fifteen-volume *Dictionary of Ancient and Modern Hebrew*, Eliezer Ben Yehuda (1857-1922) was Israel's staunchest advocate of Hebrew as a living, daily language. But he greeted Asch in Yiddish, explaining to the gathering that "I greet our honorable guest, Sholem Asch, in the language in which he creates." Asch read aloud passages from *The Little Town,* and his audience responded enthusiastically. In later years he repeatedly recalled the evening. "Very seldom," he would declare," has a reception given me so much joy as this one fifty years ago in

Jerusalem under the chairmanship of Ben Yehuda." (Quoted in Panner, p. 100.)

2. The original title was *In Eretz Yisroel* (Warsaw: Books-for-Everybody Publishing House, 1911).

3. Quoted in John K. Hutchens, "Mr. Asch at 75," *New York Herald Tribune Book Review*, 6 November 1955, p. 2; see also Girson, p. 20.

4. Quoted in Hutchens, p. 2.

5. Asch's translation appeared in 1910, in the monthly *The New Life* (*Das Naye Leben*).

6. First published in the *Yiddish Literary Monthly*, No. 3 (1908), its most recent English version is in *Kiddush Ha-Shem: An Epic of 1648 and Sabbatai Zevi: A Tragedy* (New York: Meridian, 1954). The "authorized" translation here is from the Russian version and is by Florence Whyte and George Rapall Noyes.

7. *Yugend* (Warsaw: Shimin Publishing House, 1908).

8. Information supplied by Gertrude Asch Gelber, Asch's niece, in conversation with Ben Siegel.

9. The original title was *Der Landsman.*

10. See above, Chapter Two, note 29.

11. *Earth* (Warsaw, 1910).

12. Its original title was *Kein America*. Appearing first in *The Friend* and the *Forward*, it went through several Yiddish editions, variously titled *To America* or *Joey* ("Yossele"). Translator for the American edition was James Fuchs (New York: Alpha Omega Publishing Company, 1919). All textual references are to this edition.

13. *America*, p. 97.

14. *Mary* was published first—two years after Asch wrote it—in *The Friend* (1913). *The Road to One's Self*, originally titled *Der Weg tzu Zich* (New York: Forward Publishing House, 1917-18), first appeared in *The Yiddish World* (*Die Yiddishe Velt*), a Vilna magazine.

15. Madison (1923), p. 529.

16. See Gorman, p. 398. Several years after the publication of *Mary*, Asch, having settled in America, wanted it translated into English. But as its setting was not America, Asch's publishers here rejected it; they thought *Uncle Moses*, with its New York locale, would be more acceptable to American readers. Neither *Mary* nor *The Road to One's Self* has appeared in English.

17. It has been published in Yiddish as *Churban Beth Hamikadash* and *Churban Yerusholiam* ("The Destruction of Jerusalem"); it appeared originally in *The Yiddish World*, No. 172 (1913).

18. Its original title was *Die Maisalech fun Chumosh* (Vilna: B.A. Klezkin, 1913).

19. Nathan Asch, p. 56.

20. Nathan Asch, p. 56.

21. None of these five works—including the aforementioned *The Road to One's Self* (see above, note 16)—is available in English.

22. Titled *Der Bund fun der Schwache*, it appeared originally in *The Yiddish World* (1912) and was produced at Berlin's Kamerspiel Theatre.

23. Trained for the law, Leonid Andreyev (1871-1919) turned court reporter and then author. In addition to stories and short novels, he wrote plays like *Anathema* (1904), *The Life of Man* (1907), and *King Hunger* (1909). Centering on the political unrest in Czarist Russia, most of his work tends to be bitterly pessimistic. He is best known, perhaps, for his short novel on the 1905 Revolution, *The Seven That Were Hanged* (1908).

24. Its original title was *Yiftah's Tochter* (Vilna: B.A. Klezkin,

1914). It had also appeared the previous year.

25. Its original title was *Reb Shloime Hanogid* (Vilna: B.A. Klezkin, 1913). Asch's dedication established the book's tone: "To my father, the complete Jew and the whole man; to him, whose life is a light before me like a bright star in a misty night, whom I see but cannot reach—to him I bestow this work. Father, if I cannot emulate you in my life, I want to do it in my dream." (Quoted in Madison, *Yiddish Literature*, p. 228.)

26. This is a slightly modified version of Charles Madison's translation; see Madison (1940), p. 305 and his *Yiddish Literature*, p. 229.

27. See Niger, p. 34.

28. See Meyer Waxman, "Shalom Ash," *A History of Jewish Literature* (1941; rpt. New York: Thomas Yoseloff, 1960), IV, 527.

29. Isaac Goldberg, "New York's Yiddish Writers," *The Bookman*, 46 (February 1918), 686.

30. "My Father and I," p. 57.

31. "My Father and I," p. 57.

32. "Sholem Asch: A Titan Among Us," p. 11.

33. This slip occurred in an early Yiddish version of *The Electric Chair*, published in English as *Judge Not—*.

34. "My Father and I," p. 57.

35. *A Shnirl Pearl* in the original Yiddish, the play's complete title is *A String of Pearls or The Holy Maiden*.

36. Madison (1940), p. 319.

37. The Yiddish version, *Mottke Ganef* (New York: Forward Publishing House, 1916), was followed the next year by an English translation, *Mottke the Vagabond*, trans. Isaac Goldberg (Boston:

J.W. Luce, 1917). It was reissued as *Mottke the Thief*, trans. Willa and Edwin Muir (New York: Putnam's, 1935). All textual references here are to the Muir version. Yet neither translation added much luster to the novel. Generally competent and conscientious translators, the Muirs here worked from a German rendering—rather than the original Yiddish—and produced a narrative lacking what Louis Kronenberger has aptly termed "the stewlike richness and savor of the Jewish vulgate" or the earthy humor and "emotional uniqueness" of Asch's bedeviled little people. (See Louis Kronenberger, "Sholem Asch's Novel of a Thief's Career," *New York Times Book Review*, 27 October 1935, p. 8.)

38. Madison (1941), p. 24.

39. Nathan L. Rothman, "The Earlier Asch," *Saturday Review of Literature*, 12 October 1935, p. 6.

40. *Mottke the Thief*, p. 178.

41. See Isaac Babel, *The Collected Stories* (New York: Meridian, 1960), pp. 203-34; and Isaac Bashevis Singer, *The Magician of Lublin* (New York: Noonday, 1960).

42. *Mottke the Thief*, p. 271.

43. "Sholem Asch: Still Immigrant and Alien," pp. 69-70.

CHAPTER FOUR

1. See Gorman, p. 396.

2. The three novels later were published in a single volume titled *Three Novels*, trans. Elsa Krauch (New York: Putnam's, 1938). All textual references are to this edition. *Uncle Moses* had appeared in an earlier English translation by Isaac Goldberg (New York: Dutton, 1921).

3. See Cargill, p. 72.

4. Smertenko, p. 182.

5. The play's original title was *Wer is der Foter?* and the compilations were titled *The Jewish Soldier and Other War Stories, The Destruction of Poland, Youthful Years (Yinge Yoren),* and *American Short Stories* (including "Label at Home," "Label in America," "Children of Abraham," and "Journey to California"). Of these tales several later appeared in English, but most have not.

6. In November 1918, anti-Semitic incidents flared in 110 Polish towns and villages. Nearly 200,000 Jews perished in Poland's civil wars alone, and in Rumania, Hungary, and Lithuania the number of anti-Jewish riot victims mounted daily. (See Joseph J. Schwartz and Beatrice I. Vulcan, "Overseas Aid," *The American Jew, A Reappraisal,* ed. Oscar I. Janowsky [Philadelphia: Jewish Publication Society, 1964], p. 280.)

7. "Sholem Asch Reports Distress of Lithuanian Jews," *New York Times,* 21 September 1919, p. 17, col. 4.

8. "My Father and I," p. 57; also, see above, Chapter One, note 6.

9. The war had created many new anxieties in the United States regarding the hordes of newcomers. In 1920-21, Congress was discussing the advisability of halting immigration for a year, and a popular public topic was how to make "good Americans" out of those already here. (See Editorial, "Immigration Problems in Recent Fiction," *New York Times Book Review,* 16 January 1921, p. 10.) Restrictive laws of 1921 and 1924 so reduced immigration from Eastern Europe that it ceased to be a significant political or economic factor.

10. The English translation, by Rufus Learsi (Israel Goldberg), retains the original Hebrew title, *Kiddush Ha-Shem,* and was published first in 1926 by the Jewish Publication Society. All subsequent textual references here, however, are to the more accessible *Kiddush Ha-Shem: An Epic of 1648 and Sabbatai Zevi: A Tragedy* (New York and Philadelphia: Meridian, 1959), which also uses the Learsi translation.

11. Hebrew posed no reading problems for Asch, but a Yiddish

translation (by S. Erdberg) of Friedberg's novel was available to him.

12. See Liptzin, p. 184.

13. See Panner, pp. 138-39.

14. See Shulman, p. 67.

15. Although written in 1919, and readily translated into German, Russian, Polish, and other languages, *Chaim Lederer's Return* did not appear in English until 1938 (see above, note 2). In the 1929 German-version manuscript, the title has been changed in Asch's handwriting to "Shop Krankeit" ("Shop Sickness"), and also the final paragraph has been revised in Asch's hand. (See *Catalogue of Hebrew and Yiddish Manuscripts and Books from the Library of Sholem Asch*, p. 8.) In the English version, "Shop Sickness" remains as the title of the fourteenth, or final, chapter.

16. See Cournos, "From the Yiddish," p. 21.

17. See Allen Guttmann, "The Conversion of the Jews," *Wisconsin Studies in Contemporary Literature*, 6 (Summer 1965), 163.

18. Titled originally *Der Toiter Mensch* (1920), it has not been translated into English.

19. Published also as *The Enchantress of Castile*, its original title was *Kishufmacherin fun Kastillien*. Written and published serially in 1921, it appeared as a book, in Warsaw, in 1926. This novel, too, has remained in Yiddish.

20. Madison (1941), p. 28. In this section I am indebted to the articles by Charles Madison referred to in these notes for my discussion of nature's influence on Asch's fiction.

21. Quoted in Smertenko, p. 181.

22. Translated by Madison; see his 1923 article, pp. 526-27.

23. See Smertenko, p. 181.

24. See Madison (1941), p. 28.

25. "The Red Hat," *Esquire*, 1 (April 1934), 48-49, 100.

26. *Yiddish Tales*, trans. Helena Frank (Philadelphia: Jewish Publication Society, 1912), pp. 514-28; the same tale is titled "Mama" in *From Many Countries*, pp. 68-79 and "The Mother's Reward" in *Children of Abraham*, pp. 62-74.

27. See Madison (1923), p. 525.

28. Translated by Madison; see his 1923 article, p. 524.

29. Asch's pantheism is most explicit in *The Little Town*; see *Tales of My People*, p. 64.

30. Asch, "A Word About My Collection of Jewish Books," p. viii.

31. See, for instance, "The Sinner," in *Yiddish Tales*, p. 532.

32. Cited by Madison (1923), p. 525.

33. Quoted in Madison (1923), p. 525.

34. At the European head office of the Jewish Joint Distribution Committee, Asch struck up a strong friendship with James Rosenberg, the distinguished lawyer-artist then acting as head of JDC's European activities. He introduced Rosenberg to some of the leading artists, art dealers, and writers then in Paris, and the latter did a "rapid pastel sketch" of Asch's "sorrowful profile." Rosenberg offers a curious note; he recalls that when he and Asch would start out for the Left Bank, usually in late afternoon, "We were invariably escorted or followed by two mysterious fellows, spies on or protectors of Asch. We never discovered who they were or what their business was." (James Rosenberg, *Painter's Self-Portrait* [New York: Crown, 1958], pp. 54-55.)

35. The original title was *Die Marranen* (1922).

36. It was published first in English, in *Three Novels* (see above, note 2), and later in Yiddish as *Death Penalty or The Electric Chair*

(Warsaw, 1926).

37. For a somewhat similar conclusion, see Cargill, p. 72; also, see Madison (1940), p. 315, and (1941), p. 25.

38. John Mair, "New Novels," *The New Statesman and Nation*, 12 November 1938, p. 797.

39. The phrase belongs to George Orwell, who described Rudyard Kipling as "a good bad poet." (See George Orwell, "Rudyard Kipling," *Dickens, Dali and Others* [New York: Reynal & Hitchcock, 1946], p. 156.)

40. Shalom Asch, *The God of Vengeance: Drama in Three Acts*, trans. Isaac Goldberg (Boston: The Stratford Company, 1918).

41. Mary Carolyn Davies, "Yiddish Plays," *The Nation*, 24 August 1918, p. 210.

42. Joseph Schildkraut, *My Father and I* (New York: Viking, 1959), pp. 180-81.

43. Schildkraut, p. 181.

44. See Editorial, "God of Vengeance," *The Outlook*, 6 June 1923, pp. 117-18. See also Editorial, "Drama and the Detectives," *The Nation*, 6 June 1923, p. 646; and "Sholem Asch," *Authors Today and Yesterday*, ed. Stanley Kunitz (New York: H.W. Wilson, 1933), p. 30.

45. See Lifson, pp. 576-81. For more general discussions of Asch's contribution to the Yiddish theater, see Lifson, pp. 89-93; Isaac Goldberg, ed. *Six Plays of the Yiddish Theatre*, pp. 119-22; Rebecca Drucker, "The Jewish Art Theatre," *Theatre Arts*, 4 (July 1920), 220-24.

46. See the 1930 issues of the *New York Times* for April 18, April 29, May 16, June 10, and June 20.

47. *The Nation*, 18 July 1923, pp. 59-61. The same tale is titled

"Tricked," in *From Many Countries*, pp. 155-60 and in *Tales of My People*, pp. 147-53.

48. Chaim Rozenstein, "A Half-Hour with Sholem Asch," *Our Time*, 1 February 1965, pp. 40-42. (In Yiddish)

49. Quoted in Robert van Gelder, "Asch Returns from the Past," *Writers and Writing* (New York: Scribner's, 1946), pp. 50-51.

50. Originally titled *Die Mutter* (1925), *The Mother* first was translated into English in 1930 by Nathan Ausubel and published by Horace Liveright. Unhappy with the results (and the reviews), Asch arranged for an "authorized translation" by Elsa Krauch (New York: Putnam's, 1937). (A Sun Dial Press Reprint Edition of this later translation appeared in 1950.) The reviews of both English versions generally were harsh—the earlier one being helped little by Ludwig Lewisohn's excessively laudatory preface. Indicative of the little impression Asch had made on American readers to this point was the insistence by several 1930 reviewers that *The Mother* was Asch's first novel to appear in English. It did become, however, the first selection of the newly formed Jewish-Book-of-the-Month Club.

CHAPTER FIVE

1. Issue dated October 26.

2. *Three Cities*, trans. Edwin and Willa Muir (New York: Putnam's 1933). All textual references are to this edition. The Yiddish title remained *Farn Mabl* ("Before the Flood"), but the novel was translated into German as *Die Trilogie von der Sintflut* ("The Trilogy of the Deluge") and published in three volumes (1927-32).

3. Christian Wahnschaffe is the protagonist of Wassermann's *The World's Illusion* (1913), Klim Samghin unites Gorky's four-novel cycle *The Life of Klim Samghin* (1927-36), and Pierre Bezuhov is, of course, a major figure in Tolstoy's *War and Peace* (1865-69).

4. Harry Slochower, "Spiritual Judaism: The Yearning for Status—Franz Werfel and Sholem Asch," *No Voice Is Wholly Lost:*

Writers and Thinkers in War and Peace (New York: Creative Age Press, 1945), p. 328.

5. See Louis Kronenberger, "Sholem Asch's Great Trilogy," *New York Times Book Review*, 22 October 1933, p. 1; see also Slochower, p. 241.

6. "Sholem Asch's Great Trilogy," p. 1.

7. "Sholem Asch's Great Trilogy," p. 1.

8. See, for instance, Franz Werfel, "In Praise of Schalom Asch," *Living Age*, 339 (February 1931), 598; James Hilton, "A Russian Story in the Grand Manner, *London Daily Telegraph*, 17 October 1933; and Compton Mackenzie, "The Best Novel I Have Read About the Jewish People," *London Daily Mail*, 19 October 1933.

9. Herbert Read, "Fiction," *The Spectator*, 27 October 1933, p. 592.

10. Moshe Nadir, "Don't Eat Your Heart Out, Sholem Asch," *Polemic* (New York: Yidburo Publishers, 1936), pp. 80-84. (In Yiddish)

11. See Nathan Asch, p. 59.

12. For legal actions against Nathan Asch's *Pay Day*, see the 1930 issues of *The New York Times* for April 29, May 16, June 10, and June 20.

13. The Bund, or the General Jewish Workers Union, was the first Jewish labor party. Founded in 1897, it was also the largest Jewish socialist party in pre-Bolshevik Russia and proved strongly opposed to Zionism.

14. Quoted in Rosenberg, *Face to Face*, p. 34.

15. See Werfel, p. 598. For Stefan Zweig's comments, see A.A. Roback, *Curiosities of Yiddish Literature* (Cambridge, Mass: Sci-Art Publishers, 1933), pp. 122-23.

16. The *Catalogue of . . . the Library of Sholem Asch* mentions 277 such letters, post cards, and telegrams; see p. 16, Item 101.

17. See Rosenberg, *Face to Face*, pp. 34-35.

18. Asch employed an orthography, according to Rosenberg, as "antiquated as his Hanukah lamps." And in addition to ignoring the usual rules of grammar, he would "forget" to include the vowels and would confuse masculine and feminine forms. Only when Rosenberg pointed out to Asch that his later novels had been published in the most modern Yiddish orthography did Asch allow him to transcribe his manuscripts with the more recent spellings. (See Rosenberg, *Face to Face*, p. 28.)

19. Quoted in van Gelder, p. 49.

20. Quoted in Rosenberg, *Face to Face*, p. 71.

21. Quoted in van Gelder, p. 50.

22. See Hutchens, "Mr. Asch at 75," p. 2.

23. Quoted in Rosenberg, *Face to Face*, pp. 47-48, 50.

24. Quoted in Madison, *Yiddish Literature*, p. 244.

25. Maurice Samuel, *Little Did I Know: Recollections and Reflections* (New York: Knopf, 1963), p. 275.

26. Quoted in Zara, p. 11.

27. Quoted in van Gelder, p. 51.

28. Nathan himself did not always come off as well with Hemingway. Once when both were shadowboxing, he hit Hemingway accidentally, and the latter, angered, struck Nathan in the mouth, knocking him down. That evening a contrite Hemingway appeared at Nathan Asch's door to declare: "I couldn't go to sleep until you forgave me. . . . You've got a lot of talent. You've got more of everything than any of us." (Quoted in Denis Brian, "The Importance of Knowing Ernest," *Esquire*, 77

[February 1972], 101.) But despite his contriteness here, Hemingway was not above making slighting comments about Nathan behind his back. (See Carlos Baker, *Ernest Hemingway: A Life Story* [New York: Scribner's, 1969], p. 135.)

29. *Midrashim* (plural of *midrash*) are compilations of early interpretations of—or commentaries on—Biblical texts. *Musar* books stem from a late nineteenth-century movement among orthodox Jewish groups in Lithuania devoted to moral self-criticism and to the study of traditional ethical literature (*musar*).

30. Quoted in van Gelder, p. 51.

31. See Rosenberg, *Face to Face*, pp. 77-78.

32. See Rosenberg, *Face to Face*, p. 70.

33. Asch's desire for the Nobel Prize, Maurice Samuel has reported, proved "a kind of mania with him. He didn't understand why Thomas Mann should have got it and not he." (Letter from Maurice Samuel to Ben Siegel, 29 April 1965.)

34. See Rosenberg, *Face to Face*, p. 64.

35. The complete title was *God's Prisoners, or The Lot of a Woman* (Warsaw, 1933). (In Yiddish: *Gots Gefangene*)

36. For a somewhat parallel discussion leading to a different estimate of *God's Prisoners*, see Madison, *Yiddish Literature*, pp. 238-39.

37. See Robie Macauley, "PEN and the Sword," *New York Times Book Review*, 15 August 1965, pp. 26-27.

38. See Rosenberg, *Face to Face*, pp. 66-68.

39. See Lifson, p. 587, Appendix B.

40. Dated 15 October 1936, the letter is in the Asch collection at Yale. (See *Catalogue of . . . the Library of Sholem Asch*, p. 2.) Charles Madison states that Asch returned the medal (*Yiddish*

Literature, p. 244), but the letter's presence in the collection indicates it was not mailed—and thus the medal not returned. Also in the collection are letters (1933) from officers of Warsaw's Yiddish PEN Club urging Asch not to decline the honor tendered him by the Polish government. (See *Catalogue,* p. 17, Item 101.)

41. Originally titled *Der Tillim Yid* (Warsaw, 1934), which translates literally as "The Psalm Jew," the novel was published in English as *Salvation,* trans. Willa and Edwin Muir (New York: Putnam's, 1951). An abridged edition of this translation had been published by Putnam's in 1934. Textual references are to the "enlarged" 1951 version.

42. Quoted in Madison, *Yiddish Literature,* pp. 244-45.

43. See Niger, p. 35.

44. "The Guilty Ones," *Atlantic Monthly,* 166 (December 1940), pp. 713-23.

45. See Irving Fineman, "A Tower of Babel in Jewish Poland," *Saturday Review of Literature,* 29 September 1934, p. 142.

46. See Eda Lou Walton, "A Prophet Arises in Israel," *New York Herald Tribune Books,* 23 September 1934, p. 2.

47. See Louis Kronenberger, "Profound Compassion," *New York Times Book Review,* 7 October 1934, p. 7.

48. See Rosenberg, *Face to Face,* pp. 97-98.

49. See Samuel Niger, *Sholem Asch: His Life and His Work* (New York: Congress of Jewish Culture, 1960). (In Yiddish)

CHAPTER SIX

1. In the Asch collection at Yale is a series of letters to Asch from Stefan Zweig, written during the period of Hitler's rise to power. They trace Zweig's life from his forced departure from Salzburg to his desperate mental state in Brazil, where, in 1942, he committed suicide.

2. Letter from Earle Balch to Ben Siegel, 14 July 1965.

3. Quoted in Rosenberg, *Face to Face*, p. 89.

4. Translated from the German by Willa and Edwin Muir (New York: Putnam's 1936), *The War Goes On* was published simultaneously in England, by Victor Gollancz, as *The Calf of Paper*. All textual references are to the American edition. (A 1937 Warsaw edition was titled *Baim Opgrunt* [*As the Tree Is Bent*].)

5. Quoted in Rosenberg, *Face to Face, p. 93.*

6. "Sholom [*sic*] Asch Arrives in U.S.," *New York Times*, 18 January 1935, p. 7, col. 3.

7. See *New York Times*, 22 February 1935, p. 19, col. 2.

8. *Saturday Review of Literature*, 6 April 1935, p. 601.

9. The stories were translated from the German by Caroline Cunningham (New York: Putnam's, 1935).

10. Nathan later denied being able to read Yiddish; if so, he could not have read these stories when they were written. See Nathan Asch, "My Father and I," p. 57. For comments (in Yiddish) on Nathan's claim, see Solomon Rosenberg, "Sholem Asch, His Son and His Critics," n. pag.

11. 28 March 1936, p. 17, col. 2.

12. Stefan and Friderike Zweig, *Their Correspondence 1912-1942*, trans. Henry G. Alsberg (New York: Hastings House Publishers, 1954), p. 274.

13. Louis Kronenberger, "Sholem Asch Dramatizes Germany's Years of Inflation," *New York Times Book Review*, 15 November 1936, p. 4.

14. See Milton Rugoff, "In a Fantastic Post-War World," *New York Herald Tribune*, 1 November 1936, p. 6.

15. "In a Fantastic Post War World," p. 6.

16. "Sholem Asch Dramatizes Germany's Years of Inflation," p. 4.

17. See Charlotte Moody, "Chaotic Lives," *Saturday Review of Literature*, 31 October 1936, p. 7.

18. Trans. Elsa Krauch (New York: Putnam's, 1938). All textual references are to this edition. (The Yiddish version, *Dos Gezang fun Tol*, appeared the same year, in Warsaw.)

19. See Rosenberg, *Face to Face*, p. 109.

20. Quoted in Rosenberg, *Face to Face*, p. 119.

21. Quoted in Rosenberg, *Face to Face*, p. 110.

22. In Sholem Asch, *Children of Abraham*, trans. Maurice Samuel (New York: Putnam's, 1942), pp. 279-85. "A Peculiar Gift" is included also in *The Seas of God*, ed. Whit Burnett (Cleveland: World, 1946), pp. 129-35 and in *From Many Countries*, pp. 338-44.

23. Translated by Meyer Levin, "Eretz Israel" appears in *Tales of My People*, pp. 243-49 and in *From Many Countries*, pp. 304-9; and as "At the Shore of Eretz Isroel" in *The Jewish Mirror* (Winter 1962), pp. 9-12.

24. The Yiddish title was *Der Man fun Notseres*.

25. "My Father and I," p. 60.

26. Quoted in Rosenberg, *Face to Face*, p. 116.

27. Issue dated 23 April 1937.

28. Quoted in Rosenberg, *Face to Face*, p. 117.

29. "Sholem Asch Here to Aid Relief Fund," *New York Times*, 23 April 1937, p. 19, col. 2.

30. See Rosenberg, *Face to Face*, pp. 127-31.

31. See *Children of Abraham*, pp. 181-235; Asch referred to "De Profundis" as "Out of the Depths."

32. See Rosenberg, *Face to Face*, p. 123:

33. Abraham Cahan, *Sholem Asch's Neier Veg* (New York, 1941); it is available only in Yiddish.

34. See Rosenberg, *Face to Face*, pp. 124-25.

35. Quoted in Rosenberg, *Face to Face*, p. 139.

36. *New York Times*, 17 May 1938, p. 26, col. 2.

37. John K. Hutchens, "On an Author: Sholem Asch," *New York Herald Tribune Book Review*, 15 April 1951, p. 2; see also Hutchens, "Mr. Asch at 75: Prophet with Honor," *New York Times Book Review*, 6 November 1955, p. 2.

38. Quoted in van Gelder, p. 49. Asch, years before, had placed these words in the mouth of the freeswinging young poet Frier, in his novel *The Mother* (p. 140).

39. "U.S. Delegates Sail for Parley on Jews," *New York Times*, 29 January 1939, p. 22, col. 3.

40. "A Word About My Collection of Books," pp. xvi-xvii.

41. Letter from Earle Balch to Ben Siegel, 14 July 1965.

42. See Madison, *Yiddish Literature*, pp. 247-48.

43. Quoted in a 1944 interview with Frank S. Mead of *The Christian Herald;* see Shulman, pp. 63-64 and Hindus, p. 20.

44. Quoted in Madison, *Yiddish Literature*, p. 248.

45. Quoted in Rosenberg, *Face to Face*, pp. 119.

46. Philip Rahv, "The Healing of a Wound," *The Nation*, 28 October 1939, p. 471.

47. Quoted in Madison, *Yiddish Literature*, pp. 248-49.

48. Ralph Thompson, "Books of the Times," *New York Times*, 19 October 1939, p. 21, col. 2.

49. See Milton Rugoff, "A Great Novel About the Life of Jesus," *New York Herald Tribune Books*, 22 October 1939, p. 3.

50. See Karl M. Chworowsky, "Jesus the Jew," *Christian Century*, 7 February 1940, p. 180.

51. See Alfred Kazin, "Rabbi Yeshua ben Joseph," *New Republic*, 1 November 1939, p. 376.

52. Quoted in Madison, *Yiddish Literature*, p. 252. See also Asch's speech to the American Booksellers Association, *New York Times*, 14 May 1940, p. 21, col. 2.

53. "The Gospel in a Modern Version," *Saturday Review of Literature*, 21 October 1939, p. 5.

54. "Rabbi Yeshua ben Joseph," pp. 375-76. (*Chaver* translates as "comrade.")

55. Quoted in Madison, *Yiddish Literature*, p. 252.

56. See Cargill, p. 74.

57. Quoted in Madison, *Yiddish Literature*, p. 252.

58. Quoted in van Gelder, p. 50.

59. For his research into Jesus' life and times, Asch assembled over the years a working library he estimated at 1200 volumes.

60. Robert Littel, "Outstanding Novels," *Yale Review*, 29 (Winter 1940), viii.

61. See Mary M. Colum, "Re-creation of New Testament History," *The Forum and Century*, 102 (December 1939), 262.

62. Peter Monro Jack, "A Nobly Conceived Novel of the Life of Jesus," *New York Times Book Review*, 29 October 1939, p. 3.

63. Albert Van Nostrand, *The Denatured Novel* (New York: Bobbs-Merrill, 1962; rpt. Charter Books, 1962), p. 43.

CHAPTER SEVEN

1. Letter from Milton G. Tunick to Ben Siegel, 2 April 1965.

2. For a lucid summary of Jewish attitudes toward Jesus, see Samuel Sandmel, *We Jews and Jesus* (New York: Oxford University Press, 1965; rpt. Oxford Paperback, 1973). An interesting but more generalized discussion is that by David Singer, "The Jewish Messiah: A Contemporary Commentary," *Midstream*, 19 (May 1973), 57-67.

3. *Los Angeles Times*, 5 April 1969, p. 18, col. 7.

4. "Sholem Asch and Anne Frank," *Carolina Israelite*, May 1957, p. 9.

5. *New York Times*, 9 November 1939, p. 20, col. 6.

6. Quoted in Chworowsky, p. 179.

7. See Madison (1940), p. 329.

8. *The Christianity of Sholem Asch* (New York, Philosophical Library, 1953).

9. *The Christianity of Sholem Asch*, p. 85. Lieberman, who repeatedly accuses Asch of plagiarizing Christian writers, was himself reproached for borrowing extended passages from Dr. Chaim Einshproch's Yiddish translation of the New Testament and of one other literary theft. (See, in Yiddish, "On the Thief's Head the Hat Burns," *The Mediator*, 25 (April-June 1952), 8. So vicious were Lieberman's attacks that they often worked to Asch's advantage. Samuel Sandmel, for instance, writes that he finds "tedious" Asch's novels on Jesus and Paul, and he warns "the

unwary that the Judaism Asch attributes to the age of Jesus is in reality that of pre-modern Poland. Antagonistic as I am to Asch's works, when I read the merciless attacks on him in Chaim Lieberman, *The Christianity of Scholem Asch*, I ended up with a deep sympathy for him." (*We Jews and Jesus*, p. 117, 39n.)

10. See Melech Epstein, "Abraham Cahan," *Profiles of Eleven* (Detroit: Wayne State University Press, 1965), pp. 104-6.

11. Cahan's letter to Asch was dated 17 March 1938.

12. Quoted in Judd L. Teller, *Strangers and Natives: The Evolution of the American Jew from 1921 to the Present* (New York: Delacorte, 1968), p. 77.

13. See Teller, p. 78.

14. *We Jews and Jesus*, p. 103; see also p. 117, 39n.

15. See Epstein, p. 105. See also Ronald Sanders, "The Jewish Daily Forward," *Midstream*, 8 (December 1962), 93.

16. Cahan, p. 4. See also Milton Hindus, "Reflections on Sholem Asch," *The Reconstructionist*, 28 November 1958, p. 20.

17. Quoted in Hutchens, "Mr. Asch at 75," p. 2.

18. Letter from Earle Balch to Ben Siegel, 14 July 1965.

19. "Young in the Thirties," *Commentary*, 41 (May 1966), 49.

20. Quoted in Madison, *Yiddish Literature*, p. 252.

21. "Sholem Asch Speaks," *The Mediator*, 25 (April-June 1952), 1.

22. Quoted in Shulman, pp. 63-64, and in Hindus, p. 20.

23. Quoted in Hutchens, "Mr. Asch at 75," p. 2.

24. Quoted in Epstein, p. 105.

25. "Sholem Asch; a Titan Among Us," p. 10.

26. Bickel and Grayzel are quoted in Hindus, p. 21.

27. "Reflections on Sholem Asch," p. 22.

28. "Reflections on Sholem Asch," p. 22.

29. See Louis Rittenberg, "Sholem Asch," *Universal Jewish Encyclopedia,* ed. Isaac Landman (New York: Universal Jewish Encyclopedia, 1939), I, 534.

30. Sponsored by the *New York Herald Tribune* and the American Booksellers Association, the forum was held at New York's Hotel Astor on 13 May 1940.

31. Letter from Charles Hinton to Ben Siegel, 28 February 1965.

32. Letter from Earle Balch to Ben Siegel, 14 July 1965.

33. "Asch Returns from the Past," p. 51.

34. "My Father and I," pp. 61-62.

35. "I Adopt an American Ancestor: A Fable," pp. 47-48.

36. "I Adopt an American Ancestor: A Fable," p. 53.

37. "The Guilty Ones," p. 723.

38. Quoted in Hindus, p. 22.

39. Quoted in van Gelder, p. 49.

40. Sholem Asch, *What I Believe,* trans. Maurice Samuel (New York: Putnam's, 1941); it was published in England as *My Personal Faith* (London: Routledge, 1942). All textual references are to the American edition.

41. *New York Times,* 20 January 1941, p. 11, col. 1.

42. Letter from Helen Grace Carlisle to Ben Siegel, 9 March 1965.

43. The Hebrew words are "Yiskadol V'Yiskadash," and under that title the story is included in *Tales of My People*, pp. 175-90 and in *From Many Countries*, pp. 245-58.

44. Sholem Asch, "In the Valley of Death," *New York Times Magazine*, 7 February 1943, p. 36.

45. See *From Many Countries*, p. vii.

CHAPTER EIGHT

1. Sholem Asch, *The Apostle*, trans. Maurice Samuel (New York: Putnam's, 1943). All textual references are to this edition. Neither *The Apostle* nor the later *Mary* has been published in Yiddish.

2. See Rosa Lyon Bludworth, "Sholem Asch and His Plea for Reconciliation," *Religion in Life*, 27 (Winter 1957-58), 91.

3. "Sholem Asch: Still Immigrant and Alien," p. 74.

4. Clifton Fadiman, "Paul," *The New Yorker*, 18 September 1943, p. 90.

5. M.J.T., "The Apostle to the Gentiles," *Christian Science Monitor Weekly*, 2 October 1943, p. 12.

6. The words here are arranged to resemble an altar—in a manner curiously reminiscent of the English metaphysical poets.

7. "Neither Jew nor Greek," *New Republic*, 1 November 1943, p. 626.

8. "A Dramatic Novel—Biography of the Apostle Paul," *New York Times Book Review*, 19 September 1943, p. 3.

9. See Kazin, "Neither Jew nor Greek," p. 627.

10. "Sholem Asch: Still Immigrant and Alien," p. 74.

11. "Paul," pp. 90, 93.

12. "Paul," p. 90.

13. Letter from Earle Balch to Ben Siegel, 17 August 1965.

14. A.A. Roback, *Psychology Through Literature: Apologia Pro Vita Yiddica* (Cambridge, Mass.: Sci-Art Publishers, 1942), p. 62.

15. While writing *The Apostle* Asch had borrowed reference books from the Yale library and had discussed his historical interpretations with Professor E.R. Goodenough, a respected Yale specialist in Hellenistic studies.

16. "A Word About My Collection," pp. xiv-xvi, xviii.

17. "Sholem Asch: A Titan Among Us," p. 10.

18. Quoted in Madison, *Yiddish Literature*, pp. 255-56.

19. "Toward a Wider Union," *Saturday Review of Literature*, 29 September 1945, p. 12.

20. Trans. Milton Hindus (New York: Putnam's, 1946). All textual references are to this edition.

21. "As far as I know," Asch stated on another occasion, "there are no other Messianic faiths, except the Jewish and the Christian, which has grown from it. All other faiths are God-found. The Messianic is God-seeking. An everlasting tragic thirst." ("Sholem Asch Speaks," p. 1.)

22. Quoted in Cargill, p. 73.

23. Trans. A.H. Gross (New York: Putnam's, 1946). All textual references are to this edition.

24. See Nathan L. Rothman, "Mr. Asch's Ambitious Novel," *Saturday Review of Literature*, 19 October 1946, p. 18.

25. The fire occurred on 25 March 1911 and consumed 146 lives;

most of the victims were young Jewish and Italian immigrant girls.

26. Information supplied by Gertrude Asch Gelber, Asch's niece, in conversation with Ben Siegel.

27. The Hebrew prayer for the dead.

28. See Harold Rosenberg, "What Love is Not," *Commentary*, 3 (June 1947), 593.

29. "Briefly Noted," *The New Yorker*, 2 November 1946, p. 124.

30. "What Love Is Not," p. 593.

31. Metro-Goldwyn-Mayer reportedly gave Asch a down payment of $150,000, with the rest of the sales price geared to book sales. But apparently the film was never made. See *New York Times*, 28 August 1946, p. 32, col. 6.

32. Co-winner that year was Pauline Kibbe, for her *Latin Americans in Texas*. See *New York Times*, 24 April 1947, p. 22, col. 7.

33. *Der Brenendiker Dorn* (New York, 1946); included here were "Yiskadol V'Yiskadosh," "Christ in the Ghetto," and "A Child Leads the Way."

34. The two volumes were published in 1948, by the *Yiddisher Kultur Farband* (YKUF or The Ekuf), a left-wing New York publishing house.

35. See above, Chapter Two, note 23.

36. See Bennell Braunstein, "Voice from the Ghetto," *New York Herald Tribune Weekly Book Review*, 28 November 1948, p. 3.

37. Discussed previously as "The Wiles of Destiny."

38. *Mary*, trans. Leo Steinberg (New York: Putnam's, 1949).

39. For a somewhat similar discussion of these points, see

Bludworth, p. 85.

40. "Neither Jew nor Greek," p. 626.

41. See Edmund Fuller, "Mother of Christ," *Saturday Review of Literature*, 8 October 1949, p. 19.

42. See Milton Rugoff, "Sholem Asch Concludes His Trilogy," *New York Herald Tribune Weekly Book Review*, 9 October 1949, p. 3.

43. Letter from Earle Balch to Ben Siegel, 14 July 1965.

44. "He was dumfounded when I refused to translate *Mary*," Samuel has written. "I would not tell him outright that I thought the book an artistic mess, but that was what my individual objections amounted to. The sympathy he had brought to his portrayals of Jesus and Paul became cloying sentimentality when he turned to Mary. Here he could indeed be unjustly suspected of secret Christological sentiments, and even of what many Christians have objected to, namely Mariolatry. The rage of his slanderers had, however, spent itself on *The Nazarene* and *The Apostle*, where it had not a shadow of justification" (*Little Did I Know*, p. 275).

45. "Miriam & Yeshua," *Time*, 7 November 1949, p. 100.

46. Here, as elsewhere, Asch underscores his characters' Jewishness by the use of Hebrew names, but he generally employs them inconsistently.

47. Interpreting, as do many Protestants, the New Testament word *adelphoi* (brethren) as "brothers," Asch insists that Mary did bear Joseph other children—four sons and a daughter. Roman Catholics (and some Protestants) translate the Greek term as "kinsmen" and hold Mary's virginity to have been lifelong.

48. See Fuller, p. 19.

49. "Sholem Asch Concludes His Trilogy," p. 3.

50. "Mother of Christ," pp. 19-20.

51. See *Mary*, pp. 293-303.

52. "Foreword," *Tales of My People*, p. ix.

53. George Jessel, *This Way, Miss* (New York: Henry Holt, 1955), pp. 138-39. Mr. Jessel would have been at least more rhetorically precise had he followed convention and said "Reb Sholem" instead of "Reb Asch."

54. Letter from Maurice Samuel to Ben Siegel, 29 April 1964. Here Samuel points out that he later translated two other novels by Asch (*Moses* and *Passage in the Night*), "tho' they were rather weak too—but they didn't offend me." Earlier he had refused to translate *East River*, "which I didn't like as a book."

55. Quoted in Shulman, pp. 64-65.

56. *Little Did I Know*, p. 275.

57. Quoted in Golden, p. 9.

58. Letter from Maurice Samuel to Ben Siegel, 29 April 1964.

59. Letter from Earle Balch to Ben Siegel, 17 August 1965.

60. Letter from Maurice Samuel to Ben Siegel, 29 April 1964.

CHAPTER NINE

1. Trans. Willa and Edwin Muir (New York: Putnam's, 1951). The first American edition of *Salvation* (1934) had troubled Asch; Putnam's had followed English publisher Victor Gollancz, who, thinking the religious detail excessive, had omitted much that Asch believed important to the narrative. The new edition restored the original material.

2. "On an Author: Sholem Asch," p. 2.

3. Sholem Asch, "Some of the Authors of 1951, Speaking for Themselves," *New York Herald Tribune Book Review*, 7 October

1951, p. 24.

4. Quoted in Hutchens, "On an Author: Sholem Asch," p. 2.

5. Quoted in Washburn, pp. 17-E, 22-E.

6. Letter from Earle Balch to Ben Siegel, 14 July 1965.

7. See *New York Times*, 27 November 1953, p. 25, col. 7.

8. Nathan Asch, "My Father and I," p. 63.

9. Josephine Herbst had described Nathan Asch to Callaghan as "an amusing talented man who was a little wistful." (See Morley Callaghan, *That Summer in Paris* [New York: Coward-McCann, 1963], pp. 53-54.)

10. Nathan Asch, p. 63.

11. Trans. Maurice Samuel (New York: Putnam's, 1951). All textual references are to this edition. Asch and Samuel were again on good working terms. In 1944 Asch had declared that Moses' shedding of human blood (that of the Egyptian overseer) prevented him from writing a Moses novel. (See Hindus, "Reflections on Sholem Asch," pp. 18-19.) Apparently he had overcome his qualms.

12. See, for example, Leslie Fiedler, "Exodus: Adaptation by Sholem Asch," *Commentary*, 13 (January 1952), 73.

13. Harold C. Gardiner, S.J., "Two Novels that Distort the Past," *In All Conscience: Reflections on Books and Culture* (New York: Doubleday, 1959), p. 73.

14. A Jewish saying declares that had Moses not brought forth the Hebrews another leader would have done so. In the *Haggadah*, a communally composed and ritualized retelling of the Passover tale, Moses is not mentioned.

15. Indeed, Asch here seems to be venting his resentments at his critics; he even personalizes his narrative by creating an Asch "ancestor" among the Israelites—one Nachshon ben Aminadab, of

the tribe of Judah—as if to validate his right to criticize his own.

16. "Exodus: Adaptation by Sholem Asch," p. 73. See also Charles J. Rolo, "Moses," *Atlantic Monthly*, 178 (November 1951), 95.

17. "Exodus: Adaptation by Sholem Asch," p. 73.

18. Trans. Maurice Samuel (New York: Putnam's 1953). All textual references are to this edition. The Yiddish version, entitled *Grossman and Son (Grossman un Zun)* was published at the same time. Asch's early working title for the novel, however, had been *Never Too Late.*

19. "The Crazy Mask of Literature," *The Nation,* 14 November 1953, p. 405.

20. See Nathan Rothman, "A Man's Conscience," *Saturday Review,* 17 October 1953, p. 27.

21. "A Word About My Collection of Jewish Books," pp. xv-xvi.

22. Quoted in Panner, pp. 45-46.

23. "Sholem Asch to Sail to Rejoin Ailing Wife," *New York Times,* 27 November 1953, p. 25, col. 7.

24. See, for example, Nathan Ziprin, "Asch to Ash," *Long Island Jewish Press,* September 1957.

25. Trans. Arthur Saul Super (New York: Putnam's, 1955). All textual references are to this edition.

26. See Rosenberg, "Sholem Asch, His Son and His Critics," n. pag.

27. See Mary Hornaday, "The Birth of the Messianic Idea," *Christian Science Monitor,* 3 November 1955, p. 6. See also Lewis Nichols, "Talk with Sholem Asch," *New York Times Book Review,* 6 November 1955, p. 26; and Hutchens, "Mr. Asch at 75," p. 2.

28. See P.J. Searles, "A Novel About Isaiah," *New York Herald*

Tribune Book Review, 6 November 1955, p. 2.

29. Quoted in Nichols, p. 26.

30. See Rosenberg, "Sholem Asch, His Son and His Critics," n. pag.

31. Quoted in Nichols, p. 26.

32. Quoted in Hutchens, "Asch at 75," p. 2.

33. This passage is a composite of remarks quoted in Hutchens, "Mr. Asch at 75," p. 2, and in Hornaday, p. 6.

34. Quoted in Nichols, p. 26.

35. See Meyer Levin, "Prophet of the Return," *New York Times Book Review*, 6 November 1955, p. 4.

36. See Judd L. Teller, "Unhistorical Novels," *Commentary*, 21 (April 1956), 394.

37. Historians view Cyrus as a shrewd strategist who wished Judea to serve as a buffer between his Persian home base and a troublesome Egypt. Some modern Jews see him, as they do Napoleon, as a champion of religious freedom. Napoleon's famous appeal to the Jews to join him in "liberating" Jerusalem, it has been suggested, was modeled on Cyrus's somewhat similar call. (See Teller, p. 395.)

38. "Prophet of the Return," p. 4.

39. See Panner, p. 48.

40. See Teller, p. 395.

41. Apocalyptic tendencies that led to both Jewish and Christian Messianic movements were apparent as early as Ezekiel, but they did not "flower" until after the Jewish return (538 B.C.) from Babylon. In fact, a Messianic movement and its related literature evolved late in the Second Commonwealth. Even then most

Messianic ideas and writings were relegated to apocryphal status and were never accepted by more than a minority.

42. See Levin, p. 4.

43. Quoted in Smertenko, pp. 180-81.

44. Lewis Gannet, Rev. of *The Prophet* in *New York Herald Tribune*, 3 November 1955, p. 21.

45. "Mixed Fiction," *Time*, 31 October 1955, p. 98.

CHAPTER TEN

1. The letter was dated 19 September 1955; see Panner, pp. 14-15.

2. I have included in my text (in parentheses) the page numbers from Panner's book, *Sholem Asch in His Final Home*, wherever such citations have seemed appropriate. Cast in journal form (and untranslated from the Yiddish), his recollections are generally brief, elliptical, and little concerned with continuity. I have recast, therefore, much of his information for use here. Of related interest is a compilation of anecdotes about Asch in Israel, collected mainly at second hand, by Itzhok Turkow-Grudberg, and published (in Yiddish) as *The Way of Sholem Asch* (Bat Yam, Israel: Sholem Asch-House, 1967); in Yiddish: *Sholem Asch dereh der Yidischen Ebigkeit*). Mr. Grudberg has been curator of Sholem Asch-House.

3. At the first Bat Yam reception for Asch, Elberg gave a deeply emotional talk, declaring: "Asch did not sin against us, but we sinned against him! He always meant our welfare. His intent was always to close the gap of hatred that exists between Christians and Jews" (Panner, p. 17). The Yiddish Writers Club also feted Asch, while *Die Goldene Keit* (*The Golden Chain*), among the world's most influential Yiddish magazines, had been publishing Asch for years and continued to do so despite the boycott. The tri-weekly newspaper *Die Leste Nies* (*The Latest News*) also supported Asch. These details help to counteract the stories—circulated so widely and long in America—of Asch's "ostracism" in Israel.

4. A small parchment scroll, the *mezuzah* contains the first two paragraphs of the *Shema* passage (Deut. 6:4-9 and 11:13-21). Rolled tightly, the scroll is placed in a cylindrical container and affixed to the upper righthand doorpost in the entrance to the Jewish home—and, if desired, to each of its living rooms.

5. An eminent Zionist, and later a member of the Rescue Committee of the Jewish Agency for Palestine, Kastner had engaged in protracted negotiations with Adolf Eichmann to ransom 100,000 Hungarian Jews. His efforts produced meager results. Eventually, 1,685 Jews, at $200 a head, were saved. Of these, 388 came from Kluj, Kastner's hometown, and of these many were his relatives. (See Sachar, pp. 455-56.)

6. Quoted in Rosenberg, *Face to Face*, p. 146.

7. See, for instance, Hindus, p. 17.

8. See Leftwich, p. 15.

9. Despite his disavowal of the role of literary "teacher," Asch neither denied nor apologized for the strong didactic element in his fiction. "To me writing represents a message," he told an interviewer, "not simply a form of entertainment. . . . If you have no message to transmit, what is there to impart?" (Quoted in Washburn, p. 17-E.)

10. Written by Jacob Ashkenazi (c. 1550-1626), the *Tz'enah u-Ré enah* ("Go forth and see, ye daughters of Jerusalem"—Song of Songs 3:11) consists of rabbinical commentaries and legends on the Pentateuch.

11. These words and sentiments were expressed by Nathan Ziprin, writing in the *Long Island Jewish Press*, September 1957.

12. Both Dingoll and Menes are quoted in Rosenberg, *Face to Face*, pp. 144-45.

13. Quoted in Shulman, p. 65.

14. Quoted in Rosenberg, *Face to Face*, pp. 145, 147-49.

15. *Little Did I Know*, p. 274.

16. Irving Howe, "Sholem [*sic*] Aleichem: Voice of Our Past," *A World More Attractive* (New York: Horizon Press, 1963), p. 215.

17. "My Father and I," p. 64.

18. "In his successful books," Maurice Samuel noted, Asch "kept an eye on the outside world and translatability—which is why I found him so easy to translate." (Maurice Samuel, "My Three Mother-Tongues," *Midstream*, 18 [March 1972], 56.)

19. See Madison (1940), p. 336.

20. Several commentators have suggested this comparison, but the most authoritative observation would seem that of Maurice Samuel. Asch's "Yiddish style was primitive," Samuel has stated, "it had to be corrected continuously in translation. There was something about him that reminded me of Dreiser." (Letter from Maurice Samuel to Ben Siegel, 29 April 1965.)

21. Smertenko, p. 181.

22. "Reflections on Asch," p. 19.

23. Quoted in Rosenberg, *Face to Face*, p. 86.

24. Quoted in Rosenberg, *Face to Face*, p. 117.

25. Quoted in Smertenko, p. 181.

26. See Madison, *Yiddish Literature*, pp. 243-44.

27. See Hindus, p. 19.

28. *Little Did I Know*, p. 272.

29. Alfred Kazin, "Imagination and the Age," *The Reporter*, 5 May 1966, p. 35.

30. "Reflections on Asch," p. 19.

31. See Madison (1940), p. 331.

32. Quoted in Madison (1940), pp. 332-33.

33. Asch develops this idea at length in the early chapters of *Salvation;* see especially Chapter Five ("Morning Service").

34. Quoted in Madison (1940), p. 333; see also pp. 334-36.

35. Letter from Louis Zara to Ben Siegel, 13 April 1965.

Selected Bibliography

PRIMARY SOURCES

(Only Asch's works in English translation are listed here. For his Yiddish titles and their publication data, see NOTES AND REFERENCES.)

NOVELS

America. Trans. James Fuchs. New York: Alpha Omega Publishing Company, 1918.

The Apostle. Trans. Maurice Samuel. New York: Putnam's, 1943. Toronto: G. Allen, 1943. London: Macdonald, 1949. New York: Pocket Books, 1957.

The Calf of Paper. See below, *The War Goes On.*

East River. Trans. A.H. Gross. New York: Putnam's, 1946. Toronto: G. Allen, 1946. London: Macdonald, 1948.

Kiddush Ha-Shem: An Epic of 1648. Trans. Rufus Learsi (Isaac Goldberg). Philadelphia: Jewish Publication Society of America, 1912, 1926. This translation was reprinted in *Kiddush Ha-Shem: An Epic of 1648 and Sabbatai Zevi: A Tragedy.* New York: Meridian Books and Philadelphia: Jewish Publication Society of America, 1959. (*Kiddush Ha-Shem* is referred to in my text as *Sanctification of the Name.*)

Mary. Trans. Leo Steinberg. New York: Putnam's, 1951. London: Macdonald, 1950. Toronto: G. Allen, 1950. New York: Pocket Books, 1957.

Moses. Trans. Maurice Samuel. New York: Putnam's, 1951. London: Macdonald, 1952. New York: Pocket Books, 1958.

The Mother. Trans. Nathan Ausubel. New York: Horace Liveright, 1930. London: G. Routledge, 1937. New York: AMS Press, 1970.

_____. Trans. Elsa Krauch. New York: Putnam's, 1937. Toronto: G. Allen, 1937. New York: Grosset, 1940. Garden City, N.Y.: Sun Dial Press, 1950.

Mottke the Thief. Trans. Willa and Edwin Muir. New York and London: Putnam's, 1935. London: V. Gollancz, 1936. Toronto: Reyerson, 1936. Westport Conn.: Greenwood Press, 1970.

Mottke the Vagabond. Trans. Isaac Goldberg. Boston: J.W. Luce, 1917.

The Nazarene. Trans. Maurice Samuel. New York: Putnam's, 1939. Toronto: G. Allen, 1939. London: G. Routledge, 1939, 1941, 1949, 1956. New York: Pocket Books, 1947, 1956.

A Passage in the Night. Trans. Maurice Samuel. New York: Putnam's, 1953. Toronto: G. Allen, 1953. London: Macdonald, 1954.

The Prophet. Trans. Arthur Saul Super. New York: Putnam's, 1955. London: Macdonald, 1956. Toronto: G. Allen, 1956. New York: Pocket Books, 1958.

Salvation. Trans. Willa and Edwin Muir. New York: Putnam's, 1934. London: V. Gollancz, 1934. Toronto: Reyerson, 1934.

_____. Revised Edition. Trans. Willa and Edwin Muir. New York: Putnam's, 1951. Toronto: G. Allen, 1951. London: Macdonald, 1953. New York: Schocken Books, 1968.

Song of the Valley. Trans. Elsa Krauch. New York: Putnam's, 1939. London: G. Routledge, 1939. Toronto: G. Allen, 1939.

Three Cities: A Trilogy. Trans. Willa and Edwin Muir. New York: Putnam's, 1933, 1943. London: V. Gollancz, 1933, 1937. Toronto: Reyerson, 1933, 1937. London: Macdonald, 1955. New York: Bantam Books, 1967.

Three Novels: Uncle Moses, Chaim Lederer's Return, Judge

Not—. Trans. Elsa Krauch. New York: Putnam's, 1938. London: G. Routledge, 1938. Toronto: G. Allen, 1938.

Uncle Moses. Trans. Isaac Goldberg. New York: E.P. Dutton, 1920. London: Fisher Unwin, 1922.

The War Goes On. Trans. Willa and Edwin Muir. New York: Putnam's, 1936. English Edition: *The Calf of Paper*. Trans. Edwin and Willa Muir. London: V. Gollancz, 1936, 1938. Toronto: Reyerson, 1936.

PLAYS

The God of Vengeance: Drama in Three Acts. Trans. Isaac Goldberg. Boston: The Stratford Company, 1918. Girard, Kans.: Haldeman-Julius, Little Blue Book No. 416.

_____. Trans. Joseph C. Landis. In *The Dybbuk and Other Great Yiddish Plays*. Ed. Joseph C. Landis. New York: Bantam Books, 1966. Pp. 69-113.

_____. Trans. Joseph C. Landis. In *The Great Jewish Plays*. Ed. Joseph C. Landis. New York: Horizon Press, 1972. Pp. 69-113 (Published originally as *The Dybbuk and Other Great Yiddish Plays*).

"Night." Trans. Jack Robbins. In *Fifty Contemporary One-Act Plays*. Ed. Frank Shay and Pierre Loving. Cincinnati: Stewart & Kidd, 1920. Pp. 537-44.

_____. In *Fifty One-Act Plays*. Ed. Constance M. Martin. London: V. Gollancz, 1934. Pp. 769-81.

Sabbatai Zevi: A Tragedy in 3 Acts and 6 Scenes. Trans. Florence Whyte and George Rapall Noyes. Philadelphia: Jewish Publication Society of America, 1930.

_____. In *Kiddush Ha-Shem: An Epic of 1648 and Sabbatai Zevi: A Tragedy*. New York: Meridian Books and Philadelphia: Jewish Publication Society of America, 1959.

"The Sinner." Trans. Isaac Goldberg. In *Six Plays of the Yiddish*

Theatre. Ed. Isaac Goldberg. Boston: J.W. Luce, 1916. Pp. 151-75.

_____. In *A Golden Treasury of Jewish Literature.* Ed. Leo W. Schwarz. New York: Farrar & Rinehart, 1937. Pp. 528-36.

"Winter." Trans. Isaac Goldberg. In *Six Plays of the Yiddish Theatre.* Ed. Isaac Goldberg. Boston: J.W. Luce, 1916. Pp. 123-49.

STORIES: *Collected*

Children of Abraham: The Short Stories of Sholem Asch. Trans. Maurice Samuel. New York: Putnam's, 1942.
(Contents: The Boy Saint, Yoshke the Beadle, The Song of Hunger, The Mother's Reward, The Lucky Touch, God's Bread, The Carnival Legend, From the Beyond, My Father's Greatcoat, The Rebel, Young Years, All His Possessions, De Profundis, The Stranger, The Footsteps, Sanctification of the Name, A Letter to America, The Heritage, A Peculiar Gift, The Last Jew, White Roses, The Magic of the Uniform, Dust to Dust, The Quiet Garden, Fathers-in-Law, Heil, Hitler!, A Royal Table, The Pull of the City, His Second Love.)

From Many Countries: The Collected Short Stories of Sholem Asch. Trans. Maurice Samuel and Meyer Levin. London: Macdonald, 1958.
(Contents: Dedicatory Foreword: "One of Six Million." Part One: "From Many Countries": The Boy Saint, My Father's Greatcoat, The Mother's Reward, The Last Jew, The Quiet Garden, The Heritage, The Rebel, The Dowry, A Divorce, His Second Love, Tricked, From the Beyond, A Royal Table, The Magic of the Uniform, Dust to Dust, Sin.
Part Two: "Tales from the Shadow of Death": Yiskadal V'Yiska-dash, The Song of Hunger, A Child Leads the Way, Jewish Eyes, The Duty to Live, Eretz Israel, Mama, Christ in the Ghetto, The Finger, A Peculiar Gift, The Carnival Legend, God's Bread, Sanctification of the Name, The Stranger, The Footsteps.

In the Beginning. Trans. Caroline Cunningham. New York: Putnam's, 1935.
(Thirty-five "children's stories" based on the Old Testament,

beginning with "Adam" and "Eve" and ending with "Jacob's Burial.")

Tales of My People. Trans. Meyer Levin. New York: Putnam's, 1948. Toronto: G. Allen, 1948.
(Contents: The Little Town, Tricked, A Divorce, The Dowry, Yiskadal V'Yiskadash, A Child Leads the Way, The Duty to Live, Jewish Eyes, Eretz Israel, Mama, The Finger.)

STORIES: *Uncollected*

"Abandoned." In *Great Short Stories of the World: A Collection of Complete Short Stories Chosen from the Literature of All Periods and Countries.* Ed. Barrett H. Clark and Maxim Lieber. New York: Robert M. McBride, 1928. Pp. 740-43.

"I Adopt An Ancestor: A Fable," *American Mercury,* 56 (January 1943), 47-53.

"Katie Stieglitz," *Common Ground,* 3 (Spring 1943), 19-23.

"Kola Road." Trans. Joseph Leftwich. In *Yisroel: The First Jewish Omnibus.* Revised Edition. Ed. Joseph Leftwich. New York: Thomas Yoseloff, 1963. Pp. 456-70.
Also: "Kola Street." Trans. Norbert Guterman. In *A Treasury of Yiddish Stories.* Ed. Irving Howe and Eliezer Greenberg. New York: Meridian Books, 1958. Pp. 260-75.

"The Red Hat," *Esquire,* 1 (April 1934), 48-49, 100.

"A Simple Story." Trans. Helena Frank. In *Yiddish Tales.* Ed. Helena Frank. Philadelphia: Jewish Publication Society of America, 1912. Pp. 493-505.

"The Sinner." Trans. Helena Frank. In *Yiddish Tales.* Ed. Helena Frank. Philadelphia: Jewish Publication Society of America, 1912. Pp. 529-39. (This story should not be confused with the one-act play of similar title.)

"Through the Wall." Trans. Isabel Shostac. In *Current Literature,*

49 (October 1910), 461-63.

"A Village Tsaddik." Trans. Shifra Natanson and N.B. Jopson. In *Slavonic Review*, 13 (July 1934), 41-45.

STORIES: *Alternate Titles*

"At the Shore of Eretz Isroel." In *The Jewish Mirror* (Winter 1962), pp. 9-12. Also "Eretz Israel" in *From Many Countries*, pp. 304-9 and in *Tales of My People*, pp. 243-49.

"Exalted and Hallowed." Trans. Marie Syrkin. In *Jewish Frontier Anthology 1934-1944*. New York: Jewish Frontier Association, 1945. Pp. 395-407. Also "Yiskadal V'Yiskadash" in *From Many Countries*, pp. 245-58 and in *Tales of My People*, pp. 175-90.

"A Jewish Child." Trans. Helena Frank. In *Yiddish Tales*. Ed. Helena Frank. Philadelphia: Jewish Publication Society of America, 1912. Pp. 506-13. Also "The Rebel" in *Children of Abraham*, pp. 107-13 and in *From Many Countries*, pp. 95-108.

"A Scholar's Mother." Trans. Helena Frank. In *Yiddish Stories*. Ed. Helena Frank. Philadelphia: Jewish Publication Society of America, 1912. Pp. 514-28. Also "The Mother's Reward" in *Children of Abraham*, pp. 62-74 and "Mama" in *From Many Countries*, pp. 68-79.

"A Quiet Garden Spot." Trans. Moishe Spiegel. In *A Treasury of Yiddish Stories*. Ed. Irving Howe and Eliezer Greenberg. New York: Meridian Books, 1958. Pp. 519-23. Also "The Quiet Garden" in *Children of Abraham,* "pp. 326-31 and in *From Many Countries*, pp. 90-94.

"The Wiles of Destiny." In *The Nation*, 18 July 1923, pp. 59-61. Also "Tricked" in *From Many Countries*, pp. 155-60 and in *Tales of My People*, pp. 147-53.

BOOKS: *Non-Fiction*

One Destiny: An Epistle to the Christians. Trans. Milton Hindus.

New York: Putnam's, 1945. Toronto: G. Allen, 1945.

What I Believe. Trans. Maurice Samuel. New York: Putnam's, 1941. Toronto: G. Allen, 1941.
English Edition: *My Personal Faith.* Trans. Maurice Samuel. London: G. Routledge, 1942.

ARTICLES

"Dedicatory Foreward: One of Six Million," *From Many Countries: The Collected Short Stories of Sholem Asch.* Trans. Maurice Samuel and Meyer Levin. London: Macdonald, 1958. Pp. ix-xvii.

"The Guilty Ones," *Atlantic Monthly,* 166 (December 1940), 713-23.

"In the Valley of Death," *New York Times Magazine,* 7 February 1943, pp. 16, 36.

"A Word About My Collection of Jewish Books," *Catalogue of Hebrew and Yiddish Manuscripts and Books from the Library of Sholem Asch.* Comp. Leon Nemoy. New Haven: Yale University Library, 1945. Pp. vii-xx.

Secondary Sources

BIBLIOGRAPHIES

Cohen, Libby Okun. "Shalom Asch in English Translation: A Bibliography," *Bulletin of Bibliography,* 22 (January-April 1958), 109-11. (This compiles the Asch works published in English, including their different editions and reprints. It does not list materials *about* him.)

Reisen, Zalman. "Sholem Asch," *Lexicon of Yiddish Literature and Press.* Ed. Samuel Niger. Warsaw: Central Publishing House, 1914. Pp. 76-80. In Yiddish. (Lists titles and dates of some early

SELECTED BIBLIOGRAPHY 281

Asch works [1899-1914], with brief critical comments.)

_____. "Sholem Asch," *Lexicon of Yiddish Literature.* Warsaw: Central Publishing House, 1926-30. I, 183-85. In Yiddish. (Lists Asch's works in Yiddish—and their translations in Hebrew, Russian, Polish, and German—until 1925. Included is a limited bibliography of articles about Asch.)

Zylbercwaig, Zalmen and Jacob Mestel, eds. *Lexicon of the Yiddish Theater.* Warsaw: Hebrew Actors Union, 1931. I, 105-11. In Yiddish. (Lists Asch's dramas and comedies—their translations into foreign languages and their first productions on Yiddish and foreign-language stages—until 1930. Included is a limited bibliography of articles dealing with Asch as dramatist.)

GENERAL BACKGROUND

Anderson, George K. *The Legend of the Wandering Jew.* Providence, R.I.: Brown University Press, 1965.

Babel, Isaac. *The Collected Stories.* Intro. Lionel Trilling. New York: Meridian Books, 1960.

Baker, Carlos. *Ernest Hemingway: A Life Story.* New York: Scribner's, 1969. (References to Hemingway and Nathan Asch)

Baron, Salo W. "Rebirth of Literature and the Arts," *Great Ages and Ideas of the Jewish People.* Ed. Leo W. Schwarz. New York: Random House, 1956. Pp. 384-87.

Bercovici, Konrad. "The Greatest Jewish City in the World," *The Nation,* 12 September 1923, pp. 259-61.

Brian, Denis. "The Importance of Knowing Ernest," *Esquire,* 77 (February 1972), 101. (References to Hemingway and Nathan Asch)

Browne, Lewis. "Is Yiddish Literature Dying?" *The Nation,* 2 May 1926, pp. 513-14.

Callaghan, Morley. *That Summer in Paris: Memories of Tangled Friendships with Hemingway, Fitzgerald, and Some Others.* New York: Coward-McCann, 1963. Pp. 53-54. (Callaghan's recollections of Nathan Asch)

Corbin, John. "Drama and the Jew," *Scribner's Magazine,* 93 (May 1933), 295-300.

Drucker, Rebecca. "The Jewish Art Theatre," *Theatre Arts Magazine,* 4 (July 1920), 220-24.

Eliashev, Isidor. "New Talent," *Selected Works.* New York, 1953. I, 133-37. In Yiddish. (Eliashev's pen name, "Bal Makhshoves," is Hebrew for the "man of thought.")

Epstein, Melech. "Abraham Cahan," *Profiles of Eleven.* Detroit: Wayne State University Press, 1965. Pp. 51-109. (See "The War Against Sholem Asch," pp. 104-6.)

Goldberg, Fred. "Translator's Introduction," *My Memoirs: Isaac Leib Peretz.* New York: Citadel Press, 1964. Pp. 9-19.

Goldberg, Isaac. *The Drama of Transition: Native and Exotic Playcraft.* Cincinnati: Stewart & Kidd Company, 1922.

Hindus, Milton. "Yiddish on Stage," *Midstream,* 19 (August-September 1973), 76-78.

Howe, Irving. "Sholem Aleichem: Voice of Our Past," *A World More Attractive.* New York: Horizon Press, 1963. Pp. 207-15.

_____ and Eliezer Greenberg, eds. *Voices from the Yiddish: Essays, Memoirs, Diaries.* Ann Arbor: University of Michigan Press, 1972.

_____. "The World of I.L. Peretz," *Commentary,* 57 (January 1974), 43-48.

"Immigration Problems in Recent Fiction," *New York Times Book Review,* 16 January 1921, p. 10.

Jessel, George. *This Way, Miss.* New York: Henry Holt, 1955, pp. 138-39.

Kazin, Alfred. "Imagination and the Age," *The Reporter,* 5 May 1966, pp. 32-35.

Leftwich, Joseph, ed. "Foreword to the Revised Edition," *Yisroel: The First Jewish Omnibus.* New York: Thomas Yoseloff, 1963. Pp. 9-18.

Macauley, Robie. "PEN and the Sword," *New York Times Book Review,* 15 August 1965, pp. 26-27.

Minkin, Jacob S. "I.L. Peretz," *The Shaping of the Modern Mind: The Life and Thought of the Great Jewish Philosophers.* New York: Thomas Yoseloff, 1963. Pp. 350-67.

"On the Thief's Head the Hat Burns," *The Mediator,* 25 (April-June 1952), 8. In Yiddish.

Potok, Chaim. "Martin Buber and the Jews," *Commentary,* 41 (March 1966), 43-49.

Rich, Jacob C. "Yiddish Literature," *American Writers on American Literature: By Thirty-Seven Contemporary Writers.* Ed. John Macy. New York: Tudor Publishing Company, 1934. Pp. 452-63.

Roback, A.A. *Curiosities of Yiddish Literature.* Cambridge, Mass.: Sci-Art Publishers, 1933.

_____. *Psychology Through Yiddish Literature: Apologia Pro Vita Yiddica.* Cambridge, Mass.: Sci-Art Publishers, 1942. Pp. 61-62.

Sachar, Howard Morley. *The Course of Modern Jewish History.* Cleveland: World Publishing Company, 1958. New York: Dell Publishing Company, 1963.

Samuel, Maurice. "My Three Mother-Tongues," *Midstream,* 18 (March 1972), 52-57.

Sanders, Ronald. "The Jewish Daily Forward," *Midstream*, 8 (December 1962), 79-94.

Sandmel, Samuel. *We Jews and Jesus*. New York: Oxford University Press, 1965. New York: Oxford Galaxy Paperback, 1973.

Schwartz, Joseph J. and Beatrice I. Vulcan. "Overseas Aid," *The American Jew, A Reappraisal*. Ed. Oscar I. Janowsky. Philadelphia: Jewish Publication Society of America, 1964. Pp. 277-99.

Singer. David. "The Jewish Messiah: A Contemporary Commentary," *Midstream*, 19 (May 1973), 57-67.

Singer, Isaac Bashevis. *The Magician of Lublin*. New York: Noonday Press, 1960.

Teller, Judd L. *Strangers and Natives: The Evolution of the American Jew from 1921 to the Present*. New York: Delacorte Press, 1968.

Trilling, Lionel. "Young in the Thirties, *Commentary*, 41 (May 1966), 43-51.

W.S. "Yiddish Art Theatre Opens," *New York Times*, 29 September 1939, p. 19.

Zweig, Stefan and Friderike Zweig. *Their Correspondence 1912-1942*. Trans. Henry G. Alsberg. New York: Hastings House Publishers, 1954.

BIOGRAPHY

Asch, Nathan. "My Father and I," *Commentary*, 39 (January 1965), 55-64.

Asch, Sholem. "Sholem Asch Speaks," *The Mediator*, 25 (April-June 1952), 1.

_____. "Some of the Authors of 1951, Speaking for

Themselves," *New York Herald Book Review,* 7 October 1951, p. 24.

Ashkenazi, Touvia. "Sholem Asch," *National Jewish Monthly,* 72 (February 1958), 8-9. Reprinted in *Jewish Digest,* 5 (August 1960), 51-54.

Chadotov, Nikolai N. *Near and Far.* Moscow and Leningrad, 1962. Pp. 209-11. In Yiddish.

"Drama and Detectives," *The Nation,* 6 June 1923, p. 646.

Girson, Rochelle. "The Author: Sholem Asch," *Saturday Review of Literature,* 8 October 1949, p. 20.

"The God of Vengeance," *The Outlook,* 6 June 1923, pp. 117-18.

Golden, Harry. "Sholem Asch and Anne Frank," *Carolina Israelite,* May 1959.

Greenberg, Hayim. "Sholem Asch's Christological Writings," *The Inner Eye.* Ed. Shlomo Katz. New York, 1964. II.

Howe, Irving and Eliezer Greenberg, "Sholem Asch," *A Treasury of Yiddish Stories.* Ed. Irving Howe and Eliezer Greenberg. New York: Meridian Books, 1960. Pp. 78-79.

Hutchens, John K. "Mr. Asch at 75: Prophet with Honor," *New York Herald Tribune Book Review,* 6 November 1955, p. 2.

——————————. "On an Author: Sholem Asch," *New York Herald Tribune Book Review,* 15 April 1951, p. 2.

JK-SH. "Sholem Asch," *Biographical Dictionary of Modern Yiddish Literature.* New York: Congress for Jewish Culture, 1956. I, 183-92. In Yiddish.

Kunitz, Stanley J., ed. "Sholem Asch," *Authors Today and Yesterday.* New York: H.W. Wilson, 1933. Pp. 29-31.

——————————. "Sholem Asch," *Twentieth Century Authors: A*

Biographical Dictionary of Modern Literature. First Supplement.
New York: H.W. Wilson Company, 1955. Pp. 30-31.

_____ and Howard Haycraft, eds. "Sholem Asch,"
*Twentieth Century Authors: A Biographical Dictionary of Modern
Literature.* New York: H.W. Wilson Company, 1942. Pp. 45-46.

Lewisohn, Ludwig. "God of Vengeance," *The Nation,* 28 February
1923, p. 250.

Lieberman, Herman (Chaim). *The Christianity of Sholem Asch: An
Appraisal from the Jewish Viewpoint.* New York: Philosophical Library, 1953. (This extended diatribe is more personal than critical.)

Magill, Frank N., ed. "Sholem Asch," *Cyclopedia of World
Authors.* New York: Harper & Brothers, 1958. Pp. 52-54.

Meisel, Nachman. *Sholem Asch to His Twenty-Fifth Year of
Creation.* Warsaw: B. Klezkin, 1926. In Yiddish.

Nadel, Chazkel. "The Popularity of Sholem Asch," *The Soviet
Homeland,* 8 (February 1968), 138-39. In Yiddish.

Nadir, Moshe. "Don't Eat Your Heart Out, Sholem Asch," *Polemic.*
New York: Yidburo Publishers, 1936. Pp. 80-84. In Yiddish.

Nichols, Lewis. "Talk with Sholem Asch," *New York Times Book
Review,* 6 November 1955, p. 26.

Panner, Itzak. *Sholem Asch in His Final Home.* Tel Aviv: I.L.
Peretz Library, 1958. In Yiddish.

Rapoport, I. *Sholem Asch's Literary Victories and Defeats.*
Melbourne, 1953. In Yiddish.

Rittenberg, Louis. "Sholem Asch," *Universal Jewish Encyclopedia.*
Ed. Isaac Landman. New York: Universal Jewish Encyclopedia,
Inc., 1939. I, 533-34.

Rosenberg, James N. *Painter's Self-Portrait.* New York: Crown

Publishers, 1958. Pp. 54-55.

Rosenberg, Solomon. *Face to Face with Sholem Asch*. Miami: Aber Press, 1958. In Yiddish.

_____. "Sholem Asch, His Son and His Critics," *Free Worker's Voice*, 1 August 1965. In Yiddish.

Roth, Cecil, ed. "Sholem Asch," *Standard Jewish Encyclopedia*. Garden City, N.Y.: Doubleday, 1959. Pp. 175-76.

Rozenstein, Chaim. "A Half-Hour with Sholem Asch," *Our Time*, 1 February 1965, pp. 40-42. In Yiddish.

Samuel, Maurice. *Little Did I Know: Recollections and Reflections*. New York: Alfred A. Knopf, 1963. Pp. 271-75.

Schildkraut, Joseph. *My Father and I*. New York: Viking Press, 1959.

"Sholem Asch," *Encyclopedia Britannica*. 14th ed. XXIII, 892.

"Sholem Asch Reports Distress of Lithuanian Jews," *New York Times*, 21 September 1919, p. 17, col. 4.

Van Gelder, Robert. "Asch Returns from the Past," *Writers and Writing*. New York: Scribner's, 1946. Pp. 49-51. (Reprinted from *New York Times Book Review*, 28 April 1940, p. 16.)

Warfel, Harry R. "Sholem Asch," *American Novelists of Today*. New York: American Book Company, 1951. Pp. 15-16.

Washburn, Beatrice. "Sholem Asch Writes Novels By Hand in Old World Aura," *Miami Herald*, 1 February 1953, pp. 17-E, 22-E.

Werfel, Franz. "In Praise of Schalom Asch," *Living Age*. 339 (February 1931), 596-99.

Witham, W. Tasker. "Sholem Asch," *Panorama of American Literature*. Oneonta, N.Y.: Stephen Daye Press, 1947. Pp. 260-62.

Zara, Louis. "Sholem Asch: A Titan Among Us," *Chicago Jewish Forum*, 1 (Winter 1942-43), 9-11.

Ziprin, Nathan. "Asch to Ash," *Long Island Jewish Press*, September 1957.

CRITICAL ESSAYS

Bludworth, Rosa Lyon. "Sholem Asch and His Plea for Reconciliation," *Religion in Life*, 27 (Winter 1957-58), 85-94.

Cahan, Abraham. *Sholem Asch's New Way*. New York, 1941. In Yiddish.

Cargill, Oscar. "Sholem Asch: Still Immigrant and Alien," *College English*, 12 (November 1950), 67-74. Also in *English Journal*, 39 (November 1950), 483-90.

Cournos, John. "Three Novelists: Asch, Singer and Schneour," *Menorah Journal*, 25 (Winter 1937), 81-91.

Finkelstein, Sidney. "Sholem Asch: A Symposium—Three Comments on A Great Writer," *Jewish Currents*, 12 (January 1958), 12-15.

George, Ralph W. "Sholem Asch—Man of Letters and Prophet," *Religion in Life*, 20 (Winter 1950), 106-13.

Goldberg, Isaac. "New York's Yiddish Writers," *The Bookman*, 46 (February 1918), 684-89.

Goldberg, Sarah. "Sholem Asch: A Romantic Realist," *B'nai B'rith Magazine*, 41 (June 1927), 389-91.

Gorman, Herbert S. "Yiddish Literature and the Case of Sholom Asch," *The Bookman*, 57 (June 1923), 394-400.

Hindus, Milton. "Reflections on Sholem Asch," *The Reconstructionist*, 28 (November 1958), 17-22.

Kramer, Aaron, "Sholem Asch: A Symposium—Three Comments on a Great Writer," *Jewish Currents*, 12 (January 1958, 11-12.

Landis, Joseph C. Introduction to *God of Vengeance*, in *The Dybbuk and Other Great Yiddish Plays*. Ed. Joseph C. Landis. New York: Bantam Books, 1966. Pp. 69-72.

Levine, Ben. "Sholem Asch: A Symposium—Three Comments on a Great Writer," *Jewish Currents*, 12 (January 1958), 9-11.

Lifson, David S. "Sholem Asch," *The Yiddish Theatre in America*. New York: Thomas Yoseloff, 1965. Pp. 89-93.

Liptzin, Sol. "Sholem Asch," *The Flowering of Yiddish Literature*. New York: Thomas Yoseloff, 1963. Pp. 178-89.

Madison, Charles A. "Scholom Asch," *Poet Lore*, 34 (Winter 1923), 524-31.

_____. "Sholem Asch," *Books Abroad*, 15 (Winter 1941), 23-29.

_____. "Sholem Asch," *Poet Lore*, 46 (Winter 1940), 303-37.

_____. "Sholem Asch: Novelist of Lyric Intensity," *Yiddish Literature: Its Scope and Major Writers*. New York: Frederick Unger, 1968. Pp. 221-61.

Niger, Samuel. "Sholem Asch," *Columbia Dictionary of Modern European Literature*. Ed. Horatio Smith. New York: Columbia University Press, 1947. Pp. 34-35.

_____. *Sholem Asch: His Life and His Work*. New York: Congress for Jewish Culture, 1960. In Yiddish.

Roback, A.A. "Sholem Asch," *Contemporary Yiddish Literature*. London: Lincolns-Prager Publishers, 1957. Pp. 29-34.

_____. "Sholem Asch," *The Story of Yiddish Literature*. New York: Yiddish Scientific Institute, 1940. Pp. 216-23.

Rogoff, Hillel. "Sholem Asch," *Nine Yiddish Writers*. New York: The Forward, 1931. Pp. 97-107.

Shulman, Charles E. "Sholem Asch," *What It Means to Be a Jew*. New York: Crown Publishers, 1960. Pp. 62-67.

Slochower, Harry. "Franz Werfel and Sholem Asch: The Yearning for Status," *Accent*, 5 (August 1945), 73-82. Reprinted as "Spiritual Judaism: The Yearning for Status: Franz Werfel and Sholem Asch." In Harry Slochower. *No Voice Is Wholly Lost: Writers and Thinkers in War and Peace*. New York: Creative Age Press, 1945. Pp. 229-42.

——————————. *Three Ways of Modern Man*. New York: International Publishers, 1937. Pp. 156-58.

Smertenko, Johan J. "Sholom Asch," *The Nation*, 14 February 1923, 180-82.

Van Nostrand, Albert. "How to Denature a Novel," *The Denatured Novel*. Indianapolis and New York: Bobbs-Merrill, 1960. Indianapolis and New York: Charter Books, 1962. Pp. 29-47.

Waxman, Meyer. "Shalom Ash," *A History of Jewish Literature*. New York: Thomas Yoseloff, 1941, 1960. IV, 526-43.

REVIEWS

The Apostle

Chworowsky, Karl M. "St. Paul the Jew," *Christian Century*, 6 October 1943, p. 1136.

Fadiman, Clifton. "Paul," *The New Yorker*, 18 September 1943, pp. 90, 93.

Feld, Rose. "St. Paul, Great Prophet, Great Politician," *New York Herald Tribune Weekly Book Review*, 19 September 1943, p. 3.

Kazin, Alfred. "Neither Jew Nor Greek," *New Republic*, 1

November 1943, pp. 626-27.

M.J.T. "The Apostle to the Gentiles," *Christian Science Monitor Weekly*, 2 October 1943, p. 12.

Prescott, Orville. "Outstanding Novels," *Yale Review*, 33 (Autumn 1943), vi, viii.

Roberts, R. Ellis. "Sholem Asch's Story of Paul," *Saturday Review of Literature*, 18 September 1943, p. 17.

"Talmud for the Acts," *Commonweal*, 1 October 1943, pp. 588-89.

Wagenknecht, Edward. "A Dramatic Novel-Biography of the Apostle Paul," *New York Times Book Review*, 19 September 1943, p. 3.

Werner, Alfred. "St. Paul and the New Faith," *The Nation*, 1 January 1944, pp. 21-22.

Children of Abraham

Cournos, John. "Mr. Asch's Stories," *New York Times Book Review*, 26 April 1942, p. 6.

"New Songs of Zion," *Christian Science Monitor*, 8 August 1942, p. 11.

Rothman, Nathan L. "Asch . . . ," *Saturday Review of Literature*, 9 May 1942, p. 11.

Rugoff, Milton. "Stories of Triumphant Faith," *New York Herald Tribune Books*, 26 April 1942, p. 2.

East River

Bullock, Florence Haxton. "The East Side as a Land of Living Religion," *New York Herald Tribune Weekly Book Review*, 27 October 1942, p. 5.

Lee, Lawrence. "A Novel of Man and His Destiny," *New York*

Times Book Review, 20 October 1946, pp. 1, 36.

Prescott, Orville. "Outstanding Novels," *Yale Review,* 36 (Winter 1947), 383.

Rosenberg, Harold. "What Love Is Not," *Commentary,* 3 (June 1947), 592-94.

Rothman, Nathan L. "Mr. Asch's Ambitious Novel," *Saturday Review of Literature,* 19 October 1946, pp. 18-19.

God of Vengeance

Davies, Mary Carolyn. "Yiddish Plays," *The Nation,* 24 August 1918, p. 210.

Mary

Fuller, Edmund. "Mother of Christ," *Saturday Review of Literature,* 8 October 1949, pp. 19-20.

"Miriam & Yeshua," *Time,* 7 November 1949, pp. 100, 102, 104.

Rugoff, Milton. "Sholem Asch Concludes His Trilogy," *New York Herald Tribune,* 9 October 1949, p. 3.

Moses

Fiedler, Leslie. "Exodus: Adaptation by Sholem Asch," *Commentary,* 13 (January 1952), 72-75.

Fuller, Edmund. "Portrait of the Lawgiver," *Saturday Review of Literature,* 22 September 1951, p. 16.

Gardiner, Harold C., S.J. "Two Novels That Distort the Past," *In All Conscience: Reflections on Books and Culture.* New York: Doubleday, 1959. Pp. 70-74.

Harrison, Joseph G. "Epic Novel of Moses," *Christian Science Monitor,* 27 September 1951, p. 7.

Lowenthal, Marvin. "Eloquent Retelling of Moses' Story," *New York Herald Tribune Book Review*, 23 September 1951, p. 4.

Oesterreicher, John M. "Moses," *Commonweal*, 28 September, 1951, p. 602.

Rolo, Charles J. "Moses," *The Atlantic*, 178 (November 1951), 95.

The Mother

Ehrlich, Leonard. "Jewish Life," *Saturday Review of Literature*, 8 November 1930, p. 307.

Gregory, Horace. "The Frontier on Avenue A," *New York Herald Tribune Books*, 26 October 1930, p. 21.

Robbins, Frances Lamont. "Six Novels," *Outlook and Independent*, 1 October 1930, p. 188.

Strauss, Harold. "An Early Indiscretion," *The Nation*, 25 December 1937, p. 724.

Untermeyer, Louis. "An Intimate Saga," *Saturday Review of Literature* 30 October 1937, p. 15.

Mottke the Thief

Kronenberger, Louis. "Sholem Asch's Novel of a Thief's Career," *New York Times Book Review*, 27 October 1935, pp. 8, 24.

"Mottke," *New York Times Book Review*, 23 December 1917, p. 570.

Rothman, Nathan L. "The Earlier Asch," *Saturday Review of Literature*, 12 October 1935, p. 6.

Walton, Eda Lou. "Teeming, Humorous, Pathetic," *New York Herald Tribune Books*, 13 October 1935, p. 8.

The Nazarene

Bates, Ernest Sutherland. "The Gospel in a Modern Version," *Saturday Review of Literature*, 21 October 1939, p. 5.

Chworowsky, Karl M. "Jesus the Jew," *Christian Century*, 7 February 1940, pp. 179-80.

Colum, Mary M. "Re-creation of New Testament History," *The Forum and Century*, 102 (December 1939), 261-62.

Cournos, John. "The Nazarene," *Atlantic Monthly*, 164 (November 1939), n. pag.

Jack, Peter Monro. "A Nobly Conceived Novel of the Life of Jesus," *New York Times Book Review*, 29 October 1939, pp. 3, 30.

Kazin, Alfred, "Rabbi Yeshua ben Joseph," *New Republic*, 1 November 1939, pp. 375-76.

Littell, Robert. "Outstanding Novels," *Yale Review*, 29 (Winter 1940), viii.

McGarry, William J. "Historical Fiction That Misrepresents Facts," *America*, 4 November 1939, pp. 105-6.

Rahv, Philip. "The Healing of a Wound," *The Nation*, 28 October 1939, p. 471.

Rugoff, Milton. "A Great Novel About the Life of Jesus," *New York Herald Tribune Books*, 22 October 1939, p. 3.

Thompson, Ralph. "Books of the Times," *New York Times*, 19 October 1939, p. 21.

One Destiny: An Epistle to the Christians

Mumford, Lewis, "Toward a Wider Union," *Saturday Review of Literature*, 29 September 1945, p. 12.

Werner, Alfred. "Christian and Jew," *New Republic*, 8 October 1945, p. 474.

Wilson, P.W. "Epistle to Christians," *New York Times Book Review,* 7 October 1945, p. 8.

A Passage in the Night

Bullock, Florence Haxton. "A Rich, Close-Woven Novel About Man and Conscience," *New York Herald Tribune Book Review,* 18 October 1953, p. 4.

Favre, George H. "Probing the Sense of Guilt," *Christian Science Monitor,* 10 December 1953, p. 9.

Geismar, Maxwell. "The Crazy Mask of Literature, "*The Nation,* 14 November 1953, pp. 404-5.

Rothman, Nathan L. "A Man's Conscience," *Saturday Review,* 17 October 1953, p. 27.

The Prophet

Gannett, Lewis. "Book Review: *The Prophet,"* *New York Herald Tribune,* 3 November 1955, p. 21.

Hornaday, Mary. "The Birth of the Messianic Idea," *Christian Science Monitor,* 3 November 1955, p. 6.

Levin, Meyer. "Prophet of the Return," *New York Times Book Review,* 6 November 1955, p. 4.

"Mixed Fiction," *Time,* 31 October 1955, p. 98.

Searles, P.J. "A Novel About Isaiah," *New York Herald Tribune Book Review,* 6 November 1955, p. 2.

Smith, Bradford. "The Life of Isaiah-II," *Saturday Review,* 5 November 1955, pp. 18, 31.

Teller, Judd L. "Unhistorical Novels," *Commentary,* 21 (April 1956), 393-96.

Salvation

Fineman, Irving. "A Tower of Babel in Jewish Poland," *Saturday Review of Literature*, 29 September 1934, p. 142.

Kronenberger, Louis. "Profound Compassion," *New York Times Book Review*, 7 October 1934, p. 7.

Lewisohn, Ludwig. "Epic Art," *The Nation*, 17 October 1934, pp. 451-52.

Pick, Robert. "Mystics and Miracles," *Saturday Review of Literature*, 25 August 1951, p. 26.

Plomer, William. "Fiction," *The Spectator*, 14 September 1934, p. 374.

Walton, Eda Lou. "A Prophet Arises in Israel," *New York Herald Tribune Books*, 23 September 1934, p. 2.

Song of the Valley

Cournos, John. "A Novel of Palestine," *New York Times Book Review*, 2 April 1939, p. 26.

Rothman, Nathan L. "Promised Land," *Saturday Review of Literature*, 25 March 1939, pp. 13-14.

Walton, Eda Lou. "New Novels Pastoral, Realistic and Poetic," *New York Herald Tribune Books*, 26 March 1939, p. 10.

Tales of My People

Braunstein, Bennell. "Voices from the Ghetto," *New York Herald Tribune Weekly Book Review*, 28 November 1948, p. 3.

Lipsky, Eleazer. "Folk Living & Dying," *Saturday Review of Literature*, 4 December 1948, p. 33.

Three Cities: A Trilogy

Colum, Padriac. "A Tale of Three Cities," *Saturday Review of Literature*, 4 November 1933, pp. 229-30.

Hilton, James. "A Russian Story in the Grand Manner," *London Daily Telegraph,* 17 October 1933.

Kronenberger, Louis. "Sholem Asch's Great Trilogy," *New York Times Book Review,* 22 October 1933, p. 1.

Lowenthal, Marvin. "What Is Man That Thou Art Mindful of Him?" *New York Herald Tribune Books,* 15 October 1933, p. 7.

Mackenzie, Compton. "The Best Novel I Have Read About the Jewish People," *London Daily Mail,* 19 October 1933.

Read, Herbert. "Fiction," *The Spectator,* 27 October 1933, p. 592.

Schneider, Isidor. "A Novel of Revolution," *The Nation,* 18 October 1933, pp. 450-51.

Three Novels: Uncle Moses, Chaim Lederer's Return, Judge Not—

Cournos, John. "From the Yiddish," *New York Times Book Review,* 2 October 1938, p. 21.

Mair, John. "New Novels," *The New Statesman and Nation,* 12 November 1938, p. 797.

Strauss, Harold. "Sholem Asch: Three Novels," *The Nation,* 15 October 1938, pp. 387-88.

Sylvester, Harry. "Three Novels," *Commonweal,* 11 November 1938, p. 78.

Walton, Eda Lou. "Of Jews in America," *New York Herald Tribune Books,* 23 October 1938.

Uncle Moses

Morris, C. Edward. "Uncle Moses," *New York Times Book Review and Magazine,* 20 February 1921, p. 24.

The War Goes On

Butcher, Fanny. "The War Goes On," *Chicago Daily Tribune,* 31

October 1936, p. 14.

Kronenberger, Louis. "Sholem Asch Dramatizes Germany's Years of Inflation," *New York Times Book Review*, 15 November 1936, p. 4.

Madison, Charles A. "The Golem in Germany," *The Nation*, 7 November 1936, pp. 555-56.

Moody, Charlotte. "Chaotic Lives," *Saturday Review of Literature*, 31 October 1936, pp. 6-7.

Plomer, William. "Fiction," *The Spectator*, 9 October 1936, p. 610.

Reid, Forrest. "From Berlin to New York," *Manchester Guardian Weekly*, 9 October 1936, p. 294.

Rugoff, Milton. "In a Fantastic Post-War World," *New York Herald Tribune Books*, 1 November 1936, p. 6.

Woodward, Helen. "Battle In a Mist," *New Republic*, 9 December 1936, pp. 184-85.

What I Believe

Behrenberg, A.H. "Lament for Our Day," *Christian Century*, 7 May 1941, p. 625.

Lehman, Milton. "Plain, Shockproof Faith," *New York Herald Tribune Books*, 6 April 1941, p. 23.

Chronology

(Unless otherwise designated, titles are of novels published after 1911, in English.)

1880 Born to Moshe and Malka Asch, in Kutno, Poland, Sholem Asch is the eleventh of his father's fifteen children.

1896 He submits his first literary sketches to publisher Reuben Brainin, who rejects them.

1897 He teaches Hebrew in neighboring village, then begins two-year stay in the Vistula port city of Wloclawek, holding a variety of odd-jobs.

1899 Leaving Kutno for literary career in Warsaw, Asch is welcomed by Isaac Leib Peretz, who suggests he write in Yiddish rather than Hebrew.

1900 His first stories, "Little Moses" and "On the Way," are published, followed quickly by sketches in Warsaw's Yiddish newspapers.

1901 He marries Matilda ("Madja") Spiro.

1902 Asch publishes two small story-collections in Hebrew. Nathan Asch is born.

1903 His first book of Yiddish sketches, *In An Evil Time*, receives favorable reviews.

1904 His *The Little Town*, a novella, is published serially and establishes Asch as a significant Yiddish writer. His play *The Return* launches his career as a dramatist and is produced successfully by the Cracow Polish Theater. He follows it with *The Liar*, a one-acter.

1906 He writes another short play, *Winter*, and then a longer one,

Times of the Messiah, which is produced as *The Return to Zion,* starring the Russian actress W.P. Komisarjevsky.

1907 Komisarjevsky produces his *God of Vengeance,* in St. Petersburg, in Russian.

1908 Asch publishes *Moments* (impressions of the 1905 Warsaw uprising), *Youth* (collected tales from 1902-7), and *Sabbatai Zevi* (a play). He visits Palestine and then participates in Yiddish Language Conference in Czernowitz. His stories appear in America, in the *Jewish Daily Forward.*

1909 He publishes two plays, *Prestige* and *Amnon and Tamar,* and makes his first trip to America.

1910 In New York, he writes and has produced *The Landsman.* He publishes his first story in English translation, "Through the Wall," and translates the Book of Ruth into Yiddish. He also publishes *Earth* (a novel, in Yiddish, of Jewish and Polish life). His impressions of America appear in *The Forward.*

1911 He publishes two novels, *Mary* (in Yiddish, on the 1905 Warsaw revolt) and *America* (in English, on American-Jewish life). Max Reinhardt stages *God of Vengeance* in Berlin, in German.

1912 Asch moves his family to France. He publishes a play, *League of the Weak,* which is produced at Berlin's Kamerspiel Theatre.

1913 He publishes, in Yiddish, *Reb Shlomo Nagid* (a novel of *shtetl* life); *Stories from the Bible* (for children); *Destruction of the Temple* (a "prose poem" on the pillaging of Jerusalem); and three plays—*The Inheritors, Jephthah's Daughter,* and *When Spring Comes.*

1914 He publishes, in Yiddish, *Our Faith* (a play) and *The Road to One's Self* (the novel sequel to *Mary*). He transfers his family to New York and goes on his second trip to Palestine.

1915 The New York Neighborhood Playhouse stages *With the*

Current (formerly *The Return*). Asch helps raise funds for Jewish war victims.

1916 He publishes, in Yiddish, *A String of Pearls* (a play) and *Mottke the Vagabond* (a rogue-hero novel).

1917 He publishes *Uncle Moses* (a novel of American immigrant life) and the English version of *Mottke the Vagabond.*

1918 He publishes, in Yiddish, two plays, *Who Is the Father?* and *Dance of Death.*

1919 Jacob Ben-Ami's Jewish Art Theatre presents *With the Current.* Asch publishes two novels, *Chaim Lederer's Return* and *Sanctification of the Name.* He visits Europe for the American Jewish Relief Committee.

1920 He publishes a play, *The Dead Man,* and he becomes an American citizen. Committee formed, headed by J.L. Magnes, to publish Asch's collected works.

1921 He publishes *The Witch of Castile* (a novel, in Yiddish). His collected works are published, in Yiddish, in twelve volumes. *Mottke the Thief* (originally *Mottke the Vagabond*) is a stage success. Asch visits Warsaw and Paris.

1922 He publishes, in Yiddish, both a play, *The Marranos,* and a play collection, *Dramatic Writings.*

1923 He publishes a novel, *Judge Not —.* The New York production of *God of Vengeance* results in controversy and the arrest of producer and star.

1924 Asch publishes *Joseph: A Shepherd Story in Five Scenes* (a play, in Yiddish). His collected works are again published, in Yiddish, in eighteen volumes; he visits Warsaw for the occasion.

1925 He publishes *The Mother* (a novel, in Yiddish). He and Matilda resettle in Europe, at Bellevue, near Paris.

1926 He publishes *My Journey in Spain* (travel sketches, in Yiddish) and an open letter to Marshal Pilsudski that stirs controversy.

1927 He publishes *The Reverend Dr. Silver* (a play, in Yiddish).

1928 He publishes *Coal* (a play, in Yiddish).

1929 Asch publishes *Petersburg* (a novel, in Yiddish). He attends International PEN Congress in Warsaw and makes his third trip to Palestine. Moshe Nadir attacks him in a satiric open letter.

1930 Asch publishes *Warsaw* (a novel, in Yiddish). His collected writings are again published—as are his more recent plays, as *New Dramas;* both collections are in Yiddish. He celebrates a "double jubilee" in Warsaw and Vienna, and he hires Solomon Rosenberg to be his secretary. *The Mother* is published in English.

1931 Asch publishes *Moscow* (a novel, in Yiddish).

1932 He and Matilda move to Nice. Asch is elected honorary president of the Yiddish PEN Club.

1933 Asch publishes, in English, *Three Cities* (*Petersburg, Warsaw, Moscow*) and a short novel, in Yiddish, *God's Prisoners.* He is nominated (unsuccessfully) for Nobel Prize. He denounces Nazis at International PEN's Eleventh Congress. He accepts medal from the Polish government and sparks controversy.

1934 He publishes *Salvation* (abridged English version). Villa Shalom is completed.

1935 Asch publishes *In the Beginning* (English rendering of *Stories from the Bible*) and *Mottke the Thief* (new English translation). He tours U.S. for the Joint Distribution Committee. The New York Art Troupe devotes an evening to his works. He attends the 19th Zionist Congress in Lucerne.

1936 Asch publishes *The War Goes On* (in England, *The Calf of Paper*). Ludwig Lewisohn lists him among the "World's Ten Greatest Living Jews." He makes his fourth visit to Palestine.

1937 He arranges "authorized translation" of *The Mother*. He is again attacked by Yiddish writers. He tours America to raise funds for Europe's Jews, and he receives an honorary degree (Doctor of Hebrew Letters) from the Jewish Theological Seminary.

1938 He publishes *Song of the Valley* (a novel, in Yiddish). Malka Asch (his mother) dies. Abraham Cahan urges him not to complete *The Nazarene*. He and Matilda arrive in America for short stay—remain 15 years. He goes to London to discuss free Jewish immigration to Palestine.

1939 Asch publishes, in English, *Song of the Valley* and *The Nazarene;* the latter evokes a torrent of abuse, but Yale's Sterling Library requests the holograph manuscript.

1940 He and Matilda purchase home in Stamford, Connecticut.

1941 Abraham Cahan attacks Asch in his *Sholem Asch's New Way* (Yiddish). The latter sets forth his religious views in *What I Believe* (in England, *My Personal Faith*). Asch is nearly asphyxiated when his Stamford house catches fire.

1942 He publishes *Children of Abraham* (collection of stories, in English).

1943 He publishes *The Apostle*, which rekindles attacks on him, and he finally finds a Yiddish publisher for *The Nazarene*. With other Yiddish publications closed to him, he places his fiction in the Communist newspaper *The Freiheit*.

1944 Several critics urge Nobel Prize Committee to award Asch its 1943 literature award; their efforts fail.

1945 He summarizes his views on Jewish-Christian relations in *One Destiny: An Epistle to the Christians*. He donates some rare books and documents to the Yale Library.

1946 He publishes *East River* and a story collection, *The Burning Bush* (Yiddish).

1948 He publishes a third story collection, *Tales of My People* (English), and a two-volume gathering of shorter novels entitled "Selected Works" (Yiddish).

1949 He publishes *Mary* (not to be confused with 1911 novel), which angers many Jews and Catholics and causes an open break with Maurice Samuel.

1950 Turning seventy, Asch determines to confine himself to Jewish subjects and figures.

1951 He publishes *Moses* and a restored version of *Salvation*. He and Matilda move to Miami Beach, where a street assault on him is attempted.

1952 Asch appears several times before Senator Joseph McCarthy and the House Committee on Un-American Activities.

1953 He publishes *A Passage in the Night* (in Yiddish: *Grossman and Son*). Herman (Chaim) Lieberman publishes, in English, his savage attack on Asch, *The Christianity of Sholem Asch*. Asch and Matilda return to Europe, and for more than two years divide their time between London and Nice.

1955 Asch publishes *The Prophet. The Nazarene* is translated into Hebrew.

1956 Asch and Matilda settle in Israel, in Bat Yam. Asch devotes himself to a new novel, *Jacob and Rachel. Song of the Valley* appears in Hebrew. Asch suffers first stroke.

1957 Asch dies in London and is buried there.

1958 A collection of 30 Asch stories is published in London and titled *From Many Countries*.

INDEX